VOTING RIGHTS OF REFUGEES

Voting Rights of Refugees develops a novel legal argument about the voting rights of recognised 1951 Geneva Convention refugees. The main normative contention is that such refugees *should* have the right to vote in the political community where they reside, assuming that this community is a democracy and that its citizens have the right to vote. The book argues that recognised refugees are a *special* category of non-citizen residents: they are unable to participate in elections of their state of origin, do not enjoy its diplomatic protection and consular assistance abroad, and are unable or unwilling, owing to a well-founded fear of persecution, to return to it. Refugees deserve to have a place in the world, in the Arendtian sense, where their opinions are significant and their actions are effective. Their state of asylum is the only community in which there is any realistic prospect of political participation on their part.

DR RUVI ZIEGLER is a tenured Lecturer in Law at the University of Reading, where he is Director of the LLM Programmes in International Law, Human Rights, and Advanced Legal Studies. He is Editor-in-Chief of the Working Paper Series, Refugee Law Initiative, University of London; Academic Fellow of the Inner Temple; Research Associate, Refugee Studies Centre, University of Oxford; and the Civil Liberties and Human Rights Section Convenor of the Society of Legal Scholars. Dr Ziegler is also a researcher at the Israel Democracy Institute, analysing questions of immigration, asylum, and citizenship as part of the 'Democratic Principles' project.

VOTING RIGHTS OF REFUGEES

RUVI ZIEGLER

University of Reading

CAMBRIDGE
UNIVERSITY PRESS

CAMBRIDGE
UNIVERSITY PRESS

University Printing House, Cambridge CB2 8BS, United Kingdom

One Liberty Plaza, 20th Floor, New York, NY 10006, USA

477 Williamstown Road, Port Melbourne, VIC 3207, Australia

4843/24, 2nd Floor, Ansari Road, Daryaganj, Delhi - 110002, India

79 Anson Road, #06-04/06, Singapore 079906

Cambridge University Press is part of the University of Cambridge.

It furthers the University's mission by disseminating knowledge in the pursuit of education, learning and research at the highest international levels of excellence.

www.cambridge.org
Information on this title: www.cambridge.org/9781107159310
DOI: 10.1017/9781316671443

First published 2017

A catalogue record for this publication is available from the British Library.

Library of Congress Cataloging-in-Publication Data
Names: Ziegler, Reuven, 1979– author.
Title: Voting rights of refugees / Ruvi Ziegler.
Description: Cambridge [UK] ; New York : University of Reading, [2017] |
Includes bibliographical references and index.
Identifiers: LCCN 2016028975 | ISBN 9781107159310
Subjects: LCSH: Refugees – Legal status, laws, etc. | Convention Relating to the Status of Refugees (1951 July 28) | Suffrage. | Citizenship.
Classification: LCC K3230.R45 Z54   2017 | DDC 342/.072086914 – dc23
LC record available at https://lccn.loc.gov/2016028975

ISBN 978-1-107-15931-0 Hardback

CONTENTS

FOREWORD

Refugees, almost by definition, are those without a community, other than their own, circumscribed by flight and loss. Much of the work to improve their legal status, typified today by the 1951 Convention and 1967 Protocol Relating to the Status of Refugees, sprang from the fact that refugees were often unable to benefit from treaties, where entitlement depended on nationality and reciprocity. Access to the labour market, to legal assistance, and to the courts was commonly restricted, hence the push for recognised refugees to receive national treatment wherever possible.

This insightful study takes the argument one necessary step further along the path to an effective, lasting solution. Unlike other non-citizens, as Dr Ziegler notes, refugees are protected against return to their country of origin. How long they will enjoy asylum, however, remains indeterminate, whether this is because of the obstacles (legal, practical, social, psychological) that can stand in the way of naturalisation or because no one can know for sure when the conditions that gave rise to their fear of persecution will cease and refugees may be able to go back.

Dr Ziegler takes note of these essentials, which he then combines with the logic of protection and a subtle and sophisticated analysis of the logic of political participation. He questions the all-too-simple assumption that 'citizenship' is alone or generally a sufficient basis for the attribution and enjoyment of political rights. Instead, he opens up the subject of community membership to deeper inquiry. He looks at the intellectual underpinnings of the state itself, at the concept of membership, and at the particular, protected status of the refugee recognised under the 1951 Convention. He highlights the critically close link between determining eligibility to vote, on one hand, and defining a political community, on the other, showing why political participation is so very important to individual dignity and sense of worth, and, equally, what also are the advantages to the community of an *inclusive* approach.

His analysis cuts a clear line between competing views of the citizenship–residence divide, and he concludes with a strong case for the enfranchisement of recognised Convention refugees as 'normatively desirable' – they are indeed a special category of resident non-citizens, without the privilege or benefit of being able to return home, let alone to participate in the politics of their own country. Such refugees may be non-returnable, but their situation also has that worryingly indeterminate aspect, mentioned earlier, which can be ameliorated by bringing them into full membership of the political community.

Dr Ziegler's special concern is with the recognised refugee, and he explains clearly and powerfully why such refugees need and should receive the imprimatur of community membership that is reflected in eligibility and entitlement to vote in their country of asylum. His work breaks into new territory, and although he might well disclaim any such intention, it also has important implications beyond the refugee paradigm. Its grounded combination of international law and political theory offers valuable insights and encouragement to other groups similarly situated, who are no less politically disenfranchised while just as rooted in their state of residence.

Guy S. Goodwin-Gill
All Souls College
Oxford

ACKNOWLEDGEMENTS

This book originates in a doctoral thesis at the University of Oxford. The physical and legal journey of the refugee ideally takes her from displacement to emplacement, from vulnerability to protection, and from exclusion to participation. One could only wish for refugees to enjoy in their states of asylum the kind of supportive, welcoming, and enfranchising environment that I have enjoyed at Oxford as a member of Lincoln College and of the Faculty of Law.

I was fortunate to reside throughout my doctoral studies at the Menasseh Ben Israel room, named after a great seventeenth-century Jewish scholar whose life journey took him from Madeira, which his family had to flee when he was a toddler because of the Inquisition, to the Netherlands. I am grateful to Leonard Polonsky for his generosity and to Carmella Elan-Gaston and Louise Durning at Lincoln College for their care and support. I was lucky to serve on the Middle Common Room committee as its academic officer and have acquired many dear friends who are (in)conveniently scattered across nearly all continents.

My research was further facilitated by the generosity of the Anglo-Israel Association's Kenneth Lindsay scholarship, the Anglo-Jewish Association's Karten scholarship, and the British Friends of Hebrew University's Hailsham scholarship. I am grateful to Sylviane Colombo, Chaim Gans, Ruth Gavison, Sandra Fredman, Menachem Mautner, and Christopher McCrudden for kindly supporting my applications.

As I was climbing the 'Oxford pyramid' (as the Faculty of Law website used to describe the myriad of post-graduate degrees, the BCL, the MPhil, and the DPhil), I was inspired by tutors, colleagues, and friends. My fellow post-graduate research students entrusted me with representing them at the Law Faculty board. I also had the opportunity to co-convene (together with Nicolas Croquet and Sarah Steele) the faculty's Human Rights Discussion Group. The faculty's administration was very helpful throughout, with special thanks to Gerladine Malloy.

The amicable environment of the Public International Law research seminar's Wednesday morning tea and cookies galore at All Souls' Wharton room was something to look forward to even on a (rare) rainy day – not to mention the twice-yearly gluttonous affairs of Chez Sally and Vaughan Lowe. These culinary expeditions may well have contributed to my taking up proper running (though my international law colleagues are likely to cast doubt on whether they meet the attribution test). Whether at All Souls, the Missing Bean, Turl Street Kitchen, or elsewhere across the city of dreaming spires, Eirik Bjorge, Brad Blitz, Steve Dimelow, James Grant, Jarrod Hepburn, Lawrence Hill-Cawthorne, Kubo Mačák, Violeta Moreno-Lax, Martins Paparinskis, and others offered friendly and firm challenges to my views. Long may they continue (to try).

Late in the (DPhil) day, I discovered the richness of the Refugee Studies Centre, where I am now Research Associate. I had stimulating conversations with many of the centre's fellows and associates, including Alexander Betts, Cathryn Cosello, Jean-François Durieux, María-Teresa Gil-Bazo, Matthew Gibney, Katy Long, and Jane McAdam. Thank you for your insights.

It would be fair to say that I have done quite a bit of (academic) travelling: indeed, the conferencing, chattering, glass clinching, and power-pointing 'bug' that has penetrated my system is now (probably) irremovable. I spent the autumn of 2010 as a visiting researcher at Harvard Law School, affiliated with its Immigration and Refugee Clinic and its Human Rights Center (with special thanks to Adrian Vermule and Deborah Anker). At Harvard, I had stimulating encounters with Jacqueline Bhabha, Vicky Jackson, Duncan Kennedy, Alexander Keyssar, Gerald Newman, Adam Shinar, and Jed Shugerman. Popping over (in American terms) to New Haven, I had engaging conversations with Selya Benhabib, Heather Gerken, Michael Reisman, Patrick Weil, and Stephen Wizner.

I am also reminiscent of a Geneva trip, when I was sifting through the archives of the League of Nations, searching in vain for references to voting rights in the inter-war period; exploring records of the Inter-Parliamentary Union (thanks to Anders Johnsson); and brought back to contemporary (legal) reality by colleagues at UNHCR (thanks to Alice Edwards).

On frequent visits to Israel at different stages of this project, I had the good counsel of dear colleagues, including Shlomo Avineri, Eyal Benvenisti, Tomer Broude, Aeyal Gross, Alon Harel, Guy Harpaz, Moshe Hirsch, Shai Lavi, Yaël Ronen, Ilan Saban, and Yuval Shany.

During the years of research, I paved several collaboration paths which I continue to tread. Rainer Bauböck at the European University Institute inspires much of my theoretical thinking on the franchise; I am lucky to continue to benefit from his expertise and kind advice. David Cantor at the Refugee Law Initiative, University of London, invited me to join an ambitious collaborative project which brings together refugee law scholars the world over. Mordechai Kremnitzer at the Israel Democracy Institute welcomed me to the institute's Democratic Principles project, where (Don Quixote–like) I research and write about access to the Israeli asylum system. Prior to the completion of my DPhil, I have taken up a lectureship at the School of Law of the University of Reading, where I am truly graced with excellent colleagues.

At the viva, Jeremy Waldron and Hélène Lambert gave me a good run for my money with their rigorous, invigorating, and stimulating challenges. It was exactly the experience I was hoping for. My utmost thanks also go to the book's anonymous reviewers for their helpful comments, and to Finola O'Sullivan and Lorenza Toffolon at Cambridge University Press for their guidance and assistance.

I feel incredibly honoured and privileged to have had Guy S Goodwin-Gill as my supervisor: to 'tap into' his rich knowledge and astonishingly ironclad memory and to enjoy his continuous guidance throughout the research, thinking, and writing process. Groucho Marx may disapprove, but the exclusive club of Guy's supervisees is one to which I am proud to belong.

Mark Twain said that 'all generalizations are false, including this one', so I better not generalise by suggesting that one cannot complete a research project without supportive friends. However, I will say that, when one is blessed to have them, the journey is not just far more enjoyable but also far more worthwhile. I could not possibly 'name and fame' all those who have extended a helping hand, offered a gracious thought, or were just there to listen, but several comrades who have dutifully done so from afar deserve recognition: Aran Barniv, Guy Carmi, Maya Crabtree, Yonina R Murciano-Goroff, Shir Parsai-Barniv, Anat Shapira, and Guy Zinman.

Last, but most empathically not least, I owe an enormous debt of gratitude to my family: to my sisters, Karni, Naama, and Tammy – it means the world to know that you are always there, ready to support and encourage – and to my absolutely wonderful parents, Ilana and Zvi Ziegler, whose wisdom, encouragement, advice, and love recognise no boundaries. I could not have asked for more.

ABBREVIATIONS

CEDAW	Convention on the Elimination of All Forms of Discrimination against Women
CFMs	conflict forced migrants
CJEU	Court of Justice of the European Union
CoE	Council of Europe
CRC	Convention on the Rights of the Child
CSR1951	Convention Relating to the Status of Refugees
ECHR	European Convention on Human Rights and Fundamental Freedoms
EComHR	European Commission of Human Rights
ECtHR	European Court of Human Rights
EU	European Union
First Additional Protocol	Protocol 1: Enforcement of certain Rights and Freedoms not included in Section I of the Convention (the ECHR)
GA	General Assembly (of the United Nations)
GC	Grand Chamber (of the European Court of Human Rights)
HoL	House of Lords (UK)
HRA	Human Rights Act 1998 (UK)
HRC	Human Rights Committee
IACtHR	Inter-American Court of Human Rights
ICCPR	International Covenant on Civil and Political Rights
ICERD	International Convention on the Elimination of All Forms of Racial Discrimination
ICESCR	International Covenant on Economic, Social, and Cultural Rights
ICJ	International Court of Justice
ILC	International Law Commission
IOM	International Organisation for Migration
MoU	Memorandum of Understandings
MS	Member State (of the European Union)

MWC	International Convention on the Protection of the Rights of All Migrant Workers and Members of Their Families
OAU	Organisation of African Unity
OCV	out-of-country voting
PACE	Parliamentary Assembly (of the Council of Europe)
PCIJ	Permanent Court of International Justice
RSD	refugee status determination
SC	Supreme Court
TEC	Treaty of Amsterdam amending the Treaty on European Union, the Treaties establishing the European Communities, and certain related acts
TFEU	Treaty on the Functioning of the European Union
UDHR	Universal Declaration on Human Rights
UN	United Nations
UNHCR	United Nations High Commissioner for Refugees
UNRWA	United Nations Relief and Works Agency for Palestine Refugees in the Near East
VCCR	Vienna Convention on Consular Relations
VCDR	Vienna Convention on Diplomatic Relations
VCLT	Vienna Convention on the Law of Treaties

TABLE OF CASES

European Court of Human Rights

New Zealand

Permanent Court of International Justice

Scotland

South Africa

United States

TABLE OF STATUTES

TABLE OF TREATIES AND OTHER INTERNATIONAL INSTRUMENTS

~

Introduction

A General Framework

This book concerns voting rights of persons recognised as refugees based on the criteria set in Article 1A(2) of the 1951 Geneva Convention Relating to the Status of Refugees (CSR1951 refugees).[1] It is assumed that, following their recognition, they reside in a CSR1951 Contracting State[2]

---

[1] Convention relating to the Status of Refugees (adopted 28 July 1951, entered into force 22 April 1954) 189 UNTS 137. While the book concerns refugees recognised according to art 1A(2), it should be noted that the provisions of CSR1951 also apply to 'any person considered a refugee under earlier international arrangements'; Ibid, art 1A(1). The United Nations Economic and Social Council appointed the Ad Hoc Committee on Statelessness and Related Problems to, *inter alia*, 'consider the desirability of preparing a revised and consolidated convention relating to the international status of refugees and stateless persons and, if they consider such a course desirable, draft the text of such a convention'; ECOSOC Res 248 (IX) of 8 August 1948, [a]. Following the conclusion of the work of the Ad Hoc Committee, the General Assembly decided to convene a Conference of Plenipotentiaries to complete the drafting of a Convention; GA/Res/429 (V) of 14 December 1950 [1]. The Conference met in Geneva (2–25 July 1951), culminating in the adoption of CSR1951. For a historical account of CSR1951, see Guy S Goodwin-Gill, *The United Nations Audiovisual Library of International Law*, http://untreaty.un.org/cod/avl/pdf/ha/prsr/prsr_e.pdf.

[2] The scope of the CSR1951 was limited to those who had become refugees as a result of events occurring in Europe before 1 January 1951. Subsequent developments have demonstrated that movements of refugees were by no means confined to the Second World War and its immediate aftermath. As new refugee groups emerged, it has become increasingly necessary to adapt CSR1951 to make it applicable to new refugee situations. With this aim in mind, States have ratified the subsequent Protocol relating to the Status of Refugees (adopted 31 January 1967, entered into force 4 October 1967) 666 UNTS 267. Art 1 thereof extends the substantive provisions of CSR1951 ('Articles 2 through 34 inclusive') to all recognised refugees 'as if the words . . . 1 January 1951 . . . were omitted'. See also Paul Weis, 'The 1967 Protocol Relating to the Status of Refugees and Some Questions Relating to the Law of Treaties' (1967) *British Yearbook of International Law* 39, 60 (maintaining that '[w]ith the entry into force of the Protocol there exist, in fact, two treaties dealing with the same subject matter'). There is almost a full overlap between State Parties to the 1967 protocol and State Parties to CSR1951 (Madagascar has only ratified CSR1951, while Cape Verde, the USA and Venezuela are only parties to the 1967 Protocol). In addition, Turkey, Congo, Madagascar and Monaco have kept the geographic limitation to Europe, in accordance with art 7(2) of

which aims to comply with its treaty obligations in good faith.[3] The book explores the unique *political* predicament of recognised CSR1951 refugees in the period following their recognition, when they reside in their states of asylum as *non-citizens*.[4] It appraises the legal obligations of states of asylum towards 'their' recognised CSR1951 refugees, with particular emphasis on their voting rights therein.

The United Nations High Commissioner on Refugees (UNHCR)[5] asserts that CSR1951 and the 1967 Protocol 'continue to serve as the cornerstone of the international refugee protection regime'.[6] The Executive Committee of UNHCR (an advisory body currently composed of representatives of ninety eight contracting states) has affirmed that '[t]he 1951 Convention Relating to the Status of Refugees and its 1967 Protocol are the foundation of the international refugee protection regime and have enduring value and relevance in the Twenty-First century'.[7]

the 1967 Protocol. See declarations and reservations to CSR1951 and the 1967 Protocol, www.unhcr.org/3d9abe177.pdf, and www.unhcr.org/4dac37d79.html, respectively.

[3] Vienna Convention on the Law of Treaties (adopted 23 May 1969, entered into force 27 January 1980) 1155 UNTS 331 art 26 ('every treaty in force is binding upon the parties to it and must be performed by them in good faith'). Cf. Jack L Goldsmith and Eric A Posner, *The Limits of International Law* (Oxford University Press 2005) 193 (juxtaposing international and domestic laws, situating compliance with the former in the claim that individuals would be better off in a world in which states had an obligation to comply with international law).

[4] NB CSR1951 art 1C(3). James C Hathaway, *The Rights of Refugees under International Law* (Cambridge University Press 2005) 916 (noting that '[i]f a refugee opts to accept an offer of citizenship [in the state of asylum], with entitlement fully to participate in all aspects of that state's public life, his or her need for the surrogate protection of refugee law comes to an end. There is no need for surrogate protection in such a case, as the refugee is able and entitled to benefit from the protection of his or her new country of nationality'). See e.g. the Court of Appeal decision in *DL (DRC) v the Entry Clearance Officer, Pretoria* [2008] EWCA Civ 1420 [29].

[5] The UNHCR began operating on 1 January 1951, following the adoption of its Statute as an annex to UNGA Res 428 (V) of 14 December 1950. Its mandate was initially set for three years (Statute [5]), and was subsequently extended several times for fixed periods. The mandate was extended in 2003 until 'the refugee problem is resolved'; UNGA Res 58/153 of 22 December 2003 [9]. UNHCR's task is [1] to provide 'international protection' to refugees' and seeking 'permanent solutions for the problem of refugees'. According to CSR1951, art 35(1), '[c]ontracting States undertake to co-operate' with UNHCR, which has assumed the 'duty of supervising the application of the provisions of this Convention'. UNHCR was preceded by the International Refugee Organisation; UNGA Res 62 (I) of 15 December 1946.

[6] UNHCR EXCOM Conclusion No 103 'Provision of Diplomatic Protection including through Complementary Forms of Protection' (7 October 2005).

[7] UNHCR EXCOM 'Note on International Protection' (1–5 October 2012) Annex Ministerial Communiqué [2].

Notably, CSR1951 attends to the protection needs of a defined group. According to Article 1A(2), CSR1951 refugees are persons who have crossed an international border and are outside their state of origin and have a well-founded fear of persecution in *that state* for reasons of race, religion, nationality, membership of a particular social group, or political opinion; they are either unable or, owing to their fear of persecution, unwilling to avail themselves of the protection of their state of origin. CSR1951 refugees are entitled to a host of social, economic, and civil rights in their states of asylum. However, CSR1951 is silent regarding their political rights, including their *voting* rights.

CSR1951 was drafted shortly after the adoption by the UN General Assembly (UNGA) of the Universal Declaration on Human Rights (UDHR).[8] The CSR1951 protection regime is rooted in general principles of human rights; it aims to 'assure[s] refugees the widest possible exercise of [their] fundamental rights and freedoms'.[9] Hence, the CSR1951 drafters envisaged that additional protection may be granted to CSR1951 refugees.[10] Article 5 stipulates that '[n]othing . . . shall be deemed to impair any rights and benefits granted by a Contracting State to refugees apart from this Convention'. Indeed, it has been suggested that contemporary refugee status is 'an amalgam of principles drawn from both refugee law and the human rights Covenants'.[11]

The leading international treaty in the area of political rights is the International Covenant on Civil and Political Rights (ICCPR)[12] to which 168 states have acceded to date, including nearly all Contracting States of CSR1951 and the 1967 Protocol.[13] Article 2(1) of the ICCPR requires Contracting States to respect, protect and promote a range of rights, including some political rights, of all persons in their territories and subject to their jurisdiction, including CSR1951 refugees. However, the ICCPR draws distinctions along (political) membership lines regarding

---

[8] UNGA Res 217 (III) of 10 December 1948.

[9] CSR1951 Preamble §2. See also Erika Feller, 'International Refugee Protection 50 Years On: The Protection Challenges of the Past, Present and Future' (2001) 83 (843) *International Review of the Red Cross* 581, 582.

[10] Representatives of the following states participated in the drafting process (alongside representatives of Non-Governmental Organisations): Belgium, Brazil, Canada, China, Denmark, France, Israel, Sweden, Turkey, the UK, the USA, and Venezuela.

[11] Hathaway Rights (n 4) 9.

[12] (adopted 16 December 1966, entered into force 23 March 1976) 999 UNTS 171.

[13] Of State-Parties to CSR1951 and 1967 Protocol, only Antigua and Barbuda, Fiji, the Holy See, St. Kitts and Nevis are *not* also parties to the ICCPR, http://treaties.un.org/Pages/ParticipationStatus.aspx.

two rights. Article 12(4) enunciates that 'no one' shall be 'arbitrarily deprived' of the right to enter '*his own country*',[14] endorsing sovereign exercise of migration control. In turn, Article 25 stipulates that 'every *citizen*' shall 'without unreasonable restrictions' have the right to vote in 'genuine periodic elections . . . by universal and equal suffrage'.[15] Hence, enfranchisement of non-citizen residents is treaty-compatible but is not required.[16]

Indeed, all democratic states set eligibility criteria for elections of their institutions of governance notwithstanding the appeal of the principle of universal suffrage. Broadly speaking, such criteria fall into two categories: The first, falling outside the remit of this book, concerns individual competence, primarily age, mental capacity, and conviction of a criminal offence.[17] The second, lying at the heart of this book, is (full) membership of a political community, connoted commonly though not exclusively by (state) citizenship.[18]

---

[14] See Human Rights Committee, General Comment No 27: *Freedom of Movement* (Article 12) (2 November 1999) [20] (positing that '[t]he scope of "his own country" is broader than the concept "country of his nationality"'. It is not limited to nationality in a formal sense, that is, nationality acquired at birth or by conferral; it embraces, at the very least, an individual who, because of his or her special ties to or claims in relation to a given country, cannot be considered to be a mere alien'); Human Rights Committee, *Stewart v. Canada* (1996) Comm No 538/1993 [12.4]. See also Marc J Bossuyt, *Guide to the Travaux Preparatoires of the International Covenant on Civil and Political Rights* (Martinus Nijhof Publishers 1987) 261. Cf. UDHR art 13(2).

[15] Emphasis added. See also UDHR art 21(3) (pronouncing the right of 'everyone . . . to take part in the government of his state').

[16] See Guy S Goodwin-Gill, 'Migration: International Law and Human Rights' in Bimal Ghosh (ed), *Managing Migration* (Oxford University Press 2000) 160, 167 (postulating that human rights treaties acknowledge the continuing authority of the state to maintain distinctions between citizens and non-citizens in certain areas of activity). Cf. Rainer Bauböck, 'Rights and Duties of External Citizenship' (2009) 13(5) Citizenship Studies 475, 476 (arguing that decisions about democratic inclusion cannot be based on pure procedural legitimacy; rather, they should refer to a substantive conception of the *demos*).

[17] For an appraisal of the disenfranchisement of convicted adult citizens, see generally Reuven (Ruvi) Ziegler, 'Legal Outlier, Again? U.S. Felon Suffrage Policies: Comparative and International Human Rights Perspectives' (2011) 29(2) *Boston University International Law Journal* 197.

[18] It should be noted that, the term *citizenship* is usually used in domestic law, and refers to the relations between the individual and her state, whereas the term *nationality* is used in international law to connote legal status and concomitant rights and obligations. However, as there is no 'fixed' rule, the terms may co-exist. Ivan Shearer and Brian Opeskin, 'Nationality and Statelessness' in Brian Opeskin, Richard Perruchoud and Jillyanne Redpath-Cross (eds), *Foundations of International Migration Law* (Cambridge University Press 2012) 93. Unless otherwise specified, *citizenship* and *nationality* are used throughout the book interchangeably.

Ninety-seven per cent of the global population habitually resides in their state of citizenship and are not adversely affected by citizenship-based eligibility, even in 'the age of migration'.[19] The remaining three per cent are made up of divergent groups who are residents, often long term, of states in which they are not citizens, including recognised CSR1951 refugees

It is submitted that most recognised CSR1951 refugees *qua* non-citizen residents are excluded from participation in elections of their states of asylum. Concomitantly, they are generally protected *qua* recognised CSR1951 refugees from expulsion from their state of asylum:[20] their (conditional) security of residence therein is retained until one or more of the conditions stipulated in a closed list of six cessation clauses are satisfied.[21] Importantly, neither recognised CSR1951 refugees nor their state of asylum know when or indeed *whether* such changes will occur. A state of asylum may, at its discretion, offer naturalisation;[22] failing that, recognised CSR1951 refugees are expected to reside in their state of asylum as non-citizens for an *indeterminate* period; during such period, they are likely to be excluded from participation in some or all of the elections held in their state of asylum.

The Final Act of the Conference of Plenipotentiaries convened to draft CSR1951 recommended that refugees be entitled 'to special protection on account of their position'.[23] Oppenheim famously noted that '[t]he concept of a "source" of a rule of law is important, since it enables rules of law to be identified and distinguished from other rules (in particular from

---

[19] See generally T Alexander Aleinikoff, *Citizenship Policies for an Age of Migration* (Carnegie 2002).

[20] CSR1951 art 32. States are only permitted to expel refugees in exceptional circumstances, on grounds of national security or public order; expulsion is subject to procedural constraints (art 32(2)) as well as to the prohibition on *refoulement* (art 33); expulsion depends on the willingness of another state to admit the (allegedly recalcitrant) CSR1951 refugee. See discussion in Chapter 1.

[21] CSR1951 art 1C.

[22] CSR1951 art 34 (stipulating that '[t]he Contracting States shall as far as possible facilitate the assimilation and naturalisation of refugees'). Chapter 8 considers the refugee integration requirements ensuing from this provision. Botswana, Chile, Honduras, Latvia, Malawi, Malta, Mozambique, Papua New Guinea, and Swaziland retain reservations to art 34, https://treaties.un.org/pages/ViewDetailsII.aspx?src=TREATY&mtdsg_no=V-2&chapter=5&Temp=mtdsg2&lang=en.

[23] See Final Act of the United Nations Conference of Plenipotentiaries on the Status of Refugees and Stateless Persons, unanimous recommendation 'D', *International Cooperation in the Field of Asylum and Resettlement*, Geneva, 28 July 1951.

rules *de lege ferenda*).[24] This book identifies a gap in international refugee law and international human rights law: it argues that enfranchisement of recognised CSR1951 refugees in elections of their states of asylum is normatively desirable.[25] As such, the book is 'an exercise in progressive development of the law'.[26] The question of refugees 'is international in scope and nature';[27] hence, the book's inquiry is situated in the international domain, and concerns, in principle, all states which admit and recognise CSR1951 refugees.

B   Structure of the Book

Part I lays the (international) law foundations for appraising the political predicament of recognised CSR1951 refugees. Chapter 1 ('Recognised CSR1951 Refugees in Context') situates CSR1951 in a contemporary global legal order in which the global refugee regime is a qualified exception to the discretionary power of sovereign states to control entry to

---

[24] Robert Jennings and Arthur Watts (eds), *Oppenheim's International Law* (9th edn Oxford University Press 2008) (1905) vol I: Peace 23.

[25] The *lex ferenda* question, namely whether recognised CSR1951 refugees *ought* to be enfranchised in their state of asylum, may be addressed in light of Mill's observation in John Stuart Mill, *The Collected Works of John Stuart Mill, X., Essays on Ethics, Religion and Society* (JM Robert ed, University of Toronto Press 1969) 250 (stipulating that '[w]hen we call anything a person's right, we mean that he has a valid claim on society to protect him in the possession of it either by the force of law or by that of education and opinion. If he has what we consider a sufficient claim on whatever account to have something guaranteed to him by society we say that he has a right to it . . . to have a right then is . . . to have something which society ought to defend me in the possession of'). Regarding recognition of rights in international law, see e.g. Robert Jennings, 'Speech on the Report of the International Court of Justice' (1992) 86 *American Journal of International Law* 249, 254 (contending that '[a] right – even human rights – does not amount to much in practice unless it is established and seen to be established as an integral part of the whole system of international law which alone can create effective corresponding obligations in the international community').

[26] Charter of the United Nations (adopted 26 June 1945, entered into force 24 October 1945) 3 Bevans 1153 art 13(1) (stipulating that '[t]he General Assembly shall initiate studies and make recommendations for the purpose of: a. encouraging the progressive development of international law and its codification'). For a recent reference to 'progressive realisation' of international law, see ILC, Draft Articles on Diplomatic Protection, Commentary art 8 [2], published as part of the ILC Report, 58th session (2006) GAOR Supp No 10 UN Doc A/61/10 (addressed in Chapter 7).

[27] UNGA Res 319A (IV) of 3 December 1949 preamble. See e.g. Astri Suhrke, 'Burden-Sharing during Refugee Emergencies: The Logic of Collective versus National Action' (1998) 11(4) *Journal of Refugee Studies* 396, 399–400 (arguing that refugee protection can be considered, to some extent, a global public good).

their territory and residence therein. The chapter presents general criteria for recognition as a CSR1951 refugee, and considers limits on expulsion of refugees in view of the International Law Commission (ILC) Draft Articles on Expulsion of Aliens.

Chapter 2 ('Rights of CSR1951 Refugees and Citizenship Voting Qualifications') considers the nature of state obligations towards their refugees *qua* non-citizen residents. It explores interrelations between CSR1951 and leading international human rights instruments, most pertinently the ICCPR, concluding that they are complementary and mutually reinforcing. It is suggested that the permissibility of citizenship voting qualifications in international human rights law facilitates the ubiquitous exclusion of CSR1951 refugees from participation in elections of their states of asylum.

Part II explores theoretical perspectives of voting and citizenship. Chapter 3 ('Perspectives on the Meaning and Purposes of Voting Eligibility') considers four grounds for regarding the right to vote as fundamental for individuals: enhancement of human agency and autonomy; the expressive character of voting; human dignity; and enjoyment of equal worth, concern, and respect. It is further contended that the instrumentality of voting (as a means for protecting individual interests and for expressing preferences) and its expressive role (as a manifestation of non-domination and self-governance) should be considered as mutually reinforcing. The chapter offers three perspectives on the collective nature of the electoral process: 'liberal', 'republican', and 'deliberative democracy'. The chapter concludes by responding to possible 'cultural relativity' challenges to the universality of the right to vote, and by applying the conceptual distinction between 'core' and 'penumbra' of rights to questions of voting eligibility.

Chapter 4 ('Perspectives on the Meaning and Purposes of State Citizenship') situates the legal institution of state citizenship within an extra-legal multi-dimensional framework. The chapter follows Joseph Carens' depiction of citizenship as encompassing three dimensions: legal, psychological, and political. Divergent meaning and purposes of citizenship are explored from 'liberal', 'republican', and 'communitarian' perspectives. In tandem with Chapter 3, this chapter lays the foundations for an appraisal in Chapter 5 of the plausibility of citizenship voting qualifications.

Chapter 5 ('Citizenship Voting Qualifications: Normative Appraisals') offers a brief exploration of the development of citizenship voting qualifications, using the US as a case study. The chapter presents three general positions on the desirability of interrelations between voting and citizenship: the 'inseparability' position; the 'contingent' position; and the 'disaggregation' position. It then considers six propositions. Three general propositions in support of citizenship-based eligibility: community cohesion and common identity; loyalty to the state and to its long-term well-being; and electoral inclusion as a catalyst for naturalisation. Three general propositions in support of residence-based eligibility: vulnerability of non-citizen residents absent state accountability; the disjuncture between burden sharing and political participation; and the significance of 'exit' options, or lack thereof, in assessing subjection of non-citizens to coercive authority.

Part III builds on the legal and normative foundations laid in Parts I and II to offer critical scrutiny of the political predicament of recognised CSR1951 refugees. Chapter 6 ('Out-of-Country Voting: The Recognised CSR1951 Refugee Context') highlights an emerging global trajectory to enfranchise non-resident citizens (otherwise referred to as 'expatriates') and set in place Out-of-Country Voting (OCV) procedures which enable them to vote from abroad. The chapter distinguishes between three types of non-resident citizens: voluntary migrants, including migrant workers and members of their families; Conflict Forced Migrants (CFMs); and recognised CSR1951 refugees. It is contended that, while CSR1951 refugees may have a strong(er) normative claim to be given access to OCV procedures, they are highly likely *qua* CSR1951 refugees to be constrained in their ability to vote from abroad, leaving them effectively disenfranchised.[28]

Chapter 7 ('Protecting Recognised CSR1951 Refugees outside Their States of Asylum') considers the predicament of CSR1951 refugees when they travel outside their state of asylum. Their legal status entails *ipso facto* that they do not enjoy the protection abroad of their state of nationality. It is contended that, state protection abroad retains its pedigree and significance, a view which the ILC shares.[29] It is argued that states often

---

[28] Cf. Convention on the Protection of the Rights of All Migrant Workers and Members of their Families (adopted 18 December 1990, entered into force 1 July 2003) 2220 UNTS 3 (Migrant Workers Convention) arts 41(1) and 41(2) (respectively stipulating that '[m]igrant workers and members of their families shall have the right to participate in public affairs of their State of origin and to vote and to be elected at elections of that State', and that '[t]he States concerned shall, as appropriate and in accordance with their legislation, facilitate the exercise of these rights').

[29] See UNGA Res 62/67 of 6 December 2007 [1] and [3] (respectively welcoming 'the conclusion of the work of the International Law Commission and its adoption of the draft articles [on diplomatic protection] and commentary on the topic', and commending 'the articles . . . to the attention of governments').

come to the aid of their nationals abroad, notably in criminal proceedings, and that a qualified duty to exercise state protection or to be expected to provide justifications for its refusal may be emerging.[30] In turn, CSR1951 requires states of asylum to issue Convention Travel Documents (CTDs) to recognised refugees, assuring them an unqualified right to return to the issuing state as if they were its nationals.[31] It is submitted that, in appropriate cases, states ought to protect their nationals abroad, and that states of asylum should protect their recognised CSR1951 refugees when they travel abroad using CTDs that these states have issued to them as if such refugees were their nationals.

Nevertheless, the political predicament of CSR1951 refugees is most evident as non-citizen residents in their states of asylum. Chapter 8 ('Enfranchisement of Recognised CSR1951 Refugees in Elections of Their States of Asylum') presents the central claim of this book, namely that, due to their political predicament, CSR1951 refugees are a special category of non-citizen residents: even if their states of asylum generally base voting eligibility on citizenship, recognised CSR1951 refugees ought to be entitled to vote in elections of these states until the occurrence of legal or factual changes leading to cessation of their CSR1951 refugee status.

In view of the analyses offered in Chapters 6 and 7, Chapter 8 considers political vulnerabilities of CSR1951 refugees *qua* non-citizen residents. It applies the Chapter 3 rationales for considering the right to vote to be fundamental, and revisits the Chapter 5 contentions concerning citizenship voting qualifications. The chapter then explores the expressive meaning of CSR1951 refugee recognition, the state's treaty obligations regarding refugee integration, and the public resistance challenge.

C   Some Issues Which Fall Outside the Remit of the Book

The underlying assumption of this book is that all the persons concerned have been recognised and granted CSR1951 refugee status by a state of asylum, and that they reside therein lawfully. Hence, questions concerning

---

[30] See e.g. Migrant Workers Convention art 23 (stipulating that '[m]igrant workers and members of their families shall have the right to have recourse to the protection and assistance of the consular or diplomatic authorities of their State of origin').
[31] CSR1951 art 28 and schedule art 13(1) (the latter provision stipulating that '[e]ach Contracting State undertakes that the holder of a travel document issued by it in accordance with article 28 of this Convention shall be readmitted to its territory at any time during the period of its validity').

the treatment of asylum seekers as well as responsibility-sharing in refugee protection fall outside its purview.[32] Moreover, the book does not appraise the predicament of persons falling under the CSR1951 Article 1D exclusion clause (deemed to be receiving assistance from the United Nations Relief and Works Agency for Palestine Refugees in the Near East)[33] or of persons falling under one or more of the subsections of the Article 1F exclusion clauses.[34]

Other issues beyond the scope of this book's analysis include an appraisal of regional instruments such as the Organisation of African Union (OAU) Convention,[35] which apply the term 'refugee' to persons satisfying the CSR1951 Article 1A(2) stipulation[36] *and* 'to every person who, owing to external aggression, occupation, foreign domination or events seriously disturbing public order in either part or the whole of his country of origin or nationality, is compelled to leave his place of habitual residence in order to seek refuge in another place outside his country of origin or nationality'.[37]

Similarly, the book does not consider the introduction of additional protection bases for climate-induced displacement[38] or for

---

[32] See e.g. CSR1951 Preamble [4] ('considering that the grant of asylum may place unduly heavy burdens on certain countries, and that a satisfactory solution of a problem of which the United Nations has recognized the international scope and nature cannot therefore be achieved without international co-operation'). See also UNGA Res 60/128 of 24 January 2006 [12] (urging countries 'in a spirit of international solidarity and burden and responsibility-sharing, to cooperate and to mobilize resources with a view to enhancing the capacity of and reducing the heavy burden borne by host countries, in particular those that have received large numbers of refugees and asylum-seekers').

[33] CSR1951 art 1D; UNHCR statute (n 5) [7(c)].

[34] For general discussion, see e.g. Guy S Goodwin-Gill and Jane McAdam, *The Refugee in International Law* (3rd edn Oxford University Press 2007) ch 4.

[35] Convention Governing the Specific Aspects of Refugee Problems in Africa (adopted 10 September 1969, entered into force 20 June 1974) 1001 UNTS 45 art 1 (definition of the term 'Refugee').

[36] The Preamble to the OAU Convention stipulates that the parties recognise 'that the United Nations Convention of 28 July 1951, as modified by the Protocol of 31 January 1967, constitutes the basic and universal instrument relating to the status of refugees and reflects the deep concern of States for refugees and their desire to establish common standards for their treatment' and calls upon states which have not yet done so to accede to the treaties and in the interim to apply the provisions. Art 1(1), (3) repeat the CSR1951, art 1A(2) (except the temporal and geographical restrictions which the 1967 Protocol removed). See similarly the *non-binding* Cartagena Declaration on Refugees (adopted 22 November 1984) (concerning refugees in the Americas).

[37] Ibid art 1(2).

[38] See e.g. Jane McAdam, *Climate Change, Forced Migration, and International Law* (Oxford University Press 2012).

poverty-induced displacement.[39] Furthermore, the book does not address the predicament of persons *not* recognised as CSR1951 refugees who may benefit from other forms of protection against *refoulement*[40] including temporary protection,[41] subsidiary protection,[42] and complementary protection.[43] It also does not consider the predicament entailed by *internal* displacement.[44]

Finally, recognised CSR1951 refugees may be either *citizens* of their country of origin or *stateless* persons. Statelessness is neither necessary nor a sufficient condition for obtaining CSR1951 refugee status,[45] and statelessness *per se* does not give rise to a claim to refugee status.[46] As the

---

[39] See e.g. Richard Falk, 'Accountability, Asylum and Sanctuary: Challenging Our Political and Legal Imagination' in Ved P Nanda (ed), *Refugee Law and Policy: International and US Responses* (Greenwood Press Inc 1989) 23. See also James C Hathaway, 'A Reconsideration of the underlying Premise of Refugee Law' (1990) 31 *Harvard International Law Journal* 129; Tally Kritzman-Amir, *Socioeconomic Refugees* (PhD dissertation, Faculty of Law, Tel-Aviv University 2009) (arguing that refugee protection should be granted on social-economic grounds; on her account, it would still be possible to differentiate these claimants from migrant workers, granting refugee protection only to claimants whose fundamental rights would otherwise be harmed).

[40] See e.g. Convention against Torture and other Cruel, Inhuman or Degrading Treatment or Punishment (adopted 10 December 1984, entered into force on 26 June 1987) 1465 UNTS 85 art 3; ECHR art 3 (as interpreted by the European Court of Human Rights).

[41] See e.g. Council Directive 2001/55/EC of 20 July 2001 on Minimum Standards for giving Temporary Protection in the event of a Mass Influx of Displaced Persons and on Measures Promoting a Balance of Efforts between Member States in receiving such Persons and Bearing the Consequences Thereof.

[42] See e.g. Directive 2011/95/EU of the European Parliament and of the Council of 13 December 2011 on Standards for the Qualification of Third-Country Nationals or Stateless Persons as Beneficiaries of International Protection, for a Uniform Status for refugees or for persons Eligible for Subsidiary Protection, and for the Content of the Protection Granted (recast) (EUQD), art 2(f) (a person who 'does not qualify as a refugee but in respect of whom substantial grounds have been shown for believing that the person concerned if returned to his or her country of origin . . . would face a real risk of suffering serious harm . . .').

[43] See generally Jane McAdam, *Complementary Protection in International Refugee Law* (Oxford University Press 2007).

[44] Adam Roberts, 'More Refugees, Less Asylum: A Regime in Transformation' (1998) 11(4) *Journal of Refugee Studies* 375; David A Korn, *Exodus within Borders: An Introduction to the Crisis of Internal Displacement* (Brookings Institution Press 1999); Francis Mading Deng, 'The UN and the Protection of Human Rights: The Global Challenge of Internal Displacement' (2001) 5 *Washington University Journal of Law and Policy* 141.

[45] The Convention Relating to the Status of Stateless Persons (adopted 28 September 1954, entered into force 6 June 1960) 5158 UNTS 360 art 1 defines a stateless person as 'a person who is not considered as a national by any State under the operation of its law'.

[46] See e.g. *Refugee Appeal No 72635/01* (RSAA, 6 September 2012) (New Zealand) [151–57]. For discussion of varying causes of statelessness and their interrelations with refugee

primary concern of this book is the treatment and status of recognised CSR1951 refugees in their state of asylum, predicament of stateless persons *qua* stateless persons are not engaged save for drawing relevant comparisons.

status, see e.g. Hélène Lambert, 'Comparative Perspectives on Arbitrary Deprivation of Nationality and Refugee Status' (2015) 64 *International and Comparative Law Quarterly* 1, 3.

PART I

Status and Rights of Recognised 1951 Convention
Refugees in International Law

1

Recognised CSR1951 Refugees in Context

'[f]or refugees the world is divided into places where they cannot live and places into which they cannot enter'[1]

A   Introduction

The world is exhaustively divided between sovereign states. The Charter of the United Nations enunciates that, as a membership organisation, it is based on the principle of the 'sovereign equality of all its members'.[2] The state is conventionally thought to be 'the organisation capable of and responsible for carrying on relations in respect of a territory with the people or peoples of that territory'.[3] Each state determines its membership criteria, controls access to its territory, and residence therein. Thus, state citizenship (or nationality) serves critical international functions.[4]

---

[1]   Chaim Weizmann, Minutes of Evidence before the Palestine Royal Commission (25 November 1936) published in Barnet Litvinoff (ed), *The Letters and Papers of Chaim Weizmann: Series B – Papers* (Transaction Publishers 1984) vol II no 22.

[2]   Charter of the United Nations (adopted 26 June 1945, entered into force 24 October 1945) 3 Bevans 1153 art 2(1). At the time of writing, there are 193 UN member states. The principle of sovereign equality of states in the Declaration on Principles of International Law concerning Friendly Relations and Co-operation among States in Accordance with the Charter of the United Nations, UNGA Res 2625 (XXV) of 24 October 1970.

[3]   Timothy Endicott, 'The Logic of Freedom and Power' in Samantha Besson and John Tasioulas (eds), *The Philosophy of International Law* (Oxford University Press 2010) 245, 257.

[4]   Stephen Legomsky, 'Citizens' Rights and Human Rights' (2010) 43 *Israel Law Review* 67, 77. Citizenship is generally acquired in one of the following three ways: acquisition by birth on the territory of the state (ius soli); acquisition by patrilineal or matrilineal descent (ius saguinis); and naturalisation. In principle, a coordinated ius soli would leave no-one stateless; however, the incongruent application by states of jus soli and jus sanguinis dictates that new cases of statelessness still occur. See e.g. Ayelet Shachar, *The Birthright Lottery: Citizenship and Global Inequality* (Harvard University Press 2009) 141.

This chapter situates the international legal regime in which sovereign states recognise individuals as refugees according to the criteria set in Article 1A(2) of the Convention Relating to the Status of Refugees (CSR1951)[5] as a (qualified) exception to migration control. Section B presents the current global legal order which locates migration control at the heart of state sovereignty. It is submitted that sovereign discretion to admit aliens and to expel them, subject to certain safeguards, remains resilient to 'open borders' challenges.

In turn, Section C considers the (legal) exceptionality of CSR1951 refugees who, in view of their predicament, are recognised as persons in need of international protection; nonetheless, no individual refugee has a right to be granted asylum in a particular state: hence, CSR1951 refugees do not enjoy a 'choate' right to asylum.

Section D considers the absence of centralised decision making and judicial review bodies from the CSR1951 structure,[6] leading (perhaps inevitably) to non-uniform application of its 'inclusion' clause.[7] As the book concerns individuals whose refugee claim had been processed and found valid by a Contracting State, and who subsequently (lawfully) reside in that state,[8] interpretive queries concerning the interpretation of the inclusion criteria will *not* be thoroughly explored.

Finally, Section E considers the conditional protection from expulsion that recognised CSR1951 refugees enjoy in their states of asylum, and its ramifications.

B   Migration Control and State Sovereignty

'The question of sovereignty... [has] always been at the centre of the system of public international law'.[9] 'The power to admit, exclude and expel aliens was among the earliest and most widely recognised powers

---

[5] (adopted 28 July 1951, entered into force 22 April 1954) 189 UNTS 137.

[6] Cf. art 38 (stipulating that '[a]ny dispute between Parties to this Convention relating to its interpretation or application, which cannot be settled by other means, shall be referred to the International Court of Justice at the request of any one of the parties to the dispute'). No state has submitted reservations. Notably, rather than a judicial review procedure, the provision illustrates the inter-state character of CSR1951.

[7] Ibid art 1A(2).

[8] Ulrike Davy, 'Article 32: Expulsion' in Andreas Zimmermann (ed), *The 1951 Convention Relating to the Status of Refugees and its 1967 Protocol: A Commentary* (Oxford University Press 2011) 1277, 1301.

[9] Robert Jennings, 'Sovereignty and International Law' in Gerard Kreijen (ed), *State, Sovereignty and International Governance* (Oxford University Press 2002) 27, 27.

of the sovereign state';[10] it is perhaps inherent therein.[11] Walzer considers it to be an essential element of (collective) self-determination of existing state members.[12] Nevertheless, from an international law perspective, this power *not* to admit is not unlimited: it is subject to the state's treaty obligations as well as to applicable customary international law norms.[13]

After the First World War, it has become an accepted norm that, while a state has a right to deport or expel aliens as an extension of its sovereign right to exclude them,[14] it has a (parallel) obligation to admit its nationals when other states wish to exercise their sovereign discretion and expel them.[15] Equally, a state cannot 'banish' its own nationals, since no other state would be required to admit them.[16] As Schwarzenberger submitted 'the practice of states had insisted on the duty of the home State to receive back any national expelled from a foreign State'.[17] Indeed, if states were to refuse readmission of their nationals, forcing other states to retain aliens on their soil whom they have the right to expel under international law, such action would constitute a violation of the territorial supremacy of the latter states.[18]

---

[10] *R (European Roma Rights Centre) v Immigration Officer at Prague Airport* [2004] UKHL 55 [11] (Lord Bingham) (referring to the sovereign power possessed by the Crown).

[11] Joseph H Carens, 'Aliens and Citizens: The Case for Open Borders' (1987) 49 *Review of Politics* 251, 251–52.

[12] Michael Walzer, *Spheres of Justice: A Defense of Pluralism and Equality* (Basic Books 1983) 31; see also Tom Farer, 'How the International System Copes with Involuntary Migration' (1995) 17 *Human Rights Quarterly* 72, 88.

[13] Guy S Goodwin-Gill, *International Law and the Movement of Persons Between States* (Clarendon Press 1978), 309.

[14] Bridget Anderson, Matthew J Gibney, and Emanuela Paoletti, 'Citizenship, Deportation, and the Boundaries of Belonging' (2011) 15 *Citizenship Studies* 547, 548.

[15] See e.g. Guy S Goodwin-Gill, 'Voluntary Repatriation: Legal and Policy Issues' in Gil Loescher and Laila Monahan (eds), *Refugees and International Relations* (Clarendon Press 1989) 255, 257 (noting that a legal relationship comes into existence whenever one state admits the national of another state: the general rule in international law is that a state is required to admit its nationals if they are expelled from other states, as nationality represents not only the relationship between individual and their state, but is also a legally relevant fact having consequences in international law). For an early treaty stipulating this principle, see Convention on Status of Aliens (adopted 20 February 1928, entered into force 29 August 1929) 132 LNTS 301 art 6(2) ('States are required to receive their nationals expelled from foreign soil who seek to enter their territory'.)

[16] See e.g. Hans Kelsen, *General Theory of Law and State* (Anders Wedberg Trans, Russell & Russell 1961) 236.

[17] Georg Schwarzenberger, *International Law* (3rd edn Stevens 1957) vol 1, 361.

[18] Paul Weis, *Nationality and Statelessness in International Law* (2nd edn Sijthoff and Noordhoof 1979) 45.

Torpey suggests that control over movement as manifest in the emergence of immigration controls and passports is 'an essential aspect of the state-ness' of states.[19] The passport, which ensures the 'returnability' of the individual to the issuing state, has become indispensable for international travel.[20] Chapter 7 considers the (required) issuance for CSR1951 refugees of CTDs and their protection abroad.

The (legal) ability of the state to control its sovereign borders sits uneasily with 'liberal' principles[21] according to which allocation of morally significant goods based on morally arbitrary considerations is suspect.[22] Hence, it is perhaps unsurprising that, in *The Law of Peoples*,[23] John Rawls steers clear of immigration-related questions, despite his contention in *A Theory of Justice* that each person is inviolable and should not be favoured or disfavoured based on natural chance or the contingency of social circumstances.[24]

In contradistinction, Joseph Carens has asserted (based on Rawlsian principles) that birthplace and parentage are arbitrary natural contingencies, and that community membership largely based on these contingencies is a modern equivalent of 'feudal privilege', namely an inherited status that greatly enhances one's life chances.[25] On this view, individuals should be able to join the political community of their choosing pursuant to accepting the terms of its 'social contract';[26] migration control should restrict such movement only when the well-being of

---

[19] John Torpey, *The Invention of the Passport: Surveillance, Citizenship and the State* (Cambridge University Press 1999), 1–3. See also Boldizsar Nagy, 'The Frontiers of the Sovereign' in Anne Bayefsky (ed), *Human Rights and Refugees, Internally Displaced Persons and Migrant Workers* (Nijhoff, 2006) 91, 97. Cf. Human Rights Committee, General Comment No 27: *Freedom of Movement* (Article 12) (2 November 1999) CCPR/C/21/Rev.1/Add.9 [9] (noting that '[s]ince international travel usually requires appropriate documents, in particular a passport, the right to leave a country must include the right to obtain the necessary travel documents. The issuing of passports is normally incumbent on the State of nationality of the individual').

[20] Movement of Persons (n 13) 24–25. See also Alan Dowty, Closed Borders: The Contemporary Assault on Free Movement (Yale University Press 1997) 62.

[21] Matthew J Gibney and Randall Hansen, *Deportation and the Liberal State: the Forcible Return of Asylum Seekers and Unlawful Migrants in Canada, Germany and the United Kingdom* (UNHCR 2003) 1, 15.

[22] See e.g. Ronald Beiner, *What's the Matter with Liberalism* (University of California Press 1992) 102.

[23] See generally John Rawls, *The Law of Peoples* (Harvard University Press 1999).

[24] John Rawls, *A Theory of Justice* (Harvard University Press 1971) 3.

[25] Open Borders (n 11) 252.

[26] Joseph H Carens, 'Who Belongs? Theoretical and Legal Questions about Birthright Citizenship in the United States' (1987) 37 *University of Toronto Law Journal* 413, 417–18.

current citizens pursuant to admission of migrants is expected to fall below that of refused potential applicants.[27]

Carens' conceptualisation of 'open borders' has been criticised for its impracticability[28] and for its potentially adverse effects on developing states, where arguably only the well-off could afford to migrate, thereby leading to a (further) 'brain-drain'.[29]

In contradistinction, Michael Walzer offers a principled defence of migration control; he asserts that political communities ought to retain 'the collective right of admission and refusal'.[30] Without control over decisions regarding admission and exclusion 'there could not be communities of character, historically stable on-going associations of men and women with some special commitment to one another and some special sense of their commune life'.[31] According to Walzer '[t]he distinctiveness of cultures and groups depends upon closure without [which] it cannot be conceived as a stable feature of human life'.[32]

Nevertheless, the next section suggests that the fact that states currently are and, on Walzer's account, should be institutionally capable to make

---

[27] Open Borders (n 11). Cf. Seyla Benhabib, 'Citizens, Residents and Aliens in a Changing World' (1999) 66(3) *Social Research* 709, 711 (contending that state sovereignty ought to be constrained by human rights considerations). Elsewhere, Benhabib argues that, while states should grant aliens a right to first admittance and temporary sojourn or hospitality (in a Kantian sense), they ought to retain sovereign discretion as to full membership. See generally Seyla Benhabib, 'Response to Bhikhu Parekh' in Kate Tunstall (ed), *Displacement, Asylum, Migration* (Oxford Amnesty Lectures, 2004 Oxford University Press 2006) 44. Cf. Mark FN Franke, 'Political Exclusion of Refugees in the Ethics of International Relations' in Patrick Hayden (ed), *The Ashgate Research Companion to Ethics and International Relations* (Ashgate 2009) 309, 319 (asserting that a sovereign right to territory brings with it the possibility, and hence possibly the expectation, of hospitality).

[28] See e.g. Stephen Perry, 'Immigration, Justice and Culture' in Warren Schwartz (ed), *Justice in Immigration* (Cambridge University Press 1995) 96, 106.

[29] John Woodward, 'Commentary: Liberalism and Migration' in Brian Barry and Robert Goodin (eds), *Free Movement: Ethical Issues in the Transnational Migration of People and of Money* (Harvester Wheatsheaf 1992) 59, 64–65.

[30] Spheres of Justice (n 12) 44.   [31] Ibid 62.

[32] Ibid 38–39. Cf. Bhikhu Parekh, 'Three Theories of Immigration' in Sarah Spencer (ed), *Strangers and Citizens: A Positive Approach to Migrants and Refugees* (Rivers Oram Press 1994) 91, 102–05 (arguing that the communitarian vision of homogeneous, fixed or close-knit societies appears rather outmoded, even when describing indigenous sections of society); Will Kymlicka, 'Social Unity in a Liberal State' (1996) 13(1) *Social Philosophy and Policy* 105, 117–19 (maintaining that, there is little evidence that immigration as such poses a threat to the unity or stability of a nation-state); Perry (n 28) 114 (asserting that, as long as demographic changes are sufficiently gradual, political communities seem to be capable of adjusting to diversification or transformation of the dominant culture, while maintaining institutional stability).

(first) admissions decisions does not necessarily entail that their discretion in making such decisions should be unconstrained.

C   CSR1951 Refugees as a (Qualified) Exception to Migration Control

1   Distinguishing Claims of CSR1951 Refugees from Other Migrants

The international refugee regime manifests a tension between, on the one hand, the right of states to control and limit immigration as a necessary incident of sovereignty, and on the other, persons at risk of persecution in their state of origin from which that state will not or cannot protect them.[33]

Emmerich de Vattel's stipulation regarding qualified admission of 'exiles' provides an interesting comparator: '[n]o nation can, without good reasons, refuse even a perpetual residence to a man driven from his country...' but 'if particular and substantial reasons prevent her from affording him an asylum, this man no longer has any right to demand it – because in such a case the country inhabited by the nation cannot at the same time serve for her own use and of that of this alien'.[34]

The refugee question concerns the individual's relationship with a polity and the relationships between polities.[35] The responsibility to admit refugees is a secondary, derivative duty. A CSR1951 Contracting State has a responsibility to admit refugees only because another state has failed to carry out its primary moral duty. Indeed, if the state is presumed to be the primary guardian of its citizens, then a person has a claim for assistance from the international community (funnelled through a state) only when her state is unable or unwilling to perform that role of guardian.[36] Carens submits that, given the moral presuppositions of the state system, states'

---

[33] Kristen Walker, 'Defending the 1951 Convention Definition of Refugee' (2002–2003) 17 *Georgetown Immigration Law Journal* 83, 85.

[34] Emmerich de Vattel, *The Law of Nations or the Principles of Natural Law* (1758) Bk I § 231. He argued that 'an exile is a man driven from the place of his settlement, or constrained to quit it, but without a mark of infamy. Banishment is a similar expulsion, with a mark of infamy annexed'. Ibid § 228.

[35] Gervase JL Coles, 'The Human Rights Approach to the Solution of the Refugee Problem: A Theoretical and Practical Enquiry' in Alan E Nash and John P Humphrey (eds), *Human Rights and the Protection of Refugees under International Law* (The Institute for Research on Public Policy 1988) 195, 196–7.

[36] Joseph H Carens, 'The Philosopher and the Policymaker: Two Perspectives on the Ethics of Immigration with Special Attention to the Problem of Restricting Asylum' in Kay Hailbronner et al (eds), *Immigration Admissions: The Search for Workable Policies in Germany and the United States* (Berghahn Books 1997) 3, 14.

desire to set (numerical) limits to their obligations to admit refugees is understandable; nevertheless, they would 'almost never' be justified in turning away genuine refugees.[37]

Nevertheless, the special responsibility that a state has towards its citizens is derived from moral considerations similar to those underlying its general duty towards refugees.[38] As Walzer notes, notwithstanding his defence (above) of migration control, 'there is one group of needy outsiders whose claims can only be met by taking people in. This is the group of refugees whose need is for membership itself... which is a non-exportable good'.[39]

To qualify as a refugee according to Article 1A(2) of CSR1951, a person must be outside her state of origin; must have a well-founded fear of persecution for one (or more) of five specified reasons: race, religion, nationality, membership of a particular social group, or political opinion; and must be either unable or, owing to such fear of persecution, unwilling to avail herself of the protection of their state of origin. In turn, refugees are either unable or unwilling to avail themselves of the protection of their state of origin if that state is unable to provide them a basic level of safety and security that arguably serves as the very foundation of the legitimacy of state power.[40]

It is often contended that the conceptual distinction between 'economic' migrants and refugees is fundamental to understanding the CSR1951 regime.[41] It is presumed that, unlike a 'voluntary' migrant, a

---

[37] Joseph H Carens, *The Ethics of Immigration* (Oxford University Press 2013) 218–19.

[38] See e.g. Robert Goodin, 'What Is So Special about Our Fellow Countrymen?' (1988) 98 *Ethics* 663, 684–5.

[39] Spheres of Justice (n 12) 48. Walzer nonetheless cautions against a mass influx of refugees, arguing that the right to restrain the flow remains a feature of communal self-determination. Ibid 51. Cf. Matthew E Price, 'Politics or Humanitarianism? Recovering the Political Roots of Asylum' (2004) 19 *Georgetown Immigration Law Journal* 277 (contending that, in a world of closed borders, a refusal to admit is functionally equivalent to a decision to extradite: an asylum seeker who is refused admission may have nowhere else to go but back home where she will face persecution). See also Rainer Bauböck, *Transnational Citizenship: Membership and Rights in International Migration* (Edward Elgar 1994) 66 (asserting that, if refugees are denied admission, their 'fundamental natural rights' will be infringed).

[40] Walter Kälin, 'Non-State Agents of Persecution and the Inability of the State to Protect' (2000–2001) 15 *Georgetown Immigration Law Journal* 415, 427. Cf. Emma Haddad, 'The Refugee: The Individual between Sovereigns' (2003) 17(3) *Global Society* 297, 309 (suggesting that the refugee phenomenon is a feature of an international system characterised by the predominance of states).

[41] UNHCR, Note on International Protection UN Doc A/AC/96/830 (1994). See Erika Feller, 'Refugees Are Not Migrants' (2005) 25(4) *Refugee Survey Quarterly* 27, 27 (positing that

'refugee' does not enjoy the protection of her government.[42] UNHCR contends that the 'need for international protection... most clearly distinguishes [CSR1951] refugees from other aliens'.[43] Refugees' well-founded fear of persecution is at the heart of their physical alienage, distinguishing their predicament from that of other expatriates.[44]

Moreover, CSR1951 is not designed to protect victims of general human rights violations.[45] Persecution and alienage, together manifesting the severance of a bond between refugees and their state which constitutes the normal basis of society, must be present to sustain a CSR1951 refugee claim.[46] CSR1951 enables a person who no longer has the benefit of protection against persecution in her own country to turn to the international community for protection. As the Canadian Supreme Court held in *Ward*, 'international refugee law was formulated to serve as a back-up to the protection one expects from the State of which one is a national. It was meant to come into play only in situations where that protection is unavailable...'.[47] Carens defends the physical alienage requirement, suggesting that it is not morally arbitrary: if asylum seekers are denied

'[i]t is dangerous and detrimental to refugee protection to confuse the two groups terminologically or otherwise, even though a refugee situation may be part of a broader migratory movement or may even itself develop into one'). Erika Feller, 'Asylum, Migration and Refugee Protection: Realities, Myths and the Promise of Things to Come' (2006) 18 (3–4) *International Journal of Refugee Law* 509, 525 (suggesting that CSR1951 is not and was never intended to be a migration control tool). Similarly, see James C. Hathaway, 'A Reconsideration of the Underlying Premise of Refugee Law' (1990) 31 *Harvard International Law Journal* 129, 146.

[42] Part III of the book explores substantive differences between voluntary migrants and CSR1951 refugees in terms of their ability to retain a functioning civil bond with their state of origin through participation in its elections, access to its protection abroad, and most fundamentally, an effective and practicable right to return.

[43] James C Hathaway, 'Why Refugee Law Still Matters' (2007) 8 *Melbourne Journal of International Law* 89, 98 (arguing that 'a refugee is not just a fundamentally disenfranchised human rights victim but is by definition someone who has managed to get outside his or her own country').

[44] The centrality of fear in the CSR1951 refugee definition places a greater emphasis on the experience and circumstances of the individual than the treaties which preceded CSR1951. See Chapter 7.

[45] See generally Animesh Ghoshal and Thomas M Crowley, 'Refugees and Immigrants: A Human Rights Dilemma' (1983) 5(3) *Human Rights Quarterly* 327. See also UNHCR, Handbook and Guidelines on Procedures and Criteria for Determining Refugee Status under the 1951 Convention and the 1967 Protocol Relating to the Status of Refugees (reissued December 2011) [54] (maintaining that '[n]ot every breach of a refugee claimant's human rights constitutes persecution').

[46] Andrew Shacknove, 'Who Is a Refugee?' (1985) 95 *Ethics* 274, 275.

[47] *Canada (AG) v Ward* [1993] 2 SCR 689, 689 (Can).

entry and sent back to their state of origin, then the sending state becomes directly involved in what happens to them.[48]

The conceptual significance of emphasising protection rather than economic predicament lies in the contention that, when states accept refugees 'they are responding to extremity, not equality'.[49] The ordinary inequalities of the modern world do not give rise to a moral claim for admission *as a refugee*.[50] While many CSR1951 refugees fit the vision of those most in need that is conjured in part of the theoretical discussion, others who are equally or more destitute are not refugees;[51] destitution is neither necessary nor sufficient criterion for recognition as a CSR1951 refugee.

2 An 'Inchoate' Right to Asylum

The UDHR proclaims that '[e]veryone has the right to seek and to enjoy in other countries asylum from persecution'.[52] Shortly after its adoption, the Institute of International Law defined asylum as 'the protection which a State grants on its territory or in some other place under the control of certain of its organs, to a person who comes to seek it'.[53]

Article 1 of the 1967 UN Declaration on Territorial Asylum pronounces that 'asylum granted by a state, in the exercise of its sovereignty . . . shall be respected by all other states'.[54] Indeed, it could be argued that,

---

[48] Joseph H Carens, 'Who Should Get in? The Ethics of Immigration Admissions' (2003) 17(1) *Ethics and International Affairs* 95, 101.

[49] Matthew J Gibney, *The Ethics and Politics of Asylum: Liberal Democracy and the Response to Refugees* (Cambridge University Press 2004) 211.

[50] Cf. Carens (n 48) 102–3 (contending that, while in his view the CSR1951 refugee definition is too restrictive, any attempt to modify the definition would be a mistake, because in the current political climate, any change would likely lead to a contraction). Elsewhere, he cautions that '[i]n seeking to advance the interests of refugees and other needy people, we should be careful not to undermine the legitimacy of one of the few institutions that offer them any sort of protection and hope, however limited and inadequate it may be in many respects'. Joseph H Carens, 'Refugees and the Limits of Obligation' (1992) 6 *Public Affairs Quarterly* 31, 41–42.

[51] Catherine Dauvergne, 'Amorality and Humanitarianism in Refugee Law' (1999) 37(3) *Osgoode Hall Law Journal* 597, 617.

[52] UNGA Res 217 (III) (10 December 1948) art 14(1). See Guy S Goodwin-Gill and Jane McAdam, *The Refugee in International Law* (3rd edn Oxford University Press 2007) 358 (noting that when art 14 was being drafted, states were divided between those that regarded asylum as their sovereign prerogative like the UK and those which saw it as a duty of the international community like France; the former view prevailed).

[53] Resolution adopted by the Institute of International Law (September 1950) art 1, published in (1951) 45(2) *American Journal of International Law* 15, 16.

[54] UNGA Res 2312 (XXII) of 14 December 1967.

conceptually, if states may *exclude* aliens in the exercise of their sovereignty, they may also *admit* them at will. The above declaration defines the grant of territorial asylum as 'a peaceful and humanitarian act' that cannot be regarded as unfriendly by any other State'.[55] This is notwithstanding the observation that 'the problem of refugees can never be entirely non-political'.[56] Article 2 acknowledges that the plight of asylum seekers is of international concern. Crucially, however, Article 1(3) states that 'it shall rest with the state granting asylum to evaluate the grounds for the grant of asylum'.

It is submitted that the right to asylum is inchoate, as it fails to satisfy the first of the following three requirements: first: right of entry to a given state; second: protection from forced return; third: entitlements while remaining. Article 33(1) of CSR1951 pronounces that '[n]o Contracting State shall expel or return (refouler) a refugee in any manner whatsoever to the frontiers of territories where his life or freedom would be threatened on account of his race, religion, nationality, membership of a particular social group or political opinion', while Articles 3 to 32 and 34 list entitlements of CSR1951 refugees.[57] Yet, there is no binding obligation on a Contracting State to grant asylum to any individual applicant[58] nor can such an obligation be derived at present from general principles of international law.[59]

---

[55] Declaration on Territorial Asylum, Preamble. See also UNHCR Statute art 2, adopted on 14 December 1950 as an annex to UNGA Res 428 (V)) ('the work of the High Commissioner shall be of an entirely non-political character'). For discussion, see generally William T Worster, 'The Contemporary International Law of the Right to Receive Asylum', http://papers.ssrn.com/sol3/papers.cfm?abstract_id=2025410.

[56] Guy S Goodwin-Gill, 'The Politics of Refugee Protection' (2008) 27(1) *Refugee Survey Quarterly* 8, 8.

[57] See Chapter 2. Section E considers the conditional protection from expulsion which recognised CSR1951 refugees enjoy in their state of asylum.

[58] See e.g. the ECtHR judgment in *Saleh Sheekh v The Netherlands* App no 1948/04 (Third Section Chamber ECHR, 11 January 2007) [135] (holding that '[c]ontracting States [to CSR1951] have the right, as a matter of well-established international law and subject to their treaty obligations including the Convention, to control the entry, residence and expulsion of aliens. The right to political asylum is not contained in either the Convention or its Protocols'). Cf. Goodwin-Gill and McAdam (n 52) 357 (emphasising on the one hand the close relationship between the issue of refugee status and the principle of non-refoulement, and on the other hand the concept of asylum). See also Tom Clark, 'Rights Based Refuge, the Potential of the 1951 Convention, and the Need for Authoritative Interpretation' (2004) 16(4) *International Journal of Refugee Law* 584, 587.

[59] Agnes Hurwitz, *The Collective Responsibility of States to Protect Refugees* (Oxford University Press 2009) 209; Guy S Goodwin-Gill, Declaration on Territorial Asylum, http://untreaty .un.org/cod/avl/ha/dta/dta.html. Cf. Charter of Fundamental Rights of the European Union (adopted 7 December 2000, entered into force 1 December 2009) OJ C 364/01

CSR1951 does not designate an ascertainable agent that would bear the duty of admission correlative to the claim of any particular refugee.[60] As Guy Goodwin-Gill argues, the framework of CSR1951 is 'one of obligations between Contracting States. The refugee is a beneficiary, with a status to which certain standards of treatment and certain guarantees attach'.[61]

Vincent Chetail posits that territorial sovereignty is both the foundation and the limit of the CSR1951 regime.[62] On the one hand, refugees are protected against persecution from their own states as a consequence of the territorial jurisdiction of states of asylum. The duty of every state to respect the territorial integrity of others means that states of origin can no longer exercise any act of authorities upon their nationals who found asylum abroad. On the other, states of asylum do not have a correlative obligation to grant protection to these nationals in their territory.

The legal consequences of recognition of a person as a CSR1951 refugee and of her lawful residence in an asylum-granting state, including (pertinently for this book) conditional protection from expulsion,[63] as well as a commitment to facilitate assimilation and naturalisation,[64] may explain the reluctance of states to endorse a choate right to asylum.[65]

---

art 18 (stating that 'the right to asylum shall be guaranteed with due respect for the rules of the Geneva Convention of 28 July 1951 and the Protocol of 31 January 1967 Relating to the Status of Refugees and in accordance with the Treaty on European Union and the Treaty on the Functioning of the European Union'); Grundgesetz für die Bundesrepublik Deutschland [grundgesetz] [GG] [Basic Law], 23 May 1949, BGB I, art 19(2) (Ger) art 16, cited by Dan Diner, 'Nation, Migration and Memory: On Historical Concepts of Citizenship' (1998) 4(3) *Constellations* 293, 296 (positing that the German Basic Law expresses the promise of a sovereign entity to those who, by definition, stand outside of the political community).

[60] Frank Michelman, 'Parsing 'a Right to have Rights'' (1996) 3(2) *Constellations* 200, 203. Hohfeld has famously asserted that for each claim-right there is a correlative duty; that a right is infringed when the correlative duty is not carried out, is violated when it is unjustifiably infringed, and is overridden when it is justifiably infringed. See e.g. Alan Gewirth, 'Are there any Absolute Rights?' In Jeremy Waldron (ed), *Theories of Rights* (Oxford University Press 1984) 91, 93.

[61] Guy S Goodwin-Gill, 'Refugees and Their Human Rights' (RSC Working Paper No 17 August 2004) 8.

[62] Vincent Chetail, 'Are Refugee Rights Human Rights? An Unorthodox Questioning of the Relations between Refugee Law and Human Rights Law' in Ruth Rubio-Marin (ed), *Human Rights and Immigration* (Oxford University Press 2014) 19.

[63] See Section E.   [64] See Chapter 8.

[65] Cf. Joan Fitzpatrick, 'Revitalizing the 1951 Refugee Convention' (1996) 9 *Harvard Human Rights Journal* 229, 245–49 (lamenting the absence of a right to asylum); Giorgio Agamben, *Homo Sacer: Sovereign Power and Bare Life* (Stanford University Press 1998) 21 (arguing that '[t]he figure of the asylum-seeker disrupts the holy trinity of nation-state-territory').

D Recognition: Beyond Non-uniform Interpretation

Refugee recognition under CSR1951 is *declarative*. UNHCR emphasises that 'a person is a refugee within the meaning of the 1951 Convention as soon as he fulfils the criteria contained in the definition. This would necessarily have occurred prior to the time at which his refugee status is formally determined. Recognition of his refugee status does not therefore make him a refugee but declares him to be one. He does not become a refugee because of recognition but is recognised because he is a refugee'.[66] Nevertheless, because refugees rely on their state of asylum for rights protection, a Refugee Status Determination (RSD) process is significant.

General international law dictates that '[a] state may not invoke the provisions of its internal law as justification for its failure to perform a treaty'.[67] A Contracting State which refuses to determine and identify the status of refugees is in breach of its CSR1951 obligations.[68] An assessment as to whether an applicant qualifies for CSR1951 refugee status is incumbent upon Contracting States.[69] Read together, Articles 1 and 33 of CSR1951 require Contracting States to grant, at a minimum, access to RSD processes.[70]

The CSR1951 regime is global in character: putative refugees arrive from different states of origin to different states of asylum; as an international treaty, universal standards are called for. However, since each Contracting State has to implement CSR1951 through its domestic legislation, and to interpret and apply its provisions through its legal procedures, assessment criteria are non-uniform. The CSR1951 drafters have refrained from regulating RSD procedures;[71] consequently, Chetail argues that there exist as many refugee statuses as Contracting States, in so far as the content of the applicable standards to aliens and nationals is determined by the legislation of each state.[72]

Almost every term in the Article 1A(2) stipulation is subject to divergent interpretations. Most pertinently, UNHCR observes that there is no

---

[66] Handbook (n 45) [2].

[67] Vienna Convention on the Law of Treaties (adopted 23 May 1969, entered into force 27 January 1980) 1155 UNTS 331 art 27.

[68] Guy S Goodwin-Gill, 'International Law and Human Rights: Trends Concerning International Migrants and Refugees' (1989) 23(3) *International Migration Review* 526, 536.

[69] Handbook (n 45) [2].

[70] Alice Edwards, 'Human Rights, Refugees and the Right to "Enjoy" Asylum' (2005) 17(2) *International Journal of Refugee Law* 295, 302.

[71] Itamar Mann, 'Refugees' (2011) 2e *Mafteah* 81, 85.   [72] Chetail (n 62) 28.

universally accepted definition of 'persecution'.[73] The 'well-founded fear' contains a subjective element (namely, that the individual personally has fear[74]) and an objective element (namely, that the fear is well-founded[75]), and its interpretation is challenging, not least due to its prospective nature.

Equally, the appropriate interpretation of 'for reasons of', namely whether an enumerated ground should be considered a dominant or a contributing factor to the well-founded fear of being persecuted,[76] and the scope of each of the five 'reasons' for persecution is subject to on-going debate,[77] not least due to their historical pedigree.[78]

Another challenge concerns the appropriate standard of proof that a claimant must satisfy. In RSD processes, it is necessary to look to the

---

[73] Handbook (n 45) [51]. Regarding the role of UNHCR, see e.g. Erika Feller, 'The UN and the Protection of Human Rights: The Evolution of the International Refugee Protection Regime' (2001) 5 *Washington University Journal of Law and Policy* 129, 130. Cf. EUQD art 9 (stipulating that persecutory acts must be 'sufficiently serious by their nature or repetition' to constitute 'a severe violation of basic human rights'). See also generally Deborah Anker and Fatma E Marouf, 'Socioeconomic Rights and Refugee Status: Deepening the Dialogue between Human Rights and Refugee Law' (2009) 103(4) *American Journal of International Law* 784, 784–5 ('persecution is now widely understood as sustained or systemic violation of basic human rights demonstrative of a failure of state protection').

[74] Handbook (n 45) [38]. See also The Refugee in International Law (n 52) 54 ('given the nature of the definition, the assessment of claims to refugee status thus involves a complex of subjective and objective factors').

[75] Ibid.

[76] UNHCR advocates the latter view: see e.g. 'Guidelines on International Protection: The application of Article 1A(2) of the 1951 Convention and/or 1967 Protocol Relating to the Status of Refugees to victims of trafficking and persons at risk of being trafficked' (7 April 2006) [29].

[77] See e.g. Guy S Goodwin-Gill, 'Editorial: Asylum 2001 – A Convention and a Purpose' (2001) 13 *International Journal of Refugee Law* 1, 1–2 (contending that the claims that CSR1951 is 'functionally inefficient, overly legalistic, complex, and difficult to apply within a world of competing priorities' can be partly addressed by invoking human rights law to fill in the 'grey areas', inter alia, in the interpretation of terms such as persecution and social groups). Regarding the latter issue, see e.g. Michigan Guidelines on Nexus to a Convention Ground, Guidelines Reflecting the Consensus of Participants at the Second Colloquium on Challenges in International Refugee Law, Ann Arbor, 23–25 March 2001 [13].

[78] See generally James C Hathaway, 'The Evolution of Refugee Law' (1984) 33(2) *International and Comparative Law Quarterly* 348 (contending that the enumerated grounds were based on the events of the time of drafting: from the persecution of Russians and Armenians and of the opposition in Spain, and especially of Jews and other groups in Nazi Germany, to the developing politics of the Cold War). See also Daniel J Steinbock, 'Interpreting the Refugee Definition' (1998) 45 *UCLA Law Review* 743, 766 (noting that the ethnicity, religion and nationality categories followed the 'archetypical' example of the persecution of Jews by the Nazis).

future and ask whether if returned to their state of origin, the claimant would face a serious risk of persecution, and to try to quantify that risk. Hence, every RSD process risks 'false positives' (granting refugee status to someone who does not qualify) as well as 'false negatives' (denying refugee status to a deserving applicant).[79]

This book concerns *recognised* CSR1951 refugees; hence, the above questions will not be examined here. It is nonetheless helpful to highlight two key areas.

The first area concerns the agents of persecution. Neither CSR1951 nor the *Travaux* say much about the source of persecution feared by the refugee.[80] The paradigmatic form of persecution is undertaken by the central organs of the state such as police officers, civil servants, the military or other members of the armed forces, or state security personnel.[81] However, fear of persecution by non-state agents may also substantiate a CSR1951 refugee claim: according to the prevailing 'protection theory' (*Compare* 'accountability theory'), the test is whether the state is unable or unwilling to protect individuals from serious harm.[82] Hence, as per

---

[79] See e.g. EUQD art 4(4) (stipulating that the fact that an applicant has already been subject to persecution or serious harm or to direct threats of such persecution or such harm is a serious indication of the applicant's well-founded fear of persecution or real risk of suffering serious harm, unless there are good reasons to consider that such persecution or serious harm will not be repeated). The Ethics of Immigration (n 36) ch 10: Refugees (suggesting that, in the asylum context, the analogy to the presumption of innocence should be a presumption that the claimant is a refugee; the burden of proof would rest on the state to disprove the legitimacy of the applicant's claim beyond a reasonable doubt).

[80] Goodwin-Gill and McAdam (n 52) 98. Cf. Matthew E Price, *Rethinking Asylum: History, Purpose and Limits* (Cambridge University Press 2009) (proposing an 'accountability' theory); Chapter 8 critically appraises Price's propositions.

[81] James C Hathaway and Michelle Foster, *The Law of Refugee Status* (2nd edn Cambridge University Press 2014) 297–98. See e.g. *Minister of Immigration and Multicultural Affairs v Respondent S152* [2004] HCA 18 (21 April 2004) (Australia) [67] (Hayne and Haydon JJ) (holding that '[w]here the State is involved in persecution, it will certainly be in breach of its duty to protect its citizens from persecution').

[82] Regarding the accountability theory, see e.g. *R v Secretary of State for the Home Department, ex parte Adan* [2001] 2 AC 477, 512. See also Law of Refugee Status (n 81) 305 (arguing that the accountability theory is inconsistent with the object and purpose of CSR1951, as the need for protection may be just as pressing in the case of state inability to protect as in the case of state unwillingness to do so). For academic discussion, see Volker Türk, 'Non-State Agents of Persecution' in Vera Gowlland-Debbas and Vincent Chetail (eds), *Switzerland and the International Protection of Refugees* (Kluwer 2002) 95 (arguing that the Travaux are silent on the question of agents of persecution, and do not reflect a discussion on a possible restriction that would stem from any tight correlation between the risk of persecution and the State. The EUQD art 6 includes non-state actors among 'actors of persecution'. See also Handbook (n 45) [65].

Shah, 'persecution', emanates from the combination of serious harm and failure of state protection.[83]

The second, related area concerns the absence of state protection. CSR1951 refugees are outside their state of origin; hence, protection could be read (just) as protection *abroad,* namely protection that a state (may) extend to its nationals outside its borders.[84] However, it is submitted that the absence of access to protection abroad may be seen as an extension of the absence of protection at home, namely that rights and physical security of refugees are not effectively protected by the state and its institutions operating on its territory.

As Goodwin-Gill notes, the protection normally to be expected of the government is either lacking or denied to CSR1951 refugees.[85] Fear of persecution cannot be said to exist if it is established that meaningful national protection is available to the claimant.[86] In contrast, the absence of protection in their state of origin prevents refugees from exercising their internationally recognised right to return to their 'own country'.[87] Recognition of this predicament is at the heart of their general protection from expulsion from their state of asylum, explored below.

E   After Recognition: Conditional Protection from Expulsion

The CSR1951 regime mandates that after CSR1951 refugee status has been granted, it is retained unless the recognised CSR1951 refugee comes within the terms of one or more of the *exhaustive* list of six cessation clauses.[88] In 1939, Michael Hansson posited that 'the refugee ceases to be one ... when he is either repatriated to his country of origin or becomes naturalized ... naturalization ... of course ... requires the consent of both ... the refugee and the state concerned ... meanwhile, the refugee must be enabled to live under conditions which are as satisfactory

[83] *R v Immigration Appeal Tribunal and another, ex parte Shah* [1999] 2 AC 629, 653 (per Lord Hoffmann).

[84] See also Chapter 7.

[85] Guy S Goodwin-Gill, 'Non-refoulement and the New Asylum Seekers' (1986) 26(4) *Virginia Journal of International Law* 897, 901.

[86] Law of Refugee Status (n 81) 289.

[87] Covenant on Civil and Political Rights (adopted 16 December 1966, entered into force 23 March 1976) 999 UNTS 171 art 12(4); see also the Introduction to the book.

[88] CSR1951 art 1C. See Handbook (n 45) [112]. The cessation clauses are considered in Chapter 8.

and as possible to him and to the country of refuge'.[89] Today, reference is usually made to three 'durable' solutions for refugees: repatriation, local integration (in the first state of asylum), or resettlement (in a state other than the first state of asylum).[90]

Importantly, while a refugee 'has duties' to her state of asylum, breaching these duties should not in of itself entail cessation of status.[91] Moreover, a serious non-political crime committed in the state of asylum is *not* an acceptable basis for cessation of refugee status; recognition of a person as a CSR1951 refugee entails a commitment on the part of the state of asylum to offer her protection as long as the well-founded fear of being persecuted persists.[92]

Article 32 of CSR1951 pronounces that, a recognised CSR1951 refugee is generally protected from expulsion from her state of asylum, save on grounds of national security or public order, in pursuance of a decision reached in accordance with due process of law.[93] In view of the dire implications of expulsion for recognised refugees, these grounds ought to be narrowly construed.[94] According to Article 32, after lawful presence is established, a refugee may be expelled only to a state *other* than the state

---

[89] Michael Hansson, *Survey of the Principal Legal Aspects of the Refugee Question at the Present Time*, ch II *Certain Legal Aspects of the Problem of the Settlement of Refugees* (1939) Annex 4, §I.

[90] Cf. Statute (n 56) art 1 (denoting the role of UNHCR as, inter alia, 'seeking permanent solutions for the problem of refugees by assisting . . . to facilitate the voluntary repatriation of such refugees, or their assimilation within new national communities'. See also art 9 (stipulating that UNHCR 'shall engage in such additional activities, including repatriation and resettlement').

[91] CSR1951 art 2. See also Chapter 2.

[92] James C Hathaway, 'What's in a Label?' (2005) 5 *European Journal of Migration and Law* 1, 2 (stating that 'as a matter of international law, there was and is no impediment to seeing refugee status as requiring only protection for the duration of risk').

[93] Reservations to art 32 are retained by Botswana, Mexico, Papua New Guinea and Uganda. See e.g. *Secretary of State of the Home Department v ST* (Eritrea) [2012] UKSC 12, where the UK Supreme Court held that a refugee was not entitled to the protection of art 32 unless she had been granted 'lawful presence' in the state in question. As the underlying assumption of this book is that the persons concerned are recognised by their respective states of asylum and reside lawfully therein, the merits of this judgment will not be discussed.

[94] See e.g. Davy (n 8) 1310–11 (positing that the 'national security' ground excludes criminal activities with respect to life and limb or the property of other individuals that have no bearing on the very existence of the country or the government; moreover, national security is not threatened when aliens are sick, unemployed or destitute. Similarly, the 'public order' ground is not applicable when individuals concerned are sick, unemployed or poor and thus in need of social assistance or other social benefits).

in relation to which his or her well-founded fear of persecution has been established.[95]

The commission of a serious non-political crime by a recognised refugee may be taken into account by her state of asylum should it wish to expel her.[96] However, a reprehensible refugee is still a refugee: unless she is able to take up residence elsewhere, her expulsion will not be feasible.[97] The CSR1951 drafters recognised this difficulty: Article 32(2) stipulates that the state must allow the refugee a reasonable period within which to seek admission to another state other than her state of origin.

Article 32 thus incorporates three distinct elements: restrictions on state power to expel aliens *qua* refugees; procedural safeguards in the case of an expulsion order being made; and an obligation to grant CSR1951 refugees a reasonable period of time within which they may seek legal admission to another state which, if unsuccessful, would prevent the state of asylum from expelling the CSR1951 refugee.[98]

The ILC Draft Articles on Expulsion of Aliens[99] stipulate that states may expel an alien from their territory 'in accordance with the present draft articles and other applicable rules of international law, in particular those relating to human rights'.[100] An expulsion may only be undertaken 'in

---

[95] Hence, art 32 complements the (qualified) art 33 prohibition on refoulement of refugees.

[96] See e.g. *EI/OS (Russia) v Secretary of State for the Home Department* [2012] EWCA Civ 357 (22 March 2012) (upholding the expulsion of a Chechen refugee 'on the grounds that his presence here was not conducive to the public good, based on the threat that he was assessed to present to national security').

[97] See e.g. Marjoleine Zieck, *UNHCR and Voluntary Repatriation of Refugees* (Nijhoff 1997) 101–2 (noting that 'as long as a person satisfies the definition of [CSR1951] refugee . . . he remains . . . un-repatriable and consequently benefits from the prohibition of forced return').

[98] Davy (n 8) 1295.

[99] Report of the International Law Commission on the Work of its Sixty-Sixth Session, UN GAOR 69th Sess Supp No 10 pp 11–77; UN Doc A/69/10 (2014). The ILC took into account views provided by States both in writing and orally before the UNGA's Sixth Committee (Legal) in relation to the draft articles and commentaries produced in 2012 See Sean D Murphy, 'The Expulsion of Aliens (Revisited) and Other Topics: The Sixty-Sixth Session of the International Law Commission' (2015) 109 American Journal of International Law 125, 126. Murphy notes that the ILC recommended that the UNGA 'take note of the draft articles', that it 'encourage their widest possible dissemination', and that it 'consider, at a later stage, the elaboration of a convention on the basis of the draft articles'. Report 11 [42].

[100] Draft Articles art 3. An alien is defined in art 2(b) as 'a person who does not have the nationality of the state engaging in the expulsion'. According to art 9, a State cannot make its national an alien by deprivation of nationality for the sole purpose of expelling him or her. Human rights considerations may include interference with the right to

pursuance of a decision reached in accordance with the law' which 'shall be assessed in good faith and reasonably'.[101] A state cannot expel a refugee 'except on grounds of national security or public order'.[102] Hence, while *general* expulsion power is subject to both procedural and substantive constraints, the threshold for expulsion of *refugees* is set significantly higher in view of their predicament, in congruence with the CSR1951 stipulation.

John Finnis, writing about aliens in general, asserts that, even if the genuine risk that the presence of an alien in the community poses to the rights of others, to national security, public safety, the prevention of crime, the protection of health or morals or maintenance of *l'ordre public*, or to anything else of 'public interest in a democratic society' is 'relatively slight', it nevertheless *need not be accepted*; such risk can properly be sought to be prevented by exclusion or terminated by expulsion. Finnis argues that a political community cannot shift to other political communities the risks presented by one of its nationals (members) but it need not unconditionally accept risks presented by aliens.[103]

However, by recognising a person as a CSR1951 refugee, a state of asylum acknowledges that, unlike other aliens, she does not have a state to which she *can* return.[104] Consequently, a state of asylum may have to endure risks from recognised CSR1951 refugees which ordinarily it perhaps could (and, on Finnis' view, should) avert.

Crucially, the length of this recognition-led constraint is *indeterminate*, as it applies until such time as the legal or factual circumstances that serve as the basis for refugee recognition change so that a CSR1951 refugee has secured an alternative form of enduring national protection and is no longer in need of international protection.[105] However, neither the state

---

family life; see e.g. Committee on the Elimination of Racial Discrimination, General Recommendation No 30: *Discrimination against Non-citizens* (10 January 2004) [28].

[101] Ibid arts 4, 5.

[102] Ibid art 6. Interestingly, as Thailand and Malaysia are not parties to relevant refugee protection treaties, they reserved their position regarding this provision. UNGA 67th Sess, Sixth Committee, 18th meeting, debate on the ILC report, GA/L/3446, 1 November 2012.

[103] John M Finnis, 'Nationality, Alienage and Constitutional Principle' (2007) 123 *Law Quarterly Review* 417, 423.

[104] In contrast, voluntary repatriation presupposes that CSR1951 refugees are able to exercise their right to return, and that their state of origin accepts them. See e.g. Vincent Chetail, 'Voluntary Repatriation in Public International Law: Concepts and Contents' (2004) 23(3) *Refugee Survey Quarterly* 1, 26.

[105] UNHCR, *The Cessation Clauses: Guidelines on Their Application* (UNHCR 1999) §1. Cf. judgment of the Court of Justice of the European Union in *Salahadin Abdulla and Others*

of asylum nor the recognised CSR1951 refugee know when or, indeed, *whether* this will happen.[106] Hence, the CSR1951 refugee has no effective 'exit' option out of her state of asylum, and is fully dependent on that state's protection during her residence therein; in turn, the state of asylum is bound to protect 'its' recognised CSR1951 refugee as long as such protection is required.

F Concluding Remarks

This chapter situated the CSR1951 protection regime in an international legal order that considers migration control as a fundamental tenet of state sovereignty. It was suggested that the granting of asylum remains a sovereign decision. Moreover, assessment of asylum applications is done autonomously by each Contracting State; outcomes vary accordingly.

This book concerns individuals recognised as CSR1951 refugees under divergent RSD procedures. The state of asylum may offer its recognised CSR1951 refugees a naturalisation path; should it do so, and should the refugees accept that offer, cessation of their refugee status would generally ensue. Failing that, refugee status is retained for an indeterminate period, the length of which is *unknown* to both the CSR1951 refugees and to their state of asylum. During such time, unlike other aliens, CSR1951 refugees are generally protected from expulsion, subject to two narrowly construed exceptions.

Meanwhile, enjoying conditional security of residence, their political predicament is dire; Chapter 2 demonstrates that neither CSR1951 nor international human rights law presently require states of asylum to entitle their recognised CSR1951 refugees to participate in their elections. Concomitantly, a constitutive condition of their refugee status is that such persons are unable or unwilling, owing to fear of persecution, to return to their state of origin. The implications are that, for an indeterminate period of time, CSR1951 refugees are effectively excluded

---

v Bundesrepublik Deutschland, C-175/08, C-176/08, C-178/08, C-179/08, 2 March 2010 [76] ('having regard to a change of circumstances of a significant and non-temporary nature in the third country concerned the circumstances which justified the person's fear of persecution . . . no longer exist and that person has no other reason to fear being "persecuted"').

[106] See also Matthew Lister, 'Who Are Refugees' (2013) 32(5) *Law and Philosophy* 645, 667 (noting that, to some extent, the inability to predict the length of time during which protection will be required is a consequence of the fact that the asylum- granting state has no duty to directly end the root cause of the danger).

from the political community of their state of origin while they remain non-members of the political community of their state of asylum.

Luke Lee claims that '[t]hrough the grant of asylum the refugee enters ... into a special legal relationship with the state of asylum. This relationship is similar to the legal advantages of nationality'.[107] This book contends that CSR1951 refugees *ought* to have a relationship with their state of asylum which reflects their political predicament and should hence be similar to that which the state of asylum has with its nationals (for the indeterminate period during which CSR1951-based protection is required). However, while CSR1951 permits such a relationship to exist, and (as Chapter 8 suggests) even encourages it, states of asylum are, at present, not required to accept such an obligation.

---

[107] Luke T Lee, *Consular Law and Practice* (Oxford University Press 1991) 358, text next to n 34.

2

Rights of CSR1951 Refugees and Citizenship Voting Qualifications

A   Introduction

The starting point of the analysis of this chapter is the characterisation of the modern state as 'an answer to the question of who is responsible to whom in the modern world: states are responsible to their own citizens'.[1] This conceptualisation empowers citizens and enhances the importance of citizenship. While the Universal Declaration of Human Rights ceremoniously proclaims that 'everyone' has a 'right to a nationality',[2] the right to nationality remains inchoate.[3] Hence, reliance on a state to act as the principal guarantor of human rights may expose a weakness of the

---

[1] Matthew J Gibney, *The Ethics and Politics of Asylum: Liberal Democracy and the Response to Refugees* (Cambridge University Press 2004) 211. UNHCR notes that '[i]t is the responsibility of States to protect their citizens. When governments are unwilling or unable to protect their citizens, individuals may suffer such serious violations of their rights that they are forced to leave their homes, and often even their families, to seek safety in another state. Since, by definition, the governments of their home states no longer protect the basic rights of CSR1951 refugees, the international community steps in to ensure that those basic rights are respected'. UNHCR, 'Refugee Protection: A Guide to International Refugee Law' (1 Dec 2001), www.unhcr.org/refworld/docid/3cd6a8444.html.

[2] Adopted 10 December 1948 UNGA Res 217 A (III) (UDHR) art 15(1).

[3] Laura Van Waas, *Nationality Matters* (Intersentia 2008) 299 (noting the failure of the Convention Relating to the Status of Stateless Persons (adopted 28 September 1954, entered into force 6 June 1960) 5158 UNTS 360 to address the political disempowerment of stateless persons). See also Matthew J Gibney, 'Statelessness and the Right to Citizenship' (April 2009) 32 *Forced Migration Review* 49, 49 (asserting that, in a world where all human beings must live on the territory of one nation-state or another, having a nationality is a fundamental principle of justice); James Griffin, *On Human Rights* (Oxford University Press 2008) 202 (arguing that 'in some states one can vote and enjoy the protection of the police and army without being a citizen, but only citizenship makes their possession secure. The case for saying that there is a human right to nationality is powerful'); see also Yaffa Zilbershats, *The Human Right to Citizenship* (Transnational 2002).

international system of rights protection,[4] notwithstanding states' treaty obligations.[5]

It was noted in the book's introduction that recognised CSR1951 refugees may be either citizens of their states of origin or stateless persons. In their state of *asylum*, following recognition of refugee status, they are non-citizen residents. This chapter considers the entitlements of CSR1951 refugees in their states of asylum and the ubiquitous exclusion of non-citizen residents, including CSR1951 refugees, from elections of their states of residence.

Section B examines the interrelations between CSR1951 and other leading international human rights instruments, most pertinently the ICCPR,[6] concluding that they are complementary and mutually reinforcing.

In turn, Section C considers provisions of CSR1951 that engage political activities of CSR1951 refugees in states of asylum; it is contended that CSR1951 neither prescribes nor proscribes such activities.

Section D explores rights that CSR1951 refugees enjoy under the ICCPR *qua* non-citizens. It is submitted that, while the ICCPR entitles CSR1951 refugees to (some) political rights in their states of asylum, Contracting

---

[4] See Lassa Oppenheim, *International Law: A Treatise* (Longmans, Green 1912) 369 (contending a century ago that '[a]s far as the Law of Nations is concerned, apart from morality there is no restriction whatever to cause a State to abstain from maltreating to any extent such stateless individuals'). The US Federal Supreme Court Chief Justice Warren's observation in *Perez v Brownell* 356 US 44, 64 (1958) that '[c]itizenship is man's basic right for it is nothing less than the right to have rights' has arguably been influenced by Hannah Arendt's account in *The Origins of Totalitarianism* (Harcourt 1967) 290–92. Arendt lamented the loss of a place to call home, which 'meant the loss of the entire social texture into which they [the stateless] were born and into which they established for themselves a distinct place in the world'. She argued that, while the rights of man have been defined as 'inalienable' because they were supposed to be independent of all government, it turned out that the moment human beings lacked their own government and had to fall back upon their minimum rights, no authority was left to protect them and no institution was willing to guarantee them.

[5] Cf. David Weissbrodt and Stephen Meili, 'Human Rights and Protection of Non-Citizens: Whither Universality and Indivisibility of Rights?' (2009) 28(4) *Refugee Survey Quarterly* 34, 34 (contending that, while in theory, the universality and indivisibility of human rights in the context of non-citizens is expanding, significant obstacles to the universal and indivisible application of human rights remain as increased human rights protections 'on the books' are not always translated into actual improvements in the lives of non-citizens). Regarding the predicament of stateless persons, see Carol Batchelor, 'Statelessness and the Problem of Resolving Nationality Status' (1998) 10 *International Journal of Refugee Law* 156, 182; Brad Blitz and Maureen Lynch, *Statelessness and the Benefits of Citizenship* (Oxford Brookes 2009) 7.

[6] Adopted 16 December 1966, entered into force 23 March 1976, 999 UNTS 171.

States undertake a commitment to secure voting rights in their elections (only) for their *citizens*.

It is contended that, currently, international human rights treaties do not require states of asylum to enfranchise recognised CSR1951 refugees *qua* non-citizen residents.[7] While enfranchisement of (some) non-citizens in local and regional (national) elections is increasingly practised, the territorial state continues to define the limits of the democratic community, most evidently in national elections.

Section E demonstrates that the Convention on the Protection of the Rights of All Migrant Workers and Members of Their Families (Migrant Workers Convention) has recently affirmed the resilience of an accepted link between voting and citizenship in international human rights treaties.[8]

Section F explores the unsuccessful attempt by the ILC to establish a 'protected person' status in international law. It was intended that the 'protected person' status be awarded to stateless persons, entitling them to all rights 'except political rights'. The emphasis that was placed during the drafting process on *voting* as a distinguishing factor between nationals and non-nationals is noteworthy.

B   Interrelations between CSR1951 and the ICCPR

CSR1951 entitles recognised refugees to (qualified) protection by their states of asylum.[9] It is not concerned with the obligations of states of

---

[7] Tony Evans, *The Politics of Human Rights* (2nd edn Pluto Press 2005) 111. See also Penelope Mathew, 'Lest We Forget: Australia's Policy on East Timorese Asylum Seekers' (1999) 11(1) *International Journal of Refugee Law* 7, 23; Ruth Gavison, 'Immigration and the Human Rights Discourse' (2010) 43(2) *Israel Law Review* 1, 27.

[8] Adopted 18 December 1990, entered into force 1 July 2003, 2220 UNTS 3.

[9] David Owen, 'In Loco Civitatis: On the Normative Basis of the Institution of Refugeehood and Responsibilities for Refugees' in Sarah Fine and Lea Ypi (eds), *Migration in Political Theory: The Ethics of Movement and Membership* (Oxford University Press 2016) ch 13. Regarding the present and desirable scope of protection of CSR1951 refugees, see discussion in Chapters 7 and 8. The pronouncement that refugees have rights irrespective of their nationality exhibited a shift from the inter-war approach that treated refugees in terms of their membership of national groups, for instance, in the context of various minority treaties aiming to protect rights of ethnic minorities in newly created states. John Torpey, *The Invention of the Passport* (Cambridge University Press 1999) 144. Traditionally, the treatment of aliens was regulated through reciprocal bilateral agreements between sovereign states; absent such an agreement, the state was (only) expected to offer a minimum international standard of treatment. Riccardo P Mazzeschi, 'The Relationship between Human Rights and the Rights of Aliens and Immigrants' in Ulrich Fastenrath, Rudolf Geiger et al (eds), *From Bilateralism to Community Interest* (Oxford University Press 2011)

origin towards refugees that have left them.[10] The primary purpose of CSR1951 is to ensure that refugees can exercise their fundamental rights and freedoms in the state of asylum.[11]

It was noted in Chapter 1 that recognition as a CSR1951 refugee is declaratory of status; nevertheless, it is also constitutive of rights: a recognised CSR1951 refugee can claim treatment in accordance with the CSR1951. Articles 3–34 of CSR1951 enunciate substantive rights to which refugees are entitled in their states of asylum. The accruing of rights is incremental, based on the refugee's level of attachment to the state of asylum; the longer the refugee remains in the territory of the state party, the broader the range of her entitlements.[12] A basic set of rights inheres as soon as a CSR1951 refugee comes under the state's jurisdiction; a second set of rights applies upon entering the state's territory; additional rights follow lawful presence in the territory, lawful stay therein, and durable residence, respectively.[13]

CSR1951 was adopted shortly after the adoption of the UDHR; its preamble explicitly proclaims a commitment to human rights, and it was arguably intended to contribute to the achievement of the purposes and principles of the UN, which include the advancement of human rights.[14] It

---

552, 553. Cf. Christian Joppke, *Immigration and the Nation-State* (Oxford University Press 1999) 271 (suggesting that, since the 1789 French Declaration on the Rights of Man and Citizens, domestic constitutions have conceived of civil and social rights as rights of persons residing in territory of the state, irrespective of their citizenship status).

[10] Myron Weiner, 'Ethics, National Sovereignty and the Control of Immigration' (1996) 30 *International Migration Review* 171, 188 (suggesting that the refugee 'emerges as a result of the state's unwillingness or failure to secure the ordinary protection offered to its citizens'). Chapter 1 considered the failure of states of origin to secure effective protection in the light of the criteria for CSR1951 refugee status.

[11] Niraj Nathwani, *Rethinking Refugee Law* (Nijhoff 2003) 18. Cf. Chaloka Beyani, 'Introduction' in Paul Weis, *The Refugee Convention 1951: The Travaux Preparatoires Analysed with a Commentary* (Cambridge University Press 1995) 8 (contending that, while the ideal would be to place refugees on an equal footing with nationals of the state of refuge in conformity with the principles of non-discrimination set forth in the Universal Declaration, 'it was not possible to grant refugees exactly the same treatment as nationals').

[12] James C Hathaway and Alexander Neve, 'Making International Refugee Law Relevant Again' (1998) 10 *Harvard Human Rights Law Journal* 115, 158–59.

[13] See e.g. James C Hathaway, *The Rights of Refugees under International Law* (Cambridge University Press 2005) 154; Guy S Goodwin-Gill and Jane McAdam, *The Refugee in International Law* (3rd edn Oxford University Press 2007) 305–7.

[14] Charter of the United Nations (adopted 24 October 1945) 1 UNTS 16 art 1(3), declaring that one of the aims of the United Nations is 'to achieve international co-operation in . . . promoting and encouraging respect for human rights and for fundamental freedoms for all'; and art 55, declaring that '[t]he United Nations shall promote . . . universal respect for and observance of human rights and fundamental freedoms for all'.

was the first comprehensive human rights instrument to apply to a special category of persons.[15] Subsequently, binding human rights instruments were adopted to extend state obligations towards both citizens and non-citizens,[16] including CSR951 refugees.[17] It may be argued that such treaties are expressions in positive international law of a moral idea that there are inviolable rights inherent in each human being and that sovereign states have an obligation to respect, protect, and fulfil these rights. Indeed, it may be argued that obligations assumed by states towards all those on their territory or subject to their jurisdiction are a corollary of their sovereignty.[18]

The (global) human rights project, far from being a project that is essentially antithetical to the inter-state order, primarily requires *states* to assume obligations.[19] The fact that states accede freely to human

---

[15] Nevertheless, the CSR1951 drafters have envisaged that additional protection will be granted to CSR1951 refugees by subsequent treaties. See discussion in Section D.

[16] These treaties include, *inter alia*, the ICCPR; the Covenant on Economic, Social, and Cultural Rights (adopted 16 December 1966, entered into force 3 January 1976), 993 UNTS 3; the Convention on the Elimination of All Forms of Racial Discrimination (adopted 7 March 1966, entered into force 4 January 1969), 660 UNTS 195; the Convention on the Elimination of All Forms of Discrimination against Women (adopted 18 December 1979, entered into force 3 September 1981), 1249 UNTS 13; the Convention against Torture and Other Cruel, Inhuman, or Degrading Treatment or Punishment (adopted 26 June 1987, entered into force 26 June 1987), 1465 UNTS 85; the Convention on the Rights of the Child (adopted 20 November 1989, entered into force 2 September 1990), 1577 UNTS 3.

[17] See e.g. Tom Clark and François Crépeau, 'Mainstreaming Refugee Rights: The 1951 Refugee Convention and International Human Rights Law' (1999) 17(4) *Netherlands Quarterly of Human Rights* 389, 393; cf. Daniel J Steinbock, 'Interpreting the Refugee Definition' (1998) 45 *UCLA Law Review* 733, 785 (contending that there may be a disjunction between general international human rights treaties and CSR1951, as the former are designed to ensure individuals their basic rights within their own states, the primary place of protection); Jane McAdam, *Complementary Protection in International Refugee Law* (Oxford University Press 2007) 12 (contending that, while general international human rights treaties enhance refugees' rights, CSR1951 'creates a mechanism by which entitlements attach and which does not permit derogation'). For a critical approach, see e.g. Jacqueline Bhabha, 'Internationalist Gatekeepers? The Tension between Asylum Advocacy and Human Rights' (2002) 15 *Harvard Human Rights Journal* 155, 166–67.

[18] Guy S Goodwin-Gill, 'Asylum 2001: A Convention and a Purpose' (2001) 13 *International Journal of Refugee Law* 1, 2; cf. Michael Kagan, 'We Live in a Country of UNHCR: The UNHCR Surrogate State and Refugee Policy in the Middle East' (New Issues in Refugee Research No 201 February 2011) 19 (submitting that UNHCR is not a full substitute for an actual state which should be assigned responsibility for protecting rights).

[19] Matthew Craven, 'Human Rights in the Realm of Power: Sanctions and Extraterritoriality' in Fons Coomans and Menno T Kamminga (eds), *Extraterritorial Application of Human Rights Treaties* (Hart 2004) 233, 255; Louis Henkin, 'Protecting the World's Exiles: The Human Rights of Noncitizens' (2000) 22(1) *Human Rights Quarterly* 280, 296 (arguing that

rights treaties should be seen as an affirmation of their international legal sovereignty rather than as a challenge thereto.[20]

Yaesmin Soysal, advocating *universal personhood* as a basis of political membership, notes that the power of personhood 'comes across most clearly in the case of political refugees whose status in the host polities exclusively rests on an appeal to human rights'.[21] Nonetheless, their appeal to protection has to be heeded by a territorial state, which remains the main venue for decision making and rights protection;[22] in terms of effective protection, physical presence in a state matters.[23]

To date, no international treaty enunciates the rights of non-citizens *qua* non-citizens[24] (note the non-binding Declaration on the Rights of

human rights are not really international; rather, they are obligations undertaken within a national system. The purpose of the international movement is to get national systems to work better). See also Fernando Tesón, *A Philosophy of International Law* (Westview Press 1998) 16 (contending that human rights subscribe to a Kantian international order where governments exist in the first place to protect human rights); Randall Hansen, 'The Poverty of Post-nationalism: Citizenship, Immigration, and the New Europe' (2009) 38(1) *Theory and Society* 1, 7–8 (arguing that human rights norms and conventions are most effective when they are incorporated into domestic legislation and form part of the jurisprudential frame of reference of domestic courts).

[20] Seyla Benhabib and Judith Resnik, 'Introduction' in Seyla Benhabib and Judith Resnik (eds), *Migrations and Mobility: Citizenship, Borders and Gender* (NYU Press 2009) 1, 4 (contending that, when states join together to promulgate legal commitments to universal norms that transcend sovereign boundaries and that constrain sovereign prerogatives, they do so through conventions reliant on national authority for implementation). Cf. Stephen Krasner, *Sovereignty, Organized Hypocrisy* (Princeton University Press 1997) 118.

[21] Yasemin N Sosyal, *The Limits of Citizenship* (Chicago University Press 1994) 140. See also Yaesmin N Soysal, 'Changing Citizenship in Europe: Remarks on Postnational Membership and the National State' in David Cesarani and Mary Fulbrook (eds), *Citizenship, Nationality, and Migration in Europe* (Routledge 1996) 17, 24 (describing a 'deterritorialised expansion of rights despite the territorialised closure of polities').

[22] See e.g. Christian Joppke, *Immigration and the Nation-State: The United States, Germany, and Great Britain* (Oxford University Press 2000) 6 (arguing that, absent a supra-national polity with implementation force, denizenship does not represent a new model of membership that entails the decline of traditional citizenship; rather, it is an inherently vulnerable status).

[23] See e.g. Linda Bosniak, 'Persons and Citizens in Constitutional Thought' (2010) 8(1) *International Journal of Constitutional Law* 9 (noting that, to vindicate rights claims of non-citizens *qua* persons, personhood plus territorial presence is required).

[24] See e.g. Lydia Morris, 'Managing Contradiction: Civic Stratification and Migrants' rights' (2003) 37(1) *International Migration Review* 74, 79 (contending that international human rights instruments offer 'no obvious means of addressing the different legal statuses occupied by non-citizens or the stratified nature of their rights'). Cf. David Weissbrodt, *The Human Rights of Non-Citizens* (Oxford University Press 2008) 5 (postulating that '[i]t is useful to see the human rights of non-citizens not as an amalgamation of the rights

RIGHTS OF CSR1951 REFUGEES   41

Individuals Who Are Not Nationals of the Country in Which They Live[25]).
In contradistinction, CSR1951 addresses, *inter alia*, concerns specific to
CSR1951 refugees which are not dealt with under general human rights
treaties, such as their need for travel and other identity documents.[26]
CSR1951 aims to 'assure refugees the widest possible exercise of [their]
fundamental rights and freedoms'.[27]

UNHCR posits that the human rights base of CSR1951 roots it quite
directly in the broader framework of human rights instruments of which
it is an integral part, albeit with a very particular focus: CSR1951 and
the 1967 New York Protocol 'were carefully framed to define minimum
standards without imposing obligations going beyond those that States
can reasonably be expected to assume'.[28] As refugees benefit from protection both under CSR1951 and under general human rights protections,
Section D demonstrates that resort to the ICCPR is pertinent in areas that
are not covered by CSR1951.[29]

---

of various non-citizen subgroups . . . but rather as a unified domain' and follow general
principles applying to the treatment of non-citizens). Weissbrodt asserts that 'the principal
challenge for advocates and scholars today is one of implementation, nor elaboration', as
non-citizens suffer from discriminatory treatment and social vilification, demonstrating
the need for a unified movement for their protection. Ibid 244. Nevertheless, Caroline Bettinger-Lopez and Bassina Farbernblum, 'Book Review of David Weissbrodt, *The
Human Rights of Non-Citizens* (Oxford University Press 2008)' (UNSW Research Series
Paper No 46 2010) 5–7 contend that the goals and circumstances of each group of non-
citizens are not always sufficiently common so that a unified approach will achieve the
best outcome, not least regarding CSR1951 refugees.

[25] GA/RES/40/144 of 13 December 1985. Cf. Rosalyn Higgins, 'Derogations under Human
Rights Treaties' (1976–1977) 48 *British Yearbook of International Law* 281, 282 (positing
that 'international human rights treaties undoubtedly contain elements that are binding as principles which are recognised by civilised states and not only as mutual treaty
commitments').

[26] Jason Pobjoy, 'Treating Like Cases Alike' (2010) 34(1) *Melbourne University Law Review*
181, 192. See also Chapter 7. Conversely, as Harvey notes, 'where applicable human rights
guarantees go further than refugee law they can and should be used'. Colin Harvey, 'Time
for Reform? Refugees, Asylum-Seekers, and Protection under International Human Rights
Law' (2015) 34 *Refugee Survey Quarterly* 43, 46.

[27] CSR1951 Preamble §2.

[28] UNHCR, *Note on International Protection*, UN Doc A/AC.96/951 (13 September 2001)
[4] and [107].

[29] Santhosh Persau, 'Protecting Refugees and Asylum-Seekers under the ICCPR' (New Issues
in Refugee Research No 132 November 2006) 5–6. Cf. Vincent Chetail, 'Are Refugee Rights
Human Rights? An Unorthodox Questioning of the Relations between Refugee Law and
Human Rights Law' in Ruth Rubio-Marin (ed), *Human Rights and Immigration* (Oxford
University Press 2014) 19 (arguing that human rights law, especially the ICCPR, is an

The ICJ has held that 'an international instrument has to be interpreted and applied within the framework of the entire legal system prevailing at the time of the interpretation'.[30] In turn, the Vienna Convention on the Law of Treaties (VCLT) stipulates that a treaty 'shall be interpreted in good faith in accordance with the ordinary meaning to be given to the terms of the treaty in their context and in the light of its object and purpose'.[31] If one of the (primary) objects and purposes of CSR1951 is protection of refugee rights (notwithstanding the inter-state framing of obligations therein[32]), then the interrelations between CSR1951 and other rights instruments such as the ICCPR ought to be considered as complementary and mutually reinforcing,[33] and their respective interpretations should be accordingly engaged.[34] Thus, it is submitted that the scope of protection in CSR1951 should be considered and interpreted in light of international human rights instruments.

essential and primary source of refugee protection which supplements and reinforces refugee status).

[30] *Legal Consequences for States of the Continued Presence of South Africa in Namibia*, ICJ Rep (1971) 16, 31.

[31] Adopted 23 May 1969, entered into force 27 January 1980, 1155 UNTS 331 art 31(1). See also James C Hathaway and Michelle Foster, *The Law of Refugee Status* (2nd edn Cambridge University Press 2014) 7. Furthermore, art 31(3)(c) pronounces that 'any relevant rules of international law applicable in the relations between the parties' will be taken into account together with the treaty's context; art 32 stipulates that the Travaux Préparatoires should be engaged as 'supplementary means of interpretation' when the meaning of the text is 'ambiguous or obscure' or leads to a result which is 'manifestly absurd or unreasonable'. See also Goodwin-Gill and McAdam (n 13) 8.

[32] See e.g. Guy S Goodwin-Gill, 'Refugees and Their Human Rights' (RSC Working Paper No 17 2004) 7 (noting that '[t]he formal scheme of the Convention, however, remains one of obligations between states. The refugee is a beneficiary, beholden to the state, with a status to which certain standards of treatment and certain guarantees attach').

[33] See e.g. Alice Edwards, 'Human Rights, Refugees, and the Right to "Enjoy" Asylum' (2005) 17(2) *International Journal of Refugee Law* 297, 330. See also David Weissbrodt and Stephen Meili, 'Human Rights and the Protection of Noncitizens' (2009) 28(4) *Refugee Survey Quarterly* 35, 54 (suggesting that, because many problems frequently faced by non-citizens are covered by more than one treaty, it would be desirable for each of the treaty bodies to take into account the jurisprudence of their counterparts to establish a consistent, structured approach to the protection of the rights of non-citizens). Javaid Rehman, *International Human Rights Law* (2nd edn Pearson 2010) 641 (positing that it is no longer possible to interpret or apply CSR1951 'without drawing on the text and jurisprudence of other human rights treaties', and vice versa).

[34] Jonas Christoffersen, 'Impact on General Principles of Treaty Interpretation' in Menno T Kamminga and Martin Scheinin (eds), *The Impact of Human Rights Law on General International Law* (Oxford University Press 2009) 37, 60–61.

C Political Activities of Refugees under the CSR1951

1 Introduction

CSR1951 does not explicitly address political activities of refugees in their states of asylum, in contradistinction to (some of) their social and economic rights, civil status, and identity.[35] Hence, CSR1951 neither prescribes nor proscribes states entitling refugees to vote in their states of asylum. Nonetheless, several CSR1951 provisions *implicitly* address the scope of political activities of refugees: Article 1E, regarding exclusion from refugee status; Article 2, regarding the obligations of refugees towards their states of asylum; Article 15, regarding non-political associations; and Article 34, regarding assimilation and naturalisation.

2 Article 1E

Article 1E excludes from CSR1951 status 'a person who is recognised by the competent authorities of the country in which he has taken residence [*not* the state of asylum] as having the rights and obligations which are attached to the possession of the nationality of that country'. The interpretation of this provision may be helpful in contextualising the political status of refugees vis-à-vis citizens.

The provision was included to prevent post–Second World War displaced Germans residing in neighbouring states from claiming refugee status.[36] Guy Goodwin-Gill and Jane McAdam argue that, while Article 1E was not intended to require that, to be excluded, the individual in question must enjoy the *full range* of rights incidental to citizenship,[37] the rights to enter the state and remain therein were considered to be essential, given the fundamental objective of CSR1951, namely

---

[35] See also Frank Krenz, 'The Refugee as a Subject of International Law' (1966) 15(1) *International and Comparative Law Quarterly* 90, 109 (postulating that general international law is silent on the question of political rights of refugees in their states of residence).

[36] The Berlin (Potsdam) Conference, 17 July–2 August 1945, explicitly discussed in art XII the 'orderly transfer of German populations', stipulating that 'the transfer to Germany of German populations, or elements thereof, remaining in Poland, Czechoslovakia and Hungary, will have to be undertaken . . . [and] should be effected in an orderly and humane manner'. See also Law of Refugee Status (n 31) 500.

[37] Goodwin-Gill and McAdam (n 13) 162. See e.g. *Refugee Appeal No 75091/04*, NZRSAA 208 (28 June 2004) (holding that, in view of art 1E, an asylum applicant who has obtained refugee status and permanent residence in a third state cannot raise a claim to protection under the refugee convention in respect of any state of former habitual residence).

protection.[38] Arguably, an entitlement to a 'political rights' threshold would have been tantamount to the provision applying only to persons who have the nationality of their states of residence 'whereas such persons were already excluded from the refugee definition by Article 1A(2)'.[39]

3   Article 2

Article 2 stipulates that '[e]very refugee has duties to the country in which he finds himself, which require in particular that he conform to its laws and regulations as well as to measures taken for the maintenance of public order'. Article 2 is 'an imperfect obligation', much like Article 29 of the UDHR (stipulating that '[e]veryone has duties to the community in which alone the free and full development of his personality is possible'): non-observance of a duty covered by Article 2 does not entail loss of any particular right guaranteed under CSR1951 nor cessation of refugee status. As noted in Chapter 1, CSR1951 refugees are protected from expulsion unless their behaviour is deemed serious enough to qualify under Article 32 or 33(2).[40]

Pertinently for this chapter's analysis, the *Travaux* indicate that the Ad Hoc Committee rejected a French proposal to include a provision entailing that '[t]he High Contracting Parties reserve the right to restrict the political activity of refugees'.[41] It was feared that such a provision could be misunderstood as approving limitations on areas of activity of refugees which are unobjectionable. States were reassured that 'in the absence of a provision to the contrary any sovereign government retained the right

[38] See also UNHCR, *Handbook on Procedures and Criteria for Determining Refugee Status under the 1951 Convention and the 1967 Protocol Relating to the Status of Refugees* (reissued December 2011) [145] (referring to the status of a person qualifying under art 1E as 'largely assimilated' to that of a national of the state, including full protection against deportation or expulsion 'like a national').

[39] Reinhard Marx, 'Article 1E' in Andreas Zimmermann (ed), *The 1951 Convention Relating to the Status of Refugees and 1967 Protocol* (Oxford University Press 2011) 571, 574. Note, in this regard, Judge Hill's statement in *Barzideh v Minister for Immigration and Ethnic Affairs* (1996) 69 FCR 417, 429 ('I do not think that the Article is rendered inapplicable merely because the person who has de facto national status does not have the political rights of a national. That is to say the mere fact that the person claiming to be a refugee is not entitled to vote, does not mean that the person does not have de facto nationality') quoted approvingly in *NAGV and NAGW of 2002 v Minister for Immigration and Multicultural and Indigenous Affairs* [2005] HCA 6 (Australia) [51–53].

[40] Hélène Lambert, 'Article 2: General Obligations' in Zimmermann (n 39) 625 [48].

[41] The Ad Hoc Committee on Statelessness and Related Problems, UN Doc E/1618 and E/AC.32/5 (1950) 41.

it has to regulate any activities on the part of an alien which it considers objectionable'.[42]

4 Article 15

Article 15 requires states to accord to 'refugees lawfully staying in their territory the most favourable treatment accorded to nationals of a foreign country, in the same circumstances' regarding '*non-political* and non-profit-making associations and trade unions' (emphasis added).

The drafters debated the extent to which refugees should be permitted to engage in *political* activities, namely whether the article should be modified to authorise states of asylum to restrict political activities of refugees. The French representative, echoed by the Swiss representatives, argued that refugees like other non-citizens were under an obligation to refrain from taking part in internal politics until they had become naturalised citizens.[43]

In contrast, the American representative, seconded by the Canadian representative, questioned whether, in light of their predicament, refugees should not be granted better treatment than aliens generally. He expressed concern that the French proposal can be interpreted as prohibiting expression of political opinion, an area of human activity in which refugees should have 'at least as much right to engage as other aliens'.[44] Ultimately, the French or Swiss view did not prevail (nor did the American or Canadian), and the provision as well as CSR1951 as a whole remained silent regarding political activities of refugees.

5 Article 34

Article 34 stipulates that 'the Contracting States shall as far as possible facilitate the assimilation and naturalisation of refugees'. The

---

[42] Weis (n 11) 32. Cf. Convention Governing the Specific Aspects of Refugee Problems in Africa (adopted 10 September 1969, entered into force 20 June 1974) 1001 UNTS 45 (OAU Convention) art 3 (demanding that refugees 'abstain from any subversive activities against any Member State of the OAU'). Moreover, the provision requires Member States to 'prohibit refugees residing in their respective territories from attacking any State Member of the OAU by any activity likely to cause tension between Member States'. See Lambert (n 40) [20] (noting that the CSR1951 drafters had not agreed to include an equivalent provision).

[43] Weis (n 11) 90–93. Regarding rights of CSR1951 refugees to participate in political associations under the ICCPR, see discussion in Section D.

[44] Michael Teichmann, 'Article 15' in Zimmermann (n 39) 909, 914.

provision, which may trigger one of the six bases for cessation of status under CSR1951 (acquisition of a new nationality[45]), is further discussed in Chapter 8. For this chapter's purposes, the potential significance of 'assimilation' of refugees into their host communities should be considered. The Israeli representative was concerned about the sociological connotation of the term *assimilation*, noting that it may be regarded as 'form[ing] an attack on the spiritual independence of the refugees' and offering in its stead the term *integration*.[46] However, his concerns were not shared by other representatives, who contended that assimilation inferred integration.[47] Notably, there was no discussion of how electoral inclusion of CSR1951 refugees or other political engagement in the state of asylum may affect assimilation (or integration) and, ultimately, facilitate naturalisation.

D   Refugee Rights under CSR1951 and the ICCPR

1   The General Principle

It was suggested in Section C that no CSR1951 provision regulates the extent to which refugees ought to enjoy political rights in their states of asylum. Article 7(1) promulgates that 'except where this Convention contains more favourable provisions, a Contracting State shall afford to refugees the same treatment as is accorded to aliens generally'.[48]

The Austrian representative to the Conference of Plenipotentiaries noted that '[i]f it were to be posited that refugees should not have rights greater than those enjoyed by other aliens, the Convention seemed pointless, since its object was precisely to provide for specially favourable treatment to be accorded to refugees'.[49] Hence, absent CSR1951 provisions concerning political rights, refugees are to be afforded the same political rights as other aliens in the state of asylum.[50]

---

[45]   CSR1951 art 1C(3): 'This Convention shall cease to apply to any person falling under the terms of Section A if ... [h]e has acquired a new nationality, and enjoys the protection of the country of his new nationality'.

[46]   Weis (n 11) 348.   [47]   Ibid. See also Chapter 8.

[48]   Notably, the OAU Convention and the Cartagena Declaration on Refugees, adopted by the Colloquium on the International Protection of Refugees in Central America, Mexico and Panama (19–22 November 1984), extends the refugee definition beyond CSR1951; however, they do not provide a new set of specific rights and standards but refer instead to those established in the 1951 Convention; see art viii (2) and iii (8), respectively.

[49]   UN Doc. A/CONF.2/SR.6.

[50]   Achilles Skordas, 'Article 7' in Zimmermann (n 39) 715, 719. CSR1951 entitles refugees to treatment at least as favourable as that accorded to citizens with respect to religion,

According to Article 7(2), refugees may enjoy rights even when such rights are ordinarily accorded to an 'alien' on the basis of *reciprocity*. Absent generally applicable human rights standards at the time of drafting (see Section B), states were inclined to grant certain aliens broader rights only if their citizens were to be reciprocally treated in these aliens' state of nationality.[51] However, the CSR1951 drafters recognised that the *raison d'être* of reciprocity requirements does not apply in the case of CSR1951 refugees who *qua* CSR1951 refugees do not enjoy the protection of their state of origin.[52]

Based on a similar rationale, Article 6 exempts CSR1951 refugees from requirements relating to length and conditions of sojourn or residence which non-refugee aliens would have to fulfil for the enjoyment of a CSR1951 right, when such requirements are by their nature such that a refugee is incapable of fulfilling. The exception from reciprocity 'was . . . intended to grant [refugees] treatment commensurate with their special situation'.[53]

2 Complementary Rights Protection

Article 5 stipulates that '[n]othing in this Convention shall be deemed to impair any rights and benefits granted by a Contracting State to refugees apart from this Convention', and Article 7(3) proclaims that states 'shall continue to accord to refugees the rights to which they were already entitled, in the absence of reciprocity, at the date of entry into force of this Convention for that state'.

---

protection of intellectual property, rationing measures, elementary education, public relief and assistance, labour legislation and social security, as well as fiscal taxes and charges. CSR1951 arts 4, 16, 20, 22(1), 23, 24 and 29. In turn, CSR1951 entitles refugees to treatment no less favourable than that accorded to aliens generally with respect to acquisition of property, wage earning employment, self-employment, professions, housing, post-elementary education, freedom of movement, and (as noted above) participation in non-political and non-profit making associations and trade unions. Ibid arts 7(1), 13, 17, 18, 19, 21, 22(2), 26, 15.

[51] Nehemiah Robinson, *The Universal Declaration of Human Rights: Its Origin, Significance, Application and Interpretation* (Institute of Jewish Affairs 1950) art 7 commentary; Hathaway (n 13) 78 (noting that refugees are unlikely to derive even indirect protection from general principles of 'Aliens Law' because they lack the relationship with a state of nationality that is legally empowered to advance a claim to protection).

[52] Weis (n 11) 47.

[53] Comment by the representative of the International Refugee Organisation; ibid 51.

Hence, it was emphasised that CSR1951 should not be construed as restricting the application of other human rights instruments.[54] Rather, the above provisions conform to the purported purpose of CSR1951: to secure the enjoyment of rights by refugees under both existing and prospective arrangements.[55] They also reinforce the need for a dynamic interpretation of CSR1951 provisions.[56]

3   Political Rights of Refugees under the ICCPR

It was noted in the introduction that 168 states are parties to the ICCPR, including nearly all states that are parties to the CSR1951 and the 1967 Protocol.[57] Article 1 of the ICCPR stipulates that a state must 'respect and ensure to all individuals within its territory and subject to its jurisdiction ... the rights recognised in the present Covenant'. The ICCPR does not sub-classify rights as 'civil' or 'political', though electoral rights quite plausibly belong to the latter category.[58]

The Human Rights Committee (HRC) comments that '[t]he enjoyment of Covenant rights is not limited to citizens of States parties but must also be available to all individuals, regardless of nationality or statelessness, such as ... refugees'.[59] Obligations must be given effect 'in good faith'.[60] Indeed, 'in general, the rights set forth in the Covenant apply to everyone, irrespective of reciprocity, and irrespective of his or her nationality or statelessness';[61] while it is 'in principle a matter for the State to decide who it will admit to its territory ... once aliens are allowed to enter the

---

[54] Penelope Mathew, 'Review: James Hathaway, *The Rights of Refugees under International Law* (Cambridge University Press 2005)' (2008) 102(1) *American Journal of International Law* 206, 207.

[55] Robinson (n 51) Commentary [2].

[56] Guidelines Reflecting the Consensus of Participants at the Fifth Colloquium on Challenges in International Refugee Law [4], Ann Arbor, 13–15 November 2009, published in (2010) 31 *Michigan Journal of International Law* 293.

[57] Of the State Parties to the 1967 Protocol, only very small (mostly island) states, Antigua and Barbuda, Fiji, the Holy See, St. Kitts and Nevis have not ratified the ICCPR.

[58] John Humphrey, 'Political and Related Rights' in Theodor Meron (ed), *Human Rights in International Law: Legal and Policy Issues* (Oxford University Press 1986) 171, 172 (suggesting that 'freedoms of expression, assembly, and association, though not exclusively political, are each in a special way part of the democratic process').

[59] HRC, General Comment No 31: Article 2: *The Nature of the General Legal Obligations Imposed on States Parties to the Covenant*, UN Doc CCPR/C/21/Rev.1/Add.13 (26 May 2004) [10].

[60] Ibid [3].

[61] HRC, General Comment No 15: *The Position of Aliens under the Covenant*, UN Doc HRI/GEN/1/Rev.7 (11 April 1986) [1].

territory of a State Party they are entitled to the rights set out in the Covenant'.[62]

Article 2(1) of the ICCPR stipulates that states 'undertakes to respect and to ensure to all individuals within its territory and subject to its jurisdiction the rights recognised . . . without distinction of any kind, such as race, colour, sex, language, religion, political or other opinion, national or social origin, property, birth or other status'. The absence of *nationality* as a prohibited distinction should not be considered 'fatal' because 'the list clearly is intended to be illustrative and not comprehensive . . . [and] nationality would appear to fall into the category of "distinction of any kind"'.[63]

The HRC notes that 'the general rule is that each one of the rights of the Covenant must be guaranteed without discrimination between citizens and aliens. Aliens receive the benefit of the general requirement of non-discrimination in respect of the rights guaranteed in the Covenant as provided for in Article 2'.[64] Indeed, '[n]on-discrimination, together with equality before the law and equal protection of the law without any discrimination, constitutes a basic and general principle relating to the protection of human rights'.[65] Moreover, the centrality of the concept of non-discrimination 'imbu[ed] and inspire[ed] similar protection in every other major international human rights instrument'.[66]

Nevertheless, the non-discrimination principle is subject to two significant qualifications. The first qualification is that 'not every differentiation of treatment will constitute discrimination, if the criteria for such differentiation are reasonable and objective and if the aim is to achieve a purpose which is legitimate under the Covenant'.[67] The burden is on the state to show that nationality is a relevant basis for differentiation; that the distinction is implemented in pursuit of a reasonable aim or objective; that it is necessary; that there is no alternative action available; and that

---

[62] HRC, General Comment No 18: *Non-Discrimination*, UN Doc HRI/GEN/1/Rev.5 (10 November 1989) [5–6].

[63] A similar question was addressed by the Committee on Economic, Social and Cultural Rights in its General Comment No 20: *Non-Discrimination in Economic, Social and Cultural Rights*, E/C.12/GC/20 (2 July 2009) [15]: 'the inclusion of 'other status' ground indicates that this list is not exhaustive and other grounds may be incorporated in this category entails a number of implied grounds'.

[64] GC15 (n 61) [2].   [65] GC18 (n 62) [1].

[66] Manfred Nowak, *UN Covenant on Civil and Political Rights: CCPR Commentary* (2nd revised edn Engel 2005) 598.

[67] GC18 (n 62) [13].

the discriminatory measures taken or contemplated are proportional to the end to be achieved.[68]

The second qualification, explored below, is that '[e]xceptionally some of the rights recognised in the Covenant are expressly applicable only to citizens (art. 25)'.[69] By comparison, the ICCPR stipulates that 'everyone' enjoys other political rights such as freedom of expression, freedom of peaceful assembly, and freedom of association without distinction based on citizenship.[70]

Hence, as with other ICCPR rights, the burden of demonstrating the validity of restrictions on the exercise of the political (non-electoral) rights lies with the protecting state. In the context of CSR1951 refugees, absent reasonable and objective justifications that concern the interests of the state of asylum rather than possible effects on a third state such as the state of origin, an imposition of greater restrictions on refugees *qua* non-citizens may constitute discrimination under the ICCPR.[71]

4 Article 25: Citizenship Voting Qualification

Article 25 of the ICCPR enunciates that every *citizen* shall have the right to vote in 'genuine periodic elections which shall be by universal and equal suffrage', and to exercise the right 'without unreasonable restrictions'.[72]

---

[68] Guy S Goodwin-Gill, 'International Law and Human Rights: Trends Concerning International Migrants and Refugees' (1989) 23(3) *International Migration Review* 526, 532.

[69] GC15 (n 61) [2]. See also GC18 (n 62) [8] where the HRC notes that '[a]rticle 25 guarantees certain political rights, differentiating on grounds of citizenship'. Guy S Goodwin-Gill, 'Migration: International Law and Human Rights' in Bimal Ghosh (ed), *Managing Migration* (Oxford University Press 2000) 160, 167 (noting that the major human rights treaties acknowledge the continuing authority of the state to maintain distinctions between citizens and non-citizens in certain areas of activity); See also Stephanie Farrior, 'International Human Rights Treaties and the Rights of Female Refugees' in Anne Bayefsky (ed), *Human Rights and Refugees, Internally Displaced Persons and Migrant Workers* (Nijhoff 2006) 283, 291. Analogously, ICESCR art 2(3) permits 'developing countries' to limit 'economic rights' of non-nationals. Ryszard Cholewinski, *Migrant Workers in International Human Rights Law: Their Protection in Countries of Employment* (Clarendon Press 1997) 58. Notably, the French Declaration of the Rights of Man (26 August 1789) used the term 'citizen' with regard to electoral participation (alongside a few other rights); art 6 thereof stipulates that '[l]aw is the expression of the general will. Every citizen has a right to participate personally, or through his representative, in its foundation'.

[70] ICCPR arts 19, 21 and 22 respectively.

[71] Ruma Mandal, 'Political Rights of Refugees' (UNHCR Department of International Protection 2003) [20].

[72] See also General Comment No 25: *The Right to Participate in Public Affairs, Voting Rights and the Right of Equal Access to Public Service* (Article 25), CCPR/C/21/Rev.1/Add.7

Article 25 is the only ICCPR provision that refers explicitly to rights of citizens.[73] In contradistinction, Article 21(3) of the UDHR pronounces 'the right of 'everyone... to take part in the government of his state, directly or through freely chosen representatives'. Article 21(3) UDHR may enjoy CIL status,[74] and Article 25 is often seen as its concretisation,[75] though its stipulation is arguably more restrictive.[76]

(12 July 1996) [6]. Hence, in some jurisdictions, certain voting qualifications are imposed on citizens such as age, mental competence, or conviction of a criminal offence. The reasonableness of the latter qualification was the subject of the inquiry in Reuven (Ruvi) Ziegler, 'Legal Outlier, Again? U.S. Felon Suffrage Policies: Comparative and International Human Rights Perspectives' (2011) 29(2) *Boston University International Law Journal* 197, and falls outside the remit of this book.

[73] In contradistinction, art 12(4) of the ICCPR stipulates that 'no one shall be arbitrarily deprived of the right to enter his own country'. See Zilbershats (n 3) 59 (suggesting that a person's 'own country' may also be a state to which she feels attached due to the fact that her ancestors lived there in the past or the members of her national or ethnic community live there in the present). The HRC has interpreted the phrase 'own country' to permit 'a broader interpretation that might embrace other categories of long-term residents including, but not limited to stateless persons arbitrarily deprived of the right to acquire the nationality of the country of such residence'. General Comment No 27: *Freedom of Movement* (Article 12), CCPR/C/21/Rev.1/Add.9 (2 November 1999) [20]. Indeed, 'there are few, if any, circumstances in which deprivation of the right to enter one's own state could be reasonable'. Ibid [21]. The provision, discussed further in Chapter 8, is of 'the utmost importance for refugees seeking voluntary repatriation'. Ibid [19]. See also Marc J Bossuyt, *Guide to the Travaux Préparatoires of the International Covenant on Civil and Political Rights* (Nijhoff 1987) 26 (suggesting that the drafters intended for the right to apply also to permanent residents). Furthermore, under art 12(3), only persons 'lawfully within the territory of a state' enjoy freedom of movement and choice of residence. However, as the book concerns recognised refugees, it is assumed that they reside lawfully in their state of asylum.

[74] See e.g. Thomas Franck, 'The Emerging Right to Democratic Governance' (1992) 86 *American Journal of International Law* 46, 61 (contending that art 21 reflects 'a customary rule of state obligation'). See also Christina M Cerna, 'Universal Democracy: An International Legal Right or the Pipe Dream of the West?' (1995) 27 *NYU Journal of International Law and Politics* 289, 294–97. Cf. Guy S Goodwin-Gill, *Free and Fair Elections* (Inter-Parliamentary Union 2006) 93 (contending that 'the provision in Article 21(3) stands as a straightforward statement of the principle of representative democracy which is now increasingly seen as essential to the legitimation of governments among the community of states').

[75] See e.g. Henry Steiner, 'Political Participation as a Human Right' (1988) 1 *Harvard Human Rights Yearbook* 77, 79; Allan Rosas, 'Article 21' in Gudmundur Alfredson and Asbjorn Eide (eds), *The Universal Declaration of Human Rights: A Common Standard of Achievement* (Nijhoff 1999) 431, 438; Gregory H Fox, 'The Right to Political Participation in International Law' in Gregory H Fox and Brad Roth (eds), *Democratic Governance and International Law* (Cambridge University Press 2000) 48, 54; Nowak (n 66) 567.

[76] Cf. Robinson (n 51) 131–32 (asserting that 'Article 21 is different than other articles as it does not deal with the rights of men but with those of citizens' and that '[t]he third

The HRC notes that '[i]n contrast with other rights and freedoms recognized by the Covenant... Article 25 protects the rights of "every citizen"'. Hence, basing eligibility on citizenship status rather than *domicile* is permissible.[77] Nonetheless, it stipulates that '[s]tate reports should indicate whether any groups, such as permanent residents, enjoy these rights on a limited basis, for example, by having the right to vote in *local* elections' (emphasis added).[78] The HRC celebrates the prominence of Article 25, positing that it 'lies at the core of democratic government

paragraph was considered to contain a political principle rather than a human right'); Common Standard (n 75) 440 (concluding that the difference between the provisions 'is apparently more symbolic than substantial').

[77] GC25 (n 72) [3]. Notably, ICERD art 1(2) excludes from the instrument's purview 'exclusions, restrictions or preferences made by a State Party to the Convention between citizens and non-citizens' as well as 'laws about nationality, citizenship or naturalization provided they do not target a particular nationality', thereby emphasising the nearly unfettered discretion that states enjoy in these matters. Thus, the CERD Committee in General Recommendation No 30: *Discrimination against Non-citizens* (10 January 2004) [3] notes that 'rights, such as the right to participate in elections, to vote and stand for election, may be confined to citizens'. Nonetheless, the Committee posits that 'human rights are, in principle, to be enjoyed by all persons. States Parties are under an obligation to guarantee equality between citizens and non-citizens in the enjoyment of these rights to the extent recognised under international law'; hence 'ICERD is fully applicable if the discrimination a person faces is on the basis of race or ethnic origin rather than alien status'. Ibid [2]. See also Report of the Committee on the Elimination of Discrimination against Women, General Recommendation No 21: *Equality in Marriage and Family Relations*, UN GAOR 49th Sess., Supp No. 38, UN Doc A/49/38 (1994), noting at [2] that '[n]ationality is critical to full participation in society... [w]ithout status as nationals or citizens, women are deprived of the right to vote or to stand for public office and may be denied access to public benefits and a choice of residence'.

[78] GC25 (n 72) [3]. See also CCPR, Observations regarding Portugal, A/58/40 vol I (2003) 56 [82(6)] (welcoming 'the granting to aliens of the rights to vote and to be elected in local elections'), and similar observations regarding Belgium (Belgium, ICCPR, A/59/40 vol I (2004) 56 [72(5)] and [72(27)]); See also the observations of the CERD Committee re Netherlands, A/59/18 (2004) 29 [147] (commending the fact that aliens who have been legally resident in the Netherlands for five years are entitled to vote and to stand for local election) and regarding Latvia (where '[t]he Committee recognizes that political rights can be legitimately limited to citizens. Nevertheless, noting that most non-citizens have been residing in Latvia for many years, if not for their whole lives, the Committee strongly recommends that the State party consider facilitating the integration process by making it possible for all non-citizens who are long time permanent residents to participate in local elections'). Cf. Raimo Pekkanen and Hans Danelius, 'Human Rights in the Republic of Estonia' (Report submitted to the Parliamentary Assembly of the Council of Europe, 17 December 1991) [36] (positing that '[I]f substantial parts of the population of a country are denied the right to become citizens, and thereby are also denied for instance the right to vote in parliamentary elections this could affect the character of the democratic system in that country').

based on the consent of the people and in conformity with the principles of the Covenant'.[79]

Article 25 reflects the idea that every person, whether a member of a majority or a minority, has the right to participate in public life.[80] Read in conjunction with Article 1, according to which 'all peoples are entitled to freely determine their political, economic and cultural destiny', Article 25 can be taken to affirm the contention that the sovereignty of the people shall find its expression, *inter alia*, in periodic and genuine elections.[81] It has even been asserted that, while international law still protects state sovereignty, it is now the people's sovereignty that it protects rather than the sovereign's sovereignty.[82]

The reference to *citizens* rather than persons or individuals in Article 25 may be seen as a reaffirmation of the state as the essential forum of political

---

[79] GC25 (n 72) [1].

[80] James Crawford, 'Democracy and the Body of International Law' in Fox and Roth (n 75) 91, 92.

[81] See e.g. Nowak (n 66) 570 (noting that art 25 implies that 'the government ultimately is responsible to the people and may also be controlled and deposed by it'); Henry Steiner, 'Do Human Rights Require a Particular Form of Democracy?' in Eugene Cotran and Adel O Sherif (eds), *Democracy, Human Rights and Islam* (Kluwer 1999) 193, 201 (explaining that art 25 is irreconcilable with the existence of any authoritarian regime that denies its citizens the right to take part in free and fair elections); Peter R Baehr, 'Democracy and the Right to Political Participation' in David P Forsythe (ed), *Encyclopaedia of Human Rights* (Oxford University Press 2009) vol I, 487, 490 (arguing that art 25 requires governments to be accountable to their citizens). The HRC notes in General Comment No 12: Article 1, UN Doc HRI/GEN/1/Rev.6 at 134 (13 March 1984) [4] and [6] that art 1 imposes specific obligations on states 'in relation to their own people' and asserts that 'it [the HRC] may take Article 1 into account when interpreting Article 25 of the Covenant'. See e.g. its conclusions in *Gillot v France*, UN Doc CCPR/C/75/D/932/2000 [13.4]. In its Concluding Observations on the Second Periodic Report of the Republic of the Congo, the HRC called 'to organize general elections as soon as possible in order to enable its citizens to exercise their rights under articles 1 and 25 of the Covenant'; UN Doc CCPR/C/79/Add.118 (27 March 2000) [20]. Cf. Rosalyn Higgins, *Problems and Process: International Law and How we Use it* (Clarendon Press 1994) 120–21 (arguing that 'while there is a close relationship between Article 25(1) and Article 1, nothing in the former requires a narrow reading of the right of self-determination. The two articles are complementary').

[82] Michael Reisman, 'Sovereignty and Human Rights in Contemporary International Law' (1990) 84 *American Journal of International Law* 866, 868–69. Thomas Franck's article (n 74) triggered a scholarly debate regarding the 'right to democratic governance': see e.g. Stephen Wheatley, *The Democratic Legitimacy of International Law* (Hart 2010) 224–28 (postulating that there is no international law norm requiring that all governments should be democratic, although democracy as a principle has a significant influence on the interpretation and application of international law norms). This debate falls beyond the remit of the book which assumes a state of asylum that holds elections and excludes CSR1951 refugees there-from.

activity and expression.[83] The *Travaux* indicate no discussion regarding
the justifications for the citizenship qualification or for the distinction
between the enjoyment of electoral rights and the enjoyment of other
political rights such as freedom of expression, assembly, and association,
almost as if this differentiation in scope of rights protection was deemed
conceptually predetermined.[84]

Subsequent regional treaties in the Americas and in Africa enunciate
a right to vote for citizens.[85] In contradistinction, the (earlier) ECHR
does not explicitly proclaim an individual right to vote.[86] Nevertheless, in
1987, the European Commission on Human Rights (EComHR) described

---

[83] Michael Goodhart, *Democracy as Human Rights* (Routledge 2005) 131 (arguing that the
territorial limits of modern democratic institutions are not mere contingencies, but are
directly related to foundational normative assumptions concerning the demos and its
sovereignty). See also Ruth Lister, 'Children and Citizenship' (2007) 8(2) *Theoretical
Inquiries in Law* 695, 703 (asserting that the right to vote in national elections is what
divides denizens, namely persons with a legal and permanent residence status, from
citizens).

[84] Myres S McDougal, Harold D Lasswell, and Lung-Chu Chen, 'The Protection of Aliens
from Discrimination and World Public Order: Responsibility of States Conjoined with
Human Rights' (1976) 70 *American Journal of International Law* 432, 459 (positing that
the stipulation reflects the 'long shared community expectation' that differentiation on
the basis of alienage is permissible in regard to participation in the making of community
decisions). Carmen Tiburcio, *The Human Rights of Aliens under International and Comparative Law* (Nijhoff 2001) xvi (positing that '[t]he basis for this exclusion [of non-citizens]
is that if the state created this right it may restrict it to whoever it deems appropriate.
Conversely, if the right was not created by the State but rather considered as inherent to
the human nature, then the State cannot restrict its enjoyment ... the right to vote, to be
elected and to work for the government ... are not inherent to human nature'). Cf. Bhikhu
Parekh, 'Finding a Proper Place for Human Rights' in Kate Tunstall (ed), *Displacement,
Asylum, Migration* (Oxford Amnesty Lectures, 2004 Oxford University Press 2006) 17,
20 (rejecting Tiburcio's distinction between inherent and created rights, and suggesting
that '[all] human rights are socially defined and validated. They are normative statements
about what human beings require to lead a life of dignity and what is therefore due to
them. They are not natural or inherent in human nature but social in origin in the sense
that we decide what is essential to their dignity and that they should receive this as of
right').

[85] African Charter on Human and Peoples' Rights (adopted 27 June 1981, entered into force
21 October 1986) 21 ILM 58 (1982) art 13; American Convention on Human Rights
(adopted 21 November 1969, entered into force 18 July 1978) 1144 UNTS 123 art 23.

[86] Protocol I to the Convention for the Protection of Human Rights and Fundamental
Freedoms, Enforcement of certain Rights and Freedoms not included in Section I of the
Convention (adopted 20 March 1952, entered into force 18 May 1954) ETS No 009 (First
Additional Protocol) art 3 (enunciating that '[t]he High Contracting Parties undertake
to hold free elections at reasonable intervals by secret ballot, under conditions which will
ensure the free expression of the opinion of the people in the choice of the legislature').

a conceptual transition 'from the idea of an "institutional" right to the holding of free elections & to "universal suffrage" & and then, as a consequence, to the concept of subjective rights of participation – the "right to vote" and the "right to stand for election to the legislature"'.[87] However, the EComHR held that '[t]he phrase "conditions which ensure the free expression of the opinion of the people in the choice of the legislature" implies essentially, apart from freedom of expression... the principle of equal treatment of all *citizens* in the exercise of their right to vote and to stand for elections' (emphasis added).[88]

Article 16 of the ECHR mandates Contracting States to impose restrictions on the 'political activity of aliens'. In 1977, the Parliamentary Assembly of the Council of Europe (PACE) called for its repeal,[89] contending that '[I]t should be borne in mind that Article 16 dates from a time when it was considered legitimate to restrict the political activity of aliens generally. Subsequent human rights treaties, such as the United Nations Covenant on Civil and Political Rights, the American Convention on Human Rights and the African Charter of Human and Peoples' Rights all do without such a clause'.[90] Regarding the case-law of the ECtHR mentioned above, the PACE report notes that 'a very small number of decisions on admissibility made reference to Article 16... [and] in no single case [had] the Court used Article 16 to justify a restriction on the provisions of the Convention'.[91]

5 Non-citizen Voting: Some Contemporary Practice

It is contended that Article 25 of the ICCPR 'begins to approximate prevailing practice', at least in terms of the removal of *un*reasonable restrictions on voting rights of citizens.[92] Meanwhile, citizenship qualifications are ubiquitous in *national* elections: only four states entitle all their non-citizen *permanent* residents to vote in national elections:[93] New Zealand

---

[87] *Mathieu-Mohin and Clerfayt v Belgium* App no 9267/81 (ECHR, 2 March 1987) [51].

[88] Ibid [54].

[89] Recommendation 799 (1977) on the Political Rights and Position of Aliens, 21st Sitting, 25 January 1977.

[90] Council of Europe, Thematic Monitoring Report presented by the Secretary General and Decisions on Follow-up Action taken by the Committee of Ministers, 943th Meeting, 19 October 2005 [38].

[91] Ibid [36].   [92] Franck (n 74) 64.

[93] Free and Fair elections (n 74) 126; André Blais, Louis Massicotte, and Antoine Yoshinaka, 'Deciding who has the Right to Vote: A Comparative Analysis of Election Laws' (2003) 20

(after one year of permanent residence); Chile (after five years); Malawi (after seven years); and Uruguay (after fifteen years).[94] In contradistinction, some states extend full voting rights to citizens of *specific* states, usually former colonies; for instance, non-citizen residents from Commonwealth states and Irish citizens are eligible to vote in UK general election, while other non-citizens are excluded therefrom (see further discussion in Chapter 8).

Participation of non-citizen residents in elections for local or regional bodies is more common.[95] States parties to the European Convention on Participation of Foreigners in Public Life at Local Level (ratified by nine members of the Council of Europe: Albania, the Czech Republic, Denmark, Finland, Iceland, Italy, the Netherlands, Norway, and Sweden) undertake 'to grant to every foreign resident the right to vote and to stand for election in local authority elections, provided that he fulfils the same legal requirements as apply to nationals and furthermore has been a lawful and habitual resident in the State concerned for the five years preceding the elections'.[96]

Electoral Studies 41, 52. See generally David C Earnest, 'Neither Citizen nor Stranger: Why States Enfranchise Resident Aliens' (2006) 58(2) *World Politics* 242; David T Graham and Nana Poku, *Migration, Globalisation and Human Security* (Psychology Press 2009) 58. The electoral practices of New Zealand will be considered in Chapter 8.

[94] See David C Eranest, 'The enfranchisement of resident aliens: variations and explanations' (2015) 22(5) *Democratization* 861, 864. For a list of countries with local voting rights for non-citizen residents, see p 865.

[95] Rainer Bauböck, 'Expansive Citizenship: Voting beyond Territory and Membership' (2005) 38 *Political Science and Politics* 683, 684 (noting that forty five States have extended the franchise to non-citizens in some form).

[96] (adopted 5 February 1992, entered into force 1 May 1997) ETS No 144 art 6(1). Art 7 stipulates that Contracting States may require a shorter period of residence. The Explanatory Report [1992] COETSER 2 [18] notes that '[f]or those who live in a local community, numerous aspects of their daily life – such as housing, education, local amenities, public transport, cultural and sports facilities – are influenced by decisions taken by the local authority. Moreover, foreign residents participate actively in the life and prosperity of the local community'. It is suggested that, while '[s]imilar considerations could be applied to some aspects of decision-making at central government level . . . it is arguable that there is a closer link between possession of citizenship and participation in procedures for determining what may be conceived of as the "national will", which would exclude participation of aliens in national political life'. Ibid [19]. Regarding the required length of residence, the report suggests that ' . . . it is clear that it should be long enough for the elector to have become familiar with the local community and its political situation and issues'. Ibid [38]. See also Andreas Gross, The State of Democracy in Europe: Specific Challenges Facing European Democracies – The Case of Diversity and Migration (Political Affairs Committee, Parliamentary Assembly, Council of Europe, Doc 11623, 6 June 2008)

In contradistinction, the European Union has special arrangements for Second Country Nationals (SCNs),[97] namely citizens of one EU Member State (MS) residing in another EU MS. SCNs may vote in local government elections of the EU MS in which they habitually reside, as well as in elections to the EU Parliament.[98] However, these arrangements are based cumulatively on residence *and EU citizenship*: they do not extend to national elections.[99]

E   Electoral Participation under the Migrant Workers Convention

The Migrant Workers Convention enunciates the right of migrant workers and members of their families to vote in elections of their state of *origin*, noting that it does not affect their legal status in a host state.[100] In contradistinction, migrant workers and their families may be entitled to vote in *local* elections in their states of employment at the discretion of these states.[101]

Draft Resolution [9] ('[t]he Assembly fails to see any justification for different treatment between long-term migrants who are lawfully resident in a country solely on the basis of their country of origin') and [10] ('one of the ultimate objectives of every democratic system should be equal opportunities for the exercise of political rights').

[97] Committee on Migration, Refugees and Demography, *Report on Participation of Immigrants and Foreign Residents in Political Life in the Council of Europe Member States*, Doc no 8916 (22 December 2000) [20] (noting that 'some aliens [EU nationals] are granted more rights than others. If this system does not change, parts of the foreign population, particularly non-Europeans, risk being excluded').

[98] Treaty of Amsterdam amending the Treaty on European Union, the Treaties Establishing the European Communities, and Certain Related Acts (10 November 1997) OJ C 340 art 19.

[99] Concomitantly, as non-resident citizens, SCNs may only vote in national elections of their EU state of citizenship if its legislation makes suitable arrangements for out-of-country voting; EU treaties do not require such arrangements. The fact that, by exercising their EU right to freedom of movement, EU citizens may be effectively disenfranchised (in national elections) has led to the initiation of a European Citizen Initiative which (if adopted by the EU) would entitle SCNs to vote in national elections of their EU state of residence. For a discussion paper, see Rainer Bauböck, Philippe Cayla and Catriona Seth (eds), *Should EU Citizens Living in other Member States Vote there in National Elections?* (EUI Working Paper RSCAS 2012/32 June 2012), http://eudo-citizenship.eu/docs/RSCAS_2012_32.pdf.

[100] Art 41. Out-of-Country Voting and the predicament of CSR1951 refugees are considered in Chapter 6.

[101] Ibid art 42(3). Receiving states are expected to facilitate, in accordance with their national legislation, the consultation and participation of migrant workers and members of their families in decisions concerning the life and administration of local communities; however, such consultations cannot be considered a substitute for electoral participation. Ibid, art 42(2). See Chapters 5, 6, and 8.

The juxtaposition of the dual obligation on the part of the host and sending states to facilitate voting of migrant workers and members of their families *qua* non-resident citizens with the non-binding recommendation to grant migrant workers *qua* non-citizen residents voting rights in local elections of their host state is a testament both of the emphasis in international human rights instruments on a link between citizens residing abroad and their state and of the resilience of the citizenship voting qualification.

F   The (Failed) Attempt to Create a 'Protected Person' Status in International Law

The ILC identified the topic of 'Nationality, including Statelessness' as suitable for codification at its first session in 1949, aiming initially to draft a comprehensive treaty concerning both refugees and stateless persons. Nevertheless, following the adoption of CSR1951, the ILC considered separately issues relating to statelessness with a view to their codification.

At its Sixth session in 1954, the ILC considered a report concerning *present statelessness* submitted by its special Rapporteur, Roberto Córdova.[102] In the discussion, ILC member El Khouri proposed the creation of a 'protected person' status which would entail 'all the civil rights with the exception of political rights'.[103] Córdova supported this proposition, suggesting that a *habitual residence* requirement be included because, in his view, states would be reluctant to grant political rights to a stateless person whose connection with the host state was not sufficiently strong.[104]

The ILC debated Córdova's draft, consisting of seven articles. Article 1 proclaimed that 'a state in whose territory a stateless person is resident shall, on his application, grant him the legal status of "protected person"'. According to Article 2, a 'protected person' 'shall be entitled to all the rights enjoyed by the nationals of the protecting state with the exception of *political* rights . . . [and] shall also be entitled to diplomatic protection' (emphasis added). The draft articles stipulated that stateless persons would be entitled to a 'protected person' status until such time

---

[102] Third Report on the Elimination or Reduction of Statelessness (Yearbook of the ILC 1954) vol II.

[103] 246th meeting A/CN.4/SR.246, 14 June 1954 [9–10].

[104] 247th meeting A/CN.4/SR.247, 15 June 1954 [44].

as they naturalise in the state of residence or elsewhere (when such protection would no longer be required). Lauterpacht's reservation that a 'protected person' status ought to be granted only upon failure to qualify for naturalisation did not prevail.[105]

Intriguingly, in justifying the new status, Córdova asserted that there was 'some analogy' between the status of 'protected persons' and 'the position of women in those countries where they had not yet received political rights'.[106] Reading this statement in context, it appears that the expression 'political rights' was probably not intended to refer to the full scope of political expression but rather to electoral rights.

The ILC included the draft articles as described above in its final report to the UNGA.[107] However, the report noted that 'in view of the great difficulties of a non-legal nature which beset the problem of present statelessness, the Commission considered that the proposals adopted though worded in the form of articles should merely be regarded as suggestions which governments may wish to take into account'.[108] The draft articles have not materialised as a treaty.[109]

G Concluding Remarks

Persons recognised as CSR1951 refugees are non-citizen residents of their state of asylum. The CSR1951 drafters have acknowledged the vulnerable status of CSR1951 refugees; they listed civil, social and economic rights which states of asylum are required to accord 'their' refugees, exempting refugees from reciprocity and other requirements that had been considered ill-suited for persons who do not enjoy the protection of their state of origin.

---

[105] 248th meeting A/CN.4/1954 [25]. SR.248, 16 June

[106] Ibid [80]. Moreover, Córdova proposed that de facto stateless persons be assimilated to de jure stateless persons as regards the right to a status of 'protected person' and the right to naturalisation, provided that they renounced the ineffective nationality they possessed. His proposal was rejected. *Nationality, including Statelessness, Report on Present Statelessness* (Yearbook of the ILC 1954) vol II [35].

[107] Ibid [31].   [108] Ibid [36].

[109] The report has led to the adoption of the Convention Relating to the Status of Stateless Persons and of the Convention on the Reduction of Statelessness (adopted 30 August 1961, entered into force 13 December 1975) 989 UNTS 175. The former treaty guarantees stateless persons a set of rights similar to those enjoyed by recognised refugees under CSR1951 and is equally silent regarding political rights; the latter convention is concerned with reducing statelessness rather than with rights of currently stateless persons.

Political rights are noticeably absent from CSR1951; their omission cannot be read as an implicit expectation that states nonetheless grant non-citizens the full gamut of political rights. Indeed, the concurrent attempt to create a 'protected person' status in international law for stateless persons that would entail enjoyment by such persons of all rights save for political rights is a clear testament that Contracting States were quite wary (at the time) of according political rights to non-citizens. Importantly, however, the CSR1951 drafters have created 'legal space' for expanding protection of CSR1951 refugees, signifying the character of CSR1951 as a human rights treaty. The subsequent adoption of the ICCPR has meant that CSR1951 refugees should enjoy some, but not necessarily full political rights, on a par with other non-citizens.

Nevertheless, while most political rights are guaranteed under the ICCPR to 'everyone', the Covenant permits states to set citizenship voting qualifications that exclude non-citizens, including refugees; regional treaties, international practice, and the recently adopted Migrant Workers Convention generally conform.

Following Mandal's taxonomy, there are activities undertaken by CSR1951 refugees that states of asylum are obliged to allow, such as political rights guaranteed under the ICCPR; activities which states of asylum are obliged to prevent, falling outside the remit of the book; activities which states of asylum may allow including participation in electoral processes.[110]

It was noted in the introduction that, the vast majority of persons hold citizenship of their state of residence; according to the ICCPR, as well as to regional rights instruments, they should have the right and the opportunity to participate in electoral processes of that state. According to the Migrant Workers Convention, the participation of migrant workers and their families in elections of their state of citizenship should be facilitated in their states of employment, maintaining their political 'bond' with their state of nationality.

CSR1951 refugees do not 'fit' the above legal and conceptual framework. Their political ties with their state of origin were severed by their fear of persecution, and their period of absence from their state of origin is indeterminate. While the state of asylum may choose to enfranchise CSR1951 refugees, neither CSR1951 nor the ICCPR can be read to *require* it to do so. Consequently, their predicament highlights a tension between two principles of the inter-national legal order, state sovereignty and

---

[110] Mandal (n 71) 45.

protection of individual rights: the former seeks to promote specifically defined citizen rights, while the latter espouses a universal application of entitlements.[111] Against this background, Part II of the book explores the nature and purposes of voting and state citizenship, and their interrelations.

[111] George Gigauri, *Resolving the Liberal Paradox: Citizen Rights and Alien Rights in the UK* (RSC Working Paper No 31 July 2008) 3.

PART II

Interrelations between Voting and State Citizenship

3

Perspectives on the Meaning and Purposes of Voting Eligibility

A Introduction

The electoral process stands at the heart of representative democracy.[1] This book considers the voting rights of recognised CSR1951 refugees. This chapter explores the meaning and purposes of the right to vote in elections for individuals *qua* voters, and for the electoral process in political communities; thereby, it facilitates analysis of the adverse effects of the (general) non-inclusion of recognised CSR1951 refugees in such processes.

Section B considers the claim that determining eligibility may be constitutive for defining membership in a political community. It sets the scene for a discussion in Chapter 4 of the meaning and purposes of state citizenship as well as for an appraisal in Chapter 5 of the interrelations between state citizenship and voting.

Section C argues that voting is fundamental for individuals on four mutually reinforcing grounds. In turn, Section D submits that, for individuals, voting plays both an instrumental role as a means for securing other rights (stemming from 'liberal' thought), and an expressive-intrinsic role in manifesting 'non-domination and self-governance' (stemming from 'republican' thought).

Section E introduces three leading perspectives on the role of electoral processes in decision making: a 'liberal' perspective, a 'republican' perspective, and a 'deliberative democracy' perspective. In turn, Section F suggests that, due to the facilitative role of voting, the 'cultural relativity' challenge to the universality of rights is less likely to be mounted against the right to vote. Lastly, Section G suggests that the distinction between 'core' and 'penumbra' of legal rights may be helpful in considering questions of voting eligibility.

---

[1] George Kateb, 'The Moral Distinctiveness of Representative Democracy' (1981) 91 *Ethics* 357, 35n7.

B   Voting Eligibility and Political Community Membership: Prelude

The world is divided into political communities; each political community sets eligibility criteria both for membership and for elections of its institutions of government.[2] This section briefly introduces the notion (which shall be explored further in Chapter 5) that determining eligibility to vote in election has a constitutive role in defining full membership in a political community;[3] namely, the claim that 'in deciding who may and who may not vote in its elections, a community takes a crucial step in defining its identity ... a community should be empowered to exclude from its elections persons with no real nexus to the community as such'.[4]

Rousseau based his 'social contract' theory on the premise that, to avoid the state of nature, man joins together with others to form a society based on an agreed 'compact' which, *inter alia*, sets conditions for membership; society, in turn, sets in place a legislative system, aiming to achieve two main objectives: liberty and equality.[5] Rousseau was averse to the notion of representative government (namely, of elections), postulating that '[s]overeignty, for the same reason as makes it inalienable, cannot be represented; it lies essentially in the general will, and does not admit of representation'.[6] However, modern manifestations of direct democracy are increasingly deemed unsuitable for effective routine governance due to increases in size of population and territory;[7] hence, they have been replaced with representative decision-making mechanism.[8] Montesquieu argued that, in a democracy, the people are sovereign, and ought to have 'the management of everything within their reach'; nonetheless 'that which exceeds their abilities must be conducted by their ministers whom they shall choose'.[9]

It is also helpful to recall Madison's distinction in *The Federalist Papers* between 'pure' democracy, in which citizens jointly administer public

---

[2] Richard Katz, *Democracy and Elections* (Oxford University Press 1997) 216.

[3] James A Gardner, 'Liberty, Community and the Constitutional Structure of Political Influence: A Reconsideration of the Right to Vote' (1997) 145(4) *University of Pennsylvania Law Review* 893, 967.

[4] Lawrence Tribe, *American Constitutional Law* (2nd edn Foundation Press 1988) 1084.

[5] Jean-Jacques Rousseau, *On the Social Contract* (first published 1762, Judith Masters tr, St Martin's Press 1978) bk II ch 11.

[6] Ibid bk III ch 15.   [7] Katz (n 2) 24.

[8] Robert Dahl, *Democracy and Its Critics* (Yale University Press 1989) 214.

[9] Charles de Secondat, Baron de Montesquieu, *The Spirit of Laws* (first published 1748, Thomas Nugent tr, Printed for J Collingwood 1823) bk II ch 2.

affairs, and a 'republic' where there is 'a government in which the scheme of representation takes place . . . a small number of citizens [are] elected by the rest'.[10] However, in principle, determination of eligibility to participate in governance should *not* be affected by the choice of governance structure: if persons would be eligible to vote directly, resort to representation should not affect their eligibility.[11]

C   The Fundamentality of Voting for Individuals: Four Grounds

1   Introduction

This section considers four grounds for the claim that voting is fundamental for individuals. First, voting manifests human agency and has an autonomy-enhancing effect. Second, voting is an expressive act that is both intrinsically worthwhile and has the capacity to legitimise other forms of political speech. Third, voting manifests human dignity. Fourth, the declarative character of suffrage is an affirmation of political equality: eligible voters enjoy equal worth, concern, and respect of society. It is argued that the effects of these grounds on eligible voters are cumulative as are the adverse ramifications of electoral exclusion.

2   Voting as Agency and Autonomy Enhancing

It may be suggested that individuals are the best judges of their own good or interests, and that freedom and well-being are features of human agency.[12] These maxims seem to resonate well with Raz's general theory of rights. Raz distinguishes between core rights and derivative rights, suggesting that the latter are grounded in the former.[13] Individuals have a core interest in being respected as autonomous beings, namely as authors of their lives who should be able to choose from a variety of acceptable options.[14]

Raz defines *legal* rights as legally protected interests.[15] He suggests that rights should be protected and considered valuable either because they

---

[10] *The Federalist Papers* No 10, www.foundingfathers.info/federalistpapers.
[11] Notably, the question whether *standing for elections* may be subjected to different eligibility criteria falls outside the scope of this book.
[12] Patrick Capps, *Human Dignity and the Foundations of International Law* (Hart 2009) 123.
[13] Joseph Raz, *The Morality of Freedom* (Clarendon Press 1986) 168.
[14] Robert Dahl, *On Democracy* (Yale University Press 1998) 86.
[15] Joseph Raz, 'Legal Rights' in Joseph Raz (ed), *Ethics in the Public Domain: Essays in the Morality of Law and Politics* (Clarendon Press 1995) 254, 266.

advance the autonomy of rights-bearers or because they advance a public culture which, in turn, facilitates the autonomy of rights-bearers.[16] It is contended that voters act as autonomous agents when they vote on questions that concern their perceptions of a worthwhile life. Voting enables individuals to display desires, beliefs, judgments, and perceptions. By voting, voters exercise control (albeit partial) over their social environment;[17] and they perform actions which, if performed by enough others, may alter the assignment of rights and duties in the political community.[18]

Raz asserts that political communities do not just have a (negative) duty to refrain from denying individuals their freedom, but also a (positive) duty to enhance it by 'creating the conditions of autonomy'.[19] Following Raz's argument, assuming a connection between voting and autonomy, it would follow that the state is obliged to allocate resources and to undertake positive and effective measures such as voter registration, campaign-financing, ballots-drawing, and vote-counting to secure the right to vote. For discussion of OCV procedures, see Chapter 6.

It may be doubted whether exercising one's right to vote actually contributes to personal autonomy, since it is hard to envision how a marginal effect over the outcome of an election could be seen as having more than a slim contribution to the autonomy of each voter.[20] One response is to highlight the *exercise* of agency rather than the direct impact of each person's vote, and to note that, while votes of others are required to elect office-holders, each person casts a ballot as an (autonomous) individual.[21]

---

[16] John Griffin, *On Human Rights* (Oxford University Press 2008) 39.

[17] Johannes Morsink, *Inherent Human Rights: Philosophical Roots of the Universal Declaration* (University of Philadelphia Press 2009) 266–67.

[18] Jeremy Waldron, *Law and Disagreement* (Clarendon Press 1999) 233. Elsewhere, Waldron suggests that voting rights have 'the character of Hohfeldian powers rather than claim rights to negative freedom' since 'each voter has the power to make a difference . . . formally no smaller than that made by anyone else- to the appointment of legislators and the passage of legislation'. Jeremy Waldron, *Liberal rights* (Cambridge University Press 1991) 343.

[19] Joseph Raz, 'Right-Based Moralities' in Jeremy Waldron (ed), *Theories of Rights* (Oxford University Press 1984) 182, 191. Eleftheriadis argues that Raz's 'perfectionist account of autonomy' cannot serve as a basis for a legal theory of rights that can be shared and followed by public institutions, since it does not grant adequate respect to other conceptions of the good which many people hold dear, such as religious observances, which do *not* see autonomy as an (the) ultimate value. Pavlos Eleftheriadis, *Legal Rights* (Oxford University Press 2008) 100–10.

[20] William Talbott, *Which Rights Should Be Universal?* (Oxford University Press 2005) 139.

[21] Joshua Douglas, 'Is the Right to Vote Really Fundamental?' (2008) 18 *Cornell Journal of Law and Public Policy* 143.

The awareness that one's agency extends to the most fundamental questions may also be autonomy enhancing. Research in the US has shown that turnout in federal elections is higher than in state or local elections, whereas the share and effect of each vote is clearly greater in the latter elections.[22] Such findings may be explained by the fact that voters consider the issues that are decided in federal elections to be more significant.

3   Voting as an Expressive Act

Voting may be performed in a multitude of ways including, *inter alia*, calling at a polling station, casting absentee ballots, and voting electronically. While in most electoral systems, individual preferences for parties, candidates, and policies are generally not disclosed in public, the fact that one *voted* is oftentimes visible and may even be celebrated.[23]

Voters may express themselves for constitutive reasons, seeking to project aspects of their identity such as their values, ideals, and experiences to exert themselves among others, even if the particular exertion will remain generally unrecognised. Hence, voting may be considered a meaningful participatory act which transforms individual (and collective) identities.[24] Some voters may wish to limit their engagement with political processes and to refrain from expressing political opinions in public; for them, voting may be a rather inexpensive (time and otherwise) means of expressing views and of pursuing political ends.

Modern communication channels increasingly enable individuals to express their views and preferences by a variety of means, including writing blogs, tweeting, or using virtual social networks to participate in online debates. Indeed, some voters may consider such channels to be more personally fulfilling, more influential and, perhaps, more 'expressive' than voting, due to the public forum element that is lacking when one casts a *secret* ballot. It is nonetheless contended that, for participants

---

[22] Adam Winkler, 'Expressive Voting' (1993) 68 *NYU Law Review* 330, 359. Cf. *McGeoch v Lord President of the Council* [2011] CSIH 679 (dismissing an EU law based motion to entitle a British national incarcerated in Scotland to vote in Scottish Parliament elections; the judgment notes that '[the] phrase [municipal elections] would naturally be understood as referring to local bodies whose responsibilities are primarily of an administrative nature, rather than a regional legislature within a state with federal or devolved arrangements for law-making').

[23] Public display of participation: 'I voted' stickers, http://blogs.wsj.com/independentstreet/ 2008/11/04/election-day-perks-businesses-hand-out-freebies-to-voters/.

[24] Winkler (n 22) 343.

in these forums, the fact that they are eligible voters may encourage their participation, enhance it, and perhaps even legitimise it. In such forums, participants will often identity as community members or will be asked to do so by others. Non-electoral means of communication may thus complement and reinforce the expressive character of voting.

4   Voting and Human Dignity

International declarations and treaties herald the assertion that all human beings have equal, inherent, and inviolable dignity.[25] Article 1 of the UDHR pronounces that 'all human beings are born free and equal in dignity and rights. They are endowed with reason and conscience and should act towards one another in a spirit of brotherhood'.[26] Similarly, the ICCPR proclaims 'the inherent dignity and inalienable rights of all members of the human family', noting that rights 'derive from the inherent dignity of the human person'.[27] Nonetheless, Christopher McCrudden asserts that a global consensus has not yet emerged in the philosophical debate concerning whether the *origin* of human dignity is metaphysical, religious, transformative, or otherwise.[28] While identifying the source of human dignity falls outside the remit of the book, it is submitted that eligibility to vote manifests human dignity, whatever its source may be.

James Gardner regards democratic rights as 'structural' rather than as fundamental, suggesting that voting has a relational aspect, concerning the way eligible voters are treated vis-à-vis fellow eligible voters; the dignity of eligible voters is associated with a socially constructed role that is unique to democracies.[29] The South African Constitutional Court held that '[t]he vote of each and every citizen is a badge of dignity and of personhood. Quite literally, [the vote] says that everybody counts'.[30] This book concerns states where elections are held, to which Gardner's notion of relational dignity applies.

---

[25] Michael Perry, 'Secular Viewpoints, Religious Viewpoints and the Morality of Human Rights' (Emory University School of Law Public Law and Legal Theory Research Paper Series 102–10) 6.

[26] GA/Res/217A (III) of 10 December 1948.   [27] ICCPR Preamble.

[28] Christopher McCrudden, 'Human Dignity and Judicial Interpretation of Human Rights' (2008) 19(4) *European Journal of International Law* 655, 679.

[29] James A Gardner, 'The Dignity of Voters' (2010) 64 *University of Miami Law Review* 435, 455.

[30] CCT 08/99 *August v Electoral Commission* (1999) (3) SA 1 [31] (South Africa).

The dignity of voters may be most clearly observed in its breach: since voting is emblematic of social standing and civic dignity, exclusion of otherwise eligible voters can be interpreted as an insult, a form of dishonour, or denigration.[31] Hence, exclusion infringes the 'role dignity' of excluded would-be voters. For instance, in the case of convicted adult citizens, their disenfranchisement (deliberately) conveys a message of inferiority (lesser dignity): they are excluded from their previously held status of eligible voters.

In contradistinction, when the state refrains from enfranchising non-citizen residents, it fails to equalise their status to that of citizens, sending a message of *non-inclusion*. Even though no denigration is meant by such act, certain dignity harms may ensue. It is contended that the non-enfranchisement of CSR1951 refugees, effectively excluded from participation in elections of their state of origin (see Chapter 6), manifests their *dual* non-membership.

5   Equal Worth, Concern, and Respect

Dahl advanced the principle of intrinsic equality, according to which we ought to treat all persons as if they possess equal claims to life, liberty, happiness, and other fundamental goods and interests.[32] In *Ghaidan*, the UK House of Lords held that '[d]emocracy is founded on the principle that each individual has equal value'.[33] In a democracy, equal suffrage may be an indication of whether individuals are treated properly by institutions and by their peers.[34]

The extent to which a political community distributes decision-making power *equally* matters.[35] When distributing opportunities or goods, governments ought not to assume that some community members are entitled to more because they are worthy of more concern and respect;[36] the 'value theory of democracy' rests on 'respect of citizens as

---

[31] Jeremy Waldron, 'Participation: The Right of Rights' (1998) 98(3) *Proceedings of the Aristotelian Society* 307, 314.

[32] *On Democracy* (n 14) 64 (stressing that his account is not meant 'to express a factual judgment . . . [or] to describe when we believe is or will be true . . .'. but instead 'to express a moral judgment about human beings').

[33] *Ghaidan v Godin-Mendoza* [2004] UKHL 30 [132] (Baroness Hale).

[34] Jeff Manza and Christopher Uggen, *Locked Out: Felon Disenfranchisement and American Democracy* (Oxford University Press 2006) 18.

[35] Ronald Dworkin, *Sovereign Virtue* (Harvard University Press 2000) 200.

[36] Ronald Dworkin, *Taking Rights Seriously* (Duckworth 1978) 272–73.

rulers'.[37] Hence, while tossing a coin instead of holding elections may give all prospective voters an equal chance, it does not allow them any influence on decision making, and so does not treat them with concern and respect.[38]

In the female suffrage debates, it was suggested that the interests of married women can be guarded by their husbands, and that women are not generally suited for politics but, rather, for other spheres of life. However, on the above account, even if it could be shown that the interests of spouses may be secured by votes of their husbands, their equal worth requires that they should have their views heard in their own voice.[39] Similarly, slaves were not entitled to participate in political community decision making regarding the abolition of slavery; rather, claims for abolition were debated by slave-owners and by other 'free' persons. The fact that these processes may have a plausible outcome does not make up for the indignity of their exclusionary nature. Equal concern and respect means recognition of individuals as the best judges of their own interests.

Now, it is generally assumed that parents are 'virtually representing' their children's interests; it could be similarly argued that rights of members of excluded groups, such as non-citizens, may be similarly protected by special representatives. However, unlike children, non-enfranchised competent adults are assumed to have the *capacity* to participate; their exclusion signifies that they are not treated by society with equal worth, concern, and respect.

On this account (which can distinguished from the pure instrumentalism which may have prompted Mill's support for weighted voting power based on the prospective voter's level of education[40]) political equality has independent value: loss of political equality cannot be 'compensated

---

[37] Corey Brettschneider, *Democratic Rights: The Substance of Self-Government* (Princeton University Press 2007).

[38] Ben Saunders, 'Majority Rule and Procedural Equality' (2010) 23(1) *Ratio Juris* 113, 118 (arguing that lottery voting, that is tossing a coin, however undemocratic, satisfies procedural equality. In turn, he concludes that procedural equality does not suffice to justify majority-rule based decision-making). Cf. the 'protective democracy' account in Section D which emphasises the ways in which suffrage effectuates protection of *other* rights.

[39] Alexander Keyssar, *The Right to Vote: The Contested History of Democracy in the United States* (Basic Books 2000) 175.

[40] See John S Mill, *Considerations of Representative Government* (Bibliobazaar 2007) (1862) ch viii: On the Extension of Suffrage ('... [t]he distinction in favour of education, right in itself, is farther and strongly recommended by its preserving the educated from the class legislation of the uneducated; but it must stop short of enabling them to practice class legislation on their own account . . .').

for' by having a more equitable redistribution.[41] Following Rawls, it is submitted that persons ought to conceive of themselves and of other members of their society both as possessing the moral power to have a conception of the good and as self-authenticating sources of valid claims which they are able to make in the political process.[42]

For Rawls, political equality stems from mutual recognition of individual equal worth and capacities. Political liberties are thus a 'public affirmation of the status of equal citizenship for all', and individuals who possess them retain their self-respect and self-confidence.[43] Eligibility to participate in political processes demonstrates that a person possesses *de jure* equal voice in 'settling the ways in which basic social conditions are to be arranged' in a given political community.[44] In contrast, exclusion serves as a mark of (social) inferiority.[45] Participation is not only a 'status symbol' but also facilitates feelings of 'belongingness' among members of the polity.[46] The participatory experience may generate a sense of belonging and transcendence.[47] Enfranchisement may have a constitutive effect on one's sense and conception of membership.[48]

Moreover, when persons are respected and treated as equals by their peers, it may confirm their own sense of value. Consequently, enfranchisement may enhance their self-esteem and give voters a sense of (political) competence. In this context, Nussbaum's contention that individuals are both capable and needy is helpful. She argues that an appropriate institutional environment is required to provide affirmative support for all relevant individual capabilities; settling for a (liberal) sphere of non-interference would be insufficient.[49] Hence, because enfranchisement symbolises equal concern and respect, it can help persons who are capable

---

[41] Wojciech Sadurski, 'Legitimacy, Political Equality and Majority Rule' (2008) 21 *Ratio Juris* 39, 53.

[42] John Rawls, *Political Liberalism* (Columbia University Press 1996) 30–32.

[43] John Rawls, *A Theory of Justice* (Harvard University Press 1971) 545.   [44] Ibid 233–34.

[45] Jesse Furman, 'Political Illiberalism: The Paradox of Disenfranchisement and the Ambivalence of Rawlsian Justice' (1997) 106 *Yale Law Journal* 1197, 1217.

[46] Carol Paternan, *Participation and Democratic Theory* (Cambridge University Press 1970) 22, 27.

[47] Winkler (n 22) 367.

[48] Ibid 377. See also Stephan Tontrup and Rebecca Morton, 'The Value of The Right to Vote' (NYU School of Law, Public Law Research Paper No 15–52 November 2015) (empirical research demonstrating that individuals in Western democracies derive strong utility from eligibility, independent of whether they actually exercise their participation rights), http://papers.ssrn.com/sol3/papers.cfm/abstract_id/2692760.

[49] Martha Nussbaum, *Capabilities as Fundamental Entitlements: Sen and Social Justice* (Hitotsubashi University 2002) 21.

beings yet are also in need of social support to fulfil their potential and, in turn, to contribute to society.

D   Functions of Voting: Protection and Non-domination

1   Introduction

This section considers two primary functions of voting: First, an instrumental function: the utilisation by individuals of their vote, *inter alia*, to advance their interests and those of members of their social groups (a rights-protective account). Second, an intrinsic-expressive function, namely the contention that eligible voters are not subject to the arbitrary rule of others, perceives of voting as an expression of non-domination and self-governance. It may be argued that, despite emanating from 'liberal' and 'republican' schools of thought, respectively, these functions are compatible and indeed mutually reinforcing: eligible voters are better placed to protect their interests, and they are (symbolically) non-dominated whether or not they choose to exercise their right to vote.

2   Rights-Protective Account

It may be suggested that governments can be trusted to protect and reinforce rights only when they are accountable to those whose lives they govern. The US Constitution ceremoniously declares that '[w]e hold these truths to be self-evident, that all men are created equal, that they are endowed... with certain inalienable rights... Life, Liberty and the Pursuit of Happiness. That to secure these rights, Governments are instituted among men, deriving their just powers from the consent of the governed'.[50] Notwithstanding the selective nature of the rights that the Declaration listed, and the property, gender and other non-benign voting qualifications that were applied at that time,[51] the principle that governments are elected by individuals to secure their rights has become a prominent tenet of liberal thought.[52]

---

[50] *The Unanimous Declaration of the Thirteen United States of America* (4 July 1776), www .ushistory.org/declaration/document/index.htm.

[51] Keyssar (n 39) xviii. See the discussion in Chapter 5.

[52] Some of these perceptions can be traced back to John Locke, *Two Treatises of Government* (first published 1690, Peter Laslett ed Cambridge University Press 1960). Locke constructed a theory of tacit consent of the governed, seeing that few people entering an established civil society affirmatively consent to its government.

On this account, the right to vote is a necessary (though not a suffi-cient) condition for securing other rights.[53] In contrast, electoral exclu-sion leaves individuals with an inadequate ability to influence outcomes of political decision making on matters which would secure their rights. John Stuart Mill asserted that, to protect their rights and interests from governmental abuse, individuals should participate in determining the conduct of government; he postulated that '[m]en, as well as women, do not need political rights in order that they may govern, but in order that they may not be misgoverned'.[54]

Along similar lines, the US Supreme Court held that since 'the right to exercise the franchise in a free and unimpaired manner is preservative of other basic civil and political rights, any alleged infringement of the right of citizens to vote must be carefully and meticulously scrutinized'.[55] Elsewhere, it ruled that '[n]o right is more precious in a free society than that of having a voice in the election of those who make the laws under which as good citizens we must live. Other rights, even the most basic, are illusory if the right to vote is undermined'.[56]

On a rights-protective account, voters are *expected* to exert power and advance their interests as well as interests of their social groups in the elec-toral process.[57] Hence, for instance, even if convicts are arguably 'biased' and choose to vote for candidates who support laxer punishments, their supposed bias cannot justify their disenfranchisement, because voting *is* about expressing biases, loyalties, commitments, and personal values.[58]

In this context, the electoral process may be a useful channel for vulnerable communities to enter the social discourse, especially in light of the fact that other channels may be effectively blocked.[59] For this reason, dominant groups ('the ins') may have an incentive to 'choke'

---

[53] Gregory Fox, 'The Right to Political Participation in International Law' (1992) 17 *Yale Journal of International Law* 539, 595.

[54] Mill (n 40) ch viii. Mill asserted that '[t]he limitation of the power of government over individuals loses none of its importance when the holders of power of government are regularly accountable to the community that is to the strongest party therein'. Ibid ch i.

[55] *Reynolds v Sims* 377 US 533, 561–62 (1964). See also Dora Kostakopoulou, *The Future Governance of Citizenship* (Oxford University Press 2008) 21 (noting that, in liberal theory, political participation is viewed as a condition necessary to secure personal liberties).

[56] *Wesberry v Sanders* 376 US 1, 17 (1964) (Black J).

[57] Adam Cox, 'Temporal Dimension of Voting Rights' (2007) 93 *Virginia Law Review* 361, 362.

[58] George Fletcher, 'Disenfranchisement as Punishment: Reflections on the Radical Uses of Infamia' (1999) 46 *UCLA Law Review* 1895, 1906.

[59] John H Ely, *Democracy and Distrust: A Theory of Judicial Review* (Harvard University Press 1980) 103.

off the channels of political change, block members of disempowered groups ('the outs') from entering the political process, and consequently further marginalise them.

Electoral exclusion of individuals adversely affects their respective communities, which consequently lack the (collective) ability to choose representatives that are sensitive to their needs.[60] A rights-protective account would regard electoral exclusion as adversely affecting both individuals and their social groups, enhancing their vulnerability.

3   Non-domination and Self-Governance

It may be argued that even a consensual transfer of power from individuals to the government entails a risk of abuse: hence, the government ought to leave individuals enough latitude to choose their own ends.[61] Note Isaiah Berlin's notion of liberty as 'negative' freedom or non-interference. On Berlin's account, electorally excluded individuals could be free(r) living under a liberal-minded despot than as enfranchised members of a participatory democracy which adopts personal freedom-infringing policies. Liberty, in this sense, is not incompatible with some kinds of autocracy, or at any rate with the absence of self-government as it is principally concerned with the area of control, not with its source. Berlin concluded that there is no necessary connection between individual liberty and democratic rule.[62]

In contradistinction, on an account of liberty as 'positive' freedom or as non-domination and self-governance, a person is dominated by the mere possibility of arbitrary interference even if such interference does

---

[60] David Mitchell, 'Undermining Individual and Collective Citizenship: The Impact of Exclusion Laws on the African-American Community' (2007) 34 *Fordham Urban Law Journal* 833, 856. See also On Democracy (n 14) 77 (asserting that 'the fundamental interests of adults who are denied opportunities to participate in governing will not be adequately protected and advanced by those who govern').

[61] For instance, the Tenth Amendment to the US Constitution (1791), enunciating that '[t]he powers not delegated to the United States by the Constitution, nor prohibited by it to the States, are reserved to the States respectively, or to the people', arguably reflects a perception that government ought to have limited powers.

[62] See Isaiah Berlin 'Two Concepts of Liberty' In Isaiah Berlin (ed) *Four Essays on Liberty* (Oxford University Press 1969) 155, 164 (arguing that 'liberty is liberty, not equality or fairness or justice or culture, or human happiness or a quiet conscience. If the liberty of myself or my class or nation depends on the misery of a number of other human beings, the system which promotes this is unjust and immoral. But if I curtail or lose my freedom in order to lessen the shame of such inequality, and do not thereby materially increase the individual liberty of others, an absolute loss of liberty occurs. This may be compensated for by a gain in justice or in happiness or in peace, but the loss of freedom – 'social' or 'economic' – is increased').

not occur; the relevant question to be asked is 'by whom am I ruled'. Hence, even if the rights of excluded individuals may be theoretically secured by a benevolent ruler, the excluded are dominated by the very fact that policies that affect them are decided in their (political) absence.

Enfranchisement is a manifestation of non-domination and self-governance: having one's rights affected by a decision in which one had the opportunity to participate is qualitatively different than having that decision made in one's (political) absence.[63] Only rights of political participation ground the citizen's reflexive, self-referential legal standing.[64] On this view, domination is averted even if participatory rights are not exercised in actuality;[65] enfranchisement, that is entitlement to participate, prevents the risk of being subjected to the arbitrary will of others.[66] Freedom as self-governance entails having the capacity to deliberate and change the terms of democratic cooperation, which in turn means having normative power over the consequent distribution of normative powers.[67]

On this account, electoral participation is conceptually grounded in a pre-political right to *individual* self-determination.[68] In turn, self-determination mandates that individuals play an equal part in making collective decisions which subsequently bind them. Each enfranchised individual possesses a fraction of sovereign power that is equal to their share of the population that is subject to that sovereign power. Now, the relations between voters as lawmakers and the electorally excluded should not be described as slavery because, unlike slave-masters, lawmakers cannot exercise absolute arbitrary power; but they can be described as subjection, namely of lawmakers imposing rules of behaviour on (competent) adults without consulting them.[69] Hence, the right to participate may be sufficient to secure freedom as non-domination.

---

[63] Peter Jones, *Rights* (Macmillan 1994) 181.

[64] Jürgen Habermas, *Between Facts and Norms* (Polity Press 1996) 504.

[65] See e.g. Michael Ignatieff, 'The Myth of Citizenship' in Ronald Beiner (ed), *Theorizing Citizenship* (SUNY Press 1995) 53.

[66] Michael Goodhart, *Democracy as Human Rights: Freedom and Equality in the Age of Globalization* (Routledge 2005) 147.

[67] James Bohman, *Democracy across Borders: From Demos to Demoi* (MIT Press 2007) 7.

[68] Michael Cholbi, 'A Felon's Right to Vote' (2002) 21 *Law and Philosophy* 543, 549. The right to self-determination is often considered a 'collective' right; cf. Antonio Cassese, *UN Law/Fundamental Rights: Two Topics in International Law* (Sijthoff & Noordhoff 1979) 137 (arguing that the opening sentence of art 1 of the ICCPR, '[a]ll peoples have the right of self-determination . . . ' should be read as enunciating an individual right to participate in national affairs). The collective aspects of self-determination fall *outside the scope of this book.*

[69] Jeffrey Reiman, 'Liberal and Republican Arguments against Felon Disenfranchisement' [2005] *Criminal Justice Ethics* 3, 12.

Enfranchised individuals who choose not to vote signal their willingness to go along with an outcome decided by others; by taking this decision they are not being dominated by others, as they retain the right to change their minds and participate.[70]

Nevertheless a 'strong' (Aristotelian) account of self-governance holds that participation is *intrinsic* to the 'good life' and individuals must live together in political associations to reach their full potential; *actual* political participation has intrinsic value that is superior to forms of merely private enjoyment which relate to their family, neighbourhood, and profession.[71] On this view, most persons who, at present, do not engage with the political process live an unsatisfying life: a good man must be also a good citizen; a good polity is an association constituted by good citizens; and good citizens possess civic virtue that is the predisposition to seek the good of all in public matters.

In contradistinction, several contemporary scholars contend that laws and norms can embody the common good even without universal participation of citizens in their formation. Kymlicka and Norman consider Aristotelian contentions to be artificial and archaic. They posit that Aristotle's supposedly ideal political life was made artificially possible by slavery and other forms of domination of non-citizens which are no longer tolerated.[72] Moreover, private life has become richer and consequently encompasses a greater part of individuals' lives; participation is thus inevitably occupying a lesser, though still important, part of individuals' lives.

E The Electoral Process and Social Decision Making: Three Perspectives

1 Introduction

The previous sections discussed the fundamentality of voting for individuals. This section turns to the *collective* nature of the electoral process,[73]

---

[70] Ben Saunders, *Republicanism and Abstention* (unpublished manuscript) (on file with author).

[71] Aristotle, *Politics* (350 BCE) Book VII, http://classics.mit.edu/Aristotle/politics.html.

[72] Will Kymlicka and Wayne Nomran, 'Return of the Citizen: A Survey of Recent Work on Citizenship Theory' in Ronald Beiner (ed), *Theorizing Citizenship* (SUNY Press 1995) 293.

[73] Richard Pildes, 'What Kind of Right Is "the Right to Vote"' (2007) 93 *Virginia Law Review in Brief* 43, 44–45 (suggesting that 'the right to vote can be violated when election structure dilute[s] the voting power of particular groups through the way in which those structures aggregate individual votes ... an individual voter can be disenfranchised but no vote can

in the spirit of the famous maxim that government is constituted 'of the people, by the people, for the people'.[74] It may be contended that the right to vote is qualitatively different than, for instance, the right to freedom of conscience: whereas the latter right is realised by individuals *qua* individuals, individual votes are given meaning when they are counted and given effect as part of a system of collective decision making.[75]

The electoral process is arguably a vehicle for initiating social, economic, and political change.[76] It enables governments to receive feedback on how to solve collective action problems.[77] Democratic governance, to a substantially greater degree than any alternative, provides an orderly and peaceful process for a majority of citizens to induce their government to do what they most want it to do, and to avoid doing what they most want it not to do.[78] Sound collective decisions require assembling diverse perspectives and experiences.[79]

Three perspectives concerning the purposes and ends of electoral processes will be presented: A 'liberal' perspective according to which the electoral process is an aggregation of competing individual and group preferences; individual voters are expected to vote according to their interests; as the protective democracy account in Section D suggested, having a voice matters, personally. In contrast, a 'republican' perspective views the electoral process as an attempt by the political community as a whole to construct a 'common good'; the role of each voter is to contribute to this effort. Lastly, a 'deliberative democracy' perspective diverges from the 'liberal' perspective by attributing a transformative character to inclusive deliberation.

2 A 'Liberal' Perspective

On a liberal account, individuals are considered to be the best judges of their own interests and to have divergent interests and preferences.

---

be diluted in and of itself). Queries related to the *structure* of electoral processes fall outside the scope of the book.

[74] The phrase was famously coined by Abraham Lincoln in the Gettysburg Address (19 November 1863), http://myloc.gov/Exhibitions/gettysburgaddress/Pages/default .aspx.

[75] Law and Disagreement (n 18) 237.

[76] Ludvig Beckman, *The Frontiers of Democracy: The Right to Vote and Its Limits* (Palgrave Macmillan 2009) 1.

[77] Talbott (n 20) 158.   [78] Democracy and Its Critics (n 8) 95.

[79] Jeremy Waldron, 'A Right-Based Critique of Constitutional Rights' (1993) 13(1) *Oxford Journal of Legal Studies* 18, 36.

On this account, the electoral process aggregates individual preferences to influence collective decisions.[80] A political will which does not (necessarily) reflect a 'common good' is thus constituted.[81] It is assumed that individuals bring with them divergent understandings of the good of society to the electoral process; inclusive suffrage helps ascertain the well-being of society, which, in turn, is made up of the well-being of its members.

Talbott's moderated liberal perspective suggests that, the reason that democratic decision making is required is that people are neither angels nor devils: if they were angels, there would be no need for external enforcement, whereas if they were devils, they would not be willing to incur even small costs in cases in which they have no strong countervailing personal interests.[82] To reflect individual preferences accurately, the electoral process must be inclusive. Hence, alongside their fear of majoritarian biases that (absent constitutional guarantees) can marginalise participating minorities, liberals are concerned that that 'the channels of political change' will be 'choked off' by parliamentary majorities.[83] If majorities succeed, then not only excluded individuals and their social groups but society as a whole will be adversely affected.

In this context, it is worth reflecting on Sen's famous account of famines, arguing that they do not occur in democracies both because of pressure exerted by those directly suffering from them and because the rest of the population signals to the authorities that famines cannot be tolerated.[84] Process-theory liberals advocate participation-oriented, representation-reinforcing approach to ensure that attempts to cast weaker and marginalised individuals or groups out of the political process will fail.[85]

---

[80] Thomas Christiano, 'Voting and Democracy' (1995) 25(3) *Canadian Journal of Philosophy* 394, 395–97.

[81] David Held, *Democracy and the Global Order: From the Modern State to Cosmopolitan Governance* (Polity Press 1995) 64.

[82] Talbott (n 20) 155.   [83] Ely (n 59) 87.

[84] Amartya Sen, *Development as Freedom* (Oxford University Press 1999) 150.

[85] See e.g. Ely (n 59). Cf. Waldron in Law and Disagreement (n 18) 299–303 (suggesting that, in a democracy, all rights are 'up for grabs' including democratic rights; it does not follow from the fact that a majority of men has no moral right to decide in the name of the whole political community whether women should have a right to vote that others institutions, like courts, can legitimately determine the answer; questions of voting eligibility are a 'legitimacy-free zone').

3   A 'Republican' Perspective

A 'Republican' perspective notes that the electoral process is designed to arrive at an autonomous substantive *common* interest or good that is independent of the sum of interests of individual participant.[86] Community members are expected to engage in the electoral process with 'the common good' in mind, and to support policies which, in their view, cumulatively advance the good of society as a whole, even if they do not also advance their personal interests or the interests of the social group to which they belong.

While on a 'liberal' account, a more inclusive process better reflects the divergent interests that exist in society, and facilitates the aggregation thereof (and the subsequent formation of a public will), a 'republican' account values participation because of the contribution that each person makes to the *joint* project of identifying a 'common good'. Citizens may disagree in good faith over which principles best serve the public will despite overlooking the personal interests and differences that separate them as private persons in favour of their shared interest in the common good. These differences are mediated through the political process: participation has a transformative effect on positions that citizens are willing to adopt and hold.

4   A 'Deliberative Democracy' Perspective

On a 'deliberative democracy' account, the electoral process is the institutionalisation of public use of reason in a decentralised society that is jointly exercised by autonomous persons.[87] When individuals are required to articulate their arguments in public forums, they are forced to think of reasons that others involved in the process may consider plausible: hence, a deliberative setting can shape outcomes that will be formed independently of the participants' motives.[88]

On this account, personal ends are 'discovered' through participation rather than, as the liberal perspective suggests, predetermined prior to

---

[86] Frank Michelman, 'Conceptions of Democracy in American Constitutional Argument: Voting Rights' (1989) 41 *Florida Law Review* 439, 445.

[87] See e.g. Jürgen Habermas, 'Three Normative Models of Democracy' in Seyla Benhabib (ed), *Democracy and Difference: Contesting the Boundaries of the Political* (Princeton University Press 1996) 21.

[88] Jon Elster, 'Deliberation and Constitution Making' in Jon Elster (ed), *Deliberative Democracy* (Cambridge University Press 1998) 97, 104.

and independently of individual engagement in the process.[89] This feature makes the electoral process transformative rather than aggregative. However, a deliberative democracy perspective is conceptually closer to a liberal perspective insofar as the electoral process is not expected to produce a 'common good'. Rather, the prospective outcome of a successful process is a better understanding by all community members of their needs vis-à-vis other members.

F 'Cultural Relativity' Challenges and Electoral Rights

1 The General 'Cultural Relativity' Challenge to Universality of Rights

A global commitment to the universality of human rights is oftentimes proclaimed.[90] The 'Vienna Declaration and Programme of Action' was unanimously adopted by representatives of 171 states that participated in the World Congress on Human Rights. The above declaration pronounces that 'it is the duty of States, regardless of their political, economic or cultural systems, to promote and protect all human rights and fundamental freedoms'.[91] However, the *content* of many rights that are proclaimed universally remains highly contentious. Note, for instance, the divergent approaches to prohibitions on Islamic head coverings, which some societies consider to be an infringement of freedom of religion, while in others they are presented as a means to advance gender equality.[92]

Consequently, 'cultural relativity' challenges are mounted against the presumed universal character of human rights obligations.[93] An-Na'im contends that claims of the international human rights system to 'universal cultural legitimacy should be based on a moral and political 'overlapping consensus' among major world cultural traditions' that has not yet

---

[89] Heather Lardy, 'Citizenship and the Right to Vote' (1997) 17(1) *Oxford Journal of Legal Studies* 76, 87.

[90] Jack Donnelly, *Universal Human Rights in Theory and Practice* (2nd edn Cornell University Press 2003) 157.

[91] UN Doc A/CONF 157/24 (Part 1) at 20 (1993) art 8.

[92] See e.g. Reuven (Ruvi) Ziegler, 'The French Headscarves Ban: Intolerance or Necessity?' (2006) 40(1) *John Marshall Law Review* 235.

[93] For a discussion of cultural relativism, see generally Jack Donnelly, 'Cultural Relativism and Universal Human Rights' (1984) 6 *Human Rights Quarterly* 400. In recent decades, there has also been a particular focus on a purported 'Asian values' dimension of the cultural relativism claim. See e.g. Damien Kingsbury, 'Universalism and Exceptionalism in "Asia"' in Leena Avonius and Damien Kingsbury (eds), *Human Rights in Asia: A Reassessment of the Asian Values Debate* (Palgrave Macmillan 2008) 19.

fully emerged.[94] Mutua asserts that human rights documents are 'veiled attempts' to universalise particular civil and political rights that are either accepted or aspired to by Western liberal democracies.[95]

However, the notion of cultural relativity seems to be self-contradictory, since it is premised on a *universal* tenet, namely that everyone should follow and be defined by their culture.[96] Moreover, it may be argued that the suggestions that 'Europe' has a longstanding democratic tradition or that there is an 'Asian' tradition of obedience to authority are erroneous. Indeed, if respect for human rights has emerged from Europe despite its despotic and intolerant past, then it can be plausibly contended that human beings possess some characteristics by virtue of which *any* cultural tradition can and should respect human rights.[97]

2   The Facilitative Role of the Right to Vote

The right to vote has been characterised as 'the right of rights':[98] as was noted in Section D, voters participate in decision-making processes that impact the protection of other rights. This characterisation does not imply that the right to vote has moral priority over other rights; rather, it points to the fact that, reasonable right-bearers resolve through the electoral process disagreements about rights that they may or may not have.[99]

Ronald Dworkin famously characterised legal rights as 'trumps' that are shielded from majoritarian decision making;[100] hence, they protect vulnerable minorities from the 'tyranny of the majority'.[101] However,

---

[94] Abdullahi Ahmed An-Na'im, 'State Responsibility under International Human Rights Law to Change Religious and Customary Laws' in Rebecca Cook (ed), *Human Rights of Women: National and International Perspectives* (University of Pennsylvania Press 1994) 167, 173.

[95] Makau Mutua, *Human Rights: A Political and Cultural Critique* (University of Pennsylvania Press 2002) 173.

[96] James Sweeney, 'Margin of Appreciation, Cultural Relativity, and the European Court of Human Rights in the Post Cold-War Era' (2004) 54 *International and Comparative Law Quarterly* 459, 461.

[97] Talbott (n 20) 40.

[98] Law and Disagreement (n 18) 232 citing William Cobbett, *Advice to Young Men and Women, Advice to a Citizen* (1829) quoted in Leslie J MacFarlane, *The Theory and Practice of Human Rights* (Dartmouth Publishing 1985) 142. This phrase should not be confused with Arendt's depiction of nationality as the 'right to have rights' (see Chapters 2 and 4). Hannah Arendt, *The Origins of Totalitarianism* (Harcourt 1967) 293.

[99] Law and Disagreement (n 18) 282.   [100] TRS (n 36) 328.

[101] See e.g. On Democracy (n 14) 64 (arguing that '[d]emocratic governments can also inflict harm on a minority of citizens who *possess* voting rights but are outvoted by majorities-the tyranny of the majority').

even if one rejects Dworkin's account, the right to vote has special characteristics: it legitimates and facilitates majoritarian decision making that follows its exercise.[102] Hence, support for inclusive electoral processes can be based on divergent perceptions of individual and community life.[103] For instance, McGinnis and Somin assert that 'controversial substantive rights' are better left to domestic democratic processes, and that international law should instead establish global norms facilitating democracy to ensure that governments are periodically held accountable to their peoples.[104]

'Democratic rights' are absent from the list of 'basic rights' in John Rawls' *Law of Peoples*.[105] His list includes the rights enunciated in Articles 3 to 18 of the UDHR (civil rights) whereas the political rights in Articles 19–21 (freedom of expression, assembly and association and democratic rights of participation) are described by Rawls as 'liberal aspirations'.[106] Rawls labels non-democratic societies that respect basic rights, but not political rights, as 'decent' and 'hierarchical'.[107]

Now, Rawls' account does *not* advocate cultural relativism, since he clearly posited that *basic* rights should be considered 'binding on all peoples and societies', and that their violation is 'equally condemned by both reasonable liberal peoples and decent hierarchical peoples'.[108] Hence, Rawls' universality 'test' seems to correspond to Sen's contention that we cannot judge the universality of a value by whether it commands the assent of everyone at a given point in time but, rather, by whether people anywhere may have reasons to consider it valuable.[109] *Contra* Sen, Rawls opted for a non-universal application of the political equality principles of 'theory of justice', suggesting these principles apply (only) to liberal societies.

---

[102] Goodhart (n 66) 147.

[103] Joshua Cohen, 'For a Democratic Society' in Samuel Freeman (ed), *The Cambridge Companion to Rawls* (Cambridge University Press 2003) 86, 109–10.

[104] John McGinnis and Ilya Somin, 'Democracy and International Human Rights Law' (2009) 84(4) *Notre Dame Law Review* 1739, 1742–47.

[105] John Rawls, *The Law of Peoples* (Harvard University Press 1999) 80.

[106] Ibid 80–82. *Compare* Fabienne Peter, 'The Human Right to Political Participation' (2013) 7(2) *Journal of Ethics & Social Philosophy* 1, 1 (arguing that 'human rights will fail to secure political legitimacy if the right to political participation is excluded from the set of basic rights'

[107] Ibid 63–67.   [108] Ibid 79–80.

[109] See generally Amartya Sen, 'Human Rights and Economic Achievements' in Joanne R Bauer and Daniel A Bell (eds), *The East Asian Challenge for Human Rights* (Cambridge University Press 1999) 88.

A plausible interpretation of Rawls' account considers his objection to the use of force by international actors against 'decent hierarchical' regimes that do not engage in the most extreme forms of human rights violations to be grounded in international relations. It is nonetheless possible to interpret *Law of Peoples* as (morally) legitimating such regimes.[110] Hence, Rawls' account can be seen either as an exercise in *realpolitik* or as a conceptual challenge to the universality of 'the right to democratic governance'.[111]

G 'Core' and 'Penumbra' of Rights

German constitutional law arguably draws a distinction between the *core* or *essence* of basic rights, which legislation may not infringe under any circumstances, and their *penumbra* (which may be restricted pursuant to generally applicable laws).[112] It is contended that, eligibility to vote, namely the determination *whether* a person may vote in particular elections, is at the *core* of the right to vote, whereas the conditions and procedural regulations which facilitate or hinder the *exercise* of a pre-determined right to vote are at its *penumbra*.

Non-invidious procedural requirements may inconvenience voters. For instance, in all representative democracies, including those based on proportional representation, political parties need to pass an effective percentage bar due to the limited number of seats in the legislature(s). Consequently, voters who support very marginal parties may have to 'settle' for a second preference, or having their votes discounted. Some electoral systems require prior registration that may impose technical difficulties. However, provided that such restrictions are benign and that eligible voters are still effectively able to exercise their rights (an assumption that has been proven rather shaky in certain states), they affect the penumbra of the right to vote. In contrast, disenfranchisement of eligible voters is an infringement of the *core* of their aforementioned right.

---

[110] Fernando Tesón, *A Philosophy of International Law* (Westview 1998) 107.

[111] See e.g. Thomas Franck, 'The Emerging Right to Democratic Governance' (1992) 86 *American Journal of International Law* 46, 46.

[112] German Basic Law, art 19(2). See also the jurisprudence of the Human Rights Committee e.g. General Comment No 27: *Freedom of Movement* (Article 12) (2 November 1999) CCPR/C/21/Rev.1/Add.9 [13] ('in adopting laws providing for restrictions permitted by Article 12, paragraph 3, States should always be guided by the principle that the restrictions must not impair the essence of the right').

In an England and Wales Court of Appeal judgment concerning the compatibility of domestic legislation that disenfranchises prisoners with the First Additional Protocol,[113] Lord Justice Kennedy held that

> [o]f course as far as an individual prisoner is concerned, disenfranchise-ment does impair the very essence of his right to vote, but that is too simplistic an approach, because what Article 3 of the First Protocol is really concerned with is the wider question of universal franchise, and the free expression of the opinion of the people in the choice of the legislature.[114]

The above judgment seems to frame the question in terms of how disenfranchisement affects the 'very essence' of universal suffrage as a *collective* enterprise. However, Article 3 has been consistently interpreted by the ECtHR as manifesting an *individual* right to vote.[115]

A broader debate between 'relative' and 'absolute' theories of legal rights concerns the question whether legal rights have (or should have) a 'core'. Robert Alexy draws a distinction between *rules* and *principles*, suggesting that rules are definitive, non-balanceable norms, whereas principles are competing optimisation requirements which should be implemented to the 'greatest possible extent'.[116] On this account, if rights are to be regarded as principles, it would entail that they do not have inviolable 'core' content; rather, the 'core' of a right is what remains *after* balancing has taken place.

However, it may follow from Alexy's structural approach that the question whether a right is a (non-balanceable) rule or a (balanceable) principle does not depend on the nature, fundamentality, or content of the right which the analysis engages but, rather, on linguistic formulae. Consequently, the right to vote may be regarded either as a rule *or* as a principle, depending on the particular legal stipulation. Rivers argues that the 'problem with the "very essence" of a right is that it is almost

---

[113] Art 3.

[114] *R (Pearson and Martinez)* v *Home Secretary; Hirst* v *Attorney General* [2001] EWHC 239 (Admin) [41] cited in *Hirst* (No 2) v *UK* (GC) App no 74025/01 (Grand Chamber ECHR, October 2005) [16]. In *Hirst*, the ECtHR held that §3(1) of the Representation of the People Act 1983 c2 (mandating blanket disenfranchisement of prisoners serving a custodial sentence) is incompatible with Protocol I, art 3, above.

[115] See e.g. Ziegler (n 92). See e.g. *Gitonas and others* v *Greece* App no 18747/91 (Grand Chamber ECHR, 1 July 1997) [39] (the court 'has to satisfy itself that the conditions do not curtail the rights in question to such an extent as to impair their very essence and deprive them of their effectiveness'). See also the discussion of ECtHR art 3 jurisprudence in Chapter 2.

[116] Robert Alexy, *A Theory of Constitutional Rights* (Oxford University Press 2002) 47.

impossible to define usefully without reference to competing public interest'.[117]

In contrast, Kai Möller asserts that normative assessments regarding the importance of rights or interests relative to one another ought to determine which rights or interests should *generally* take precedence when a conflict arises between them.[118] On this account, if one accepts that eligibility is at the core of the right to vote, then it is reasonable to argue that eligibility should not be subjected to individualised balancing or proportionality assessment; rather, it should reflect the respective meanings of enfranchisement and of membership.

H   Concluding Remarks

This chapter explored aspects of the fundamentality of voting for individuals and for polities in view of individual rights and capacities as well as the collective nature of the electoral process. The constitutive nature of voting as a manifestation of membership in a political community will be explored further in subsequent chapters, as will the ramifications of rights-protective and non-domination accounts.

Following Waldron, it may be argued that voters take at times a 'Benthamite' self-interest path and at other times a 'Rousseauian' general will path;[119] both paths, separately and jointly, offer solid justifications for considering the right to vote to be fundamental. In a 'Benthamite' democracy, individuals ought to be allowed to assert their interests, whereas in a 'Rousseauian' democracy, all opinions should be respected, voiced in debate, and given an effective opportunity to win supporters. It was further contended that the right to vote is less susceptible to 'cultural relativity' challenges to universality of rights, and hence a global cross-cultural consideration of questions of voting eligibility should be less contentious. Finally, it was asserted that, following the analytical distinction between core and penumbra of rights, questions of *eligibility* stand at the core of the right to vote.

---

[117] Julian Rivers, 'Proportionality and Variable Intensity of Review' (2006) 65 *Cambridge Law Journal* 174, 187.

[118] Kai Möller, 'Balancing and the Structure of Constitutional Rights' (2007) 5(3) *International Journal of Constitutional Law* 453, 465.

[119] Jeremy Waldron, *Liberal Rights* (Cambridge University Press 1993) 408, 415 (suggesting that, while in a 'Benthamite' democracy, the minority has to also be protected against majoritarianism, in a 'Rousseauian' democracy institutional decision-making need not be constrained by counter-majoritarian mechanisms).

It will be argued in Chapter 8 that, in view of the diverse yet complementary accounts and roles of voting eligibility, the non-inclusion of
CSR1951 refugees in elections of their states of asylum aggravates their
political predicament and that, conversely, their enfranchisement would
be both intrinsically and instrumentally significant.

Perspectives on the Meaning and Purposes of State Citizenship

A   Introduction

The traditional claim in international law that 'acquisition and loss of citizenship is, in principle, regulated by national legal orders' appears to holds firmly.[1] As Chapter 1 demonstrated, absent a 'world state',[2] states are responsible for and are unconstrained in determining their membership as long as such determination does not conflict with principles of international law.[3]

Citizenship is the term usually used to denote (full) membership in a statist political community with its own governing institutions (otherwise referred to as a polity); references to 'citizen' in other contexts are made analogously or metaphorically.[4] States do not lay claim to the entire globe

---

[1] See e.g. Hans Kelsen, *General Theory of Law and State* (Anders Wedberg Trans, Russell & Russell 1961) 233 (asserting that 'acquisition and loss of citizenship is in principle regulated by the national legal orders').

[2] See e.g. Immanuel Kant, *Perpetual Peace: A Philosophical Sketch* (W Hastie trans 1891) (1795) 17. Ayelet Shachar, *The Birthright Lottery: Citizenship and Global Inequality* (Harvard University Press 2009) 47–49 (arguing that a world citizenship or a 'world government' may lead to the disintegration of social bonds and of mutual responsibilities that bind people together, motivating them to redistribute benefits gained from membership. It may also cause cultural and social capital losses of rich and diverse forms of modern statehood such as history, identity narratives, political struggles, social experiments, and linguistic diversity). See also Michael Walzer, 'Spheres of Affection' in Joshua Cohen (ed), *For Love of Country: Debating the Limits of Patriotism* (Beacon Press 1996) 125, 126–7 (claiming that he is 'not even aware that there is a world such that one could be a citizen of it').

[3] Convention on Nationality (adopted 12 April 1930, entered into force 1 July 1937) 179 LNTS 89 art 1 (proclaiming that '[i]t is for each State to determine under its own law who are its nationals. This law shall be recognized by other States in so far as it is consistent with international conventions, international custom, and the principles of law generally recognized with regard to nationality'). The latter qualification indicates that, while sovereign, states are not free of constraints on the international plane.

[4] See Richard Ford, 'City-States and Citizenship' in T Alexander Aleinikoff and Charles Klusmeyer (eds), *Citizenship Today: Global Perspectives and Practices* (Carnegie 2001) 209, 210. Cf. Jeremy Waldron, 'Teaching Cosmopolitan Right' in Kevin McDonough and Walter

and to its people(s). Rather, they (attempt to) lay a sovereign claim to control over finite sections of the globe (the territorial dimension) and over finite groups of persons (the human dimension).[5]

In the territorial dimension, boundaries are physical referents; in the human dimension, they serve as a function of the legal institution of state citizenship. For individuals, membership in the international community funnels through membership in a statist political community. Brubaker described 'nationality' as 'an international filing system, a mechanism for allocation of persons to states'.[6]

Paraphrasing Mark Twain, reports of the death of citizenship are greatly exaggerated. A person cannot freely choose to become a member of a statist political community, nor can a person substitute their political community membership for membership in another political community at their pleasure.[7] State citizenship effectively serves as 'a powerful instrument of social closure'.[8] Indeed, citizenship is *janus* faced: it is both a unifier (offering members a common set of rights, entitlements, privileges and obligations under law that link them to each other and to the state) and a divider (membership status for some designates others as non-members).[9] By distinguishing between members and

Feinberg (eds), *Citizenship and Education in Liberal-Democratic Societies* (Oxford University Press 2003) 23, 41 (noting that 'citizenship means more than formal participation', and asserting that 'the phrase "citizen of the world" should not be regarded as meaningless in the absence of a constituted world government. If anything, the absence of a coercive institution to secure and sustain necessary structures of life and practice at a global level . . . makes it all the more important for use to use "citizens of the word" as an idea regulating our actions').

[5] David R MacDonald, *Difference and Belonging: Liberal Citizenship and Modern Multiplicity* (PhD thesis, LSE 2002) 161. Convention on the Rights and Duties of States (adopted 26 December 1933, entered into force 26 December 1934) 16 LNTS 19 art 1 (listing four conditions for recognising a state as a legal person in international law: a permanent population; a defined territory; a government; and the capacity to enter into relations with other states). *Notably, questions of state recognition fall outside the remit of this book.*

[6] Rogers Brubaker, *Citizenship and Nationhood in France and Germany* (Harvard University Press 1992) 31. See also Paul Weis, 'The United Nations Convention on the Reduction of Statelessness 1961' (1962) 11(4) *International and Comparative Law Quarterly* 1073, 1073 (suggesting that '[f]rom the point of view of international law, the stateless person is an anomaly, nationality still being the principal link between the individual and the Law of Nations'.).

[7] Cf. Yaffa Zilbershats, *The Human Right to Citizenship* (Transnational 2002) (advocating recognition of a 'human right to citizenship').

[8] Brubaker (n 6) x.

[9] Matthew J Gibney, 'The Rights of Non-Citizens to Membership' in Caroline Sawyer and Brad K Blitz (eds), *Statelessness in the European Union* (Cambridge University Press 2011) 41.

non-members, political communities are exclusive:[10] the articulation of the existence of a community is itself a symbol whose purpose is to invoke boundaries.[11]

Bauböck offers a conceptual distinction between freedom of association (regarding membership in associations other than the state) and membership in the state itself; he posits that, in liberal societies, non-statist associations are founded on three assumptions: First: becoming a member of an association is a voluntary act. Second: every member of an association is free to leave it. Third: every person is entitled to join with others and set up a new association.[12]

For state membership (citizenship), the first and third assumptions do not generally hold: the world is exhaustively divided between states which, in turn, enjoy discretion in defining their membership. The second assumption may, in principle, apply (at least in liberal states which do not restrict renunciation of citizenship). Nevertheless, citizenship is increasingly considered a 'protective shield', and renouncing citizenship may have dire implications: citizens have a much stronger interest to remain members of their statist association than respective members of voluntary associations, not least due to the security of residence which citizenship entails in a world characterised by migration control, and to the prioritisation of citizens (considered below).

Hence, the (paradigmatic) state is a political unit that controls a bounded territory with a national community, most of which habitually resides in that territory, and which has the power to impose its (political) will within these boundaries.[13] Nonetheless, the state's territorial and human dimensions do *not* fully overlap: not every person who resides in the territory of a state at a given time belongs to its corresponding political community and a person does not cease to belong to an association simply by leaving its territory and residing abroad. Indeed, as Part III of this book demonstrates, citizenship is a 'bundle' of rights that occasionally

[10] Paulina Tambakaki, *Human Rights, or Citizenship?* (Birkbeck Law Press 2010) 35.
[11] Elizabeth Frazer, *The Problems of Communitarian Politics: Unity and Conflict* (Oxford University Press 1999) 81.
[12] Rainer Bauböck, *Immigration and the Boundaries of Citizenship* (Centre for Research in Ethnic Relations University of Warwick 1992) 13.
[13] See e.g. Stephen Castles and Alastair Davidson, *Citizenship and Migration: Globalization and the Politics of Belonging* (Routledge 2000) 12. See also generally Nicholas Barber, *The Constitutional State* (Oxford University Press 2011) (stipulating that the state claims legitimate, supreme, and effective authority over its people, and that the state is a social group that exists to benefit its members).

'transcend the boundaries of the political and territorial entities in whose political institutions these rights are embodied'.[14]

Section B argues that, state citizenship has both legal and extra-legal dimensions, and that the latter significantly affect the extent to which rights (not least, electoral rights) are disaggregated from citizenship status. In turn, Sections C, D, and E, respectively, explore the meaning and purposes of citizenship from 'liberal', 'republican', and 'communitarian' perspectives.[15] Alongside the exploration of meaning and purposes of voting in Chapter 3, this chapter contextualises the appraisal of citizenship voting qualifications in Chapter 5. Concordantly, Part II offers divergent bases for appraising (in Part III of the book) the political predicament of recognised CSR1951 refugees.

B   The Multi-dimensional Character of State Citizenship

Citizenship is the quintessential *legal* relationship between individuals and their state.[16] State citizenship determines both the legal criteria of (full) membership, and the nature of the 'conversation' between the state and its (full) members.[17]

Kelsen argued that domestic legal orders (at the time of his writing) usually reserve for their citizens 'the so-called political rights'; such rights include the right to vote which 'affords the individual the legal possibility of participating in the creation or execution of legal norms'. He asserted that it is for each state to decide if to enfranchise all, some or none of its citizens, as well as all, some or none of its non-citizens.[18] On Kelsen's account, states could exist just with subjects, namely without *citizens*, except insofar as they wish to require parts of their populations to perform duties of military service; according to his reading of international law, such duties may only be imposed on citizens.[19]

---

[14] Bauböck (n 12) 1.
[15] The exposition below should not be considered exhaustive; there are multiple variations of each perspective, and considerable overlaps between them.
[16] Barber (n 13) 48–49 (outlining other types of relationships that an individual can have with a state: on his account, resident non-nationals may have a relationship with their host state even though they are not members; friendly aliens can trade with nationals of the state, and receive its protection while in its territory; enemy aliens are considered a threat to the state).
[17] David Jacobson, *Rights across Borders: Immigration and the Decline of Citizenship* (Johns Hopkins University Press 1996) 7.
[18] Kelsen (n 1) 238.
[19] Ibid 240. Kelsen does not explain the distinction between military service and e.g. taxation. See also Protocol Relating to Military Obligations in Certain Cases of Double Nationality

Kelsen's depiction, seen through a contemporary lens, arguably suffers from two fundamental flaws: it downplays the significance of *legal* rights of citizenship; and it fails to address the extra-legal dimensions of state citizenship that may explain social choices concerning the assignment of legal rights and obligations. In its oft-quoted *Nottebohm* judgment, the International Court of Justice (ICJ) held that 'nationality is a legal bond having as its basis a social fact of attachment, a genuine connection of existence, interest and sentiments, together with the existence of reciprocal rights and duties'.[20]

Chapter 2 described how state parties to international human rights treaties assume (some) obligations towards all persons in their territories and subject to their jurisdiction. The wording in (some) contemporary bills of rights is similarly inclusive, securing the enjoyment of rights without regard to citizenship status. Thus, it was submitted that, in the 'age of human rights',[21] considering state citizenship to manifest the 'right to have rights'[22] is an overstatement.[23] As US Supreme Court Justice Frankfurter noted, '[t]he very substantial rights and privileges that the alien . . . enjoys under the Federal and State Constitutions puts him in a very different condition from that of an outlaw in Fifteenth-Century England'.[24]

Nonetheless, as Part I of this book demonstrated, two fundamental rights remain typically attached to state citizenship: the unconditional right to enter the state or return to it, coupled with immunity from involuntary removal; and the right to elect representatives to its governing institutions and to be governed by self-given laws.[25]

(adopted 12 April 1930, entered into force 25 May 1937) 178 LNTS 227 (implicitly assuming that only nationals will be liable for conscription).

[20] Nottebohm (*Lichtenstein v Guatemala*) Judgment of 6 April 1955, ICJ Rep 1955, 4, 22.

[21] Louis Henkin, 'Refugees and Their Human Rights' (1994–1995) 18 *Fordham International Law Journal* 1079, 1079.

[22] *Trop v Dulles* 356 US 86, 102 (per Warren CJ) (holding provisions stripping certain convicts of their US citizenship to be unconstitutional).

[23] See e.g. T Alexander Aleinikoff, 'Theories of Loss of Citizenship' (1986) 84 *Michigan Law Review* 1471, 1486.

[24] *Trop* (n 22) 127 (Frankfurter J, dissenting). See also Jeremy Waldron, 'Special Ties and Natural Duties' (1993) 22(1) *Philosophy and Public Affairs* 3, 15 (noting that, historically, communities were established to avoid conflict and violence, leading to an evolution of a limited system of justice that was not duly concerned with temporary migrants).

[25] Shai Lavi, 'Citizenship Revocation as Punishment: On the Modern Duties of Citizens and Their Criminal Breach' (2011) 61(4) *University of Toronto Law Journal* 783, 797. See e.g. Charter of Fundamental Rights of the European Union (18 December 2000) OJ 2000 C364 ch v: citizens' rights. Cf. Linda Bosniak, 'The Meaning of Citizenship' (2011) 9 *Issues in Legal Scholarship* (Article 12), 14 (asserting that, 'if citizenship is a term that we

Chapter 1 argued that the immigration control regime is at the heart of the present international legal order. It was emphasised that the granting of CSR1951 refugee status is a sovereign decision which emphasises the general resilience of migration control. Chapter 2 demonstrated that, even when states generally adhere to their international human rights obligations and adopt inclusive bills of rights (above), these instruments do not require states to extend voting rights to their non-citizen residents.

As Chapter 3 contended, elections matter, *inter alia*, because the electoral process gives legal effect and legitimacy to collective decisions regarding allocation of finite resources. On a 'liberal' account, voters protect their interests by expressing their preferences; on a 'republican' account, the enfranchised are expected to seek (the) common good, which they collectively define. Interests and preferences of the electorally excluded are under-represented for potentially protracted periods; thus, it is unsurprising that the outcomes of these processes tend to disfavour their needs.

While the book appraises the *legal* exclusion of CSR1951 refugees *qua* non-citizen residents from voting in elections of their states of asylum, it is nevertheless suggested that the extra-legal dimensions of state citizenship (absent from Kelsen's account) affect both the criteria for naturalisation of non-citizens and their electoral exclusion.

Zilbersahts posits that state citizenship operates on 'vertical' and 'horizontal' planes.[26] On the 'vertical' plane, it is a legal status bestowed on those considered to be full and equal members of the political community, engendering the rights and duties of individuals vis-à-vis their state. On the 'horizontal' plane, it is a 'nexus' between persons and their state and between political community members themselves. Carens suggests that citizenship has three interrelated dimensions: legal, political, and psychological.[27] As an institution, citizenship may be regarded both as a bundle of rights and obligations and as a set of political, cultural, and social practices.[28]

Citizenship status affects citizens who, in turn, affect the changing character of citizenship. In an ideal form, citizenship manifests political equality and is (nearly) irrevocable; citizens have control over their

conventionally deploy to talk about a range of political and social relationships, it does not seem controversial to say that non-citizens enjoy aspects of citizenship or membership though obviously not others').

[26] Zilbershats (n 7) xiii. See also Aleinikoff (n 23) 1488.

[27] Joseph H Carens, *Culture, Citizenship, and Community* (Oxford University Press 2000) ch 7, esp pp 162–66.

[28] Law Commission of Canada, *Citizenship and Identity* (Sage 1999) 4.

lives, can choose the projects and relationships that they wish to pursue, and can make decisions about how to pursue such projects. Following the discussion in Chapter 3 of the fundamentally of voting, state citizenship arguably furthers both individual autonomy (in Razian terms) and non-domination (in Petitt's terms).[29] Citizens enjoy the opportunity to advance their most important interests and can exercise a wide range of moral autonomy.[30] Hence, in its ideal form, citizenship may accomplish both self-protection (on a 'liberal' account), and self-governance (on a 'republican' account).[31]

C 'Liberal' Perspectives

1 Equal Citizenship and the Role of Participation

On 'liberal' accounts, state citizenship is the creation of a political community that is a product of human imagination, coordination, and agency (rather than a creation of nature).[32] The 1789 French 'Declaration of the Rights of Man and of the Citizen' defined the relationship between states and their inhabitants in terms of rights rather than authority;[33] it adopted a Lockean notion of a political association established by individuals to secure their (natural) rights to life, liberty, and property.[34] The Declaration proclaimed that 'the preservation of the natural and indefeasible rights of man is the purpose of every political association'.[35] Notably, it enunciated universal suffrage of citizens, pronouncing that '[l]aw is the expression of the general will. Every citizen has a right to participate personally or through his representative in its foundation'.[36]

Contemporary liberals contend that state citizenship manifests equal status in a political community. Trevor Marshall portrayed the development of (British) citizenship as a process of full realisation of equality

---

[29] Barber (n 13) 55.

[30] Robert Dahl, *On Democracy* (Yale University Press 1998) 75.

[31] Melissa Williams, 'Non-Territorial Boundaries of Citizenship' in Seyla Benhabib, Ian Shapiro and Danilo Petranovic (eds), *Identities, Affiliations, and Allegiances* (Cambridge University Press 2007) 226, 247–48.

[32] Shachar (n 2) 147.

[33] Andreas Fahrmeir, *Citizenship: The Rise and Fall of a Modern Concept* (Yale University Press 2007) 1.

[34] John Locke, *Two Treatises of Government* (first published 1690, Peter Laslett ed, Cambridge University Press 1997) bk ii.

[35] The Declaration was approved by the National Assembly of France, 26 August 1789 www.hrcr.org/docs/frenchdec.html.

[36] Ibid [6].

among citizens, describing a process whereby the scope of rights has gradually increased from civil rights, to political rights, to social rights. Marshall defined the political element as the 'right to participate in the exercise of political power, as a member of a body invested with political authority or as an elector of the members of such a body'.[37]

In *A Theory of Justice*, Rawls argued that, to ensure just distribution of rights and duties, individuals possessed with inviolable rights established political associations.[38] On this account, a person is 'someone who can be a *citizen*, that is, a normal and fully cooperating member of society over a complete life' whereas citizens are 'free and equal persons'.[39]

Bauböck submits that state citizenship is a 'set of rights exercised by the individuals who hold the rights, equal for all citizens and universally distributed within a political community, as well as a corresponding set of institutions guaranteeing these rights.'[40]

On a 'liberal' account, a political community is 'an association of individuals who share an understanding of what is public and what is private within their polity'.[41] The political community provides a framework of coexistence for individuals who share a common public life yet maintain separate and occasionally divergent private lives in which members may hold loyalties to different groups and cultures.[42] The primary role of citizenship is instrumental, namely to facilitate advancement of individual interests which exist *independently* of their individual citizenship status.

On this account, not all citizens need to be equally enthusiastic about their citizenship status: the state can tolerate (some) passive, disinterested, and even partial citizens.[43] While liberals would rather see a cultural convergence around liberal norms, they do not consider such convergence critical for the state's survival.[44]

Nonetheless, the stability and health of public institutions and the political culture of the political community depend on a political community

---

[37] Trevor H Marshall and Tom Bottomore, *Citizenship and Social Class* (Pluto Press 1992) (1950) 6–8.
[38] John Rawls, *A Theory of Justice* (2nd revised edn Oxford University Press 1999) 3.
[39] John Rawls, *Political Liberalism* (Columbia University Press 2005) 18–19.
[40] Bauböck (n 12) 16.
[41] Chandran Kukathas, 'Liberalism, Communitarianism, and Political Community' (1996) 13(1) *Society Philosophy and Policy* 80, 86.
[42] Ibid 104.   [43] *Difference and Belonging* (n 5) 232.
[44] Jeff Spinner, *The Boundaries of Citizenship* (Johns Hopkins University Press 1994) 6; Stephen Macedo, *Liberal Virtues* (Clarendon Press 1991) 251.

having a sufficient number of members who value their membership, and who are consequently willing to take actions that exceed legal demands. Hence, while liberals reject an imposition of a duty to vote, they would also consider low turnout in elections as a failure.

2   Identity and Attachment

Carens usefully distinguishes between *identity* and *attachment*. He posits that a person may have a strong sense of political identity as a member of a given political community, yet lack a corresponding sense of attachment to that community.[45] On a 'liberal' account, a political community may only use non-coercive means to make state citizenship seem more valuable and enhance its psychological dimension. It may be argued that individuals have different reasons for valuing their membership in a particular polity, and that citizenship may be meaningful to them because it represents *their* full and equal membership in the political community that, in turn, they consider valuable for reasons that may differ from those of other community members.

Now, some citizens may undergo a transformative process whereby their objective belonging may turn to subjective affective belonging.[46] Jürgen Habermas suggests that, ideally, citizens adopt constitutional patriotism, namely identify with their political community because they take pride in its (democratic) principles of free, equal, and inclusive collective self-determination, and in its (liberal) principles of rights protection.[47] If citizens are able to feel 'at home' in their political community, identify with its interests, and on balance regard its major institutions (especially its political and legal ones) as valuable, then they may (freely) choose to make their citizenship a fundamental basis of their moral or personal identity.[48]

Yael Tamir asserts that most liberals 'except for some cosmopolitans and radical anarchists' are liberal nationalists who assume that states/nations exist, have been successful, and are resilient.[49] Citizens in a modern polity

---

[45] Carens (n 27) 163.   [46] Difference and Belonging (n 5) 246.

[47] See e.g. Jürgen Habermas, *Between Facts and Norms: Contributions to a Discourse Theory of Law and Democracy* (William Rehg transl, MIT Press 1996) app ii: Citizenship and National Identity 491–515.

[48] Andrew Mason, *Community, Solidarity and Belonging: Levels of Community and their Normative Significance* (Cambridge University Press 2000) 138.

[49] Yael Tamir, *Liberal Nationalism* (Princeton University Press 1993) 139.

are connected by 'the belief that [they] all belong to a group whose exis-tence [they] consider valuable'.[50] On her account, citizens value the exis-tence of the political community because of its national character. Thus, Tamir argues that 'the liberal tendency to overlook the value inherent in nationalism is mistaken'.[51]

In contradistinction, Dora Kostakopoulou considers citizenship to be a 'network good' that is characterised by the fact that a person's 'con-sumption' of a good does not hinder other persons' usage thereof.[52] She asserts that citizenship 'would mean very little if citizens belonged to borderless communities', and advocates substituting naturalisation procedures with automatic civic registration subject only to residence and non-criminality qualifications.[53] Kostakopoulou argues that liberal nationalists are 'mak[ing] a virtue out of the necessity of nations', that nation-states are not timeless constructions, and their success is less a measure of their intrinsic value than an expression of political projects and socio-political contingency.[54]

However, Kostakopoulou recognises the contemporary prominence of the state, even though she contests its normative salience by criticising contemporary liberal attempts to transform citizenship, suggesting that they are 'underpinned by citizenship that is wedded to the nation-state'.[55] It was noted in Chapter 2 that the de-territorialised notion of rights which Yaesmin Soysal offers does not negate the importance of state provision of rights protection; rather, it celebrates the advent of human rights law, and the ideal that states are no longer permitted to restrict rights to their citizens.[56] Similarly, Bauböck's transnational citizenship embraces the

---

[50] Ibid 98.

[51] Ibid 3. See also Dario Castiglione, Emilio Santoro and Richard Bellamy, *Lineages of Euro-pean Citizenship: Rights, Belonging, and Participation in Eleven Nation-states* (Palgrave Macmillan 2004) 7 (contending that national identity shapes a common civic conscious-ness and allegiance to the state and one's fellow citizens. It encourages reciprocity and solidarity in both politics and economics. National systems of education created a public political language and inducted citizens into a certain civic culture and set of values).

[52] Dora Kostakopoulou, *The Future Governance of Citizenship* (Cambridge University Press 2008) 109.

[53] Ibid 86, 196.   [54] Ibid 49.

[55] Ibid 78. Cf. Ayelet Shachar, 'The Future of National Citizenship: Going, Going, Gone?' (2009) 59 *University of Toronto Law Journal* 579, 585 (arguing that Kostakopoulou's book exhibits a prevalent tension between the desire to make citizenship free from any attachment to notions of collectivity while at the same time demanding even more robust provision of services and pathways to redistribution via the state).

[56] Yasemin Soysal, *The Limits of Citizenship: Migrants and Postnational Membership in Europe* (University of Chicago Press 1994) 512.

notion that individuals can have multiple belongings to (statist) political communities.[57] The analysis in this book endorses both contentions.

The introduction of European Union (EU) Citizenship is quite pertinent for the above consideration. Joseph Weiler argues that one of the purported aims of institutionalising EU citizenship was the attempt to create European *demos* that has communal psychological identity and a feeling of belonging that is built around a commitment to shared values. EU citizenship *supplements* rather than replaces state citizenship.[58] The decision to institutionalise citizenship and to make it contingent on MS citizenship arguably supports the claim that state citizenship remains significant and resilient.[59]

3   Prioritisation of Citizens

It was noted above that, through the electoral process, societies determine, *inter alia*, provision and allocation of finite public goods and services. On a rights-protective account, voters are advancing their individual and group preferences when making their electoral choices; non-citizens are likely to be disfavoured. The conjunction of electoral exclusion of non-citizens gives rise to a liberal difficulty. The longer non-citizens reside in a state, the more difficult it is for liberals to justify denying them benefits that citizens enjoy.

The prioritisation of citizens is often justified on two ('liberal') grounds.

The first ground suggests that membership is institutionalised by rights, benefits, and obligations which distinguish members from non-members.[60] On this view, if non-citizens are exempt from obligations such as military service and are not subject to personal taxation, then it would be reasonable to deny them equal provision of goods and services.

However, conscription may require non-citizen (male) residents to serve alongside (male) citizens, while (female) citizens may be

---

[57] Bauböck (n 12) 59.

[58] See e.g. Joseph HH Weiler, '*To be a European Citizen* – Eros and Civilization' (1997) 4(4) *Journal of European Public Policy* 495, 500.

[59] See Linda Bosniak, 'Denationalising Citizenship' in T Alexander Aleinikoff and Douglas Klusmeyer (eds), *Citizenship Today: Global Perspectives and Practices* (Carnegie 2001) 237, 241; Will Kymlicka, *Politics in the Vernacular: Nationalism, Multiculturalism and Citizenship* (Oxford University Press 2001) 320–23.

[60] Miriam Feldblum, 'Reconfiguring Citizenship in Europe' in Christian Joppke (ed), *Challenges to the Nation-State* (Oxford University Press 1998) 231, 233.

exempt.[61] Reliance on conscription as an indicator of fair distribution based on burden sharing is thus both over and under-inclusive. Such reliance would logically entail that ending conscription requires alteration of eligibility criteria. Also, extending both rights and obligations to non-citizens, rather than by denying them both, can plausibly address the presumed 'inequality'. Moreover, 'liberals' are generally wary of 'conditionality' of rights;[62] thus, they are likely to oppose denial of benefits to persons who are unable to contribute to production and services because they suffer from a severe disability.[63]

The second justification invoked by liberals for internal prioritisation is the social significance of inter-generational cooperation and of concerns for its long-term survival. Thus, it may be fair to prioritise citizens over newcomers even if they both contribute to the society's well-being.[64] However, since the same rationale could also apply to naturalised individuals *after* their naturalisation, its application would need to be qualified.

D 'Republican' Perspectives

1   Equal Citizenship and the Role of Participation

'Republican' citizenship is associated with Aristotle's assertion in *Politics* that '[a]s soon as a man becomes entitled to participate in authority, deliberative and judicial, we deem him to be citizen'.[65] Aristotle considered a person to be a 'political animal', and believed that citizens undertake a moral obligation to be actively and significantly involved in the life of their political community.

Aristotle based his analysis on Greek city-states, favouring a compact *polis* where citizens know each other's characters. Indeed, he considered Athens (with an estimated 40 000 citizens) too big.[66] Now, in Aristotle's

---

[61] *Citizenship and Migration* (n 13) 11. Some political communities recognise the special contribution of non-citizens to their armed forces by offering them expedited naturalisation. See e.g. Naturalization Information for Military Personnel (United States), www .uscis.gov/files/form/m-599.pdf.

[62] Ibid 11.

[63] Allen Buchanan, 'Justice as Reciprocity versus Subject-Centered Justice' (1990) 19(3) *Philosophy and Public Affairs* 227, 232.

[64] Stephen Perry, 'Immigration, Justice and Culture' in Warren Schwartz (ed), *Justice in Immigration* (Cambridge University Press 1995) 94, 96.

[65] Aristotle, *Politics* (350 BCE) bk iii, 1, http://classics.mit.edu/Aristotle/politics.3.three.html.

[66] Derek Heater, *What Is Citizenship?* (Polity Press 1999) 45.

Athens, citizenship was a privileged status permanently denied to *metics*, the property-less resident aliens (the majority of the polis' residents).[67] Aristotle justified this political inequality by contending that, to act in the public sphere, citizens had to possess special qualities, and that merely belonging to the human species does not suffice. He believed that since the *essence* of citizenship consists in active political participation, citizenship should be restricted to those who are capable of both ruling and being ruled.[68]

Rousseau rejected an exclusionary perception of citizenship, arguing that (all) individuals are born free, and are capable of self-rule.[69] However, on his account, they 'remain as free as before' only after the conclusion of a social contract under which no man, regardless of property or wealth, was subject to another man. Rousseau took a more inclusive approach to eligibility, viewing participation in decision making and submission to the general will as traits of universal (male) citizenship, rather than as special qualities expected of a particular class of men.[70]

Political participation, whether exclusionary or inclusionary, stands at the core of 'republican' perspectives of citizenship;[71] it serves as its 'ultimate badge'.[72] Chapter 3 explored a distinction between a 'liberal' notion of freedom as non-interference, and a 'republican' notion of freedom as non-domination;[73] the latter is manifested through participation in self-governance.[74] 'Republican' accounts consider state citizenship as personally significant *far and beyond* its legal status:[75] citizenship, like friendship, is more than a set of objective entitlements and opportunities.[76] Charles Taylor suggests that, 'in a functioning republic the citizens do care very much what others think'.[77]

---

[67] Citizenship and Migration (n 13) 10.
[68] Hannah Arendt, *The Human Condition* (The University of Chicago Press 1989) 63–64.
[69] Jean-Jacques Rousseau, *On the Social Contract*, Judith Masters (tr) (St Martin's Press New York 1978) (1762) 191–92.
[70] Ibid 203.   [71] Barber (n 13) 50.
[72] Peter Goldsmith, *Citizenship: Our Common Bond* (Ministry of Justice 2008) 43 [60], 75–76 [13].
[73] James Bohhman, *Democracy across Borders: From Demos to Demoi* (MIT Press 2007) 7.
[74] See e.g. Charles Taylor, 'Cross-purposes: the Liberal-Communitarian Debate' in Nancy Rosenblum (ed), *Liberalism and the Moral Life* (Harvard University Press 1989) 179.
[75] Richard Dagger, *Civic Virtues: Rights, Citizenship and Republican Liberalism* (Oxford University Press 1997) 101.
[76] Mason (n 48) 153.
[77] Charles Taylor, 'The Politics of Recognition' in Amy Gutmann (ed), *Multiculturalism: Examining the Politics of Recognition* (Princeton University Press 1994) 25, 46.

'Republicans' are averse to rights-centred accounts of citizenship because of their supposed failure to account for the *obligations* that citizens owe to their state and to their fellow citizens. The alleged link between liberal citizenship and phenomena like low voter turnout and exploitation of the welfare state led to a revival of a 'civic republican' citizenship discourse;[78] it also resulted in an attempted shift from a 'rights-centred' to a 'responsibilities' discourse.[79]

A 'republican' account describes citizens as office-holders with attendant responsibilities and duties, noting that citizens should manifest civic virtues.[80] Good citizens *should* vote even though requiring citizens to vote may not necessarily be wise.[81] Citizens should reflect on politics and governance, assist state officials when these officials are acting for the public good;[82] they should promote the *common* interests of the community.[83]

2   Identity and Attachment

'Republican' accounts expect a tight fit among the legal, political, and psychological dimensions of citizenship: citizens ought to feel a strong sense of emotional identification with their political community, and to draw their primary political identity from their state membership. 'Republicans' reject what they see as an instrumentalist non-collectivist conception of liberal citizenship.[84] Rather, they consider the political community as a good in and of itself, and contend that genuine political community goes beyond mere cooperation and mutual benefit: it shapes the identity of the participants.[85]

Rousseau deplored the perceived lack of a social bond in real-world politics. He advocated the formation of a 'civic religion' that is designed for sanctifying the social contract, enabling citizens to love laws, justice,

---

[78] Michael Ignatieff, 'The Myth of Citizenship' in Ronald Beiner (ed), *Theorizing Citizenship* (SUNY Press 1995) 53, 68–69.

[79] See e.g. Goldsmith (n 72) ch 3: 'Legal Rights and Responsibilities of Citizenship'.

[80] Jason Schall, 'The Consistency of Felon Disenfranchisement with Citizenship Theory' (2006) 22 *Harvard Blackletter Law Review* 53, 86.

[81] See e.g. Goldsmith (n 72) ch 6: 'Enhancing the Bond of Citizenship' [98].

[82] Barber (n 13) 52.

[83] David Miller, 'Bounded Citizenship' in Kimberly Hutchings and Roland Dannreuther (eds), *Cosmopolitan Citizenship* (Macmillan 1999) 60, 62–3.

[84] Schall (n 80) 83.

[85] Ronald Beiner, 'Introduction: Why Citizenship Constitutes a Theoretical Problem in the Last Decade of the Twentieth Century' in Ronald Beiner (ed), *Theorizing Citizenship* (n 82) 15.

and duty.[86] He stressed the need to inform and teach citizens of the value of the rights and duties attached to citizenship. Rousseau suggested that citizens in a modem state manifest their patriotism by having a sense of nationhood; on this account, if a political community does not have a national character, it has to create one.[87]

David Miller, a contemporary 'civic republican', argues that the promotion of national identity and characteristics will create the mutual trust and assurance that are necessary for promoting civic responsibilities.[88] He contends that nationality may serve as a foundation for republican citizenship as a 'partial replacement for the patriotic loyalty of the city-state'.[89] Miller suggests that a common national identity is required to preserve robust commitments to social distributive justice, to voluntary cooperation, and to meaningful democratic participation among those who belong to the polity.[90]

It may, however, be argued that compatriot feelings can also be generated on local, regional, and transnational levels of identification.[91] Moreover, Hannah Arendt critically observed that, modern national citizenship deviates from the classical ideal of citizenship; she contended that artificially constructed national identity replaced the special bond of intimacy, personalities, and duties.[92] According to 'republican' theories, current levels of cultural and national pluralism may exceed the level that may sustain a 'republican' society. Hence, to preserve the community, a culturally 'thick' and potentially exclusionary ethnic nationalism may follow making minority groups a point of dissension rather than a force for 'republican' unity.[93]

Toleration of multiple citizenships dovetails the above debate. Carens contends that the Republican reluctance to accept multiplicity in the *legal* dimension of citizenship misses the reality of multiplicity in the *psychological* dimension.[94] The 1789 French Constitution, much inspired by

[86] Rousseau (n 69) 142–52.
[87] Derek Heater, *Citizenship: The Civic Ideal in World History, Politics and Education* (Longman 1990) 51.
[88] David Miller, *Citizenship and National Identity* (Polity Press 2000) 68.   [89] Ibid 87.
[90] David Miller, *On Nationality* (Clarendon Press 1995) ch 3.
[91] See e.g. Shachar (n 2) 150.
[92] Hannah Arendt, *The Origins of Totalitarianism* (Harcourt 1967) 230–31.
[93] *Difference and Belonging* (n 5) 291.
[94] Carens (n 27) 172. See also David A Martin, 'New Rules on Dual Nationality for a Democratizing Globe: Between Rejection and Embrace' (1999) 14 *Georgetown Immigration Law Journal* 1, 8–9 (asserting that allegiance to more than one state seems possible). It will be argued in Chapter 5 that reluctance to accept multiple political identities explains not

Rousseau's work, provided for the naturalisation of a alien by undertaking a civic oath to obey the law and the constitution and renounce other allegiances.[95] In today's US, persons wishing to naturalise are required, in addition to bearing 'true faith and allegiance' to the US to 'declare, on oath, that [they] absolutely and entirely renounce and abjure all allegiance and fidelity to any foreign prince, potentate, state, or sovereignty of whom or which [they] have heretofore been a subject or citizen'.[96]

Historically, international law has been quite hostile to multiple nationalities. The Preamble to the 1930 Hague Convention stipulated that '[i]t is in the general interest of the international community to secure that all its members should recognise that every person should have a nationality and should have one nationality only . . . the ideal . . . is the abolition of all cases both of statelessness and of double nationality'.[97] Multiple citizenships are increasingly becoming more accepted, and international instruments partially conform.[98] However, it may be too early to define

---

only the objection to dual citizenship but also the unwillingness to extend suffrage to non-citizens.

[95] Heater (n 66) 49.

[96] United States Naturalization Regulations of 1929, Rule 8, Subdivision C. Interestingly, the US does not require naturalised persons to renounce their former citizenship (though their state of origin may require them to do so), manifesting a rather ambivalent approach to citizenship. Cf. the Canadian Citizenship Act 1946, which requires applicants to swear or affirm that they will be faithful and bear true allegiance to Her Majesty Queen Elizabeth II, Queen of Canada, Her Heirs and Successors, and that [they] 'will faithfully observe the laws of Canada and fulfil [my] duties as a Canadian citizen'.

[97] Hague Convention Preamble.

[98] Maarten P Vink and Gerard-Rene de Groot, 'Citizenship Attribution in Western Europe: International Framework and Domestic Trends' (2010) 36(5) *Journal of Ethnic and Migration Studies* 713, 715. Council of Europe treaties are quite instructive in this regard. Convention on the Reduction of Cases of Multiple Nationality and Military Obligations in Cases of Multiple Nationality (adopted 6 May 1963, entered into force 28 March 1968) ETS No 043 art 1 (stipulating that citizens of a contracting state who voluntarily acquire the citizenship of another contracting state *lose* their previous citizenship by operation of law). Second Protocol amending the 1963 Convention (adopted 2 February 1993, entered into force 24 March 1995) ETS No 149 amended art 1 so that, under certain conditions, voluntary acquisition of a foreign citizenship will not *necessarily* lead to loss of previous citizenship. According to the explanatory notes, 'the 1963 Convention . . . is based on the principle that dual nationality is undesirable and should therefore be avoided. However, since 1963, a number of intervening factors have meant that there should be a *relaxation of that strict principle*: labour migrations between European States leading to substantial immigrant populations, the need for integration of long-term immigrants and the recognition of the principle of equality of the sexes' (emphasis added). In [5] and [6], it is noted that, '[t]here is no doubt that for many immigrants and their children the prospect of losing their nationality of origin is often a disincentive to seeking the nationality of the country in which they live and whose nationality they would like to have . . . [a]cquisition

insistence on singular membership in a nation-state as an 'outmoded norm':[99] many states still consider renunciation of other citizenship(s) as a condition for naturalisation, while others regard acquisition of a new citizenship as *implicit renunciation* of their citizenship. In the CSR1951 refugee context, the relevance of restrictive approaches to multiple citizenships will be addressed in Chapter 8.

3 Prioritisation of Citizens

'Republican' accounts *presuppose* the autonomous (insulated) nature of particular political communities. On 'republican' accounts, a state ought to advance the well-being of *its* members.[100] 'Republicans' expect citizens who take part in self-governance to seek the good of society as a whole rather than their private interests; citizens ought to adopt policies that prioritise citizens only if such policies help society as a whole. Hence, it is up to state members, based on their understanding of the 'common good', to decide how to treat non-members.

E 'Communitarian' Perspectives: An Intermediary?

On a 'communitarian' account, to live meaningful lives, individuals need to be part of communities of shared meanings and identities to which they can feel that they belong.[101] Hence, while 'communitarian' perspectives share common ground with liberal tenets, 'communitarians' consider the 'liberal' vision of membership to be rootless and too abstract.[102]

As noted above, a 'liberal' account considers citizenship to be a status, an entitlement, and a set of rights that the citizen may choose to enjoy

of the nationality of the host country is certainly an important, even crucial factor as far as integration in that country is concerned . . . seen from the viewpoint of immigrants of long standing, who are recognised in the host country in practically all aspects, the absence of full participation in its political life can only be regarded as deplorable', http://conventios.coe.int/Treaty/EN/Repots/Html/149.htm.

[99] Stephen Castles, 'Globalisation and the Ambiguities of National Citizenship' in Rainer Bauböck and John Rundell (eds), *Blurred Boundaries: Migration, Ethnicity, Citizenship* (Ashgate 1998) 224, 238–42.

[100] Barber (n 13) 12.

[101] See e.g. Michael J Sandel, *Liberalism and the Limits of Justice* (2nd edn Cambridge University Press 1998) 179 (asserting that we ordinarily think of ourselves 'as members of this family or community or nation or people, as bearers of this history, as sons or daughters of that revolution, as citizens of this republic').

[102] Neera Badhwar, 'Moral Agency, Commitment and Impartiality' (1996) 13(1) *Social Philosophy and Policy* 1, 14.

passively or actively. Citizenship is life's outer frame, unless an individual chooses to make it otherwise. In contrast, a 'republican' account considers citizenship to be an office, a responsibility, and a burden proudly assumed, making it *the core* of each citizen's life.[103]

Communitarians borrow from Liberalism and Republicanism. While 'communities of character' are supposed to give meaning and shape to individual efforts to make *their* life choices, individuals are constituted inside the political arena and the state ought to encourage the pursuit of a common good or collective goal by its citizens.[104] Indeed, Walzer claims that '[m]an the citizen who obeys only the laws he has made, is man at his very best: free, virtuous and powerful'.[105]

'Communitarians' share with 'liberals' an anxiety as per justifying an unequal allocation of resources between citizens and non-citizens. However, they also accept the ('republican') contention that non-citizens do not yet possess the indispensable sense of belonging to the political community manifested by successful completion of a naturalisation process. Consequently, 'communitarians' emphasise the need to facilitate naturalisation: Walzer suggests that once society has made a (first admission) migration control decision (which on his account it is entitled to make), a (second admission) decision regarding full community membership, namely naturalisation, should 'never [be subject] to the ultimate constraint of closure'.[106]

F   Concluding Remarks

States regulate their 'human dimension' through migration control (*external* prioritisation of their citizens). Concomitantly, citizenship often serves as a basis for ensuring citizens tangible benefits that non-citizens do not receive (*internal* prioritisation). Meanwhile, admission as full members of the polity through naturalisation is not automatic but is rather subject to varying conditions. Dovetailing the multi-dimensional account of

---

[103] Michael Walzer, 'Citizenship' in Terence Ball, James Farr and Russell Hanson (eds), *Political Innovation and Conceptual Change* (Cambridge University Press 1982) 211, 216.

[104] Heather Lardy, 'Citizenship and the Right to Vote' (1997) 17(1) *Oxford Journal of Legal Studies* 75, 82.

[105] Michael Walzer, *Obligations: Essays on Disobedience, War, and Citizenship* (Clarion Books 1970) 210–12.

[106] Michael Walzer, *Spheres of Justice: A Defense of Pluralism and Equality* (Robertson 1983) 60.

state citizenship offered by Carens, the chapter explored three broad per-spectives on state citizenship that may account for divergent approaches to these extra-legal dimensions.

'Liberal' perspectives view citizenship as a means to (multiple) ends. Citizenship premised on political equality is designed to better the lives of (all) members of the political community by advancing individual interests which exist independently of citizenship status. To achieve these goals, it is desirable that some citizens be politically involved, while oth-ers may remain uninvolved. Some citizens may feel that their objective belonging to the state, manifested by citizenship, also entails a subjective, affective belonging, which recreates their citizenship as a primary good, while others may be apathetic towards their state or even dissent.

The adverse effects of internal prioritisation of citizens on the elec-torally excluded are a concern for liberals. Some 'liberal' accounts offer 'contractarian' and inter-generational justifications, emphasising the need for greater access to naturalisation, while others opt for full decoupling of rights and access to provision of goods and services from citizenship status.

On 'republican' accounts, the institution of state citizenship is foun-dational for each member of the political community. Self-governance stands at the core of the institution of state citizenship, with the ensuing assumption that all community members are committed and enthusias-tic citizens that are concerned with a general good shared by their fellow citizens.[107] The particular political character of the community is empha-sised. Citizenship is considered to make persons truly free, equal, and worthy of recognition by their fellow community members. The psy-chological dimension follows: citizens ought to feel a great attachment towards their (ideally exclusive) political community.

'Republicans' may accept internal prioritisation of citizens if the 'com-mon good' (as defined by citizens) so requires based on the assumption that the needs of non-citizens will be taken into account even in their (political) absence, and that non-citizens who wish to do so will ulti-mately naturalise after satisfying appropriate conditions.

In contradistinction, communitarian perspectives attribute to the institution of citizenship a strong identity element. 'Communitarians' attribute great significance to state citizenship; they thus believe that the

---

[107] Ronald Beiner, *Liberalism, Nationalism, Citizenship: Essays on the Problem of Political Community* (University of British Columbia Press 2003) 6.

solution to internal prioritisation and its ensuing predicament for non-citizens is their naturalisation. Non-citizens should not remain outside the political bounds of the polity for protracted periods: once a political community has decided to admit a non-citizen, its prerogative concerning naturalisation is restricted, in part because of the acknowledged adverse effects of electoral exclusion and their implications for facilitation of social cohesion.

5

Citizenship Voting Qualifications:
Normative Appraisals

A   Introduction

This book assumes the existing global legal order in which sovereign states make first admission decisions (immigration), second admission decisions (naturalisation), and determine eligibility for voting in their elections.[1]

Chapter 2 presented the ubiquitous practice of exclusion of non-citizen residents from elections of their states of residence, and the permissibility thereof according to international and regional human rights treaties. Chapter 3 offered perspectives on the meaning and purpose of voting and elections, concluding that there are mutually reinforcing reasons for considering the right to vote to be fundamental for individuals; and, conversely, that electoral exclusion has adverse effects. Chapter 4 offered perspectives on the meaning and purposes of state citizenship, emphasising its political and psychological dimensions which, in turn, affect the rights and obligations that are attached to citizenship as a legal status.

Against this background, this chapter appraises the plausibility of citizenship-based voting eligibility. Section B uses a US case study to offer a historical context for citizenship voting qualifications. Section C explores three normative positions concerning the interrelations between voting and citizenship: the *inseparability* position, the *contingent* position, and the *disaggregation* position. Section D presents six principal contentions in contemporary discourse, three in support of citizenship-based eligibility, and three in support of residence-based eligibility. Chapter 8 revisits citizenship voting qualifications, suggesting that the political predicament

---

[1] See e.g. Bill Jordan and Franck Duvel (eds), *Migration* (Polity Press 2003) 6. Hence, Jennings' self-determination logical paradox ('[t]he people cannot decide until somebody decides who the people are') falls outside the scope of the remit of this book. See Ivor Jennings, *The Approach to Self-Government* (Cambridge University Press 1958) 56. Similarly, questions relating to collective self-determination and secession are not engaged.

of recognised CSR1951 refugees weaken citizenship-based arguments and strengthen residence-based arguments.[2]

B   Citizenship Voting Qualifications in Historical Context: US Case Study

It is often assumed in public discourse that citizenship and voting are inseparable, especially in national elections.[3] Levinson wonders 'why do we so automatically (almost thoughtlessly) link citizenship and suffrage';[4] Brubaker attributes the absence of a 'serious challenge' to the electoral exclusion of non-citizens to forces of nationalism, even in states where long-term residents constitute a sizeable part of the population.[5]

Nevertheless, as the following US case study demonstrates, the notion that citizenship status is both necessary and sufficient voting qualification is of rather recent vintage. In 1840, the Supreme Court of the state of Illinois upheld the state constitution's grant of suffrage in state elections to those who 'although they may be neither native nor adopted citizens, have identified their interests and feelings with the state by habitation and residence, in view of the just principle of reciprocity between the government and the governing'.[6] Sixty-Four years later, the US Supreme Court reiterated that '[t]he state might provide that persons of foreign birth could vote without being naturalised'.[7]

---

[2] It was noted in Chapter 1 that persons holding CSR1951 refugee status *have not been naturalised* in their states of asylum. See CSR1951, art 1C(3), stipulating that CSR1951 will cease to apply to a person who 'has acquired a new nationality, and enjoys the protection of the country of his new nationality'. See also Susan Kneebone and Maria O'Sullivan, 'Article 1C' in Andreas Zimmermann (ed), *The 1951 Convention Relating to the Status of Refugees and its 1967 Protocol: A Commentary* (Oxford University Press 2011) 481.

[3] See Simon Caney, *Justice beyond Borders: A Global Political Theory* (Oxford University Press 2005) 64 (depicting citizenship rights as 'special rights arising from a person's membership in a political community' which 'may include the right to vote in elections', juxtaposing them against 'human rights' that are enjoyed by a person 'by virtue of being a human being'). See also Tomas Hammar, *Democracy and the Nation State: Aliens, Denizens and Citizens in a World of International Migration* (Aldershot 1990) 27 (describing non-citizen permanent residents as *denizens*. The term 'denizen' may have originated in medieval England; see www.oed.co.uk/view/Entry/49985?rskey=3JMpLI&result=1&isAdvanced=false#eid.

[4] Sanford Levinson, 'Suffrage and Community: Who Should Vote?' (1989) 41 *Florida Law Review* 545, 556.

[5] Rogers Brubaker, *Citizenship and Nationhood in France and Germany* (Harvard University Press 1992) 28.

[6] *Spragins v Houghton* 3 Ill 377, 408 (1840).

[7] *Pope v Williams* 193 US 621, 632–33 (1904). During the first 150 years of US history, non-citizens voted in many US states and territories. The 1928 Federal elections were

Suffrage, of course, was far from 'universal' at that time.[8] Citizenship was neither necessary nor sufficient for eligibility to vote: instead, race, colour, gender, and property ownership were permissible voting qualifications. It was generally assumed that the interests of the excluded will be effectively represented by wise, fair minded, endowed white men.[9] African-Americans were assumed to be 'intellectually inferior' and hence to lack the competence to vote;[10] they were disenfranchised even in states in which they were *citizens*. In its infamous *Dred Scott* judgment, the US Supreme Court ruled that 'a person may be a citizen, that is a member of the community who form the sovereignty, although he exercises no share of the political power and is incapacitated from holding particular offices'.[11]

In tandem, property qualifications were justified on two main grounds: First, property owners had unique stakes in society, and personal interests in state policies, especially concerning taxation.[12] Second, property ownership was the way to be freed from dependence: the property-less could be too easily manipulated or controlled.[13] In contrast, it was assumed

---

the first in which no non-citizen was permitted to vote. James B Raskin, 'Legal Aliens, Local Citizens: The Historical, Constitutional and Theoretical Meanings of Alien Suffrage' (1993) 141(4) *University of Pennsylvania Law Review* 1391, 1397 citing Leon E Aylsworth, 'The Passing of Alien Suffrage' (1931) 25 *American Political Science Review* 114, 114. It is now a Federal crime for non-citizens to vote in Federal elections. Illegal Immigration Reform and Immigrant Responsibility Act of 1996, Pub L 104–208, Div C, Title II, § 216(a), *codified as amended at* 18 USCA § 611(a). However, US states and local authorities may still enfranchise non-citizens in state and local elections, respectively. Joseph Fishkin, 'Equal Citizenship and the Individual Right to Vote' (2011) 86 *Indiana Law Journal* 1289, 1350 (defining this phenomenon as rendering non-citizen residents *local* citizens).

[8] Cf. Ludvig Beckman, 'Who Should Vote? Conceptualizing Universal Suffrage in Studies of Democracy' (2007) 15(1) *Democratization* 29, 42 (arguing that satisfaction of a 'universal suffrage' standard is a matter of definition; in his view, a suggestion that 'universal suffrage' should be measured in relation to eligibility of competent adult citizens masks normative assumptions about age and citizenship which ought to be acknowledged explicitly rather than disguised as objective criteria).

[9] Michael Levin, *The Spectre of Democracy: The Rise of Modern Democracy as Seen by Its Critics* (Macmillan 1992) 45.

[10] Eric Foner, *Reconstruction, America's Unfinished Revolution 1863–1877* (Harper & Row 1988) 278.

[11] *Dred Scott v Sanford*, 60 US 393 (1857) (Taney CJ).

[12] Virginia Harper-Ho, 'Noncitizen Voting Rights: The History, the Law and Current Prospects for Change' (2000) 21 *Immigration and Nationality Law Review* 477, 485 (regarding the State of Michigan 1850 Constitutional Convention).

[13] Alexander Keyssar, *The Right to Vote: The Contested History of Democracy in the United States* (Basic Books 2000) 166.

that paupers, namely recipients of public relief from the community, have surrendered their independence.[14]

Others argued that suffrage had to be 'earned' by paying taxes, by serving in the military or by labouring on public roads, since '[t]hose who bear the burdens of the state should choose those that rule it'.[15] The latter requirement was applied rather inconsistently, as women were disenfranchised despite paying taxes:[16] they were considered too delicate for the 'worldly' experiences necessary for politics.[17]

In 1885, the US Supreme Court held that '[i]t would be quite competent for the sovereign power to declare that no one but a married person shall be entitled to vote'.[18] Following the enfranchisement of African-Americans, several southern states introduced literacy tests requiring voters to demonstrate that they could understand and interpret the Federal Constitution, as well as a two-dollar poll tax, a sum which was considered prohibitively high.[19] Both types of measures withstood constitutional challenges;[20] this is despite the fact that they were intended to effectively disenfranchise African-Americans.[21]

As late as 1966, when the US Supreme Court declared the Virginia poll tax to be unconstitutional, Justice Stewart dissented, noting that 'property qualifications and poll taxes have been a traditional part of our political structure . . . these and other restrictions were gradually lifted, primarily because popular theories of political representation had changed . . . whether one agrees or not, arguments have been and still can be made in favor of them'.[22]

Times have changed, indeed. Race, gender, wealth, and literacy are no longer considered acceptable voting qualifications.[23] As Chapter 2

[14] Ibid 54.   [15] Ibid 44.   [16] Ibid.   [17] Ibid 175.
[18] *Murphy v Ramsey* 114 US 15, 43 (1885).
[19] US Const, amend xv (1870): 'The right of citizens of the United States to vote shall not be denied or abridged by the United States or by any State on account of race, color, or previous condition of servitude'.
[20] See e.g. *Williams v Mississippi*, 170 US 213 (1898). In 1920, there were nearly five million illiterate Americans, making up roughly 8 per cent of the voting age population. The impact of literacy tests was hence significant. Keyssar (n 13) 144.
[21] This may have also been the motive behind alteration of provisions sanctioning the disenfranchisement of convicts. Reuven (Ruvi) Ziegler, 'Legal Outlier, Again? U.S. Felon Suffrage Policies: Comparative and International Human Rights Perspectives' (2011) 29(2) *Boston University International Law Journal* 197, 240.
[22] *Harper v Virginia* 383 US 663, 684 (1966).
[23] See e.g. Judith N Shklar, *American Citizenship: The Quest for Inclusion* (Harvard University Press 1991) 2 (critically asserting that 'the ballot has always been a certificate of full membership in society, and its value depends primarily on its capacity to confer a minimum of social dignity'.)

demonstrated, electoral democracy premised on the maxim that ordinary people are qualified to govern themselves is now required by international and regional human rights treaties, and is increasingly practised globally.[24] In turn, *citizenship* has become (the) primary voting qualification:[25] it is the basis on which CSR1951 refugees are excluded from elections of their states of asylum.

C   The Interrelations between Citizenship and Enfranchisement: Three Positions

The analysis below presents three main positions that emerge from the contemporary discourse concerning the interrelations between citizenship and enfranchisement: the inseparability position, the contingent position, and the disaggregation position.

1   The Inseparability Position

The inseparability position maintains a strict correlation between national citizenship and voting in all electoral processes, including local and regional elections, adopting a version of the 'republican' account set in Chapters 3 and 4, namely that enfranchisement defines full membership in a self-governing polity. Seyla Benhabib asserts that there is no way to cut the 'Gordian knot' that links territoriality, representation, and democratic voice.[26] As Jean Cohn argues, the democratic participation is at the centre of full citizenship.[27] Consistent application of the inseparability position equally opposes enfranchisement of persons who are not full community members and disenfranchisement of (some) full community members.[28]

---

[24] Robert Dahl, *Democracy and Its Critics* (Yale University Press 1989) 97.
[25] Voting qualifications that affect *citizens* fall outside the scope of this book. They include age, mental competence, and current or previous criminal conviction. Regarding mental competence, see e.g. Velmer S Burton, 'The Consequences of Official Labels: A Research Note on Rights Lost by the Mentally Ill, Mentally Incompetent and Convicted Felons' (1990) 26(3) *Community Mental Health Journal* 267. Regarding age qualifications, see e.g. Aoilfe Nolan, 'The Child as "Democratic Citizen" – Challenging the Participation Gap' [2010] *Public Law* 126; Vivian E Hamilton, 'Democratic Inclusion, Cognitive Development, and the Age of Electoral Majority' (2012) 77(4) *Brooklyn Law Review* 1. Regarding disenfranchisement of convicts, see Ziegler (n 21) 199.
[26] Seyla Benhabib, *The Rights of Others* (Harvard University Press 2004) 220–21.
[27] Jean L Cohn, 'Changing Paradigms of Citizenship and the Exclusiveness of the Demos' ((1999) 14 *International Sociology* 245, 249.
[28] Richard Katz, *Democracy and Elections* (Oxford University Press 1997) 216.

Both US courts and the German Federal Constitutional Court appear to have adopted the first part of the above stipulation. The US Supreme Court held in *Cabell* that 'exclusion of aliens [non-citizens] from basic governmental processes is not a deficiency in the democratic system, but a necessary consequence of the community's process of political self-definition. Self-government, whether direct or through representatives, begins by defining the scope of the community of the governed, and thus the governors as well; aliens are by definition outside this community'.[29] The federal district court in Washington, DC, went further, upholding federal law that prohibits financial contributions to electoral campaigns by non-citizen residents; it ruled that such contributions constitute participation in governance, which states may legitimately restrict to citizens (even though the restriction was not imposed on permanent residents).[30]

The German Federal Constitutional Court held in 1990 that state (*Land*) legislation in Schleswig-Holstein enfranchising some non-citizens in local government elections was incompatible with the German Constitution (as it stood at that time).[31] It maintained that '[a]ccording to the [German] Basic Law, the people from whom state authority emanates comprises German citizens... citizenship is both the legal precondition for the equal status of individuals and the foundation for equal rights and duties; the exercise of legal rights and duties legitimates democratic state authority'.[32] The Court held that the 'German people' were designated

---

[29] *Cabell v Chavez-Salido*, 454 US 432, 438–40 (1982). The case concerned a citizenship requirement for holding a probation officer position. The Supreme Court held that 'although citizenship is not a relevant ground for the distribution of economic benefits, it is for determining membership in the political community... citizenship requirement may seem an appropriate limitation on those who would exercise and, therefore, symbolize this power of the political community over those who fall within its jurisdiction...'

[30] *Bluman et al v Federal Election Commission*, 800 F Supp 2d 281 (D.D.C. 2011) (holding that 'it is fundamental to the definition of our national political community that foreign citizens do not have a constitutional right to participate in, and thus may be excluded from, activities of democratic self-government') (*certiorari* to the Federal Supreme Court denied on 9 January 2012).

[31] Following the adoption of the Treaty on European Union in 1992, the German Basic Law had to be amended so that EU citizens residing in Germany *would* be allowed to vote in regional and local elections. Other non-citizens are still excluded. For a general discussion see e.g. Cristina M Rodriguez, 'Noncitizen Voting and the Extraconstitutional Construction of the Polity' (2010) 8(1) *International Journal of Constitutional Law* 30.

[32] *Opinion of the German Federal Constitutional Court*, 31 October 1990, BVerfGE 83 (FRG), reprinted in Donald P Kommers, *The Constitutional Jurisprudence of the Federal Republic of Germany* (Duke University Press 1997) 197.

as possessors of the constitution-giving power, and that '[e]lections in which aliens can vote cannot convey democratic legitimacy'.[33]

In a later judgment concerning similar arrangements in the State of Hamburg, the German Court held that any exercise of state authority must be supported by a 'chain of legitimation' reaching back to the sovereign people, which did not include aliens.[34] Hence, rather than adopt a perception of democracy as a means of facilitating *individual* self-determination (see Chapter 2), it took the view that democracy is a form of *collective* self-determination, and that the collective will of the community as a whole may be threatened if outsiders are enfranchised.[35]

It may be contended that, if the franchise defines the political community, and if full membership in a political community is inseparable from enfranchisement, then a disenfranchised person should no longer be considered a full member of that community;[36] rather, they are a 'second-class' or 'semi' citizen.[37] It has been suggested that disenfranchisement of otherwise full members institutionalises a double polity in which enfranchised members rule over disenfranchised members.[38] Maintaining its approach, in 2013, the German Federal Constitutional Court quashed legislation requiring German citizens living abroad to have resided in Germany at some point for three consecutive months in order to vote in national elections.[39]

According to the inseparability position, naturalisation must precede enfranchisement. In turn, states set divergent requirements for naturalisation. David Earnest argues that the predicament of non-citizen residents in *jus sanguinis* states is compounded, as such states tend to

---

[33] See Gerald Neuman, 'We the People: Alien Suffrage in German and American Perspective' (1991–1992) 13 *Michigan Journal of International Law* 259, 277.

[34] Ibid 287.   [35] Ibid 285.

[36] Ronald Dworkin, 'What is Equality?' (1987) 22 *University of Simon Fraser Law Review* 1, 4.

[37] Elizabeth Cohen, *The Myth of Full Citizenship: A Comparative Study of Semi-Citizenship in Democratic Polities* (PhD dissertation, Yale University 2003) 26 (referring to 'semi-citizenship'). Interestingly, Cohen suggests that 'some people don't need citizenship', mentioning two categories: children (who arguably have citizen-parents) and partial nationals (who arguably have full citizenship in the country that they chose to leave). Ibid 234.

[38] Katherine Pettus, *Felony Disenfranchisement in the Contemporary United States: An Ancient Practice in a Modern Polity* (PhD dissertation, Columbia University 2002) 21–22 (on file with author). See also Heather Lardy, 'Citizenship and the Right to Vote' (1997) 17 *Oxford Journal of Legal Studies* 75, 85.

[39] www.bundesverfassungsgericht.de/entscheidungen/cs20120704_2bvc000111.html (German).

provide non-citizens fewer economic, civil, and political rights as well as set higher barriers for naturalisation;[40] in contrast, *jus soli* states are more likely to engage in 'denationalising citizenship'.[41]

Ethnic nationalists support restricting access to naturalisation to applicants from similar ethnic origins to those of the (majority) state population. States which adopt ethnic naturalisation criteria are likely to host a sizeable electorally excluded non-citizen resident population for protracted periods. In contrast, 'civic republicans' and 'liberals' alike reject ethnic criteria for naturalisation purposes, taking the view that those wishing to naturalise should, in principle, be offered the opportunity to do so.[42] Nonetheless, their views diverge as to the desirable qualifications for naturalisation, as well as with regard to toleration of multiple citizenships: according to expansive approaches, any non-citizen satisfying a (reasonable) residence requirement should be entitled to naturalise, and should not have to forgo previous citizenships; restrictive views require applicants to pass language as well as citizenship or integration tests, to exhibit self-sufficiency, to pay fees and possibly to renounce other citizenship(s).[43]

David Miller, for instance, posits that states which deny citizenship to long-term immigrants 'are justifiably accused of violating democratic principles'.[44] Nevertheless, he also contends that nations legitimately wish

---

[40] See David C Earnest, *Voting Rights for Resident Aliens: Nationalism, Postnationalism and Sovereignty in an Era of Mass Migration* (PhD dissertation George Washington University 2004) (on file with author).

[41] See e.g. Linda Bosniak 'Denationalizing Citizenship' in T Alexander Aleinikoff and Charles Klusmeyer (eds), *Citizenship Today: Global Perspectives and Practices* (Carnegie 2001) 237, 241.

[42] See e.g. Peter Goldsmith, *Citizenship: Our Common Bond* (Ministry of Justice 2008) ch 4 [23] (suggesting that 'it should not be commonplace for people to live in a society for a very long time without becoming a part of that society and taking on their social responsibilities as citizens' and proposing a system whereby 'people who have come to the UK either have limited leave to be here or they have to apply to become citizens'). See also Cohn (n 27) 262–63 (contending that there are good *democratic* as well as *liberal* grounds to avoid permanent presence of a large immigrant population that is permanently denied access to citizenship).

[43] See Rainer Bauböck and Sarah Wallace Goodman, *Naturalisation* (EUDO Citizenship Policy Brief No 2 2011), http://eudo-citizenship.eu/docs/policy-brief-naturalisation_revised .pdf (analysing legislative trends regarding naturalisation requirements); Gerard Rene de Groot and Maarten Vink, *Loss of Citizenship* (EUDO Citizenship Policy Brief No 3 2012), http://eudo-citizenship.eu/docs/policy_brief_loss.pdf (analysing legislative trends regarding loss of citizenship).

[44] David Miller, 'Democracy's Domain' (2009) 37(3) *Philosophy and Public Affairs* 201, 219; David Miller, 'Immigrants, Nations and Citizenship' (2008) 16(4) *Journal of Political*

to restrict membership to those who identify themselves with the nation, culturally and otherwise; on this view, giving citizenship rights 'freely' to all non-citizen residents risks undermining the conditions of mutual trust and assurance which make 'responsible citizenship' possible.[45] Similarly, Herman Van Gunsteren advocates requiring a reasonable residence period, capacity of dialogic performance, knowledge of the language and culture of the particular political community, recognition of its political institutions, and a reasonably secure access to the means of subsistence. On his account, only those who satisfy these qualifications should be admitted to citizenship.[46]

However, it could be argued that, if enfranchisement depends on naturalisation, then *requiring* applicants to pass language, citizenship and other courses rather than *providing* such courses to applicants may effectively become a modern-day equivalent of literacy tests. Ruth Lister suggests that access to citizenship must be fairly easy and open to all who want it and who will undertake fairly limited, largely formal steps to achieve it, so that 'legal aliens' would be able to 'remove themselves from the disadvantaged class by naturalising'. Pertinently for this book, Lister's underlying assumption is that 'the non-citizen in question has a "home" state to which he could return if he found the situation in the state to which he immigrated undesirable'. She notes that '[o]bviously this condition does not apply to refugees' which thus 'speaks strongly in favour of granting a larger basket of social benefits to refugees and similarly situated individuals'.[47]

Walzer describes 'the rule of citizens over non-citizens' as 'probably the most common form of tyranny in human history'.[48] States may undertake community cohesion measures as part of the naturalisation process, but 'membership's rights and rule . . . be equally open to all those men and women who live within a political community's territory and are subject to local law'.[49] Zilbershats asserts that naturalisation should be based on

---

Philosophy 371 (arguing for citizenship tests); Cf. Jonathan Seglow, 'Arguments for Naturalisation' (2008) 57(5) *Political Studies* 788.

[45] David Miller, *On Nationality* (Oxford University Press 1995) 88.

[46] Herman R Van Gunsteren, 'Admission to Citizenship' (1988) 98 *Ethics* 731, 736–37.

[47] Ruth Lister, 'Citizenship in the Immigration Context' (2010–2011) 70 *Maryland Law Review* 175, 230.

[48] Michael Walzer, *Spheres of Justice* (Basic Books 1983) 62. Cf. Karen Knop, 'Citizenship, Public and Private' (2008) 71 *Law and Contemporary Problems* 309, 320 (basing eligibility on *domicile* can transform the construction of political membership as a two-way relationship between the individual and the state).

[49] Walzer (n 48) 60–61.

a 'nexus' to a common present and future, and should only be subject to fulfilment of residence requirements.[50] Rubio-Marin's framework is more expansive positing that naturalisation of residents should be automatic except when the state of origin of a resident non-citizen would require her to forgo its citizenship.[51]

2   The Contingent Position

The contingent position shares the conceptual stance of the insepara-bility position, namely that naturalisation should precede full electoral inclusion of non-citizens. Nonetheless, it endorses habitual residence (*ius domicile*) as a basis for participation in sub-national elections, retain-ing citizenship-based eligibility for national elections and referendums in which the issues under consideration are arguably 'fundamental' and concern the 'long-term future' of the polity.[52]

According to this view, *all citizens* should retain voting rights in national elections and referendums of their state of citizenship regardless of whether they reside therein. The fact that some voters in sub-national elections are *not* part of 'the people' is accepted: non-citizen residents are citizens 'in the making' whose integration may be facilitated by local suffrage.[53]

Hence, the inseparability and contingent positions share a perception of an inextricable link between full enfranchisement and full membership in a political community. However, the contingent position takes a

---

[50] Yaffa Zilbershats, 'Reconsidering the Concept of Citizenship' (2001) 36 *Texas International Law Journal* 689, 692. See also T Alexander Aleinikoff and Douglas Klusmeyer (eds), *Citizenship Policies for an Age of Migration* (Carnegie 2002) 46 (contending that all long-term migrants should be naturalised).

[51] See generally Ruth Rubio-Marin, *Immigration as a Democratic Challenge: Citizenship and Inclusion in Germany and the United States* (Cambridge University Press 2000).

[52] Rainer Bauböck, 'Stakeholder Citizenship and Transnational Political Participation: A Normative Evaluation of External Voting' (2006–2007) 75 *Fordham Law Review* 2393, 2429–30. Section D considers Bauböck's position. Interestingly, the US Supreme Court upheld residence-based qualifications in *municipal* elections, holding that '[a] govern-mental unit may legitimately restrict the right to participate in its political processes to those who reside within its borders'. The question whether residence *substitutes* for citizen-ship or *complements* it as a voting qualification is not addressed directly in the judgment. *Holt Civic Club v City of Tuscaloosa* 439 US 60, 68 (1978).

[53] James Hampshire, 'Becoming Citizens: Naturalisation in the Liberal State', in Gideon Calder, Peter Cole and Jonathan Seglow (eds), *Citizenship Acquisition and National Belonging* (Palgrave 2010) 74, 79. See also the Human Rights Committee, Latvia (CCPR/CO/79/LVA), 6 November 2003 [16–18].

non-binary approach to the link between membership and enfranchisement, recognising that territoriality ought to matter – at least on the
local level.[54]

3   The Disaggregation Position

The disaggregation position aims to address the non-congruence between
the 'input' and 'output' of democratic self-government, which the inseparability and contingent positions tolerate:[55] the notion that only resident
or non-resident citizens are eligible to vote in elections and referendums
that enable the enactment of laws that are applicable in a territorially
bound jurisdiction where only some of these citizens as well as non-
citizens reside habitually. Since all habitual residents are subject to the
continuous authority of the state, residence-based enfranchisement would
thus come closer to symmetry between the rulers and the ruled.[56] The
underlying assumption is that, most state legislation applies territorially,
notwithstanding extra-territorial application of certain areas of criminal
law and of personal taxation.

On this view, while the state should facilitate naturalisation of non-
citizens, especially in view of the security of residence which ensues, it
should also enfranchise non-citizen residents. The one person, one vote
rule is *not* violated when a person is eligible to vote in two separate states,
nor does such dual enfranchisement lead to dual representation.[57]

Disaggregation view-holders point to the fact that the eligibility of
citizens to vote in local and regional elections in their state is already
based on residence ('mobile' voting rights): if a person relocates to a

---

[54] See e.g. Linda Bosniak, 'Being Here: *Ethical Territoriality* and the Rights of Immigrants'
(2007) 8(2) *Theoretical Inquiries in Law* 389, 390–91.

[55] See e.g. Gerald M Rosberg, 'Aliens and Equal Protection: Why Not the Right to Vote?'
(1977) 75(5–6) *Michigan Law Review* 1092; Lea Brilmayer, 'Shaping and Sharing in Democratic Theory: Toward a Political Philosophy of Interstate Equality' (1987) 15 *Florida State
University Law Review* 389, 390 (suggesting that exclusion of residents 'separates the
shaping of the laws from the sharing of its consequences').

[56] See Beckman (n 8) 45 (asserting that '[a] perfect symmetry between rulers and ruled
is not as fanciful as it may sound. Organisations that aspire to be ruled democratically,
such as many political parties, trade unions, and even chess clubs and other voluntary
associations, typically recognize that every member has the right to vote').

[57] Similarly, enfranchising dual residents in *local* elections in two residential communities
does not result in double representation, because these residents would only vote once in
each election. Cf. EU nationals of two EU Member States whose enfranchisement in both
states arguably breaches the 'one person one vote' rule as the outcomes of such elections
determine the composition of the Council of Ministers.

different city or area, her voting rights 'migrate' as well. Hence, it is argued that a distinction may be drawn between the permanent nature of state citizenship and the (transient) nature of voting in a particular locality. A radical version of the disaggregation position entails that, since most legislation applies territorially, voting rights of non-resident citizens should become dormant after a period of non-residence, both at the local and at the national level.[58] On this account, voting rights are automatically restored if and when expatriates exercise their (unconditional) right to return and reside in their state of citizenship.

Notably for this book's purposes, most disaggregation view-holders are not 'post-nationalists': they consider voting eligibility questions through a statist prism.[59]

D   Citizenship Voting Qualifications: Six Contentions

This section explores six principal contentions in the citizenship voting qualifications discourse. The first three arguments are oft-invoked to support citizenship-based eligibility in light of the inseparability or contingent positions, discussed above. They concern community cohesion and common identity; loyalty to the state and stake-holding in its long-term well-being; and the promise of electoral inclusion as a catalyst for naturalisation. The latter three arguments advance residence-based eligibility in light of the disaggregation position. They centre on the vulnerability of non-citizen residents, absent state accountability; the

---

[58] Claudio Lopez-Guerra, 'Should Expatriates Vote?' (2005) 12 *Journal of Political Philosophy* 216, 226–27. cf. David Owen, 'Resident Aliens, Non-resident Citizens and Voting Rights' in *Citizenship Acquisition* (n 53) 63 (supporting enfranchisement of non-resident citizens, as well as of non-citizen residents).

[59] Cf. Thomas Pogge, *World Poverty and Human Rights: Cosmopolitan Responsibilities and Reforms* (Polity Press 2008) 98. David Held, *Democracy and the Global Order: From the Modern State to Cosmopolitan Governance* (Stanford University Press 1995) 223–32 (contending that citizenship rights embody a conception of empowerment that is strictly limited to the framework of the nation-state, whereas formulations of rights in treaties, regional documents, and international law, which directly transcend the claims of individual nation-states have emerged of late). Elsewhere, Held advocates a *cosmopolitan* model of democracy that entails the creation of new political institutions that would coexist with the system of states but would override states in clearly defined spheres of activities where those activities have demonstrable transnational and international consequences. David Held, *Models of Democracy* (Polity Press 1996) 304. See also James Bohman, *Democracy across Borders: From Demos to Demoi* (MIT Press 2007) 5 (asserting that 'transnational democracy . . . as realized in a variety of institutions and communities . . . is not only more democratic, but is the only feasible way . . . in which to realize the democratic minimum and the rights of members of the human political community').

apparent disjuncture between burden sharing and political participation; and the significance of 'exit' options, or lack thereof, in assessing the extent to which non-citizen residents are subjected to coercive authority.

1 Community Cohesion and Identity Formation

Fredrick Schauer suggests that political communities need organising symbols to delineate membership.[60] An inclusive nature of democratic citizenship paradoxically explains the insistence on exclusion of non-citizens.[61] On this view, today, the lines which divide members from strangers, citizens from aliens, 'we' from 'they' are drawn most sharply around political privileges; absent other voting qualifications such as the qualifications that were explored in Section B, citizenship-based eligibility facilitates social cohesion and strengthens identity formation.[62]

It may be argued that, citizenship-based eligibility increases its real and symbolic significance and improves the sense of community among (all) citizens;[63] citizens are thus considered equal partners in the common enterprise of governing the commonweal.[64] Hence, a sense of social solidarity depends on exclusion of non-citizens,[65] since even on 'liberal' accounts (see Chapter 4) democratic politics requires some shared values and understandings, as well as a commitment to cooperation among most community members.[66]

However, excluding non-citizens because they do not 'fit' in is, arguably, circular if citizenship is regarded as (the) criterion for determining whether a person 'fits in' and non-citizens are not given a reasonably accessible non-discriminatory path to attain citizenship.[67] Moreover, it

---

[60] Fredrick Schauer, 'Community, Citizenship and the Search for National Identity' (1986) 84 Michigan Law Review 1504, 1514–15.

[61] Charles Taylor, 'The Dynamics of Democratic Exclusion' (1998) 9(4) Journal of Democracy 143, 143.

[62] Seyla Benhabib, 'Citizens, Residents and Aliens in a Changing World' (1999) 66 Social Research 708, 722.

[63] Gerald L Neuman, 'Aliens and Equal Protection: Why Not the Right to Vote?' (1977) 75 Michigan Law Review 1092, 1110.

[64] Ayelet Shachar, The Birthright Lottery: Citizenship and Global Inequality (Harvard University Press 2009) 32.

[65] Frank I Michelman, 'Conceptions of Democracy in American Constitutional Argument: Voting Rights' (1989) 41 Florida Law Review 443, 456.

[66] David A Martin, 'Due Process and Membership in the National Community: Political Asylum and Beyond' (1983) 44 University of Pittsburgh Law Review 165, 198–99.

[67] T Alexander Aleinikoff, 'Citizens, Aliens, Membership and the Constitution' (1990) 7 Constitutional Commentary 9, 15.

can be argued that electoral exclusion of immigrants negatively affects social cohesion and social justice by compromising the democratic quality of representation.

2   Loyalty to the State and to Its Long-Term Well-Being

It may be suggested that, while non-citizen residents are (only) required to obey the laws of their host state, citizens are also expected to be loyal to their state. On this account, only citizens, who are full and permanent members of the polity, may be presumed to be committed to the continued success of the polity, and to have its long-term interests at heart. By comparison, non-citizens may consider their own interests rather than those of their host state, particularly on questions concerning regulation of future migration and naturalisation.[68] The alleged fear is that, in a conflict between interests of the non-citizen's state of origin and interests of the state of residence, the former may take precedence.[69] It is further contended that, if non-citizen residents forgo (for economic, familial, political, or psychological reasons) a reasonable opportunity to naturalise, their refusal may cast doubts on their long-term commitment to the well-being of the polity.[70] However, as non-citizens are not protected from deportation, they have an incentive to remain loyal to their host state.[71] Moreover, enfranchisement (signifying inclusion) may make them feel more committed and loyal.[72]

Bauböck suggests that the reason citizens should be enfranchised is because they are 'stakeholders': by virtue of their permanent membership, they have a life-long interest in the future of the polity, its survival

---

[68] Note the 'republican' view of the purposes of the electoral process (Chapter 3), namely that good citizens are expected to advance the 'common good' rather than use the process to advance their private interests.

[69] Ron Hayduk, 'Democracy for All: Restoring Immigrant Voting Rights in the United States' (2004) 26(4) *New Political Science* 499, 515.

[70] Raskin (n 7) 1448.

[71] Interestingly, the US Supreme Court held that it should not be assumed that US citizens who vote in foreign elections have thereby voluntarily renounced their US citizenship. *Afroyim v Rusk*, 387 US 253 (1967). In contrast, the German Federal Constitutional Court described dual nationality as 'an evil that should be avoided or eliminated in the interests of States as well as the interests of the affected citizens'. *Opinion of the German Federal Constitutional Court*, 21 May 1974, BVerfGE 37, cited in Richard Plender, *Basic Documents on International Migration Law* (Nijhoff 1997) 217.

[72] Hayduk (n 69) 510.

and success.[73] This rationale applies both to resident and to non-resident citizens, as the latter enjoy an unconditional right to return, but does not extend to non-citizen residents.[74] However, it may be argued that permanent residence in a political community indicates a strong commitment thereto: with the passage of time, they establish ties that bind them to their state of residence. Conversely, expatriates (especially if they hold multiple citizenships) are occasionally merely nominal citizens.[75]

Moreover, the assumption that all citizens, most of whom natural-born, share an unconditional commitment to the long-term success of their polity, which all non-citizens *prima facie* lack is contentious.[76] For instance, there is little reason to assume that persons who have chosen to leave their original homes and migrate permanently to a new polity will necessarily harbour less allegiance than those whose citizenship was purely ascriptive.[77]

3 Electoral Inclusion as a Catalyst for Naturalisation

Chapter 4 addressed the internal prioritisation of citizens, referring to the predicament of non-citizens resulting therefrom. Conversely, it has been suggested that the removal of internal prioritisation and, subsequently, the decoupling of civil, social, and economic rights from citizenship has led to a devaluation of the institution of citizenship.[78] On this account,

---

[73] See also Peter Spiro, 'Perfecting Political Diaspora' (2006) 81 *NYU Law Review* 207 (refuting the claims that expatriates are more akin to irresponsible, uninformed or undisciplined voting, as well as the contention that such participation diverts expatriates from having deeper political engagement in the place where they reside).

[74] *Stakeholder Citizenship* (n 52) 2393; Rainer Bauböck, 'The Rights and Duties of External Citizenship' (2009) 13(5) *Citizenship Studies* 476, 478–483. See also Chapter 6 (regarding non-resident citizens voting).

[75] Cf. Christian Joppke, 'The Inevitable Lightening of Citizenship' in Ricard Zapata-Barrero (ed), *Citizenship Policies in the Age of Diversity* (CIDON Foundation 2009) 37 (asserting that there is a fundamental tension between freedom of movement and the principle of solidarity).

[76] Lardy (n 38) 95.

[77] Stephen H Legomsky, 'Citizens' Rights and Human Rights' (2010) 43(1) *Israel Law Review* 67, 76.

[78] Peter Shuck, 'Membership in the Liberal Polity: The Devaluation of American Citizenship' (1989) 3 *Georgetown Immigration Law Journal* 1, 9 (suggesting that the decoupling of rights from citizenship status has led to a reduction in the number of applications for naturalisation in the United States).

non-citizens no longer feel a compelling need to naturalise, and enfranchisement will further reduce their incentives to do so.[79]

EU citizens residing in another EU MSs are often considered a case in point as they tend not to naturalise in such circumstances. However, this phenomenon can be partly explained by the fact that EU citizens enjoy several entitlements that are otherwise reserved to *citizens of their state of residence*, including diplomatic and consular protection, (conditional) freedom of movement in and out of the state, as well as enfranchisement in *local* and *EU Parliament* elections.[80]

More fundamentally, following Walzer (see Chapter 4), if citizenship signifies membership in a 'community of character' and consists of more than merely legal status and concomitant rights, then naturalisation ought to be encouraged for morally sound reasons; enticing non-citizens to naturalise by restricting access to goods and services seems questionable.

4   Accountability and Vulnerability

It may be argued that, even if *de jure* the enjoyment of non-electoral rights is generally residence-based rather than citizenship-based, then *de facto* non-citizen residents often do not enjoy equal treatment.[81] It was contended in Chapter 3 that, elected officials can benefit from taking into account the knowledge, views, and preferences of citizens

---

[79] David Jacobson, *Rights across Borders: Immigration and the Decline of Citizenship* (Johns Hopkins University Press 1996) 9. Jacobson suggests that 'the civic and even nationalist symbolism of parliamentary elections is, it appears, the last bastion and expression of nationhood'. Ibid 38.

[80] Kiran Banerjee, *Political Community of Fate or Postnational State? The Persistence of the other in Contemporary German Citizenship* 14, http://papers.ssrn.com/sol3/papers.cfm?abstract_id=1767041. The looming 23 June 2016 'Brexit' referendum on the UK's membership of the EU reportedly led to an increase in the number of naturalisation applications lodged by citizens of other EU member states resident in the UK, www.theguardian.com/politics/2015/aug/17/dual-nationality-passports-eu-migrants-fear-brexit-european-union-referendum.

[81] See e.g. Linda Bosniak, 'Citizenship, Non-citizenship and the Trans-nationalization of Domestic Work' in Seyla Benhabib and Judith Resnik (eds), *Migrations and Motilities: Citizenship, Borders and Gender* (NYU Press 2009) 127, 143 (suggesting that alienage still serves as a source of disadvantage: lack of citizenship status disqualifies aliens from enjoyment of a range of rights in many political communities). See also Vicky Jackson, 'Citizenships, Federalisms and Gender', Ibid 439, 446 (arguing that a territorially based government remains a human necessity, and that while citizenship should *not* be the only basis for rights-holding it is a concept and rhetorical trope that has been effectively invoked in connection with claims of political rights).

and non-citizens alike.[82] Nonetheless, it seems reasonable to assume that officials will have greater incentives to attend to the needs and interests of non-citizens if the latter are enfranchised;[83] hence, non-citizens may be more vulnerable *because* they lack voting rights.[84]

It may be asserted that, even if it does not satisfy the 'republican' ideal of self-governance, the extent to which non-citizens can hold authorities of their host state accountable for violations of rights through *non-electoral* means matters as it can further protection of their rights and interests.[85] On this account, non-citizen residents are less vulnerable if they are nationals of a powerful state that protects its nationals abroad, holds host states accountable for violating rights of its nationals, entitles its expatriates to vote, and to which repatriation is both possible and plausible.[86]

It may also be argued that electoral exclusion of non-citizens can be mitigated by exercising *non-electoral* political rights in the states of residence, such as demonstrating, debating in public arenas, joining parties or forming new parties.[87] However, even if *de jure* non-citizens enjoy political rights, their views and preferences may be given less weight (or discarded wholesale) because they are not eligible voters (see Chapter 3).

5   Burden Sharing and Fairness

Chapter 4 assessed a 'contractarian' burden-sharing justification for internal prioritisation of citizens. Yet the argument can be applied *mutatis mutandis* to justify enfranchisement of non-citizen residents. Following a 'no taxation without representation' principle, it may be asserted that non-citizen residents who make financial contributions to their society through taxation and engage in other contributory social activities should be entitled to vote, especially as elections are a medium through which

---

[82] Ibid.

[83] Daniel Munro, 'Integration through Participation: Non-Citizen Resident Voting Rights in an Era of Globalization' (2008) 9(1) *Journal of International Migration and Integration* 63, 74–75.

[84] Ludvig Beckman, 'Citizenship and Voting Rights: Should Resident Aliens Vote?' (2006) 10(2) *Citizenship Studies* 153, 154.

[85] Meghan Benton, 'The Tyranny of the Enfranchised Majority? The Accountability of States to their Noncitizen Population' (2010) 16(4) *Res Publica* 397, 408.

[86] The predicament of recognised CSR1951 refugees, to whom none of the above-mentioned mitigating circumstances are applicable, will be considered in Chapter 8.

[87] Citizenship Policies (n 50) 46.

societies allocate finite resources.[88] The argument also applies to expatriates who are taxed abroad or who send remittances to their state of origin. As PACE has recently stressed 'democratic legitimacy requires equal participation by all groups of society in the political process, and that the contribution of legally resident non-citizens to a country's prosperity further justifies their right to influence political decisions in the country concerned'.[89]

However, as asserted in Chapter 4, making rights protection dependent on financial contributions may be reminiscent of property qualifications: not all non-citizens work or pay taxes, nor do all citizens, so relying on financial contribution to construe eligibility would be (at least) as over and under-inclusive as it was in previous centuries. Rather than being *sine qua non* for enfranchisement, taxation can serve as an additional *indicator* of the contribution of non-citizens to the community in which they reside. Zilbershats helpfully refers to one's centre of meaningful life as part of the 'nexus' to the present and future test, asserting that 'logic requires that those who decide the nature of life in the state should be those who live, work, and educate their children [there]'.[90]

6   'Exit Options' and Subjection to Coercive State Authority

Resident non-citizens are subject to the entire corpus of laws in their state of residence, including the redistribution of public goods and services and the regulation of private behaviour.[91] Citizenship-based eligibility comes in direct tension with a basic liberal tenet (Chapter 3), namely that '[g]overnments are instituted among Men, deriving their just powers from the *consent* of the governed'.[92] On Dahl's strong principle of equality 'the criterion of inclusion stipulates that the demos should include all adults subject to the binding collective decisions of the association'.[93]

---

[88]   Hayduk (n 69) 507.
[89]   Recommendation No 1500: Participation of Immigrants and Foreign Residents in Political Life in the Council of Europe Member States, 26 January 2011 (8th sitting) ('urg[ing] the governments of member states (a) to grant the right to vote and stand in local elections to all migrants legally established for at least three years irrespective of their origin').
[90]   Yaffa Zilbershats, *The Human Right to Citizenship* (Transnational 2002) 96.
[91]   Adam Przeworski, 'Minimalist Conception of Democracy: A Defense' in Ian Shapiro and Casiano Hacker-Cordón (eds), *Democracy's Values* (Cambridge University Press 1999) 23, 47.
[92]   See United States Declaration of Independence 4 July 1776, discussed in Chapter 3. See also Peter Jones, *Rights* (Macmillan 1994) 88.
[93]   Dahl (n 24) 129.

Dahl asserted that 'every adult subject to a government and its laws must be presumed to be qualified as and has an unqualified right to be a member of the demos'.[94]

However, if all personal interests that may be affected by state-mandated action are to be included under the umbrella of the 'all affected' principle, then 'virtually (maybe literally) everyone in the world... should be entitled to vote on any proposal or any proposal for proposals'.[95] While being bound by legislation implies being affected by that legislation, being affected by legislation does not necessarily imply being bound by it.[96] Hence, a qualified version of Dahl's principle suggests that electoral participation should be considered as a presumptive right which materialises when fundamental interests are at stake:[97] for instance, permanent residents are not just affected by coercive legislation, but are also meaningfully bound by it.

Lopez-Guerra, advocating a strong disaggregation position, argues that the principle of subjection to coercive authority entails that the electorate should *exclude* non-resident citizens because they are not subject to the laws passed by the demos.[98] In contrast, Owen submits that, while habitual residents are subjected to binding decisions, non-resident citizens are often subject to coercive power of their state of nationality through personal or property taxation, liability for conscription, denial of future electoral participation, and/or restrictions on future enjoyment of goods and services; hence, it is consistent to advocate both enfranchisement of non-citizen residents and enfranchisement of non-resident citizens.[99]

Still, it may be contended that, even if non-citizens are subject to binding decisions of their state of residence, they should not necessarily have a right to participate in creating its law. Rather, like minors, they should have a right to be protected from harm by law. On this view, *most* non-citizens are not inescapably tied to the fate of the community: they have chosen to enter a society which they can leave by returning to their state of citizenship (refugees and stateless non-citizens notwithstanding).

---

[94] Ibid.
[95] Robert E Goodin, 'Enfranchising All Affected Interests, and Its Alternatives' (2007) 35(1) *Philosophy and Public Affairs* 40, 55.
[96] See e.g. Beckman (n 8) 161.
[97] Sarah Song, 'Democracy and Noncitizen Voting Rights' (2009) 13(6) *Citizenship Studies* 607, 609.
[98] Lopez-Guerra (n 58) 223.   [99] See e.g. Owen (n 58) 53.

In other words, since they have an 'exit option', they are not involuntarily subject to state coercion.[100]

However, a 'times & ties' argument would suggest that, as time passes, non-citizen residents establish social membership in a community through employment, education, housing, and community involvement; the adverse consequences of repatriation may outweigh their (*de jure*) right to return.[101] Hence, their formal 'exit option' becomes considerably weaker. It can also be argued that persons should not be expected to relinquish their right to participate in the administration of state-imposed coercive power for lengthy periods as a 'price' for migration.[102] Finally, as dual or multiple nationals have an 'exit option', the same logic can apply to them.[103]

E Concluding Remarks

Successful struggles for inclusive suffrage have led to a (legal) reality where, in democracies, almost all mentally competent adult (resident) citizens are, in principle, eligible voters in elections of their states of citizenship. The transition from exclusionary to a near-universal suffrage altered the way in which voters are perceived: political equality, rather than presumed moral virtuousness, dictates eligibility. Citizenship has thus become (the) main voting qualification.

This chapter presented three general normative propositions concerning citizenship voting qualification. The inseparability position holds that enfranchisement on all electoral levels emanates from 'the people' of a given state; it would be just as wrong to enfranchise a non-citizen as it would be to disenfranchise a citizen, wherever the latter resides. The contingent position distinguishes sub- and supra-national from national elections and referendums, basing enfranchisement in the former on domicile, and in the latter on citizenship. In contrast, the disaggregation position substitutes citizenship for residence as (the) basis for enfranchisement of non-citizen residents, leading (on some accounts) to disenfranchisement of non-resident citizens.

The inseparability and contingent positions entail exclusion of non-citizens (from all or) from national elections, respectively, until such time

---

[100] Neuman (n 63) 277. See also Seglow (n 44) 793.
[101] Cf. Joseph H Carens, 'The Case for Amnesty', *Boston Review Online* (May/June 2009), www.bostonreview.net/BR34.3/carens.php.
[102] Ibid 793.
[103] See n 71 (US and German judgments concerning multiple citizenships).

as they are legally able (and willing) to naturalise. In states which base naturalisation policies on ethnic nationalist criteria, for some non-citizens, the path to naturalisation may be either blocked or highly cumbersome, compounding their predicament. More inclusive approaches to naturalisation require applicants to satisfy conditions ranging from (on liberal views) residence and self-sufficiency requirements to (on more restrictive accounts) passing language, citizenship, and integration tests, taking oaths of allegiance, paying fees, and renouncing other citizenship(s). Pertinently, even following the least restrictive account, non-citizen residents are electorally excluded for a (potentially protracted) period of time.

The chapter then presented six contentions that feature prominently in the scholarly discourse. Preservation of community identity, loyalty to the state and to its long-term well-being, and incentives to naturalisation generally support the (partial or total) electoral exclusion of non-citizens; the absence of state accountability towards its non-citizen population, the unfairness of burden sharing without participation, and the subjection of non-citizens to coercive state authority, absent 'exit options', support residence-based eligibility. The principal tenets of the above contentions and, indeed, of Part II as a whole, will be revisited in Chapter 8 and applied to the political predicament of recognised CSR1951 refugees.

PART III

Political Predicament and Remedies

6

Out-of-Country Voting: The Recognised CSR1951 Refugee Context

A Introduction

The effective exercise of the right to vote 'imposes an obligation upon the state not merely to refrain from interfering with the exercise of the right, but to take positive steps to ensure that it can be exercised'.[1] The state's positive obligations include, *inter alia*, the promulgation of election laws that regulate the formation of political parties, facilitate registration and voting processes, and enable access to information.[2]

It was noted in Part II that all states have non-citizen resident populations and, pertinently for this chapter, have non-resident citizens (expatriates). Before considering accessibility to OCV arrangements, states must first determine *whether* their non-resident citizens remain on the electoral roll; failing that, expatriates have to exercise their (recognised) right to return to their state and to re-establish residence there in order for their (dormant) voting rights to be reactivated (see Chapter 5). In contradistinction, if expatriates remain eligible voters, an effective exercise of their right to vote may depend on accessible OCV procedures.[3] As the discussion below demonstrates, the analytically distinct questions of eligibility and accessibility are often conflated.

The book concerns voting rights of recognised CSR1951 refugees. This chapter explores their political predicament *qua* expatriates.[4] It is suggested that expatriates requiring access to OCV procedures may be

---

[1] *Richter v Minister for Home Affairs and Others*, 2009 (3) SA 615 (CC) (12 March 2009) [53].

[2] See generally Rory O'Connell, 'Realising Political Equality: The European Court of Human Rights and Positive Obligations in a Democracy' (2010) 61(3) *Northern Ireland Law Quarterly* 263.

[3] See Rainer Bauböck, 'Towards a Political Theory of Migrant Transnationalism' (2003) 37 *International Migration Review* 700, 714 (arguing that, since most states do not grant voting rights to non-citizen residents, they are deprived of any opportunity for democratic participation unless they can vote in their states of citizenship).

[4] It is acknowledged that, stateless refugees suffer from political predicament in their state of origin.

(broadly) divided to three categories: first: voluntary expatriates, including migrant workers and their families; second: CFMs; third: CSR1951 refugees. It is argued that, among expatriates, CSR1951 refugees are least likely to have access to OCV.

Section B demonstrates that, although most states consider their expatriates as eligible voters, residence-based eligibility (*in addition* to citizenship) is not explicitly proscribed by the ICCPR or by regional treaties. However, whereas OCV procedures used to be rare,[5] and *eligible* expatriates were expected to travel to the state to cast their ballot in person, research shows that at least 115 states have in place OCV procedures.[6] Concomitantly, 'soft law' instruments, most notably of the Council of Europe (CoE), advocate an expansive approach to both eligibility and to accessibility, while judicial bodies are more reluctant to demand the electoral inclusion of expatriates or (when expatriates remain on the electoral role) to require states to facilitate their expatriates' full access to OCV procedures. In addition, state parties to the Migrant Workers Convention are required to facilitate OCV of their expatriates in their states of employment.[7]

Section C considers accessibility of CFMs to OCV procedures. It is contended that, in the main, such access is made possible against the backdrop of post-conflict transformation or peace-building. In such circumstances, elections play a pivotal role in internationally sponsored agreements: CFMs participating in such elections are seen either as being symbolically (re)admitted to the political community of their state of origin or as actively participating in the (new) formation thereof.

---

[5] Peter Spiro, 'Citizenship and Diaspora: A State Home for Transnational Politics?', http://ssrn.com/abstract=1755231 (noting that, historically '[t]he grant of political rights to those who have established residence outside the national territory is anomalous').

[6] See *Voting from Abroad: The International IDEA Handbook on External Voting* (Institute for Democracy and Electoral Assistance 2007) 1–3 (positing that 'external voting' has two main purposes: ensuring the realisation of political rights for citizens living outside their state, and increasing political participation and thereby building trust and confidence in electoral processes and the democratic governments they produce). See also Michael Collyer, 'A Geography of Extra-Territorial Citizenship: Explanations of External Voting' (2014) 2(1) *Migration Studies* 55, 64 (offering a five-prong global classification: states where no elections are held; states where expatriates are ineligible; states where expatriates are eligible but no OCV is available; states where OCV is available, and expatriates vote in the district where they were most recently resident; states where expatriates elect their own representation).

[7] (adopted 18 December 1990, entered into force 1 July 2003) 2220 UNTS 3 (Migrant Workers Convention).

International organisations often offer their assistance and cooperation to secure the widest possible participation, and to enhance legitimacy and accountability. The rationale underlying OCV of CFMs and the facilitation of such procedures by states of asylum is an imminent or forthcoming repatriation of CFMs; indeed, oftentimes, the two processes take place in parallel.

Section D considers the predicament of recognised CSR1951 refugees (it is noteworthy that CSR1951 refugees may flee states that hold elections and have OCV procedures in place[8]). It is contended that, CSR1951 refugees *qua* expatriates have a normatively strong(er) claim to remain eligible voters and to have access to OCV procedures.[9] It is a constitutive element of their refugee status that they have left their state of origin involuntarily[10] and cannot or will not exercise their internationally recognised right to return to it and vote in person; hence, absent access to OCV, they are effectively disenfranchised. Additionally and importantly, CSR1951 refugees are significant stakeholders in their state's elections; indeed, their repatriation may often depend on its results. Indeed, denying CSR1951 refugees access to OCV procedures creates perverse incentives for regimes which may aim to achieve desirable political results by persecution or by failing to adequately offer CSR1951 refugees protection from persecution by non-state actors.[11]

Nevertheless, it is submitted that access of CSR1951 refugees to OCV poses largely unavoidable impediments over and above those facing voluntary expatriates and CFMs in post-conflict circumstances. CSR1951 refugees suffer alienage from the political community of their state of

---

[8] Bayard Roberts, *Guide to Forced Migration and Electoral Participation* (Forced Migration Online 2003) 16, www.forcedmigration.org/research-resources/expert-guides/forced-migration-and-electoral-participation.

[9] CFMs may not necessarily satisfy the criteria set in CSR1951, and their arrival *en masse* often results in states of asylum being unable or unwilling to conduct Refugee Status Determination procedures. CFMs failing to satisfy the CSR1951 criteria may be granted 'temporary protection' status or some form of 'subsidiary protection' (see sources cited in the Introduction to this book nn 38–40).

[10] UNHCR EXCOM Conclusion No 62 (XLI) 'Note on International Protection' (5 October 1990) (noting '... (iii) the difference between refugees and persons seeking to migrate for economic and related reasons, and the need for any refugee policy to respect fundamental distinctions between the two categories of people, and be fully consonant with the principles particular to, and essential for, the protection of refugees including... non refoulement').

[11] Jeremy Grace, *External and Absentee Voting in Challenging the Norms and Standards of Election Administration* (IFES 2007) 35, 39.

origin as a result of their well-founded fear of persecution, and their repatriation is neither imminent nor forthcoming. While international organisations may conduct OCV operations in the context of post-conflict or peace-building transitional elections, they are highly unlikely to offer such assistance to individual CSR1951 refugees.

Participation of CSR1951 refugees in OCV processes requires formal engagement with authorities of their state of origin for the purposes of identification, registration, and voting. If their well-founded fear of persecution stems from actions of a persecutory regime, it would be manifestly unreasonable to expect CSR1951 refugees to be willing to make such contact. Moreover, persecutory regimes may view deflectors as criminals and disenfranchise them, while states of asylum may ideologically refuse to facilitate or even tolerate on their territory political engagement with a persecutory regime.[12]

In contradistinction, where the fear of persecution stems from non-state actors, states of origin that are unable to provide their citizens with adequate protection from persecution may not necessarily be able to maintain functioning OCV processes. Moreover, states of asylum may view political engagement between CSR1951 refugees and officials of their state of origin as indicative of voluntary re-availing of that state's protection, and initiate proceedings for cessation of refugee status; in turn, CSR1951 refugees may be reluctant to engage with the diplomatic missions of their state of origin for fear of losing their status.

Consequently, despite having a *prima facie* normative claim to an exercisable right to vote from abroad, CSR1951 refugees normally remain *de facto* disenfranchised. Their forced alienage from the political community of their state of origin means that they can neither take part in its elections through OCV procedures nor exercise their right to return to that state. In addition, as Chapter 7 demonstrates, they do not enjoy the protection abroad of their state of origin. In light of these predicament, Chapter 8 addresses the main contention of this book, namely that CSR1951 refugees suffer unique political predicament: they are in need of citizenship-dependent rights for the indeterminate period during which they hold refugee status and this 'protection gap' can be mitigated by their enfranchisement in their state of asylum.

---

[12] Importantly, OCV takes place on the territory of the state of asylum; thus, it requires the acquiescence of that state. For a recent example, see 'Returning Officers', *The Economist Online* (2 June 2012), www.economist.com/node/21556222 (regarding OCV in Canada of French expatriates).

B   Out-of-Country Voting of Voluntary Migrants

1   *OCV and the International Covenant on Civil and Political Rights*

Article 25 of the ICCPR stipulates that '[e]very *citizen* shall have the right and the opportunity, without any of the distinctions mentioned in Article 2 and *without unreasonable restrictions*... (2) *to vote* and to be elected at genuine periodic elections which shall be by universal and equal suffrage'.[13] In tandem, Article 12(4) pronounces that every person has a right to return 'to his own country' and reside there.[14]

Chapter 2 considered Article 25 in the context of non-citizen suffrage. The HRC notes that 'the right provided for by Article 25 is not an absolute right and that restrictions of this right are allowed as long as they are not discriminatory or unreasonable.'[15] Residence is not one of the prohibited grounds in Article 2 of the ICCPR; hence, the question is whether residence may be considered a reasonable restriction on the exercise by an otherwise eligible citizen of her right to vote.[16]

---

[13] Emphasis added.

[14] The provision clearly applies to citizens, and potentially to other persons who have a strong attachment to the state. In General Comment No 27: *Freedom of Movement* (Article 12), CCPR/C/21, Rev 1, Add 9 (2 November 1999), the HRC notes that '[t]he right of a person to enter his or her own country recognizes the special relationship of a person to that country' and considers 'that there are few, if any, circumstances in which deprivation of the right to enter one's own country could be reasonable'. It emphasises that '[t]he right to return is of the utmost importance for refugees seeking voluntary repatriation'. Ibid [19] and [21].

[15] Communication 500/1992 *Joszef Debreczeny v the Netherlands* [9.2]. According to the HRC, the factors which should determine whether a particular residence requirement is reasonable are *the nature and purpose* of the election, and the effect *on the concerned population*; see Communication 932/2000 *Gillot v France* [14.2] (holding that the imposition of lengthy prior residence requirements which effectively disenfranchised French settlers in the context of a referendum on autonomy for the pacific territory of New Caledonia was reasonable).

[16] Cf. the American Convention on Human Rights (adopted 22 November 1969, entered into force 18 July 1978) 1144 UNTS 123 art 23(1): '[e]very *citizen* shall enjoy the following rights and opportunities: (b) *to vote*... in genuine periodic elections, which shall be by universal and equal suffrage...'; art 23(2): 'The law may regulate the exercise of the rights and opportunities referred to in the preceding paragraph *only on* the basis of age, nationality, *residence*, language, education, civil and mental capacity, or sentencing by a competent court in criminal proceedings' (emphases added). In contradistinction, the African Charter on Human and Peoples' Rights (adopted 27 June 1981, entered into force 21 October 1986) (1982) 21 ILM 58 art 13 pronounces that '*[e]very citizen* shall have the right to participate freely in the government of his country, either directly or through freely chosen representatives in accordance with the provisions of the law' without explicit qualifications (emphasis added).

According to Article 2(2), state parties are required to respect and ensure rights to all persons within their territories and subject to their jurisdiction. The HRC opined that the ICCPR may apply extra-territorially to 'anyone within the power or effective control of that State Party, even if not situated within the territory of the State Party'.[17] Indeed, it may be argued that a purposive interpretation of the ICCPR entails that, for the purposes of Article 25, expatriates are under effective control of their state.[18] The HRC notes that '[s]tates must take effective measures to ensure that all persons entitled to vote are able to exercise that right [to vote]'.[19] Nevertheless, it appears to acknowledge possible legitimacy of residence requirements by maintaining that 'when residence require-ments apply . . . they must be reasonable . . . and should not be imposed in such a way as to exclude the homeless from the right to vote'.[20]

2   Between 'Hard' and 'Soft' Law: OCV in the Council of Europe

The First Additional Protocol proclaims that '[t]he High Contracting Parties undertake to hold free elections at reasonable intervals by secret ballot, under conditions which ensure the free expression of the opinion of the people in the choice of the legislature'.[21] While the provision does not explicitly enunciate an individual right to vote, the EComHR held in *Mathieu-Mohin* that the provision entails a subjective 'right to vote'[22] based on the concept of 'universal suffrage'.[23] It further held that, while

[17] HRC, General Comment No 31: *The Nature of the General Legal Obligation Imposed on States Parties to the Covenant*, CCPR/C/21, Rev 1, Add 13 (29 March 2004) [10].

[18] Caroline Carter, 'The Right to Vote for Non-resident Citizens: Considered through the Example of East Timor' (2011) 46 *Texas International Law Journal* 655, 657.

[19] General Comment No 25: *The Right to Participate in Public Affairs, Voting Rights and the Right of Equal Access to public service* (Article 25), CCPR/C/21, Rev 1, Add 7 (12 July 1996) [3].

[20] Ibid [11]. The latter point may be significant in the context of CSR1951 refugees. See also Inter-Parliamentary Union, *Declaration on Criteria for Free and Fair Elections*, adopted unanimously by the Inter-Parliamentary Council in its 154th session (Paris, 26 March 1994) art 2(1): '[e]very adult citizen has the right to vote in elections on a non-discriminatory basis'; art 2(3): '[n]o eligible citizen shall be denied the right to vote or disqualified from registration as a voter, otherwise than in accordance with objectively verifiable criteria prescribed by law, and provided that such measures are consistent with the State's obligations under international law'; and art 2(5): '[e]very voter has the right to equal and effective access to a polling station in order to exercise his or her right to vote'.

[21] Art 3.

[22] *Mathieu-Mohin and Clerfayt v Belgium* App no 9267/81 (ECHR, 2 March 1987) [54].

[23] Ibid [51]. See also Guy S Goodwin-Gill, *Free and Fair Elections* (Inter-Parliamentary Union, 2006) 103–04. The ECtHR has recently subjected eligibility-restricting measures

the right to vote is not absolute, its exercise should not be curtailed to such an extent as to impair its 'very essence' and deprive it of its effectiveness.[24]

OCV features highly on the agenda of the CoE. Its Committee of Ministers adopted a recommendation stipulating that the right to vote is an essential part of the democratic process, and that every European expatriate should be *entitled* to fully exercise it.[25] PACE adopted a series of 'soft law' instruments concerning access to OCV. A 2004 recommendation entitled 'Links between Europeans Living Abroad and Their Countries of Origin' pronounced that expatriates should have 'the right to vote . . . in embassies and consulates in the host states' while maintaining their 'right of return', and called on signatories to 'take account of their expatriates' interest in policy making, in particular concerning questions of . . . political rights, including voting rights'.[26] The explanatory memorandum emphasised that '[t]he right to vote may be regarded as the principal attribute of citizenship and its exercise as the very basis of democracy' and that '[m]ember States [should] allow their expatriates to vote by post, in person at their consulates, or by proxy'.[27] In its 2005 resolution entitled 'Abolition of Restrictions on the Right to Vote',

---

to heightened scrutiny. See e.g. *Kiss v Hungary* App no 33802/06 (Second Section Chamber ECHR, 20 May 2010) (holding that a provision in the Hungarian Constitution disenfranchising persons under the partial guardianship of another due to their mental incapacity is in contravention of Article 3 of Protocol I. The ECtHR emphasised that, where a provision disenfranchises 'a particularly vulnerable group in society', the 'margin of appreciation' must be considered narrower and the state must offer very weighty reasons for its decisions). See also its recent cases concerning prisoner voting: *Scoppola* (No 3) *v Italy* App no 126/05 (Grand Chamber ECHR, 22 May 2012); *Frodl v Austria* App no 20201/04 (First Section Chamber ECHR, 8 April 2010); *Hirst* (No 2) *v UK* App no 74025/01 (Fourth Section Chamber ECHR, 30 March 2004); (Grand Chamber ECHR, 6 October 2005). For analysis of prisoner voting jurisprudence, see Reuven (Ruvi) Ziegler, 'Legal Outlier, Again? U.S. Felon Suffrage: Comparative and International Human Rights Perspectives' (2011) 29(2) *Boston University International Law Journal* 197, 222–34.

[24] *Mathieu-Mohin* (n 22) [54] and [56].

[25] Recommendation R(86), *The Exercise in the State of Residence by Nationals of Other Member States of the Right to Vote in the Elections of the State of Origin* (21 March 1986). Notably, the CoE is advocating OCV of non-resident citizens *and* enfranchisement of non-citizen residents; *Convention on the Participation* of Aliens in Public Life at Local Level, Strasbourg, 5 February 1992, CETS No 144 (see also Chapter 2).

[26] Recommendation No 1650 (2004) §5.v.d.iv [6] and [9.1.c] respectively. The PACE notes that 'it is in states' interest that their nationals should continue to exercise their nationality consciously and actively' and that 'nationals can play an important go-between role in host countries, working for better political, cultural, linguistic, economic, financial and commercial relations between their countries of origin and the countries where they live'. Ibid [3].

[27] Ibid *Explanatory Memorandum*, §4.3.1 [36].

PACE urged states to 'allow citizens living abroad to participate to the fullest extent possible in the electoral process', *inter alia*, by 'grant[ing] electoral rights to all their citizens (nationals) without imposing residence requirements'.[28]

A 2011 Venice Commission Report entitled 'Out-of-Country Voting' recommended that 'states adopt a positive approach to the right to vote of citizens living abroad, since this right fosters the development of national and European citizenship'.[29] Nonetheless, it noted that 'the Commission does not consider at this stage that the principles of the European electoral heritage require the introduction of such a right'.[30] As the analysis below demonstrates, the ECtHR has generally refrained from proscribing residence eligibility requirements and (absent such requirements) from requiring states to ensure effective access to OCV procedures.

In a case concerning eligibility, the Fourth Section Chamber of the ECtHR rejected a challenge to Lichtenstein's legislation, stipulating that only Liechtenstein nationals who ordinarily reside (*ordentlicher Wohnsitz*) in Liechtenstein one month before the date of an election or a referendum are entitled to vote. The judgment offered four rationales: First, a non-resident citizen is less directly or less continually concerned with his state's day-to-day problems and has less knowledge of them. Second, it is impracticable for parliamentary candidates to present electoral issues to citizens abroad; moreover, non-resident citizens have no influence on the selection of candidates or on the formulation of their electoral programmes. Third, there is a close connection between the right to vote in parliamentary elections and the fact of being directly affected by the acts of the political bodies so elected. Fourth, the legislature may legitimately wish to limit the influence of citizens living abroad in elections on issues which, while admittedly fundamental, primarily affect persons living in the state.[31] Importantly for this chapter's purposes, the judgment

---

[28] Resolution No 1459 (2005) [7] and [11(b)]. See also Recommendation No 1714 (2005) [1.ii].

[29] Venice Commission, *Report on Out-of-Country Voting*, adopted at its 87th plenary (17–18 June 2011).

[30] Ibid [98–99].

[31] *Hilbe v Liechtenstein* App no 31981/96 (Grand Chamber ECHR, 7 September 1999) (in French). Cf. Court of Justice of the European Union (CJEU) judgment concerning the exclusion of Dutch nationals residing in Dutch overseas territories from participation in elections for the European Parliament (C-300/04 *Eman v College van burgeneester en wethounders van Den Haag* [2006] ECR I-08055). The CJEU applied similar reasoning to uphold the reasonableness of residence requirements. For discussion, see generally Panos Stasinopolous, 'EU Citizenship as a Battle of the Concepts: Travailleur v Citoyen' (2011) 4(2) *European Journal of Legal Studies* 74.

emphasised that Mr Hilbe (residing in Switzerland) retains *an unqualified right to return* to Lichtenstein; should he choose to exercise this right, his right to vote would be restored. The (effective) right of return was thus recognised as a justification for *ineligibility* of expatriates.[32]

The Second Section Chamber upheld a challenge to a residence requirement for *candidacy*. Ukraine contended that the applicant had provided false information concerning his residence in the five years preceding the elections. The Chamber reiterated that, for candidacy, residence 'was not an unreasonable or arbitrary requirement *per se*',[33] the court noted that 'stricter requirements may be imposed on the eligibility to stand for election to parliament, as distinguished from voting eligibility' as it would 'enable [candidates] to acquire sufficient knowledge of the issues associated with the national parliament's tasks'.[34] However, in the circumstances of the case, since Ukrainian law did not distinguish between 'legal' and 'habitual' residence, the fact that the applicant's internal passport (*Propsika*) indicated that he retained legal residence should have sufficed for satisfying registration requirements.[35]

Moreover, the applicant has been granted *refugee* status in the US, and the Chamber recognised that 'he [the applicant] was in a difficult position: if he had stayed in Ukraine, his personal safety or physical integrity might have been seriously endangered, rendering the exercise of any political rights impossible, whereas, in leaving the state, he was prevented from exercising such rights'.[36] Hence, the fact the applicant was a recognised refugee strengthened his normative claim.

CoE jurisprudence regarding restrictive voting eligibility of non-resident citizens dates back to 1979, when the EComHR rejected a challenge to UK legislation restricting OCV procedures to servicemen and diplomats. The EComHR reasoned that servicemen and diplomats are distinguishable from other expatriates in that they 'are not living abroad voluntarily but have been sent to a state other than their own by their government in the performance of services to be rendered their country',

---

[32] Ibid.

[33] *Melnychenko v Ukraine* App no 17707/02 (Second Section Chamber ECHR, 30 March 2005). For discussion of legal and political theory issues raised by eligibility to stand as a candidate, see Alecia Johns, 'The Case for Political Candidacy as a Fundamental Human Right' (2016) 16 *Human Rights Law Review* 29.

[34] Ibid [56–57].

[35] Ibid [61]. Cf. Judge Loucaides (dissenting), maintaining that reliance on the applicant's 'undisputed *actual* residence rather than on the *formal* registration of such residence ... cannot be considered an arbitrary or even a wrong decision' (emphases in original).

[36] Ibid [65]. See also the analysis in Section D.

noting that 'there is... no risk of electoral fraud in their use of postal votes'.[37]

In *Doyle*, the ECtHR refrained from declaring UK legislation disenfranchising non-resident citizens absent from the UK for more than fifteen years to be incompatible with the requirements of A3P1.[38] The Fourth Section Chamber held that 'over such a time period, the applicant may reasonably be regarded as having weakened the link between himself and the UK and he cannot argue that he is affected by the acts of political institutions to the same extent as resident citizens'. Importantly for this chapter, the Court emphasised that if 'he [the applicant] returns to live in the U.K., his eligibility to vote as a British citizen will revive'.[39]

In May 2013, the Fourth Section Chamber rejected a second challenge to the UK legislation.[40] The applicant, a Second World War veteran living with his Italian wife in Italy, argued that the rationales in *Hilbe* (cited in *Doyle*) for justifying eligibility restrictions are archaic. Modern technology enables non-resident citizens to keep in contact with their state of origin, and it is entirely possible for a person living in Italy to be as informed as a person living in London on the day-to-day problems of the UK and to follow a general elections campaign. Moreover, since Mr Shindler is entitled to return to the UK, his interests are directly affected, *inter alia*, by NHS reforms, pensions, financial and banking regulations, and taxation.[41] The

---

[37] *X v United Kingdom* App No 7730/76 (ECHR, 28 February 1979), ECHR Decisions and Reports 15 p 137.

[38] *Doyle v UK* App no 30158/06 (Fourth Section Chamber ECHR, 6 February 2007).

[39] Ibid. Cf. High Court judgment in *Preston v Wandsworth Borough Council* [2011] EWHC 3174 [39–42] (HC) (rejecting a claim that the UK legislation serves as a deterrent for British citizens *qua* EU nationals wishing to exercise their EU right to freedom of movement. The High Court held that, while the right to vote is a fundamental UK constitutional right and the claimant is aggrieved by its removal, the UK government was entitled to hold that there is a legitimate objective which the rule is designed to achieve, namely to remove the right to vote from those whose links with the UK have diminished and who are not, for the most part at least, directly affected by the laws passed in the UK. According to the judgment, there is no evidence to suggest that the rule creates a barrier of any kind to freedom of movement. The judgment was upheld in *R (on the application of Preston) v Lord President of the Council*, [2012] EWCA Civ 1378 (CA).

[40] *Shindler v UK* App no 19480/09 (Fourth Section Chamber ECHR, 7 May 2013).

[41] Ibid pp 4–5 to the applicant's submission (on file with author). For a critique of the judgment's rationales, see Reuven (Ruvi) Ziegler, 'Voting Eligibility: Strasbourg's Timidity' in Katja S Ziegler, Elizabeth Wicks, and Loveday Hodson (eds), *The UK and European Human Rights: A Strained Relationship?* (Hart 2015) 165. *Compare* with the recent judgment of the Ontario Court of Appeal in *Frank v Canada (AG)* [2015] ONCA 536 (20 July 2015) (upholding the Canada Elections Act, SC 2000, c 9 s 11(d) which restricts eligibility to Canadians residing outside Canada less than five years unless they are either Members

court refrained from engaging directly with the applicant's arguments, opting instead to accord the state a wide margin of appreciation.

The ECtHR has also been reluctant to require access to OCV when non-citizen residents remain on the electoral roll. In 2010, the First Section Chamber upheld a legal challenge mounted by Greek nationals residing in Strasbourg and working for the CoE.[42] Article 51(4) of the 1975 Greek Constitution stipulates that '[t]he conditions for the exercise of the right to vote by persons living outside the country may be specified by statute adopted by a majority of two thirds of the total number of Members of Parliament'. The applicants argued that, absent legislative regulation setting up OCV procedures in Greek Embassies and Consulates, they were effectively unable to vote in Greek parliamentary elections.

The Chamber held (by a 5–2 majority, Judges Vajic and Flogaitisdissenting) that, while the applicants could have returned to Greece to vote, a *de facto* obligation to travel is expensive and disturbs professional and family life. Thus, the lack of legislative implementation in respect of OCV constitutes unfair treatment of Greek citizens living abroad, particularly of 'expatriates who, due to their financial circumstances or the fact that their place of residence is even further away, are *de facto* deprived of the opportunity to exercise their right to vote'.[43] Per *Melnychenko*, the Chamber emphasised that restrictions on the exercise of voting rights (the 'active' aspect) should be subject to greater scrutiny than restrictions on the 'passive' aspect (the right to stand for election), permitting a narrower 'margin of appreciation' to Contracting States. Drawing on the above-mentioned CoE resolutions and recommendations, as well as on legislative developments in other members of the CoE, the Chamber held that 'Greece clearly falls short of the common denominator . . . as regards the effective exercise of voting rights by expatriates'.[44]

Yet, in March 2012, the Grand Chamber (GC) unanimously reversed.[45] Its reasoning (based on *Hilbe*) appeared to conflate questions of eligibility and access to OCV. The GC maintained that 'bright line' rules are inevitable even if they may not do justice to particular

of the Canadian Forces; employees in either the federal or provincial public service who have been posted outside Canada; employees of an international organization to which Canada belongs who have been posted outside Canada; or a person who lives with a Canadian citizen in any one of these exempted groups. An appeal against the judgment, which reversed [2014] ONSC 907 (2 May 2014), is pending before the Canadian Supreme Court).

[42] *Sitaropolous v Greece* App no 42202/07 (First Section Chamber ECHR, 8 July 2010).
[43] Ibid [43].   [44] Ibid [46].
[45] *Sitaropolous v Greece* App no 42202/07 (Grand Chamber ECHR, 15 March 2012).

applicants.[46] According to the GC, Contracting States are *not* under an obligation to enable citizens living abroad to exercise their right to vote, nor is there a European consensus of which Greece supposedly falls short.[47] It held that, while travelling to Greece to exercise one's right to vote disrupts one's financial, family, and professional lives, such disruption is not 'disproportionate to the point of impairing the very essence of the voting rights in question'.[48]

This non-exhaustive survey indicates that, the questions whether expatriates should retain their right to vote, and, if so, whether they should have access to OCV procedures, receive increasing political and jurisprudential attention. While the (legal) outcomes are divergent, four assumptions appear to underlie all cases involving *voluntary* expatriates: First, states of origin can set up OCV procedures if they so wish. Second, expatriates are able to engage with diplomatic services of their states of origin to exercise their right to vote from abroad (assuming they are included on the electoral roll). Third, states of residence generally tolerate such political foreign engagements on their territory. Fourth, expatriates can return to their state to vote in person, notwithstanding potential disruption to their work and family life. As Section D demonstrates, these conditions are highly unlikely to be satisfied regarding access of CSR1951 refugees to OCV (when they remain on the electoral roll).

3   OCV and the Migrant Workers Convention

The Migrant Workers Convention concerns migrant workers and their families; *refugees* are explicitly excluded from its purview.[49] The treaty

---

[46] Ibid [68–69].   [47] Ibid [75].

[48] Ibid [80]. Cf. *Vámos and others v. Hungary*, App no 48145/14 (Second Section Chamber ECHR, 19 March 2015) (holding that, States are not generally required to implement measures to allow voting from abroad, but if they do, so such measures must be non-discriminatory). Cf. the South African Constitutional Court judgment in *Richter* (n 1), quashing domestic legislation listing professions and post-holders that may enjoy access to OCV procedures, to the exclusion of others, including the applicant (a teacher working in the United States). The Court held that 'a voter may not complain if the burden imposed does not prevent the voter from voting, as long as the voter takes reasonable steps to do so'. Ibid [56]. However, '[while] [i]t is acceptable to ask voters to travel some distances from their homes to a polling station . . . [i]t cannot be said . . . that requiring a voter to travel thousands of kilometres across the globe to be in their voting district on voting day is exacting reasonable compliance from a voter'. Ibid [68]. The Court further observed that expatriate voting is 'an expression both of . . . continued commitment to . . . [the] country and . . . civic-mindedness from which . . . democracy will benefit'. Ibid [69].

[49] Migrant Workers Convention art 3(d). Notably, the Convention steers clear of questions of migration control (art 79: 'Nothing in the present Convention shall affect the right

imposes obligations both on states of employment (defined as states 'where the migrant worker is to be engaged, is engaged or has been engaged in a remunerated activity, as the case may be') and on 'sending' states (defined as states 'of which the person concerned is a national').[50] Thus, the treaty aims to protect rights of migrants *qua non-citizen residents* as well as their rights *qua expatriates* of their sending states.[51] In contrast, Chapter 2 demonstrated that CSR1951 imposes obligations only on the state of asylum in view of the political predicament of CSR1951 refugees.

Alongside the individual right to have access to diplomatic and consular services, enunciated in Article 23 (see the discussion in Chapter 7), the Migrant Workers Convention imposes obligations on states of origin with regard to voting rights of their citizens. According to Article 41(1), '[m]igrant workers and members of their families *shall* have the right to participate in public affairs of their State of *origin* and to vote ... at elections of that State, in accordance with its legislation' (emphases added).

The *acquiescence* of the territorial state is required to regulate acts taking place outside the state's territory; hence, OCV procedures are subject to limitations imposed by host states.[52] In view of this (international) norm, Article 41(2) of the Migrant Workers Convention pronounces that states of employment 'shall, as appropriate and in accordance with their legislation, facilitate the exercise of these rights'.

Alongside the obligations regarding voting rights of migrants in elections of their states of *origin*, Article 42(3) of the Migrant Workers Convention stipulates that '[m]igrant workers may enjoy political rights in the State of employment if that State, in the exercise of its sovereignty, grants them such rights'. Hence, like the CoE, the Migrant Workers Convention considers OCV of non-resident citizens and enfranchisement of non-citizen residents as conceptually compatible.

---

of each State Party to establish the criteria governing admission of migrant workers and members of their families').

[50] Ibid art 6.

[51] Similarly to CSR1951, the Migrant Workers Convention distinguishes between rights granted to all migrant workers and members of their families regardless of legal status (enumerated in Part III) and '[o]ther rights of migrant workers and members of their families who are documented or in a regular situation' (enumerated in Part IV) which such persons shall enjoy in addition to the rights set forth in Part III.

[52] Carlos Navarro, 'The Political Rights of Migrant Workers and External Voting' in *Voting from Abroad* (n 6) 178.

The Committee on Migrant Workers (the treaty's monitoring body) receives reports concerning fulfilment of Convention obligations.[53] The Committee has commended Mali, noting 'with satisfaction that many expatriate Malians have the opportunity to participate in certain countries'.[54] Similarly, it commended Mexico, which established OCV processes in 2005, as well as Azerbaijan, BiH, Colombia, Ecuador, The Philippines, and Senegal.[55] In contrast, the Committee expressed concern that no OCV arrangements were established by Albania, Algeria, Bolivia, Chile, Egypt, El Salvador, Guatemala, Paraguay, and Sri Lanka.[56] Two states, Azerbaijan and Paraguay, indicated in their reports that they entitle non-citizen residents to vote in local elections, in accordance with the recommendation in Article 42(3).[57]

Article 8(2) of the Migrant Workers Convention further affirms the state-citizen bond by enunciating the *right* of migrant workers and members of their families 'at any time to enter and remain in their state of origin'.[58] Hence, the underlying assumption is similar to that of Article 12(4) of the ICCPR, namely that voluntary migrants *retain* their bond of citizenship with their state of origin while residing abroad, reflected in their right to return to that state at will, in the availability of protection abroad, and in the dual commitment on the part of the

---

[53] The individual complaints mechanism requires 10 accessions; so far, only two State Parties have acceded to it.

[54] CMW/C/MLI/CO/1 of 31 May 2006.

[55] CMW/C/MEX/1 of 18 November 2005 (Mexico); CMW/C/AZE/CO/1 of 19 May 2009 (Azerbaijan); CMW/C/BIH/CO/1 of 3 June 2009 (BiH); CMW/C/COL/CO/1 of 22 May 2009 (Colombia); CMW/C/ECU/2 of 26 January 2010 (Ecuador); CMW/C/PHL/CO/1 of 22 May 2009 (The Philippines); CMW/C/SEN/1 of 4 January 2010 (Senegal).

[56] CMW/C/ALB/CO/1 of 22 February 2010 (Albania); CMW/C/DZA/1 of 22 June 2008 (Algeria); CMW/C/BOL/CO/1 of 29 April 2008 (Bolivia); CMW/C/CHL/CO/1 of 19 October 2011 (Chile); CMW/C/EGY/CO/1 of 25 May 2007 (Egypt); CMW/C/SLV/CO/1 of 4 February 2009 (El Salvador); CMW/C/GTM/CO/1 of 18 October 2011 (Guatemala); CMW/C/PRY/1 of 23 February 2011 (Paraguay); CMW/C/LKA/CO/1 of 19 October 2009 (Sri Lanka).

[57] CMW/C/AZE/CO/1 of 19 May 2009 (Azerbaijan); CMW/C/PRY/1 of 23 February 2011 (Paraguay).

[58] Nonetheless, the Migrant Workers Convention has only 48 signatories. As most of the duties are imposed on states of employment, State Parties tend to be *sending* states such as Mexico and the Philippines, which consider the treaty as a vehicle to protect their citizens working abroad; states of employment are noticeably absent. Moreover, at present, the only European State Party is BiH. See Srdjan Vucetic, 'Democracies and International Human Rights: Why Is There No Place for Migrant Workers?' (2007) 11(4) *International Journal of Human Rights* 403, 418 (analysing the Travaux, Vucetic suggests that the Migrant Workers Convention was largely drafted by developing states for developing states).

sending state and of the state of employment to effective exercise of OCV.

C Out-of-Country Voting of Conflict Forced Migrants

Conflicts oftentimes cause displacement.[59] Settlements of conflicts may include elections and, occasionally, the establishment of representative institutions as part of a transition to democracy and as a key component of durable peace-building.[60] Transitional elections in which CFMs are effectively disenfranchised may be considered deficient; in contrast, participation of CFMs enhances the legitimacy of the outcomes of negotiations and of election results, and increases the commitment of CFMs to the peace-building process. Elections may help reunite a conflict-torn society around common institutions.[61]

The effective enfranchisement of CFMs in post-conflict elections has arguably played an important role in the peace-building process in cases as diverse as Angola, Bosnia-Herzegovina, Cambodia, Guatemala, Mozambique, and Nagorno-Karabakh, by providing direct opportunity for conflict victims to participate in the selection of their post-conflict leadership.[62] Indeed, Diaspora members have participated in peace-building commissions and in other forms of post-conflict political activity: for instance, the Iraqi Diaspora has played a prominent role in governance in the aftermath of the 2003 Iraq war.[63]

Recognition of a claim to effective citizenship, and consequent inclusion of CFMs in formal political activities such as elections or referendums, serve as powerful symbols of their (re)admission to the political

---

[59] Grace defines a 'Conflict Forced Migrant' as any person displaced from their home community due to a deteriorating security or human rights situation generally as a consequence of violence; notably, this is a far broader definition than that of a CSR1951 refugee. Jeremy Grace, *Enfranchising Conflict Forced Migrants* (IOM Participatory Elections Project Discussion Paper No 2 2003) 5.

[60] Jeremy Grace, 'The Electoral Rights of Conflict Forced Migrants: A Review of Relevant Legal Norms and Instruments' (IOM Participatory Elections Project discussion paper No 1 2003) 3.

[61] The Electoral Knowledge Network, *Voting from Abroad*, http://aceproject.org/ace-en/topics/va/external-voting-a-world-survey-of-214-countries. See also Voting from Abroad (n 6) 18–9.

[62] James Milner, *Refugees and the Peace-Building Process* (UNHCR 2011) 5–6.

[63] Katy Long, *Voting with Their Feet: A Review of Refugee Participation and the Role of UNHCR in Country of Origin Elections and Other Political Processes* (UNHCR 2010) 47. *Compare* 'Expats vote start Egypt's Presidential race', 20 May 2012, www.ft.com/cms/s/0/09b52072-a102-11e1-9fbd-00144feabdc0.html#axzz27qrJKOgM.

community as equal citizens.[64] The underlying assumptions behind electoral processes taking place in such circumstances are either that the conflict has ended or that it is likely to be resolved soon and, consequently, that repatriation is either imminent or forthcoming.

UNHCR notes that 'conflict settlements often include the holding of national elections, and refugees may be expected to repatriate according to a certain schedule in order to vote'.[65] Repatriation arguably plays an important part in validating the post-conflict political order. When CFMs voluntarily go back to their homeland, they are quite literally 'voting with their feet' and expressing confidence in the future of their state; enabling CFMs to repatriate and express their political preference is arguably inherent in the concept of a free, fair, and democratic election.[66]

The logic of repatriation and enfranchisement guides the interpretation of Article 5(c) of the Convention on the Elimination of All Forms of Racial Discrimination (CERD). The provision requires signatories to guarantee the enjoyment of 'political rights, in particular the right to participate in elections, to vote... on the basis of universal and equal suffrage', while Article 5(d)(ii) guarantees everyone '[t]he right to leave any country, including one's own, and to return to one's country'.[67] The Committee on the Elimination of Racial Discrimination (the treaty body supervising its implementation) emphasised that '(a) all such refugees and displaced persons have the right freely to return to their homes of origin under conditions of safety';[68] it further noted that 'after the return to their homes of origin, the right to participate fully and equally in public affairs at all levels'.[69]

Annex 7 of the Dayton agreement concerning Bosnia and Herzegovina is illustrative of the approach to participation of CFMs in post-conflict electoral processes.[70] The agreement stipulated that '[a]ll refugees and displaced persons have the right freely to return to their homes of origin' and that 'the parties confirm that they will accept the return of such persons

---

[64] Long (n 63) 13.   [65] *Handbook on Voluntary Repatriation* (UNHCR 1996) 66.

[66] *The State of the World's Refugees: A Humanitarian Agenda* (UNHCR 1997) ch 4.

[67] (adopted 21 December 1965, entered into force 4 January 1969) 660 UNTS 195.

[68] CERD Committee, General Recommendation No 22, *Article 5 and Refugees and Displaced Persons*, 49th session, UN Doc A/51/18 annex VIII at 126 (1996) [2]. The recommendation recalls 'the 1951 Convention and the 1967 Protocol Relating to the Status of Refugees as the main sources of the international system for the protection of refugees in general'.

[69] Ibid [2(a)] and [2(d)] respectively.

[70] General Framework Agreement for Peace in Bosnia and Herzegovina, *Agreement on Refugees and Displaced Persons* (14 December 1995).

who have left their territory, including those who have been accorded temporary protection by third countries'.[71] The agreement established that 'the parties shall ensure that refugees and displaced persons are permitted to return in safety, without risk of harassment, intimidation, persecution or discrimination'.[72] Crucially, the agreement pronounced that '[t]he exercise of a refugee's right to vote shall be interpreted as confirmation of his or her intention to return to Bosnia and Herzegovina' and that 'by Election Day, the return of refugees should already be underway, thus allowing many to participate in person in elections in Bosnia and Herzegovina'.[73] Had CFMs been excluded from the democratic processes, the legitimacy of these processes would be strongly compromised.

There were instances in which the linkage between elections and repatriation had arguably led states of asylum to withdraw protection prematurely while effective repatriation was impeded by local resistance.[74] Indeed, states hosting CFMs, eager to see them depart, may attempt to bring asylum to an imminent end following participation in post-conflict elections.[75] For instance, in the 1997 Liberian elections, Guinea refused re-entry to Liberians who had returned to Liberia to vote, even though international agencies argued that repatriation was unsafe.[76]

Furthermore, host states may prefer to see immediate repatriation of CFMs rather than allow OCV on their territory.[77] They may be concerned about jeopardising their security, stability, and sovereignty by allowing political party campaigning, voter education, and voter registration to take place on their soil. Thus, the international community may have to

---

[71] Ibid [1].   [72] Ibid [2].

[73] Ibid annex 3: Agreement on Elections art iv (Eligibility) [1]. See also Soeren Keil & Anastasiia Kudlenko, 'Bosnia and Herzegovina 20 Years after Dayton: Complexity Born of Paradoxes' (2015) 22(5) *International Peacekeeping* 471, 478 (discussing the significance of the refugee return clauses of the DPA).

[74] Lauren Prather and Erik S Herron, 'Enfranchising Displaced Voters: Lessons from Bosnia-Herzegovina' (2007) 6(4) *Election Law Journal* 354, 357.

[75] Jeremy Grace and Erin Mooney, 'Peacebuilding through the Electoral Participation of Displaced Populations' 28(1) (2009) *Refugee Survey Quarterly* 95, 102.

[76] Brett Lacy, *Building Accountability, Legitimacy and Peace: Refugees, Internally Displaces Persons, and the Right to Political Participation* (International Foundation for Electoral Systems 2004) 4.

[77] Liberian and Cambodian refugees refused to allow electoral activities of the home state on their territories thereby compelling refugees to repatriate if they wished to vote. Dennis Gallagher and Anna Schowengerdt, 'Participation of Refugees in Postconflict Elections' in Krishna Kumar (ed), *Postconflict Elections, Democratization, and International Assistance* (Lynne Rienner Publishers 1998) 199, 208–9.

'persuade' host states that participation of CFMs in elections will expedite their repatriation.

An Organisation for Security and Cooperation in Europe (OCSE) conference convened in 1999 resolved 'to secure the full right of persons belonging to minorities to vote and to facilitate the right of refugees to participate in elections in their countries of origin'.[78] It may be argued that effective OCV of CFMs sometimes requires international support, *inter alia*, through provision of funding, administrative assistance in issuance of documentation, registration, distribution of election material, monitoring, and verification. The International Organisation for Migration (IOM) has conducted large-scale OCV operations in transitional elections.[79] From the point of view of CFMs, the involvement of the international community creates a secure and sustaining environment auspicious to electoral participation.

It may be observed that, unlike voluntary expatriates, effective participation of CFMs in OCV is likely to require a post-conflict or peace-building context, with international assistance, and with a view to forthcoming repatriation, notwithstanding the challenges relating to premature termination of protection.

---

[78] Istanbul Summit Declaration (18–19 November 1999) [26].

[79] The IOM led OCV processes in the 1999 BiH elections through the 'Refugee Elections Steering Group' set up following the signing of a Memorandum of Understanding (MOU) between the IOM and the OSCE. IOM offices in 17 states registered 630 000 voters, and 394 000 of whom cast their ballots. The IOM provided similar assistance following the 1999 East Timor tripartite agreement (Indonesia, Portugal, and the United Nations). In 2000–2001, the IOM operated the 'Out of Kosovo Voting Programme' registering nearly 300 000 Kosovars. The IOM was also responsible for OCV of 846 000 Afghan refugees residing in Pakistan and Iran in the 2004 elections in Afghanistan; an MOU was signed with the respective governments. In 2005, the IOM assisted the Independent Electoral Commission of Iraq in registering and administering elections for the 2005 Transitional National Assembly in 14 states, registering 279 000, of whom 265 000 voted (www.iom.int/cms/home). For a recent account of external voting in Latin America and MENA since 2000, see Jean-Michel Lafleur, 'The Enfranchisement of Citizens Abroad: Variations and Explanations' (2015) 22(5) *Democratization* 840. See also UNSC Resolution 2149 (10 April 2014) s 30(b)(v) ('to devise, facilitate and provide technical assistance to the electoral process and make all necessary preparations... for the holding of free, fair, transparent and inclusive elections, including... participation of Central African Republic Internally Displaced Persons and refugees no later than February 2015'. See also George Mbella, 'Central African Republic: Tripartite Agreement Permits Voting By Refugees' (3 November 2015) (reporting that more than 109 000 out of 250 000 CAR refugees resident in Cameroon were scheduled to participate in upcoming legislative and presidential elections on 13 December 2015, following a three-partite agreement: Cameroon, CAR, and UNHCR), http://allafrica.com/stories/201511030910.html.

D   Out-of-Country Voting of CSR1951 Refugees

1   Introduction

The well-founded fear of persecution that the international community recognises as a basis for CSR1951 refugee status is a symptom of a more fundamental political rupture between the refugee-citizen and their state of origin, leaving a CSR1951 refugee without national protection and without access to a political forum.[80]

Hathaway suggests that, a CSR1951 refugee is 'by definition a person who no longer enjoys the assumed bond between citizens and the state'.[81] Because CSR1951 refugees receive a form of substitute protection, those enjoying a form of protection that negates the need for the surrogate protection of refugee law are excluded.[82] Forced displacement is an indication that the web of rights and obligations which links the citizen to her state has broken down.[83]

It is submitted that, OCV requires a cumulative tri-partite effort on part of the CSR1951 refugee, the state of origin, and the state of asylum. Notwithstanding normative commonalities with CFMs, the unique predicament of CSR1951 refugees dictates that they are unlikely to enjoy effective access to OCV.

2   CSR1951 Refugees and CFMs in Post-conflict Elections: Normative Commonalities

Section B considered jurisprudence challenging preferential access to OCV procedures of non-resident citizens serving as military personnel and diplomats. It was noted that their claims may be normatively stronger

---

[80] Long (n 63) 5. Cf. Andrew Shacknove, 'Who Is a Refugee?' (1985) 95 *Ethics 274*, 277 (arguing that persecution is a sufficient but not a necessary condition for the severing of the normal social bond; persecution is one manifestation of a broader phenomenon: the absence of protection of the citizen's basic needs, which constitutes the full and complete negation of society and the basis of refugee-hood). Shacknove asserts that 'under normal conditions, protection appends to the citizen following him into foreign jurisdictions. For the refugee, protection of basic needs is absent, even at home' and suggests that 'refugee status should only be granted to persons whose government fails to protect their basic needs, who have no remaining recourse other than to seek international restitution of these needs, and who are so situated that international assistance is possible'. Ibid 284.

[81] James C Hathaway, *The Rights of Refugees under International Law* (Cambridge University Press 2005) 210.

[82] James C Hathaway and Michelle Foster, *The Law of Refugee Status* (2nd edn Cambridge University Press 2014) 500.

[83] *The State of the World's Refugees* (n 66) ch 1: Safeguarding Human Security.

than general claims of voluntary migrants because they are sent abroad by their governments, render services to their state, and remain strongly attached thereto.

In contrast, CSR1951 refugees, like CFMs, reside outside their state of origin *in*voluntarily;[84] in seeking asylum, they have not in any way manifested a wish to relinquish their citizenship.[85] Indeed, an effective exclusion of CSR1951 refugees from OCV processes may create perverse incentives for persecutory governments to use displacement as a means of securing and legitimising their rule.[86] However, in terms of their relations with their state of origin, and their attachment thereto, CSR1951 refugees are often (though not always) in a diametrically opposed position to that of diplomats working at state embassies and consulates.

It has been suggested that OCV is particularly pertinent when non-resident citizens are stakeholders in election results rather than merely affected by them. Mr Shindler asserted before the ECtHR that his right to OCV as a non-resident British citizen stems, in part, from the fact that, should he choose to exercise his right to return to the UK, he will be subject to government policies decided in his (political) absence. For recognised CSR1951 refugees, election results may even determine *whether* they are likely to be able to exercise their right to return;[87] hence, their 'stakes' in such elections are high.

Importantly, recognised CSR1951 refugees are entitled to hold their status until one of an *exhaustive* list of six cessation clauses in Article 1C thereof can be invoked by their state of asylum, in which case they would no longer require international protection and would no longer be able to refuse to avail themselves of the protection of their state of origin.[88]

Article 1C(5) is noteworthy in this context, as it concerns changes in circumstances in the state of origin of the CSR1951 refugee that have a 'fundamental, stable and durable character' and that result both in

---

[84] Long (n 63) 25.

[85] Gallagher and Schowengerdt (n 77) 199. See also Venice Commission, 'Report on Out-of-Country Voting' (24 June 2011) c.i.v. ('if persons, in exceptional cases, have been displaced against their will, they should, provisionally, have the possibility of being considered as resident at their former place of residence').

[86] Note, in this context, the decision in *Melnychenko* (n 33).

[87] See e.g. 'Congolese refugees in Zambia await elections in their homeland before deciding to return' (2 June 2006), http://unhcr.org/cgi-bin/texis/vtx/search?page=search&docid= 448049544&query=elections.

[88] Joan Fitzpatrick, 'The End of Protection: Legal Standards for Cessation of Refugee Status and Withdrawal of Temporary Protection' (1998–1999) 13 *Georgetown Immigration Law Journal* 343, 346. See also Chapter 8.

eradication of the refugee's well-founded fear of being persecuted and in restoration of protection.[89] UNHCR has issued formal declarations of general cessation of refugee status regarding changes in a particular territory.[90] Post-conflict or peace-building transitions are often perceived in such terms.[91] The analysis below is premised on the assumption built into the CSR1951 framework: namely, that absent such changes, CSR1951 refugees are either unable or unwilling to repatriate.[92]

3 Out-of-Country Voting of CSR1951 Refugees: Impediments

a Introduction

OCV *ipso facto* takes place outside the state's territory. It requires recognition on the part of the state of origin of the need to give effect to

---

[89] UNHCR EXCOM Conclusion No 65 (XLII) (1991) recalled in EXCOM Conclusion No 69 (XLIII) (1992) [b]. UNHCR advocates a waiting period of minimum 12–18 months before assessing developments in a country of origin. UNHCR EXCOM 'The Application of the Ceased Circumstances Clause in the 1951 Convention' (20 December 1991) [12]. A similarly phrased cessation clause, art 1C(6), concerns refugees who are *de jure stateless*. The analysis in the book centres on the predicament of refugees who *are* citizens of their state of origin, and who would able to vote in its elections save for their persecution-induced involuntary non-residence. See also Joan Fitzpatrick and Rafael Bonoan, 'Cessation of Refugee Status' in Erika Feller, Volker Türk and Frances Nicholson (eds), *Refugee Protection in International Law* (Cambridge University Press 2003) 491, 495.

[90] UNHCR, *Guidelines on International Protection: Cessation of Refugee Status under Articles 1C(5) and (6) of the Convention* (2003) n 3 (references to UNHCR formal declarations of general cessation regarding the situations in Poland and Czechoslovakia, 15 November 1991; Chile, 28 March 1994; Malawi and Mozambique, 31 December 1996; Bulgaria and Romania, 1 October 1997; Ethiopia, 23 September 1999; Timor Leste, 20 December 2002).

[91] See e.g. James C Hathaway, 'The Rights of States to Repatriate Former Refugees' (2005) 20 *Ohio State Journal on Dispute Resolution* 175, 185 (suggesting that the paradigmatic change which the CSR1951 drafters conceived of was the reversion of a totalitarian regime to democratic governance).

[92] Cf. UNHCR's contention that the 'compelling reasons' clause in Article 1C(5) (textually confined to pre-convention refugees) has come to reflect a general humanitarian principle that is applicable to Article 1A(2) refugees; *Guidelines on International Protection* (n 90) [21]. UNHCR's argument was rejected by the Court of Appeal and the House of Lords in *Hoxha v SSHD* [2002] EWCA Civ 1403 [49]; [2005] UKHL 19 [26]. See also J Randal Montgomery, 'Components of Refugee Adaptation' (1996) 30 *International Migration Review* 679, 697–8 (arguing that refugees have a natural inclination to develop ties to the community within which they reside and a human need to build a new life following severe trauma); Gregor Noll, *Rejected Asylum Seekers: The Problem of Return* (UNHCR 1999) 6 (suggesting that refugees may resist repatriation 'in order to preserve the value of their integrative effort'). See also John Fitzpatrick and Rafael Bonoan, 'Cessation (Article 1C)' in Erika Feller, Volker Türk and Frances Nicholson (eds), *Refugee Protection in International Law* (Cambridge University Press 2003) 492, 502 (enclosing a table of 'ceased circumstances' situations, ranging from Sudan in 1972 to Ethiopia in 1999).

the right to vote of its expatriates. As noted above, in post-conflict or peace-building contexts, international assistance is oftentimes provided. In contrast, it seems highly improbable that international organisations will assist individual CSR1951 refugees to exercise OCV in their states of asylum.[93]

An (unpublished) UNHCR policy paper suggests that, the organisation should refrain from facilitating or promoting large-scale refugee OCV unless elections are likely to be 'transformative'.[94] It sets four cumulative parameters for such engagement that are *unlikely* to be satisfied in a 'regular' CSR1951 refugee context: First, elections have to take place in post-conflict situations, and the security situation has to be generally stable. Second, the overall political and social environment should be generally considered conducive to free and fair elections. Third, the exercise of the right to vote should foster durable solutions. Fourth, refugees must be able to participate voluntarily in national elections and not be subjected to misrepresentation, intimidation, or manipulation.

In view of the above, international involvement in cases of CSR1951 refugees is highly improbable. OCV requires, first, direct engagement of CSR1951 refugees with officials of their state of origin, at least for registration and voting purposes. Second, their state of origin has to be both willing and able to conduct OCV in the respective state of asylum, and to permit their participation. Third, the state of asylum must agree to facilitate or, at the very least, permit OCV procedures on its territory as well as, arguably, election-related activities. When the states of origin are persecutory, none of these conditions are likely to be fulfilled; when fear of persecution emanates from non-state actors, it is highly improbable that all three cumulative conditions can be satisfied.

---

[93] Long (n 63) 7.

[94] *The Participation of Refugees in Elections of their Country of Nationality and the Role of UNHCR* (UNHCR, Geneva 2010) (on file with author) 2. For instance, in 2005, UNHCR was considering whether to assist OCV of Iraqi CFMs, notwithstanding its assessment at the time that conditions in Iraq were not conducive to return, as the authorities were not yet able to protect citizens from violent attacks, and as basic services needed for a secure and stable existence could not be guaranteed. 'Iraqi election enthusiasm reflected among refugee Diaspora' (16 December 2005), www.unhcr.org/43a2e9fe4.html. The Iraqi Election Commission requested assistance from UNHCR in 2010 regarding OCV of Iraqis living in states neighbouring Iraq (Jordan, Lebanon, Syria and Egypt). The CFMs were divided on whether to participate, citing sectarian violence as the greatest threat if they return. Wafa Amr, 'Refugees Watch Iraqi Elections with Doubts and Hopes' (1 March 2010), www.unhcr.org/print/4b8bcfb36.html.

b   Well-Founded Fear of a Persecutory Regime

OCV procedures may require citizens to present themselves at embassies or consulates in order to register and vote. CSR1951 refugees whose well-founded fear of persecution stems from the actions of a predatory regime may wish to refrain from engaging with officials of their states of origin.[95] Indeed, Article 25 of CSR1951 pronounces that the state of asylum must provide administrative assistance to CSR1951 refugees that would normally be provided by their state of origin.[96] A persecutory regime may not even necessarily have diplomatic relations with the state of asylum; however, even if there OCV procedures are in place in the state of asylum, a persecutory regime is unlikely to consider itself as such, and may not permit CSR1951 refugees (whom *it* may view as criminals[97]) to participate in such elections.[98]

Article 2 of CSR1951 requires that refugees in a state of asylum 'conform to its laws and regulations as well as to measures taken for the maintenance of public order'. Hence, OCV of CSR1951 refugees requires both *de jure* and *de facto* consent of the state of asylum. When a state grants asylum to CSR1951 refugees based on their well-founded fear of persecution stemming from their state of origin, the state of asylum may object to official engagement between the refugee and their persecutory regime, just as it would refuse to accept an attempt by the latter state to exercise protection abroad on behalf of its refugee-national.[99]

c   Well-Founded Fear of Persecution Emanating from Non-state Actors

It was noted in Chapter 1 that, a well-founded fear of persecution may stem from the actions of non-state actors, where the state of origin fails to comply with its obligation to establish and operate a system of effective protection against persecution. In such circumstances, CSR1951 refugees may not fear engagement *as such* with officials of their state of origin;

---

[95] Ruma Mandal, *Political Rights of Refugees* (UNHCR 2003) 19–20.

[96] Ad Hoc Committee on Refugees and Stateless Persons, *Draft Report of the Ad Hoc Committee on Statelessness and Related Problems* (15 February 1950) annex II.

[97] Cf. *Melnychenko* (n 33) (regarding the treatment of the applicant by the Ukrainian authorities).

[98] Voting from abroad (n 6) ch 1.

[99] See Chapter 7; while states of asylum are required to issue CTDs to CSR1951 refugees, they may limit their validity so that refugees are prohibited from travelling to their state of origin.

indeed, the authorities may even be sympathetic to their cause. Nonetheless, UNHCR views with suspicion engagement of CSR1951 refugees with officials of their state of origin, especially with regard to the issuance of official documentation such as national passports.[100]

Drawing on instances of applications for national passports or renewal thereof as creating a presumption that re-availing of protection is intended, Goodwin-Gill and McAdam assert that, for the purposes of re-availing of protection, the CSR1951 refugee must not only act voluntarily, but must also intend to and actually obtain protection so as to indicate the establishment of normal relations with the authorities of the state of origin.[101]

CSR1951 refugees may fear that their state of asylum will consider their (potentially continuous) voluntary engagement with officials of their state of origin concerning OCV *qua expatriates* to be indicative of their willingness to accept the protection of their state of origin and of the ability of that state to provide adequate protection. A state of asylum may then invoke the Article 1C(1) cessation clause, which stipulates that if a CSR1951 refugee has 'voluntarily re-availed himself of the protection of the country of his nationality' she no longer requires international protection. Hathaway contends that, once a state of asylum determines that protection in the state of origin is viable, it is entitled to withdraw CSR1951 refugee status, as CSR1951 does not *require* that asylum be granted as permanent admission to a new political community.[102]

Grace and Mooney argue that 'the act of refugees voting in their home state's elections, whether in person or by absentee ballot should never be taken to signal that refugees and asylum seekers no longer require international protection'.[103] However, in reality, these acts *are* likely to be

---

[100] For instance, UNHCR advises that, once recognised, a CSR1951 refugee should not normally retain her national passport, and that if a refugee applies for and obtains a national passport or its renewal, it will (in the absence of evidence to the contrary) be presumed that she intends to avail herself of the protection of her state of nationality. UNHCR, *Handbook and Guidelines on Procedures and Criteria for Determining Refugee Status under the 1951 Convention and the 1967 Protocol Relating to the Status of Refugees* (reissued 2011) [49–50]. Notably, however, it is ordinary practice for expatriates to identify themselves using their national passports when residing abroad. See also Rosa Da Costa, *Rights of Refugees in the Context of Integration* (UNHCR 2006) 131.

[101] Guy S Goodwin-Gill and Jane McAdam, *The Refugee in International Law* (3rd edn Oxford University Press 2007) 136.

[102] James C Hathaway, 'The Meaning of Repatriation' (1997) 9(4) *International Journal of Refugee Law* 551, 551. See also Chapter 8 (regarding the distinction between naturalisation and CSR1951 refugee status).

[103] Grace and Mooney (n 75) 114.

considered as such a signal by states of asylum; moreover, it may not always be unreasonable to assume that, if a state of origin is able to conduct OCV procedures and to enable effective participation of CSR1951 refugees therein, it is also able to provide them adequate protection.

E   Concluding Remarks

Recent developments in international practice and jurisprudence suggest a trajectory towards enhancing eligibility of expatriates to vote in elections of their state of citizenship; in tandem, OCV procedures are increasingly made available, notwithstanding the fact that most expatriates are able to exercise the right to return to their state of citizenship. In post-conflict or peace-building transitional elections, internationally supported concerted efforts may be made to enhance participation of CFMs with a view to their imminent or forthcoming repatriation. In contrast, recognised CSR1951 refugees are both electorally excluded *and* unable (due to their well-founded fear of persecution) to exercise their internationally recognised right to return to their state of origin.

Thus, the analysis above suggests that the strength of normative claims of CSR1951 refugees to have access to OCV is met with a political reality in which their disenfranchisement is highly likely. CSR1951 refugees are harmed in a manner which repudiates their claim to political membership.[104] They are both effectively and symbolically, territorially and extra-territorially, shunned from the political community of their state of origin. Their vulnerability is heightened by the fact that the length of their stay in the state of asylum is indeterminate, and their repatriation is thus neither imminent nor necessarily forthcoming.

Moreover, both CSR1951 and the Migrant Workers Convention impose obligations on host states to guarantee rights of non-citizens residing in their state; the state's 'good faith' compliance is expected.[105] However, as Chapter 7 demonstrates, while migrant workers and their families can, in principle, avail themselves of the assistance and protection of their state of origin, CSR1951 refugees do not enjoy the protection abroad of their state of origin; thus, when they are ill-treated in their state of asylum, they are left without effective protection.

---

[104] Matthew E Price, *Rethinking Asylum: History, Purpose and Limits* (Cambridge University Press 2009) 70.

[105] 'Good faith' is 'one of the basic principles governing the creation and performance of legal obligations whatever their source'. See e.g. Nuclear tests case (*Australia v France*) 1974 ICJ Rep 253, 268 [46] cited in Goodwin-Gill and McAdam (n 101) 456.

In view of the above predicament and of the fact that, under CSR1951, material, administrative, and symbolic obligations are undertaken by states of *asylum*, it is argued in Chapter 8 that states of asylum should mitigate the 'protection gap' of CSR1951 refugees, *inter alia*, by enfranchising them in their elections.

7

Protecting Recognised CSR1951 Refugees outside
Their States of Asylum

A   Introduction

In a world of sovereign states, when travelling abroad, every person needs a state to play the role of 'guardian angel',[1] that is to have a state to which they can turn for protection and assistance in their dealings with other states. This chapter highlights the predicament of persons recognised as CSR1951 refugees[2] when they travel *outside* their state of asylum.

Weis famously depicted CSR1951 refugees as 'a vessel on the open sea ... not sailing under any flag'[3] and as 'internationally unprotected persons'.[4] UNHCR considers them to be persons 'in need of international protection'.[5] Indeed, according to CSR1951 (as Chapter 2 illustrated)

---

[1] Stephen Legomsky, 'Why Citizenship' (1994) 35 *Virginia Journal of International Law* 279, 300.

[2] CSR1951 Art 1A(2).

[3] Paul Weis, 'The International Protection of Refugees' (1954) 48 *American Journal of International Law* 193, 193. See Recommendation CM/Rec (2009) 13 of the Committee of Ministers to Member States (MS) on the Nationality of Children, Principle 7, https://wcd.coe.int/ViewDoc.jsp?id=1563529 (defining persons as *de facto* stateless if they possess solely the nationality of the state which they have left while they are recognised by their state of habitual residence as *de jure* refugees). See also Hugh Massey, *UNHCR and De Facto Statelessness* (UNHCR April 2010) 40 (contending that, generally, non-enjoyment of rights attached to nationality does not in of itself constitute *de facto* statelessness, the only exception being the non-enjoyment of diplomatic protection and consular assistance of the state of nationality in relation to other states).

[4] Paul Weis, 'Human Rights and Refugees' (1971) 1 *Israel Yearbook on Human Rights* 35, 35; Paul Weis, *Nationality and Statelessness in International Law* (2nd edn Sijthoff and Noordhoof 1979) 164 (advocating the use of the term 'unprotected persons' in lieu of *de facto* stateless). In an oft-quoted statement, the General Claims Commission held in *Dickson Car Wheel Company v United Mexican States*, 4 RIAA 669, 678 (July 1931) that '[a] state ... does not commit an international delinquency in inflicting an injury upon an individual lacking nationality, and consequently, no state is empowered to intervene or complain on his behalf either before or after the injury'. Notwithstanding its archaic nature, this statement illustrates a particular vulnerability of CSR1951 refugees which this chapter analyses.

[5] UNHCR, *Handbook on Procedures and Criteria for Determining Refugee Status under the 1951 Convention and the 1967 Protocol Relating to the Status of Refugees* (reissued December

when states of asylum recognise persons as CSR1951 refugees, they assume obligations towards them, acting *in loco civitatis*; CSR1951 refugees enjoy a 'bundle' of rights and entitlements in their states of asylum.

However, when recognised CSR1951 refugees travel outside their state of asylum, they are left effectively without protection. Their status entails *ipso facto* that, if they are ill-treated abroad, they cannot turn to representatives of their state of origin and request its diplomatic protection, nor can they expect to receive its consular assistance. Additionally, they do not enjoy the protection which their state of asylum offers its nationals abroad. It is submitted that a state of asylum ought to extend the scope of protection that it offers recognised CSR1951 refugees residing in its territory, and provide them diplomatic protection and consular assistance when they travel abroad as if they were its nationals.

Following a general exposition of diplomatic protection and consular assistance in Section B, the argument in this chapter is advanced in four steps. First, the advent of human rights treaties has not rendered protection of nationals abroad obsolete nor has the practice fallen into disuse. On the contrary, state protection abroad retains its pedigree and significance, as is illustrated by the ILC Draft Articles on Diplomatic Protection that were adopted by the General Assembly with a favourable view to their forthcoming codification in an international treaty;[6] by recent jurisprudence of the ICJ; and by frequent resort by states to consular assistance.

Second, while states previously enjoyed unfettered discretion regarding whether and when to protect their nationals abroad, recent developments

---

2011) [90]: '[a]s long as he [the person claiming refugee status] has no fear in relation to the state of his nationality, he can be expected to avail himself of that state's protection. He is not in need of international protection and is therefore not a refugee'.

[6] ILC Report, 58th session (2006) GAOR supp. no. 10, UN doc. A/61/10. See GA/Res/61/35, 4 December 2006, inviting governments 'to submit comments concerning the recommendation by the Commission to elaborate a convention on the basis of the articles' (ILC Articles). See also GA/Res/61/34, 4 December 2006, 'emphasising the importance of furthering the codification and progressive development of international law as a means of implementing the purposes and principles set forth in the Charter'. In its 59th session, the General Assembly adopted GA/Res/62/67, 6 December 2007 welcoming 'the conclusion of the work of the International Law Commission and its adoption of the Draft Articles [on diplomatic protection] and commentary on the topic' and commending 'the articles ... to the attention of governments' at [1] and [3], respectively. It further decided to include 'diplomatic protection' in its agenda for its 2010 session with a view to considering 'the question of a convention on diplomatic protection, or any other appropriate action, on the basis of the articles'. See also GA/Res/65/27, 6 December 2010 (the General Assembly deciding 'to further examine the question of a convention on diplomatic protection, or any other appropriate action').

in domestic jurisdictions as well as regional provisions (EU treaties) point to the potential emergence of a (qualified) duty to exercise protection or to justify its refusal; interventions by states on behalf of their nationals abroad are likely to become more prevalent, especially as states are increasingly expected to fulfil rights-protecting obligations extra-territorially.[7]

Third, CSR1951 mandates that states of asylum shall issue CTDs to refugees lawfully staying in their territory. While CTDs do not require states of asylum to provide protection abroad to CSR1951 refugees, they reflect partial recognition of the instrumental role of these states in facilitating safe refugee travel. Indeed, as was noted above, the absence of protection by their state of nationality is a constitutive element of CSR1951 refugee status. While nationals travelling abroad may turn to their state's consular officers for assistance, and (as noted above) perhaps even demand that their state come to their aid, recognised CSR1951 refugees cannot even approach the consulate of their state of nationality to request renewal of their passport, as engagement with consulate officials can trigger cessation or loss of refugee status; hence, CSR1951 refugees cannot reasonably expect to be assisted by a state which they have fled.

Fourth, the 'nationality of claims' requirement remains pivotal to the international law institution of diplomatic protection, and efforts to effectuate its general relaxation have thus far failed. As noted above, most travellers are able to receive such protection from representatives of their state of nationality; in contrast, when CSR1951 refugees travel outside their state of asylum, they are left effectively without protection. Thus, a protection-enhancing agenda has led the ILC to 'carve out' an exception to the 'nationality of claims' requirement, authorising states of asylum to provide protection abroad to their recognised refugees.[8] Chapter 8 analyses the contention that justifications for extending protection abroad to CSR1951 refugees by their states of asylum, notwithstanding nationality

---

[7] Regarding extraterritoriality, see e.g. Marko Milanović, *Extraterritorial Application of Human Rights Treaties: Law, Principles and Policy* (Oxford University Press 2011).

[8] ILC Draft Articles art 8(2). Notably, some refugees are *de jure stateless*: their vulnerability, both in international law and in domestic law, extends above and beyond their fear of persecution, and is generated first and foremost by their statelessness. The ILC Draft Articles purport to ameliorate their travel-related predicament by enunciating that '[a] State may exercise diplomatic protection in respect of a stateless person who, at the date of injury and at the date of the official presentation of the claim, is lawfully and habitually resident in that State'. Ibid art 8(1). The analysis focuses on the predicament of recognised CSR1951 refugees who *are* nationals of their state of origin, and who would be eligible for its protection abroad but for their fear of persecution.

requirements, apply *mutatis mutandis* to entitlements in their states of asylum.

B   Locating Protection of Nationals Abroad in General International Law

State protection abroad takes the form of diplomatic protection and consular assistance. As Section C demonstrates, these two forms of protection are often linked: a state whose nationals abroad are denied access to its consular assistance may wish to exercise its diplomatic protection in pursuit of a remedy.

Weis defined diplomatic protection as 'a right of the state accorded to it by customary international law to intervene on behalf of its nationals if their rights are violated by another state in order to obtain redress'.[9] The ILC Draft Articles, aiming to codify diplomatic protection in an international treaty, link it with the notion of state responsibility.[10] They define diplomatic protection as 'the invocation by a state through diplomatic action or other means of peaceful settlement of the responsibility of another state for an injury caused by an internationally wrongful act

---

[9] Paul Weis, *Nationality and Statelessness in International Law* (Stevens 1956) 35; Guy Leigh, 'Nationality and Diplomatic Protection' (1971) 20 *International and Comparative Law Quarterly* 453, 455. See, for example, Intergovernmental Committee on Refugees, *Memorandum: Statelessness and Some of Its Causes: An Outline* (UNRRA 1946) ch II: 'even where no specific (bilateral) treaties exist, a national residing abroad enjoys, according to general principles of international law, the protection of the consular and diplomatic representatives of his nationality'. Diplomatic protection has a contested history: it is associated with actions taken selectively by imperialist states in the 19th and early 20th centuries to protect their nationals who were engaged in commercial activities in developing states. John Dugard, 'Diplomatic Protection' in *Max Planck Encyclopaedia of Public International Law*, www.mpepil.com/subscriber_article?script=yes&id=/epil/entries/law-9780199231690-e1028&recno=1&searchType=Quick&query=diplomatic+protection++.

[10] Crawford points out that the articles on diplomatic protection were originally seen as belonging to the *study on state responsibility*. In 1996, the General Assembly identified diplomatic protection as a separate topic appropriate for codification and progressive development. James Crawford, 'The ILC Articles on Diplomatic Protection' (2006) 31 *South African Yearbook of International Law* 19, 20 (referring to GA/Res/51/160, supp no 1 [249], 19 December 1996). According to the Articles on Responsibility of States for Internationally Wrongful Acts, ILC Report, 53rd session (2001) GAOR supp no 10, UN Doc. A/56/10, 'every internationally wrongful act of a state entails the international responsibility of that state'. In turn, 'a state commits an internationally wrongful act when its conduct consists of an action or omission attributable to that state under international law which constitutes a breach of an international obligation of that state'. Ibid arts 1–2.

of that state to a natural or legal person that is a national of the former state'.[11]

Diplomatic protection has been commonly associated with the 'Vattelian fiction',[12] that 'whoever ill-treats a citizen *indirectly* injures the state which must protect that citizen'[13] (emphasis added). Notably, the ILC Draft Articles refrain from engaging directly with the debate surrounding the contemporary relevance of this 'fiction'.[14]

As noted above, alongside diplomatic protection, states also provide consular assistance to their nationals when they engage with foreign state authorities; such assistance is commonly required in criminal proceedings abroad and in emergency situations such as a natural disaster when search and rescue operations may be required. States of nationality also

---

[11] ILC Draft Articles art 1. The commentary notes that, in view of the customary distinction between primary and secondary rules, the Articles do not seek to define or describe the *content* of the internationally wrongful acts giving rise to the responsibility of the state for injury to an alien. Ibid [2]. Article 14 stipulates that 'local remedies' should be exhausted prior to exercising diplomatic protection, since international litigation tends to be costlier, complex and time-consuming, and since domestic courts may be better placed to appraise the facts and apply national law. Mohamed Bennouna, Special Rapporteur, *Preliminary Report on Diplomatic Protection*, ILC Report, 50th session, GA/CN.4/484 (4 February 1998) [16]; Antonio Cassese, *International Law* (2nd edn Oxford University Press 2005) 121.

[12] For general discussion, see Annemarieke Vermeer-Künzli, 'As If: The Legal Fiction in Diplomatic Protection' (2007) 18 *European Journal of International Law* 37.

[13] Emer De Vattel, *The Law of Nations or the Principles of Natural Law Applied to the Conduct and to the Affairs of Nations and Sovereigns* (1758) vol 3: Of War.

[14] The Permanent Court of International Justice (PCIJ) held in an oft-quoted judgment that '[i]t is an elementary principle of international law that a state is entitled to protect its subjects when injured by acts contrary to international law committed by another state from whom they have been unable to obtain satisfaction through the ordinary channels ... by taking up the case of one of its subjects and by resorting to diplomatic action or international judicial proceedings on his behalf, *a state is in reality asserting its own right*, the right to ensure, in the person of its subjects, respect for the rules of international law'. *Mavromartis Palestine Concessions* (1924) PCIJ Rep ser A, no 2 [10–12] (emphasis added). The *Mavromartis* ratio has triggered much critique; for instance, Vermeer-Künzli (n 12) 58 argues that the essence of the fiction is that a state *pretends* to claim its own right, while in reality it is espousing the right of its national. Indeed, it seems that when the state is claiming its own right, it is not required to resort to diplomatic protection, since a violation of a state's own substantive rights results in direct injury. See also *Advisory Opinion, Reparations for Injuries Suffered in the Service of the United Nations*, ICJ Rep 1949, 181, 184. The ILC suggests that the 'Vattelian fiction' was a means to an end at a time when the individual had no (primary) rights in the international legal order, whereas today an individual is the subject of many primary rules protecting him both at home and abroad. ILC Draft Articles commentary art 1 [3]. See Section C.

occasionally engage authorities of host states to ensure that their nationals receive proper treatment.

The customary right of states to provide consular assistance to their nationals abroad and the concomitant duty on host states to facilitate such protection were codified in Article 6 of the Vienna Convention on Consular Relations (VCCR).[15] This Convention lists 'protection in the receiving state of the interests of the sending state and of its nationals' as the first function of a consular mission,[16] alongside the issuance of passports and travel documents,[17] and representation of nationals who are unable to defend their own rights and interests before the courts and other authorities of the receiving state.[18] As the analysis in the following section demonstrates, a breach by a host state of its primary obligation to facilitate provision of consular assistance to aliens by their state of nationality may give rise to a remedial claim by the alien's state of nationality by way of diplomatic protection.[19]

C   The Pedigree of State Protection Abroad

1   The Advent of Human Rights Treaties and the Individual in International Law

In traditional international law, states alone were considered 'subjects' of international law; individuals who were ill-treated and sought a remedy had to persuade their state to exercise diplomatic protection on their

---

[15] (adopted 24 April 1963, entered into force 19 March 1967) 596 UNTS 261. The VCCR currently has 177 parties. See also Vienna Convention on Diplomatic Relations (adopted 18 April 1961, entered into force 24 April 1964) 500 UNTS 95 art 3(b) (stipulating that a diplomatic mission may protect 'in the receiving State the interests of the sending state and of its nationals within the limits permitted by international law'). This treaty has 190 parties.

[16] Ibid VCCR art 5(a). See also ILC Report, 13th Sess (1978) GAOR supp no 10 (A/4843), published in the Yearbook of the International Law Commission, vol ii pt ii 92, 96–97 [7] (noting that the function of safeguarding the interests of the sending state and of its nationals is the most important consular function).

[17] Ibid art 5(d).   [18] Ibid art 5(i).

[19] Eileen Denza, *Diplomatic Law: A Commentary on the Vienna Convention on Diplomatic Relations* (3rd edn Oxford University Press 2008) 33 (questioning whether a distinction can be easily drawn between diplomatic and consular functions). Cf. Annemarieke Künzli, 'Exercising Diplomatic Protection: The Fine Line between Litigation, Demarches and Consular Assistance' (2006) 66 ZaöRV 321, 335 (contending that the confusion arises because most diplomatic protection cases concern the deprivation of property or arrest, detention, imprisonment and trials of nationals. Künzli notes that when consular officers communicate with officials of the host state involved, their actions do *not* necessarily constitute diplomatic protection).

behalf.[20] Thus, Hersch Lauterpacht referred to diplomatic protection as one of the most important functions of the foreign service of the modern state.[21] Recent decades have seen the advent of human rights treaties recognising the prominence of the individual and establishing arrangements that enable individuals to bring claims against their state of nationality or against other states regarding their alleged maltreatment without having to obtain the assistance or prior consent of the former state.[22]

For instance, under the Optional Protocol to the ICCPR, individuals can submit written communications to the HRC regarding alleged violations of their ICCPR rights,[23] provided that the respondent state has recognised the committee's competence, and that local remedies have been exhausted.[24] Nonetheless, even when individuals are able to initiate such proceedings, remedies are limited, and are usually in the form of a declaratory statement or an observation; enforcement, when applicable, is quite challenging, especially considering the vulnerability of foreign nationals.[25] The HRC reports that very few communications are

---

[20] Rosalyn Higgins, *Problems and Process: International Law and how we use it* (Clarendon Press 1995) 49–50 (arguing that 'we have erected an intellectual prison of our own choosing and then declared it to be an unalterable constraint'; she refers instead to 'participants' in international legal decision-making processes). Cf. Riccardo Pisillo Mazzeschi, 'Impact on the Law of Diplomatic Protection' in Menno T Kamminga and Martin Scheinin (eds), *The Impact of Human Rights Law on General International Law* (Oxford University Press 2009) 211, 213 (offering to look instead at the identity of an addressee of single international norms or of the holder of single international rights or obligations. He notes that, while traditional international law was formally addressed only to states and other sovereign entities, contemporary international law is occasionally formally addressed also to individuals and directly regulates relationships between states and individuals).

[21] Hersch Lauterpacht, 'Allegiance, Diplomatic Protection, and Criminal Jurisdiction over Aliens' (1945–1947) 9 *Cambridge Law Journal* 330, 335. See also Edwin Borchard, *The Diplomatic Protection of Citizens Abroad* (Banks law publishing NYC 1922) v (contending that international law has authorised the state of which the individual is a citizen to vindicate his rights by diplomatic and other methods sanctioned by international law. This right of diplomatic protection constitutes, therefore, a limitation upon the territorial jurisdiction of the state in which the alien is present).

[22] See, for example, the ICCPR Preamble (recognising 'the inherent dignity and . . . equal and inalienable rights of all members of the human family [as] . . . the foundation of freedom, justice and peace in the world').

[23] (adopted 16 December 1966, entered into force 23 March 1976) 999 UNTS 302 arts 1–2.

[24] Individuals may also initiate proceedings concerning treaty-based rights violations before several regional courts: the Inter-American Court of Human Rights, the African Commission on Human and Peoples' Rights, and the European Court of Human Rights.

[25] Robert McCorquodale, 'The Individual and the International Legal System' in Malcolm Evans (ed), *International Law* (3rd edn Oxford University Press 2010) 284, 293–5; Higgins

submitted by asylum seekers or refugees; this may be due, *inter alia*, to the length of time for assessing applications and the inability to afford legal counsel which may not be provided for this purpose.[26]

Hence, notwithstanding the significant symbolic and practical contribution of human rights treaties to rights protection, state protection abroad remains an effective remedial rights-protecting measure for foreign nationals. Moreover, states are likely to treat a protection claim launched by another state more seriously than a complaint filed by a foreign national to a human rights monitoring body. In turn, as the case-law analysed below illustrates, states value their right to intervene on behalf of their nationals when they face criminal proceedings abroad, and appear to do so quite frequently.

It is asserted that, if the ultimate goal of diplomatic protection is protection of individuals against infringements of their rights, then it would be a setback to abandon it.[27] Consequently, diplomatic protection and human rights treaties mechanisms should be considered *complementary*.[28] Indeed, the ILC Draft Articles proclaim that '[t]he rights of states, natural persons, legal persons or other entities to resort under international law to actions or procedures other than diplomatic protection to secure redress for injury suffered as a result of an internationally wrongful act are not affected by the present draft'.[29]

(n 20) 51; Lea Brilmayer, 'From "Contract" to "Pledge": The Structure of International Human Rights Agreements' (2006) *British Yearbook of Human Rights* 163, 171 (arguing that a state's strongest reason to comply with such treaties is that the state agrees with the values that the treaty embodies; compliance is thus grounded in recognition of the underlying pre-existing norm as morally binding and not as reciprocal self-interest as per treaties that do not concern individual rights).

[26] Santhosh Persau, 'Protecting Refugees and Asylum-Seekers under the ICCPR' (UNHCR New Issues in Refugee Research No 132 November 2006) 4, quoting Michael O'Flaherty: *Human Rights and the UN: Practice Before the Treaty Bodies* (2nd edn Kluwer Law International 2002) 4 (suggesting that it takes the HRC an average of four years to issue a view on the merits). See also David Weissbrodt & Michael Divine 'Unequal Access to Human Rights: The Categories of Noncitizenship' (2015) 19(8) *Citizenship Studies* 870, 872 (noting that access to enforcement mechanisms may be hindered by fears that a complaint may cause adverse consequences worse than a violation of the right at issue, including revocation of a visa, and/or deportation).

[27] John Dugard, Special Rapporteur, *First Report on Diplomatic Protection*, A/CN.4/506 [22], [29].

[28] John Dugard, Special Rapporteur, *Seventh Report on Diplomatic Protection*, A/CN.4/567 [3].

[29] ILC Draft Articles art 16. Similarly, the ILC Articles on the Responsibility of States (n 10) art 33(2) pronounces that the obligations outlined are 'without prejudice to any

2   Protection Abroad and the Ill Treatment of Foreign Criminal Defendants

It was noted above that diplomatic protection may be invoked, *inter alia*, with regard to breaches of primary obligations of a party to the VCCR regarding access of foreign nationals to consular services of their state. The VCCR devotes particular attention to criminal proceedings: Article 36 thereof stipulates that '[t]he competent authorities of the receiving state shall, without delay, inform the consular post of the sending state if, within its consular district, a national of that state is arrested or committed to prison or to custody pending trial or is detained in any other manner'.[30] In turn, the detained foreign nationals have a *right* to communicate freely with their consulates.

Consular officers have a right to visit their nationals in prison, custody, or detention, to converse and correspond with them, and to arrange for their legal representation; however, if a detained or imprisoned individual does not wish to receive consular actions, consular officers are required to refrain from pursuance thereof.[31] The rationale behind the obligation of the host state is that, faced with proceedings in a foreign state, the state of nationality of the detainees may provide them valuable assistance and aim to ensure that their trial will be fair and that they will enjoy proper legal representation.

A state party to the VCCR may initiate proceedings against another state party for alleged breaches of its obligations if both states have acceded to the Optional Protocol to the VCCR concerning the Compulsory Settlement of Disputes.[32] In recent years, Paraguay, Germany, and Mexico have initiated proceedings before the ICJ against the US following alleged breaches of the VCCR. In all three cases, US authorities detained foreign nationals and subsequently failed to inform them of their right to

---

right arising from the international responsibility of a state which may accrue directly to any person or entity other than a state'.

[30]   VCCR art 36(1)(b).

[31]   Ibid art 36(1)(c). The Travaux Préparatoires suggest that the decision to confer individual rights elicited considerable debate and was thus made explicitly. Mark J Kadish, 'Article 36 of the Vienna Convention on Consular Relations: A Search for the Right to Consul' (1997) 18 *Michigan Journal of International Law* 565, 596.

[32]   (adopted 24 April 1963, entered into force 19 March 1967) 596 UNTS 487 art 1(2) (stating that '[d]isputes arising out of the interpretation or application of the Convention shall lie within the compulsory jurisdiction of the International Court of Justice and may accordingly be brought before the Court by an application made by any party to the dispute being a Party to the present Protocol').

consular assistance; they also failed to inform the respective consulates of the detention. All trials resulted in murder convictions and the imposition of the death penalty.

The first case concerned Angel Francisco Breard, a Paraguayan national who was sentenced to death in Virginia, and was executed on 14 April 1998, despite an interim order issued by the ICJ on 9 April 1998.[33] Following the issuance of an apology by the US, Paraguay withdrew its claim, and no merits judgment was rendered.[34]

The second case concerned two German nationals, Karl and Walter LaGrand, who were tried and convicted in Arizona. Following Karl's execution on 24 February 1999, Germany initiated proceedings on 2 March 1999 requesting a provisional measure ordering a stay of Walter's prospective execution, which the ICJ subsequently issued.[35] Walter was nevertheless executed, and Germany decided to pursue the case on its merits. It claimed to be legally acting both in its own right (demanding redress for the direct injury that it suffered by being denied an opportunity to provide consular assistance to its nationals) and on behalf of its nationals by way of diplomatic protection (demanding redress for the injury caused to them by the denial of access to consular assistance). Contrarily, the US claimed that the obligations were owed to Germany alone, not to the LaGrand brothers, since only parties held rights under the VCCR.[36]

Additionally, Germany argued that the right to receive information and to have access to the consulate of one's state of nationality are *human* rights of aliens, not just VCCR-based rights; its claim was based on Article 10 of the (non-binding) Declaration on the Human Rights of Individuals who are Not Nationals of the Country in Which They Live.[37] Notably, if the individual right to be notified and to have access to consular assistance has indeed acquired the status of a human right, its violation may call

---

[33] Breard *(Paraguay v US)* Order of 9 April 1998, ICJ Rep 1998, 266.

[34] The US Statement dated 3 November 1998 appears in John B Quigley, William J Aceves, and S Adele Shank, *The Law of Consular Access: A Documentary Guide* (Routledge 2010) 139–40.

[35] LaGrand *(Germany v US)* Order on Provisional Measures, ICJ Rep 1999, 9.

[36] LaGrand, Memorial of Germany, 16 September 1999 [7.01].

[37] GA/Res/40/144 art 10, 13 December 1985 (enunciating that '[a]ny alien [defined in art 1 as 'any individual who is not a national of the State in which he or she is present'] shall be free at any time to communicate with the consulate or diplomatic mission of the State of which he or she is a national or, in their absence, with the consulate or diplomatic mission of any other State entrusted with the protection of the interests of the State of which he or she is a national in the State where he or she resides').

into question criminal convictions that followed a procedurally flawed process.[38] Moreover, it could strengthen claims that states should be required (rather than just entitled) to provide consular assistance to their nationals.[39] The ICJ found the US in breach of its treaty obligations.[40] It accepted Germany's argument that Article 36 establishes individual treaty rights which may be invoked by the detainee's state.[41] However, it reserved judgment on whether the treaty right is a human right.[42]

The third case concerned fifty-one Mexican nationals awaiting execution in ten states of the US.[43] The Inter-American Court on Human Rights (IACtHR), in an advisory opinion requested by Mexico, opined that a detained foreign national has a fundamental human right that is recognised (rather than established) by the VCCR to be informed of the right to contact consular agents of his state of nationality.[44] The above treaty enunciates the state's right to assist its nationals through the consular officer's actions, and the correlative individual's right to contact the consular officer to obtain that assistance.[45] The court held that, fundamentally, the individual is the possessor of the right, and she may 'expressly' oppose intervention on her behalf.[46]

The IACtHR held that consular assistance can significantly affect the outcome of a criminal process;[47] 'notification of one's right to contact the consular agent of one's state will considerably enhance one's chances of defending oneself.'[48] The consul is in 'a unique position to offer information to the detainee about the legal system in which he is detained in comparison to his home legal system'.[49] Nonetheless, the IACtHR stopped

---

[38] Christina M Cerna, 'The Right to Consular Notification as a Human Right' (2008) 31 *Suffolk Transnational Law Review* 419, 442.

[39] See the discussion in Section D.

[40] LaGrand (*Germany v US*), Merits, Judgment of 27 June 2001, ICJ Rep 2001, 466.

[41] Ibid [76–77]. See also Mónica Feria-Tinta, 'Due Process and the Right to Life in the Context of the Vienna Convention on Consular Relations: Arguing the LaGrand Case' (2001) 12(2) *European Journal of International Law* 363, 364.

[42] Ibid. See also Joan Fitzpatrick, 'The Unreality of International Law in the US and the LaGrand Case' (2002) 27 *Yale Journal of International Law* 427, 429.

[43] Arizona, Arkansas, California, Florida, Illinois, Nevada, Ohio, Oklahoma, Oregon and Texas. See discussion in Annemarieke Vermeer-Künzli, 'Case Concerning Mexican Nationals' (2005) 18 *Leiden Journal of International Law* 49.

[44] *Advisory Opinion, The Right to Information on Consular Assistance in the Framework of the Guarantees of the Due Process of Law*, OC-16/99 of 1 October 1999 (1999) ser A no 16 [129].

[45] Ibid [80].   [46] Ibid [82–83].   [47] Ibid [27].   [48] Ibid [121].

[49] Linda J Springrose, 'Strangers in a Strange Land' (1999–2000) 14 *Georgetown Immigration Law Journal* 185, 195.

short of attaching obligations to the recognition of a human right to consular protection other than those explicitly noted in the VCCR.[50]

The advisory opinion was issued before the ICJ judgment in *LaGrand*, yet the international court made no reference to it. In 2003, Mexico initiated proceedings before the ICJ concerning its nationals, and asked the ICJ to declare that 'the right to consular notification under the VCCR is a human right'.[51]

The ICJ held that the US breached its VCCR obligations and ordered that the US provide 'by means of its own choosing, review and reconsideration of the convictions and sentences of the Mexican nationals'.[52] Recalling *LaGrand*, the Court ruled that Article 36 creates individual rights, and noted the 'interdependence of the rights of the individual and of the state'.[53] However, on the question of a *human* right to consular assistance, the ICJ held that 'neither the text nor the object and purpose of the Convention, nor any indication in the *Travaux*, support the conclusion that Mexico draws from its contention in that regard'.[54] On 8 July 2011, despite the ICJ ruling and pleas from the US government, the State of Texas executed Humberto Leal, one of the fifty-one Mexican nationals in *Avena*.[55]

Dissatisfaction with repeated violations of US obligations under the VCCR has led to the introduction in the US Senate of the Consular Notification Compliance Act of 2011, aiming to 'facilitate compliance with Article 36'.[56] The Senate Judiciary Committee held a hearing on

---

[50] Christina M Cerna, 'Impact on the Right to Consular Notification' in Menno T Kamminga and Martin Scheinin (eds), *The Impact of Human Rights Law on General International Law* (Oxford University Press 2009) 171, 185.

[51] Avena and Other Mexican Nationals (*Mexico v US*) Application of 9 January 2003 [281].

[52] Case concerning Avena and other Mexican Nationals (*Mexico v US*) Judgment of 31 March 2004, ICJ Rep 2004, 121 [153].

[53] Ibid [40]. In his separate opinion, Judge Sepulveda criticised this stipulation, suggesting that it introduces undesirable vagueness [21].

[54] Ibid [124]. In a subsequent case concerning a Guinean national who was expelled by the DRC following his imprisonment after residing there for 32 years, the ICJ held that the Congolese authorities breached their VCCR art 36 obligations by failing to inform Mr. Diallo upon his arrest of his right to consular assistance. The court's analysis centres on the financial ramifications of Mr. Diallo's expulsion. Case concerning Ahmadou Sadio Diallo (*Republic of Guinea v DRC*) Judgment of 30 November 2010, ICJ Rep 2010 [66].

[55] On 7 July 2011, the US Supreme Court denied a request for stay of execution in a five to four *per curiam* judgment; *Leal v Texas*, No 11–5001 (2011).

[56] http://leahy.senate.gov/imo/media/doc/BillText-ConsularNotificationComplianceAct .pdf.

the proposed bill on 27 July 2011, but it has not progressed since.[57] The primary impetus for proposing to incorporate the VCCR into US federal law was fear that, in view of repeated US treaty violations, other states may refuse to abide by their obligations under the VCCR with regard to US citizens.

John Bellinger, a former legal adviser to the US Secretary of State, asserted that the proposed bill could help protect US citizens who travel around the world and are arrested in foreign states, and suggested that the VCCR (and in particular Article 36(1)(b)) 'is one of the most important international treaties to which the U.S. is a party'.[58] Patrick Kennedy, a State Department representative and former Congressman, noted that 'in 2010 alone consular officers conducted more than 9,500 prison visits and assisted more than 3,500 Americans who were arrested abroad'; he submitted that 'consular services are extensive and indispensable'.[59]

On 10 August 2011, the Serbian government filed an *amicus curiae* brief in a case before the Court of Appeals of the US State of Nevada, seeking to stay the execution of Avram Nika, a Serbian national convicted of killing a man who had stopped to help him on a highway, on the grounds that the Serbian consulate was not informed of his arrest in 1994.[60] The Serbian government argued that, for a foreign national, the right to consular assistance, or at least the option of requesting such assistance, is vital to ensure due process and access to a fair trial.[61] The government maintained that its consulate could and would have monitored the legal team from the outset and advised, supplemented, or even replaced it as needed.[62]

It is asserted that the VCCR rights to access consular assistance (for individuals) and to provide it (for states) are frequently exercised; hence, they retain their practical and symbolic significance in the day-to-day dealings of consulates with their nationals. States are willing to invest resources and initiate international proceedings to defend their right to

---

[57] http://judiciary.senate.gov/hearings/testimony.cfm?id=3d9031b47812de2592c3baeba 62c686d&wit_id=3d9031b47812de2592c3baeba62c686d-0--1.

[58] Ibid.

[59] Ibid. Cf. *Human Rights and Democracy: The 2011 Foreign and Commonwealth Office Report* (April 2012) §vi: Human Rights for British Nationals Overseas (stating that '[s]upporting British nationals in difficulty around the world sits at the heart of FCO activity as one of the U.K. Government's three foreign policy priorities').

[60] *Nika v McDaniel, Warden and Masto, Attorney General of the State of Nevada*, case no CR94P2264, http://reprieve.org.uk/static/downloads/2011_08_10_PUB_Nika_Serbia_ Amicus_Brief.pdf.

[61] Ibid [12].   [62] Ibid [4].

offer consular assistance to their nationals and to seek redress for breaches of rights of their nationals. While the US was responsible for several violations of VCCR obligations, its breaches should not be interpreted as dismissal of the Convention's importance; rather, they can be attributed, in part, to jurisdictional questions under the US federal system;[63] indeed, the proposed Congressional legislation enjoys bipartisan support and is endorsed by the Obama administration.

While the ICJ did not follow the IACtHR in declaring the right to consular assistance as a *human* right, it nonetheless recognised its individual basis under the treaty; seeing that the VCCR has 173 state parties, such a determination carries great significance. As indicated above, the reluctance to label the right to consular assistance as a human right stems, in part, from the ramifications insofar as it may entail a concomitant duty on a national's state to provide such assistance; the next section addresses this question.

D   The Potential Emergence of a Qualified Duty to Protect Nationals Abroad

1   *The Traditional View in International Law and Its Discontents*

It is conventionally maintained that '[t]here is no duty incumbent upon a state to exercise its protection over its citizens abroad. The matter is in the discretion of every state and no citizen abroad has by *international* law a right to demand protection from his home state although he may have such a right by *municipal* law' (emphases added).[64]

The ICJ held in *Barcelona Traction* that 'a state may exercise diplomatic protection by whatever means and to whatever extent it sees fit... [s]hould the national... consider that their rights are not adequately protected, they have no remedy in international law'.[65] The ILC commentary affirmed that, in international law, a state has a right to exercise diplomatic protection on behalf of its nationals but is under no duty to do so.[66]

Section C suggested, following a rights-centred approach, that diplomatic protection may at times be the only effective means for a state to

---

[63] See, for instance, the US Supreme Court's decision in *Medellín v Texas*, 552 US 491 (2008) (concerning US compliance with the ICJ *Avena* judgment).

[64] Lassa Oppenheim and Hersch Lauterpacht, *International Law: A Treatise* (Longmans 1955) vol I, 686.

[65] ICJ Rep 1970, 3, 44 [78].   [66] ILC Draft Articles art 2 commentary [3].

protect rights of its nationals extra-territorially; hence, it may be suggested that, if a state is reasonably able to exercise protection, then it should be expected to do so in appropriate cases.[67] Indeed, the first draft published by the ILC Special Rapporteur posited that, following grave breaches of *ius cogens* norms, states of nationality should be *required* to exercise diplomatic protection upon their nationals' request, unless these nationals are able to bring their claim before a competent international court or tribunal, and unless the exercise of diplomatic protection would seriously endanger the overriding interest of the state and/or its people.[68]

However, the Rapporteur's proposal was critiqued as arguably too far-reaching.[69] The ILC Draft Articles include instead a 'soft' obligation: a recommendation that states should give 'due consideration' to the possibility of exercising diplomatic protection when significant injury has occurred, taking into account the views of the injured person 'wherever feasible'.[70] It thus appears that, at present, states are not required under international law to exercise diplomatic protection; following the ICJ's reluctance to define the right to receive consular assistance as a human right so as to require states to offer such assistance to their nationals, the ILC Draft Articles similarly opted for a cautious approach.

2 The Emergence of a Qualified Duty to Provide Protection Abroad?

Some domestic constitutions include provisions enunciating an individual right to protection abroad. For instance, Article 27(2) of the 2011 Hungarian Constitution provides that '[e]very Hungarian citizen has the

---

[67] Phoebe Okowa, 'Issues of Admissibility and the Law on International Responsibility' in Malcolm Evans (ed), *International Law* (3rd edn Oxford University Press 2010) 472, 484.

[68] Dugard First Report (n 27) art 4. See also John Dugard, 'Diplomatic Protection and Human Rights: The Draft Articles of the International Law Commission' (2005) 24 *Australian Yearbook of International Law* 75, 80.

[69] Dugard conceded that 'in all fairness it was probably too much to have expected the commission to approve art 4 *de lege ferenda* in the light of the scant evidence of state practice in its favour'. Ibid 83. In contrast, the proposal has also been criticised for being too restrictive, since breaches of *jus cogens* norms are considered breaches of *erga omnes* obligations which, according to the *Barcelona Traction* ratio, do not require the satisfaction of conditions that are necessary to trigger diplomatic protection.

[70] ILC Draft Articles art 19. See also Menno T Kamminga, 'Final Report on the Impact of International Human Rights Law on General International Law' in Menno T Kamminga and Martin Scheinin (eds), *The Impact of International Human Rights Law on General International Law* (Oxford University Press 2009) 1, 16.

right to enjoy the protection of Hungary while abroad'.[71] Concomitantly, in some common law jurisdictions, such as the UK and South Africa, that have not codified a right to protection abroad, the unfettered discretion that states traditionally enjoyed has been recently constrained.[72]

In the UK, applicants demanded that the government intervene on behalf of a British national held in Guantanamo Bay. The Court of Appeal held in *Abbassi* that, while the state is not under a duty to provide diplomatic protection, its discretion is not unlimited;[73] 'it must be a normal expectation of every citizen that if subjected abroad to a violation of a fundamental right, the British government will not simply wash their hands of the matter and abandon him to his fate'.[74] Nevertheless, while the citizen's request ought to be considered, the Foreign and Commonwealth Office retains discretion 'whether to make any representation in a particular case and if so in what form'.[75]

The South Africa Constitutional Court went somewhat farther in its *Kaunda* judgment.[76] The case concerned 69 South African citizens who were held in Zimbabwe and faced potential extradition to Equatorial Guinea where they were going to be charged with participation in an attempted coup against that state's government, and upon conviction were likely to be sentenced to death. Applicants demanded that the South African government take 'all reasonable and necessary steps' to 'seek the release and/or extradition of the applicants'.[77]

The Constitutional Court held that the application was premature, since the extradition to Equatorial Guinea has not yet taken place.[78] Nevertheless, the court maintained that, in principle, based on Section 3(2) of the South African Constitution (enunciating that all citizens 'are

---

[71] A similar provision appeared in art 69 of the previous Hungarian Constitution. Other Constitutions containing such provisions are those of Albania, Belarus, Bosnia and Herzegovina, Bulgaria, Cambodia, China, Croatia, Estonia, Georgia, Guyana, Italy, Kazakhstan, Lao People's Democratic Republic, Latvia, Lithuania, Poland, Portugal, Republic of Korea, Turkey, Ukraine and Vietnam. Dugard First Report (n 27) [80–86].

[72] See also the ECtHR judgment in *Case of Ilascu and others v Moldova and Russia* App no 48787/99 (Grand Chamber ECHR, 8 July 2004) [331] (holding that losing control over parts of its territory did not release Moldova from its obligation to use diplomatic means to secure the rights of its nationals against possible abuse by the Transdniestrian authorities).

[73] *Abbassi v Secretary of State for Foreign and Commonwealth Affairs* [2002] EWCA (Civ) 1598.

[74] Ibid [97].   [75] Ibid [98–99].

[76] *Kaunda v President of the Republic of South Africa*, CCT 23/04, 2004 (10) BCLR 1009 (CC) (S Afr).

[77] Ibid [1–4].   [78] Ibid [127].

equally entitled to the rights, privileges and benefits of citizenship') South African citizens may request that the government offer them protection against wrongful acts of a foreign state;[79] their request has to be considered and responded to appropriately,[80] even though decisions whether to offer protection and in what form are an aspect of foreign policy.[81]

Justice Ngcobo, concurring, stipulated that citizens have 'a right to request protection from the government ... in South Africa or abroad' when their human rights are violated or threatened;[82] while the government retains wide discretion, a request must be properly assessed and cannot be arbitrarily refused.[83] Moreover, it noted that states 'have not only a right but a *legal obligation* to protect their nationals abroad against an *egregious violation* of their human rights' (emphases added).[84]

Justices O'Regan and Mokgoro (dissenting with regard to the outcome of the case) similarly held that the government is constitutionally required 'to provide diplomatic protection to its citizens to prevent or repair egregious breaches of international law norms'.[85] Justice Sachs added that 'the government has a clear and unambiguous duty to do whatever is reasonably within its power to prevent South Africans abroad, however grave their alleged offences, from being subjected to torture, grossly unfair trials and capital punishment'.[86]

Thus, the UK and South African courts appear to have applied (to a different extent) a 'Wednesbury reasonableness'[87] test regarding the propriety of governmental responses to diplomatic protection requests. In South Africa, Justices Ngcobo, O'Regan, and Mokgoro held that South Africa was required to act to prevent or seek redress for egregious human rights violations against its nationals.

Notably, while both judgments acknowledged that a protection obligation cannot be derived (yet) from *international* law, they based the qualified duty to provide diplomatic protection or to justify its refusal

---

[79] Ibid [58].   [80] Ibid [67].   [81] Ibid [60–64].   [82] Ibid [185].
[83] Ibid [191–92].   [84] Ibid [169].   [85] Ibid [114–15].   [86] Ibid [275].
[87] *Associated Provincial Picture Houses v Wednesbury Corporation* [1947] 1 KB 223 (CA) ('It is true to say that, if a decision on a competent matter is so unreasonable that no reasonable authority could ever have come to it, then the courts can interfere'). Since the passage of the Human Rights Act 1998 c2, UK courts have been applying ECtHR tests in judicial review cases concerning ECHR rights (for instance, balancing or proportionality regarding arts 8–11 of the ECHR). See e.g. *R (Daly) v Secretary of State for the Home Department* [2001] 2 AC 532 (HL); *R (Huang) v Secretary of State for the Home Department* [2007] UKHL 11. Indeed, the contemporary relevance of 'Wednesbury reasonableness' in non-HRA JR cases has been questioned; see e.g. *R (Alconbury) v Secretary of State for the Environment, Transport and the Regions* [2003] 2 AC 295 (HL) (Lord Slynn).

on principles of citizenship theory, namely the legitimate expectations of citizens from their (democratic) state.[88]

3   Protection-Enhancing Regime for Citizens of the European Union

This section presents recent developments in the EU treaty regime that are designed to enhance the protection which EU citizens enjoy when they travel outside the EU. The 'Lisbon Treaty' stipulates that '[e]very citizen of the [European] Union shall, in the territory of a third state [that is, not an EU Member State] in which the Member State of which he or she is a national is not represented, be entitled to protection by the diplomatic or consular authorities of any Member State, on the same conditions as the nationals of that Member State'.[89]

The EU Charter of Fundamental Rights (CFR), which also came into force that day, includes an identical provision in a section entitled 'Diplomatic and Consular Protection'.[90] Notably, the CFR lists this entitlement alongside the right of EU citizens to vote in European Parliament elections and in local government elections taking place in a MS other than their EU state of nationality.[91] Implementation by MS of their treaty obligations is subject to judicial review by the Court of Justice of the European Union (CJEU) as well as by their national courts.[92]

---

[88] Cf. the Israeli Supreme Court judgment in HCJ 3992/04 *Mimon-Cohen v Minister of Foreign Affairs and others* (2004) PD 59 (1) 49 [22–23] (dismissing a petition for intervention on behalf of the petitioner, an Israeli citizen detained in Thailand on murder charges carrying the possible imposition of the death penalty. The Israeli court held that, in *international* law, Israel has full discretion whether to exercise its right to diplomatic protection, reserving the question whether, in *domestic* law, an individual has a right to protection that entails a corresponding duty to exercise such protection).

[89] Treaty on the Functioning of the European Union (adopted 13 December 2007, entered into force 1 December 2009) OJ C 83/47 (TFEU) art 23. The provision replaced The Treaty of Amsterdam Amending the Treaties Establishing the European Union, the Treaties Establishing the European Communities and Related Treaties (adopted 10 November 1997, entered into force 1 May 1999) OJ C 340 (TEC) art 20. TFEU art 20 establishes '[c]itizenship of the Union' to which 'every person holding the nationality of a Member State' is entitled. The provision clearly stipulates that 'citizenship of the Union shall be additional to and not replace national citizenship' (the provision replaces TEC art 17).

[90] Charter of Fundamental Rights of the European Union (adopted 7 December 2000, entered into force 1 December 2009) OJ C 364/01 art 46.

[91] Ibid arts 39, 40; TFEU art 22. Notably, 'Third Country Nationals' are generally entitled to most other rights under the Charter in line with principles of human rights treaties.

[92] TFEU art 23 includes an operative clause: 'Member States shall adopt the necessary provisions and start the international negotiations required to secure this protection'. The

A 'levelling down' interpretation could be applied to these provisions, namely that if a MS does *not* provide protection to its nationals abroad, then it would not be required to provide such protection to nationals of other MS. However, it is contended that the provisions assume that EU MS *will* provide protection to their own nationals;[93] the aim was to *expand* protection so that EU citizens will have an effective address to turn to wherever they travel globally.[94]

Indeed, the European Commission noted that more than thirty million EU citizens live in non-EU states, but only in three of these states (the US, China, and Russia) are all twenty-seven EU MS diplomatically

Council adopted Directive (EU) 2015/63 of 20 April 2015 on the coordination and cooperation measures to facilitate consular protection for unrepresented citizens of the Union in third countries (24 April 2015) OJ L 106/5. Art 2(1) thereof stipulates that 'Member States' embassies or consulates shall provide consular protection to unrepresented citizens [defined in art 4 as 'every citizen holding the nationality of a Member State which is not represented in a third country' on the same conditions as to their own nationals'. Art 9 stipulates that the consular assistance may include assistance in the following situations: arrest or detention; being a victim of crime; a serious accident or serious illness; death; relief and repatriation in case of an emergency; a need for emergency travel documents).

[93] Alessandro I Saliceti, 'The Protection of EU Citizens Abroad' (2011) 17(1) *European Public Law* 91, 100. *But compare* the judgment of the CJEU in C-650/13 *Delvigne* (request for a preliminary ruling from the Tribunal d'instance de Bordeaux (France) (6 October 2015). The case concerned the legality, under EU law, of the exclusion from voting in elections for the EU Parliament of a French national sentenced to 12 years' imprisonment for murder. Contrary to the position of the French, Spanish, and British governments that the CFR art 39 rights are reserved to EU citizens that reside in a Member State other than their Member State of nationality, thus providing only a right to *equal treatment,* the CJEU held [33] that 'citizenship of the Union, to which that right is linked, entails a status whose legal effects apply even when there is no cross-border element'. For discussion, see Reuven (Ruvi) Ziegler, 'The "Brexit" Referendum: We Need to Talk about the (General Election) Franchise', *UK Constitutional Law Blog* (7 October 2015). Elsewhere, the CJEU held that EU citizens cannot be deprived of their right to vote for the European Parliament if the national legislation which excludes them from the franchise fails a basic rationality test. C-300/04 *Eman and Sevinger v College van burgemeester en wethouders van Den Haag* [2006] ECR I-8055 (CJEU). According to a 2010 report, Five EU MS (Belgium, Cyprus, Malta, Romania and Sweden) also offer consular assistance to refugees. CARE, *Report on Consular and Diplomatic Protection: Legal Framework in the EU Member States* (2010) 619–22.

[94] EU citizenship is dependent on citizenship of an EU MS; in turn, MS retain full prerogative with regard to granting their nationality; being an EU citizen does *not* mean being a citizen of all MS. Consequently, *prima facie,* EU citizenship does not fulfil the 'nationality of claims' requirement. It is thus questionable whether non-EU states are required to respect these (internal) EU arrangements if and when an EU MS attempts to exercise protection on behalf of a national of another EU MS. Of course, non-EU states may accept a claim in accordance with provisions of bilateral or multilateral treaties between the protecting state or states and the third state or states against which protection is asserted.

represented.[95] More than 100 000 EU citizens were present in major crises areas (Libya, Egypt, and Bahrain after the uprisings; Japan and Haiti after the earthquakes), indicating EU citizens' need to have access to consular services abroad.[96]

The significance of the above provisions is threefold: First, the treaty provisions manifest the contemporary relevance of state protection abroad, in line with the domestic and international jurisprudence that was previously analysed. Second, the provisions create a judicially enforceable EU citizen's right to enjoy protection of consular and diplomatic authorities of other MS on a par with the protection that these MS provide their own nationals, though the provisions do not explicitly pronounce an individual right to protection abroad as such. Third, the provisions adopt a no-EU-citizen-left-behind agenda, and were promulgated with the declared aim of imbuing EU citizenship with substantive meaning for millions of EU citizens, and of potentially relaxing the 'traditional' nationality requirement.

Notwithstanding the ambiguity regarding the question whether the above provisions also concern the exercise of diplomatic protection on behalf of nationals of other MS and, if they do, whether EU citizenship satisfies the international law 'nationality of claims' requirement, these provisions form part of a cognisable trajectory towards expanding the individual right to receive protection when travelling abroad. As such, they call particular attention to the vulnerabilities of CSR1951 refugees: whereas the professed aim of the EU legal regime is that every EU citizen should enjoy effective protection wherever they travel, CSR1951 refugees to whom the analysis turns are in need of such protection wherever *they* travel.

E   CSR1951 Refugees as Persons in Need of International Protection

1   *Absence of Protection as a Constituent Element of CSR1951 Refugee Status*

Post–First World War international refugee law instruments were non-universal in scope; they addressed the quandaries of particular national

---

[95] European Commission, *EU Citizenship Report 2010: Dismantling the Obstacles to EU Citizens' Rights* (October 2010) 9, http://ec.europa.eu/justice/citizen/files/com_2010_603_en.pdf.

[96] Communication from the Commission, *Consular Protection for EU Citizens in Third Countries* (March 2011) 3, http://ec.europa.eu/justice/policies/citizenship/diplomatic/docs/communication_consular_protection.pdf.

groups, and were predicated on a juridical concept of protection aimed at rectifying breakdowns in the international legal order that were caused, *inter alia*, by denial by some states of diplomatic protection and consular assistance to their nationals abroad.[97] Thus, according to these instruments, state denial of protection for their nationals formed a constitutive part of refugee definitions.

For instance, a Russian refugee was defined as 'any person of Russian origin who does not enjoy or who no longer enjoys the protection of the Government of the USSR and who had not acquired another nationality', and an Armenian refugee was defined as 'any person of Armenian origin formerly a subject of the Ottoman empire who does not enjoy or who no longer enjoys the protection of the Government of the Turkish Republic and who had not acquired another nationality'.[98] The provisions of the 1938 Convention concerning Refugees Coming from Germany similarly applied to persons possessing or having possessed German nationality that are not proved to 'enjoy in law or in fact the protection of the German Government'.[99]

The scope of application of CSR1951, unlike that of its predecessors, is not restricted to those possessing a particular nationality.[100] Nevertheless,

---

[97] Jane McAdam, *Complementary Protection in International Refugee Law* (Oxford University Press 2007) 24.

[98] Arrangement with regard to the Issue of Certificates to Russian Refugees (5 July 1922) 13 LNTS 237 and Arrangement with regard to the Issue of Certificates to Armenian Refugees (31 May 1924) LN doc CL 72(a) 1924 respectively. See the later Arrangement concerning the Extension to Other Categories of Refugees of Certain Measures Taken in Favour of Russian and Armenian Refugees (30 June 1928) 89 LNTS 63. Similarly, see Arrangement with regard to 'Assyrian or Assyro-Chaldean and assimilated refugees' and 'Turkish refugees' (30 June 1928) 2006 LNTS 89 p 63; Convention with regard to 'Spanish refugees' (28 October 1933) 3663 LNTS 159 p 199.

[99] Convention Concerning the Status of Refugees Coming from Germany art 1 (10 February 1938) 192 LNTS 59. The Committee report noted that 'the fact that most of them [referring to the refugees coming from Germany] possess national passports is of no importance in view of the precarious nature of the documents in their possession and the fact that as a rule it is impossible for them to get their passports extended'. League of Nations, Committee of International Assistance to Refugees, Report by the Committee submitted to the League of Nations, C.2.M.2 1936 XII Geneva (3 January 1936). See also Protocol (14 September 1939) 4634 LNTS 198 p 141 (regarding Austrian refugees, victims of Nazi persecution).

[100] Notably, under CSR1951, states can restrict the convention's geographical application, and the convention includes a dateline (1 January 1951). However, parties to the New York Protocol relating to the Status of Refugees (adopted 31 January 1967, entered into force 13 December 1973) 666 UNTS 267 removed the geographic restriction and agreed to apply the substantive provisions of CSR1951 [arts 2 through 34] to recognised refugees as if the dateline in CSR1951 was omitted. There is almost a full overlap between parties to the 1967 protocol and parties to CSR1951, with Madagascar being only a party to CSR1951,

as noted above, the absence of protection abroad is similarly a constituent element of its refugee definition. To be recognised as a refugee, a person must be unable or, owing to fear of persecution for reasons of one (or more) of the five Convention grounds, unwilling to avail herself or himself of the *protection* of their state of nationality.[101] Persons possessing more than one nationality have to demonstrate that they lack the protection of each state.[102] Inability or unwillingness to enjoy the protection of the refugee's state of origin is a necessary (though not a sufficient) condition for CSR1951 refugee status.

Moreover, four of the six cessation clauses of CSR1951 refugee status concern the availability of protection: voluntary re-availing of the protection of the state of nationality;[103] acquisition of a new nationality (usually that of the state of asylum) and enjoyment of protection of that state;[104] voluntary re-establishment in the state of nationality;[105] and the occurrence of a fundamental change in circumstances so that refugees may no longer refuse to avail themselves of the protection of their state of nationality.[106]

The *Travaux* of CSR1951 indicate that *protection* in Article 1(A)(2) was used by the drafters as shorthand for protection abroad.[107] Domestic courts have adopted similar interpretations.[108] Grahl-Madsen argued that, even if a state of nationality wishes to 'protect' its refugee-nationals or act diplomatically on their behalf, it has lost its (otherwise internationally recognised) right to do so until such time as its refugee-nationals willingly repatriate, and that such intervention may be considered an

---

while Cape Verde, the USA and Venezuela are only parties to the 1967 Protocol. Notably, the Convention relating to the International Status of Refugees (28 October 1933) 159 LNTS 199 was the first attempt to create a comprehensive binding international legal framework for refugees, including a prohibition on expulsion and *refoulement*. This treaty had 14 parties.

[101] CSR1951 art 1A(2).   [102] Ibid.   [103] Ibid art 1C(1).

[104] Ibid art 1C(3).   [105] Ibid art 1C(4).   [106] Ibid art 1C(5).

[107] Antonio Fortin, 'The Meaning of Protection in the Refugee Definition' (2001) 12(4) *International Journal of Refugee Law* 548, 564; David Wilsner, 'Non-State Actors and the Definition of a Refugee in the United Kingdom: Protection, Accountability or Culpability?' (2003) 15(1) *International Journal of Refugee Law* 68, 108.

[108] *Minister for Immigration and Multicultural Affairs v Khawar* [2002] HCA 14 [72] (Gleeson CJ, McHugh and Gummow JJ) (Australia); *Minister for Immigration and Multicultural Affairs v Respondent S152/2003* [2004] HCA 18 [23] (Gleeson CJ) (Australia); *Canada (Attorney General) v Ward* [1993] 2 SCR 689, 724; *Horvath v Secretary of State for the Home Department* [2001] 1 AC 489, 495 (HL); *The Queen (Al Rawi and others) v Secretary of State for Foreign and Commonwealth Affairs and another* [2006] EWCA Civ 127 [28] (HL).

abuse of right.[109] Indeed, permitting officials to afford 'protection' to their refugee-nationals may subvert the foundation of the institution of (political) asylum.[110]

It is quite instructive to compare the arrangements under CSR1951 with those under the Migrant Workers Convention: Article 23 stipulates that '[m]igrant workers and members of their families shall have the right to have recourse to the protection and assistance of the consular or diplomatic authorities of their State of origin'.[111] Migrant workers are thus entitled to such protection. As noted in Chapter 6, Article 3(d) thereof stipulates that the Convention 'shall not apply to . . . *refugees* . . . unless such application is provided for in the relevant national legislation of, or international instruments in force for the state party concerned' (emphasis added).

Chapter 1 demonstrated that, in international law, the state's right to protect its nationals abroad is linked to the state's duty to readmit its nationals, should another state wish to deport them.[112] Hence, persons who avail themselves of the protection abroad of their state of nationality implicitly accept the risk that they would be considered 'deportable' to that state. Consequently, unwillingness of CSR1951 refugees to avail themselves of the protection abroad of their state of nationality need not necessarily be based on fear of being persecuted by that state's diplomatic or consulate staff but, rather, on fear of being subsequently subject to expulsion to their state of nationality where they have a well-founded fear of persecution.[113]

---

[109] Atle Grahl-Madsen, 'Protection of Refugees by Their Country of Origin' (1985–1986) 11 *Yale Journal of International Law* 362, 389–95. Notably, he contended that the granting of asylum or refugee status 'resembles acquisition of a new nationality'. Ibid 389. Cf. Niraj Nathwani, 'The Purpose of Asylum' (2000) 12 *International Journal of Refugee Law* 354, 358 (suggesting that the right to exercise diplomatic protection persists as long as a person remains a national, and if a refugee remains a national of the state of origin, that state may in theory exercise such protection). Nathwani asserts that the right of diplomatic protection is a privilege of the state under international law; refugees who do not enjoy diplomatic protection *de facto* share this fate with myriad of persons whose government chooses not to protect them for one reason or the other. Ibid 360.

[110] Luke Lee, *Consular Law and Practice* (Oxford University Press 1991) 353.

[111] (adopted 18 December 1990, entered into force 1 July 2003) 2220 UNTS 3.

[112] Richard Plender, *International Migration Law* (Revised 2nd edn, Nijhoff 1988) 468; Oppenheim and Lauterpacht (n 64) vol I 646.

[113] Fortin (n 107) 576. See e.g. *Case Regarding Cessation of Refugee Status*, VwGH No. 2001/01/0499, 15 May 2003 (Austrian High Administrative Court [*Verwaltungsgerichtshof*]) [6], www.unhcr.org/cgi-bin/texis/vtx/refworld/rwmain?docid=3f40c1584 (holding that '[T]he successful application for the issuance or extension of validity of a passport of the country of nationality can lead to a cessation of refugee status even when the

This book endorses the (prevailing) contemporary interpretations of the 'protection' element of the CSR1951 refugee definition which, in addition to the absence of state protection abroad, emphasise the pertinence of the state's failure to provide protection *in its territory* to victims or potential victims of persecution at the hands of the state or of non-state actors. Indeed, fear of persecution and lack of protection from persecution are often interrelated; the latter may create a presumption as to the likelihood of persecution and to the well-founded nature of the refugee's fear.[114] The Australian High Court held that '[a]n inability or unwillingness to seek diplomatic protection may be explained by a failure of internal protection, that is protection in the wider sense, or may be related to the possibility that seeking such protection could result in return to the place of persecution'.[115]

2 Travel Arrangements of CSR1951 Refugees: The Role of the State of Asylum

From an international law perspective, a fundamental purpose of travel documents is to provide the admitting state *prima facie* guarantee that the issuing state is prepared to readmit individuals should the admitting state choose to deport them.[116]

It was noted above that, CSR1951 refugees cannot approach the consular authorities of their state of nationality for the issuance or renewal of their passport or other travel documents issued by that state: if a CSR1951 refugee seeks and receives such protection, it may arguably trigger a CSR1951 cessation clause, in view of the stipulation in

danger of persecution remains in the country of origin and a return there is not envisaged ... where a recognised refugee insists on using a passport issued by the authorities of the country of nationality for purposes for which the Convention travel document would suffice or where a refugee wants to gain advantages bound to nationality by applying for the issuance of such a passport'). See also Refugee Protection Division, 3 August 2004 (Canada) (upholding cessation of refugee status of a Russian national, concluding that 'the fact that the Respondent went to government authorities to obtain official documents such as passports and driving permits, causes me to conclude that he has sought and received the protection of his state, and voluntarily re-established himself in Russia').

[114] Guy S Goodwin-Gill and Jane McAdam, *The Refugee in International Law* (3rd edn Oxford University Press 2007) 22–23. Fortin (n 107) 574 (noting that the query as to whether the absence of internal protection brings about well-founded fear of persecution is pertinent regarding persecution by *non-state* actors, whereas it would be awkward to describe the state's action as a breach of its 'protection' obligations when it engages in persecution).

[115] *S152/2003* (n 108) [19] (Gleeson CJ, Hayne and Heydon JJ).

[116] John Torpy, *The Invention of the Passport* (Cambridge University Press 2000) 162–63.

Article 1(C)(1)that 'this convention shall cease to apply to any person falling under the terms of section A if... [h]e has voluntarily re-availed himself of the protection of the country of his nationality'.[117]

Based on the assumption that CSR1951 refugees cannot or will not request administrative assistance from the authorities of their states of nationality, Articles 25(1) and 25(3) respectively stipulate that 'the Contracting States in whose territory he [the refugee] is residing shall arrange that such assistance be afforded to him by their own authorities or by an international authority' and that 'documents or certifications so delivered shall stand instead of the official instruments delivered to aliens or by or through their national authorities'.

To facilitate refugee travel, and in light of their inability to use their national passports even if they possess them, Article 28(1) *requires* states of asylum to issue CTDs to refugees who are lawfully staying in their territories 'unless compelling reasons of national security or public order otherwise require'.[118]

CTDs should guarantee refugees an unconditional right to re-enter the territory of the state of asylum just as if they were its passport holders,[119]

[117] Cf. Joan Fitzpatrick and Rafael Bonoan, 'Cessation of Refugee Status' in Volker Türk and Erika Feller (eds), *Refugee Protection in International Law* (Cambridge University Press 2003) 491, 525 (noting, with regard to refugees travelling through third states with a state of origin-issued passport, that an asylum state seeking to impose cessation of refugee status must still prove that the refugee in question intended to avail him or herself of national protection and that effective protection is in fact available from the State of origin... simple travel on the passport without assistance from the State of origin would not suffice to justify cessation). See also *Khawar* (n 108) [65] (McHugh and Gummow JJ) where the Australian High Court noted that 'obtaining administrative assistance from the consular authorities of the state of nationality such as renewing a passport may provide an indication that the person enjoys diplomatic protection the strict sense but is not necessarily incompatible with refugee status...'

[118] UNHCR notes that the terms 'compelling reasons', 'national security' and 'public order' should be interpreted and applied restrictively, and only concern grave and exceptional circumstances. See UNHCR, *Guide for Issuance Machine-Readable Convention Travel Documents for Refugees and Stateless Persons* (October 2012) [25], www.unhcr.org/refworld/pdfid/5081320d2.pdf. For a recent discussion of the scrutiny applied to the term 'compelling' in art 28, see *AZ v SSHD* [2015] EWHC 3695 (Admin). The issuance of travel documents to refugees has been an important function of post First World War instruments, and is most famously associated with 'Nansen certificates'; see 1933 Convention art 2. While various states have initially submitted reservations to art 28, the two remaining are Israel's and Zambia's. See reservations and declarations to the 1951 convention, www.unhcr.org/3d9abe177.pdf.

[119] CSR1951 art 28 sch [13]. Should a CSR1951 refugee lawfully take up residence in another state, the responsibility for issuing a new CTD shall be of the authorities of that state. Ibid [11].

and refugees are expected to use CTDs *instead* of passports of their states of nationality (if they possess them).[120] Pertinently, according to Article 12(3) of the ICCPR, mentioned in Chapter 2, CSR1951 refugees should enjoy the right to leave the state; refusal to issue them a CTD may infringe their right to freedom of movement. The CTD specimen does not even mention the refugee's nationality, nor does it determine or affect the national status of its holder.[121] Other parties are required to recognise CTDs as passport-equivalent.[122] States of asylum are required to make the CTD valid for the largest number of states possible, save in special or exceptional cases.[123] The exception, as noted by Jens Vedsted-Hansen, is the widespread practice of excluding the refugee's state of origin from the validity of CTDs.[124]

Thus, *de jure*, CSR1951 refugees are able to enjoy international freedom of movement on terms that are not appreciably different from those that govern the passport-based system of travel and that apply to nationals of their state of asylum.[125] However, pertinently for this chapter, the CSR1951 schedule stipulates that the issuance of CTDs 'does not in any way entitle the holder to the protection of diplomatic or consular

---

[120] See Handbook (n 5) [121] (noting that 'acquisition or renewal of a passport may raise questions about the refugee's continued need for international protection. Obtaining or renewing a passport will, in the absence of proof to the contrary [a passport does not always permit re-entry into the state origin], be presumed that he intended to avail himself of the protection of the country of his nationality').

[121] Ibid [15]; Grahl-Madsen (n 109) 391.

[122] Ibid [7]; Hélène Lambert, *Seeking Asylum: Comparative Law and Practice in Selected European Countries* (Nijhoff 1995) 163. See also Final Act of the United Nations Conference of Plenipotentiaries on the Status of Refugees and Stateless Persons, and Convention Relating to the Status of Refugees, Geneva, 2 to 25 July 1951, A/CONF.2/108/Rev.1 [iv]: Facilitation of refugee travel: 'The conference, considering that the issue and recognition of travel documents is necessary to facilitate the movement of refugees and in particular their resettlement . . . urges government which are parties to the Inter-Governmental agreement on refugee travel documents . . . to continue to issue or to recognise such travel documents and to extend the issue of such documents to refugees as defined in Article 1 of the 1951 Convention or to recognise the travel documents so issued to such persons until they have undertaken obligation under Article 28 of the said Convention'.

[123] CSR1951 art 28 sch [4].

[124] Jens Vedsted-Hansen, 'Article 28/Schedule' in Andreas Zimmerman (ed), *The 1951 Convention Relating to the Status of Refugees and Its 1951 Protocol: A Commentary* (Oxford University Press 2011) 1177, 1208 (noting that the Schedule does not stipulate that the travel document will lose its validity if the holder enters the territory of that state; however, such travel may result in *cessation of refugee status*). See also James C Hathaway, *Rights of Refugees under International Law* (Cambridge University Press 2005) 841–42.

[125] Hathaway (n 124) 874.

authorities of the state of issue and does not confer on these authorities a right of protection'.[126]

It can be argued that, while the drafters were conscious of the intuitive appeal of authorising states of asylum to exercise protection on behalf of CSR1951 refugees when they travel using travel documents that *these states* issued, they knowingly refrained from including an exception to the 'nationality of claims' requirement.

Hence, states of asylum assume a vital role in facilitating international travel of CSR1951 refugees, yet CSR1951 neither requires nor authorises them to provide protection to 'their' refugees when they travel abroad. Notably, however, states of asylum are not *precluded* by CSR1951 from providing such protection on other legal bases.[127]

F   The 'Nationality of Claims' Requirement: CSR1951 Refugees as a Special Case

1   The 'Nationality of Claims' Requirement in General International Law

It was noted above that, in general international law, following the ill treatment of a natural or legal person, a 'nationality of claims' requirement must be satisfied to render admissible a state's diplomatic protection claim.[128] The Permanent Court of International Justice (PCIJ) held in *Panevezys Saldutiskis Railways* that 'it is the bond of nationality between the state and the individual which alone confers upon the state the right of diplomatic protection ... where the injury was done to the national of some other state, no claim to which such injury may give rise falls within the scope of the diplomatic protection'.[129]

---

[126] CSR1951 sch [16].

[127] See e.g. Paul Weis, *The Refugee Convention 1951: The Travaux Analyses with a Commentary* (Cambridge University Press 1995) 267. The Council of Europe adopted the Protocol to the European Convention on Consular Functions Concerning the Protection of Refugees, 11 December 1967, CETS No 061A. The Protocol entitles the consular officer of the state in which a refugee is habitually residing to 'protect such a refugee and to defend his rights and interests in conformity with the Convention'. Ibid art 2(2). However, the Protocol and the Convention only entered into force on 9 June 2011, nearly 44 years from their inception, following the fifth ratification; the last state to ratify was Georgia, preceded by Norway, Greece, Portugal and Spain.

[128] Ian Brownlie, *Principles of Public International Law* (7th edn Oxford University Press 2008) 478.

[129] *Estonia v Lithuania*, (1939) PCIJ Rep, ser A/B no 76, 16 [65]. See also Interhandel (*Switzerland v USA*) Judgment of 21 March 1959, ICJ Rep 1959, 27. See also Edwin Borchard,

The ICJ arguably made the nationality requirement more stringent in its *Nottebohm* judgment. It held that 'nationality is a legal bond having as its basis a social fact of attachment, a genuine connection of existence, interests and sentiments, together with the existence of reciprocal rights and duties . . . nationality entitles a state to exercise protection vis-a-vis another state if it constitutes translation into juridical terms of the individual's connection with the state'.[130] According to the judgment, a respondent state may refuse to recognise a diplomatic protection claim should the claimant state fail to establish a 'genuine connection' with its national even if nationality is formally possessed.[131]

Application of the *Nottebohm* stipulation has been subject to scholarly critique.[132] The 'genuine connection' requirement cuts against a protection-enhancing approach by excluding from eligibility for diplomatic protection 'millions of persons who have drifted away from their state of nationality and made their lives in states whose nationality they never acquire';[133] also potentially excluded are 'others who have acquired nationality by birth, descent or operation of law of states with which they have a most tenuous connection'.[134]

Thus, it may be argued that the *Nottebohm* stipulation should be strictly interpreted so as to apply (only) in circumstances such as those similar to that case: after residing for decades in Guatemala, the respondent state, Mr Nottebohm has naturalised in Liechtenstein, the claimant state, shortly before the claim was filed, raising suspicion of artificiality. It is also noteworthy that the ICJ phrased the legal question rather narrowly:

'Basic Elements of Diplomatic Protection of Citizens Abroad' (1913) 7 *American Journal of International Law* 497, 515 (asserting that, due to the bond of citizenship, a state 'must watch over its citizens abroad').

[130] Nottebohm (*Lichtenstein v Guatemala*) Judgment of 6 April 1955, ICJ Rep 1955, 4, 22. See also Chittharanjan F Amerasinghe, *Diplomatic Protection* (Oxford University Press 2008) 91–92.

[131] See also United States, *Restatement (III) of Foreign Relations Law* (1987) §211 (noting that 'an individual has the nationality of a state that confers it, but other states need not accept that nationality when it is not based on a genuine link between the state and the individual'). The ICJ carefully limited its inquiry to the *international* effect of Nottebohm's nationality, preserving the state's discretion over nationality determinations for domestic law purposes. Peter Spiro, 'A New International Law of Citizenship' (2011) 105(4) *American Journal of International Law* 694, 705.

[132] See e.g. Robert Sloane, 'Breaking the Genuine Link: The Contemporary International Legal Regulation of Nationality' (2009) 50 *Harvard International Law Journal* 1, 3–4 (arguing that 'the genuine link theory . . . as a purported general norm of international law originates in a misreading of *Nottebohm*').

[133] Dugard First Report (n 27) [117].   [134] Ibid.

'whether the nationality conferred on Nottebohm can be relied upon by Lichtenstein against Guatemala'.[135]

The ICJ held in *Barcelona Traction* that there are some obligations that states owe to the international community as a whole (*erga omnes*) because they concern 'basic human rights'. In such cases, as all states may have a legal interest in protection regarding such violations, the nationality requirement is unnecessary. However, the ICJ clarified that *erga omnes* obligations 'are not of the same category' as 'obligations the performance of which is the subject of diplomatic protection'.[136] The judgment thus hints at the possibility of interventions by states other than states of nationality regarding violations of basic human rights, yet the contours of this exception are unclear. Hence, the *lex lata* nature of the nationality requirement as such was affirmed.[137]

2   The ILC Draft Articles and the Refugee Exception

The 'nationality of claims' requirement entails that, in principle, CSR1951 refugees can only receive diplomatic protection from their state of nationality. In turn, CSR1951 refugee status entails the *absence* of such protection (see Section E), and while CSR1951 sets arrangements for refugee travel abroad, the CTD as such does not entitle CSR1951 refugees to the protection abroad of their state of asylum.[138]

The ILC Draft Articles follow the general maxim that '[t]he state entitled to exercise diplomatic protection is the state of nationality'.[139] Notably, CSR1951 pronounces that '[a] refugee shall be accorded in . . . [matters pertaining to access to the courts] . . . in states other than that in which he has his habitual residence the treatment granted to a national of the country of his habitual residence'.[140] In *Al Rawi*, the UK Court of Appeal held, based on the general maxim above that, when Article 16 rights of

---

[135]   *Nottebohm* (n 130) 18. See also Sloane (n 132) 22.

[136]   *Barcelona Traction* (n 65) [33–34].

[137]   Leigh (n 9) 470 (advocating that diplomatic protection should be made independent of formal nationality, and that states should be allowed to bring claims on behalf of any individual effectively connected with them irrespective of whether the individual is also a national of the respective state in the formal sense).

[138]   Enrico Milano, 'Diplomatic Protection and Human Rights before the International Court of Justice: Refashioning Tradition?' (2005) 35 *Netherlands Yearbook International Law* 85, 100.

[139]   ILC Draft Articles art 3(1).   [140]   CSR1951 art 16(3).

CSR1951 refugees are violated abroad, they do not have resort to the diplomatic protection of their states of asylum.[141]

Nevertheless, the ILC Draft Articles 'carve out' an exception to the 'nationality of claims' maxim, authorising a state of asylum to exercise diplomatic protection 'in respect of a person who is recognised as a refugee by that state, in accordance with internationally accepted standards' provided that the person resides legally and habitually in its territory'.[142] The commentary considers the provision to be 'an exercise in progressive development of the law';[143] it emphasises the predicament of refugees who may lose their status by availing themselves of protection of their state of nationality.[144]

The provision sets a higher threshold for exercising diplomatic protection ('lawfully and habitually staying') than the threshold for issuance of travel documents set by CSR1951 ('lawfully staying').[145] Notwithstanding the undesirable ramifications of setting a higher threshold for protection

---

[141] The case concerned two foreign nationals (a Jordanian and a Libyan) recognised by the UK as CSR1951 refugees who were in possession of UK-issued CTDs. The claimants were held by the US in Guantanamo bay where they were, allegedly, denied access to fair court proceedings in contravention of CSR1951 art 16. UNHCR, acting as an intervener, argued that, as both the UK and the US are parties to the 1967 Protocol the UK is entitled to demand that the US fulfil its CSR1951 art 16 obligations in good faith and may invoke principles of state responsibility for alleged breaches of these obligations. UNHCR further argued that it is wrong to treat citizenship as a formal requirement for the exercise of diplomatic protection on behalf of a recognised refugee who requires protection in another State party to the Convention/Protocol. It further argued that, as UK CTD holders, the claimants had a right to return to the UK, which other state parties had to respect, and which the UK can and should protect through legal means. Guy S Goodwin-Gill, '*The Queen (Al Rawi and others) v Secretary of State for Foreign and Commonwealth Affairs* (UNHCR intervening)' (2008) 20(4) *International Journal of Refugee Law* 675; see also www.refworld.org/cgi-bin/texis/vtx/rwmain?docid=45c350974. The Court of Appeal refused to grant the sought relief. *The Queen (Al Rawi and others) v Secretary of State for Foreign and Commonwealth Affairs* [2006] EWCA Civ 1279. The judgment stipulated that, since the claimants were not British nationals, *lex lata* does not entitle the UK to exercise diplomatic protection [118]. The court further held that, if it were demonstrated that CSR1951 art 16 rights were violated (a determination which would require prior investigation into US detention practices and Federal law), the UK would not be able to demand release of the detained (and their consequent return to the UK), as such a demand would constitute an extension of a right of diplomatic protection: the relevant demand would be that the US fulfil its treaty obligations and treat the detainees properly [124–29].

[142] ILC Draft Articles art 8(2) and art 3(2) (stipulating that 'diplomatic protection may be exercised by a state in respect of a person that is not its national in accordance with draft article 8').

[143] ILC Draft Articles commentary art 8 [2].   [144] Ibid [6].   [145] CSR1951 art 28.

of CSR1951 refugees abroad,[146] it may be argued that, setting a similar threshold regarding enfranchisement of CSR1951 refugees in their states of asylum would not be unreasonable; indeed, most CSR1951 refugees become habitual residents of their states of asylum due to the protracted nature of their fear of persecution and would thus be eligible for protection (see discussion in Chapter 8).

The proposed provision attracted mixed reactions. The UK government noted the *lex ferenda* nature of the provision; it posited that, while the Crown will be prepared to make representations on behalf of refugees in exceptional cases, *stricto sensu* it would not be an exercise of diplomatic protection.[147] Other states have generally approved of the provision.[148] In the deliberations, concern was raised that authorising the exercise of diplomatic protection on behalf of refugees could be seen as a first step towards conferral of nationality of the state of asylum, and may therefore create a disincentive for states to grant CSR1951 refugee status.[149] Consequently, the commentary emphasises that the exercise of diplomatic protection should *not* be seen as giving rise to a legitimate expectation of conferment of nationality.[150] It further notes the discretionary nature of Article 8 which (it argues) follows *a fortiori* from the unfettered state discretion in deciding whether to exercise diplomatic protection.[151]

Moreover, Article 8(3) of the ILC Draft Articles qualifies the state of asylum's right to exercise diplomatic protection, stipulating that such protection cannot be exercised in respect of an injury caused by 'an

---

[146] Paula Escarameia, 'Professor Dugard as an Innovator in the World of the International Law Commission' (2007) 20 *Leiden Journal of International Law* 931, 933 (criticising the higher threshold set by the ILC by noting that refugees may desperately need the protection of their state of asylum prior to habitually residing in that state).

[147] Comments and Observations received from Governments, UN Doc A/CN.4/561/Add. 1, 3 April 2006.

[148] See, for example, a statement by the group of Nordic states. Austria and El Salvador expressed reservations about the fact that the arrangement is not strictly limited to CSR1951 refugees, and argued that an open meaning of the term 'refugee' means that the respondent state would have to rely on the definition of the term 'refugee' by the claimant state. Comments and observations received from Governments, UN doc. A/CN.4/561, 27 January 2006.

[149] ILC Report, 52nd session (2000), GAOR supp no 10 (A/55/10) 171.

[150] ILC Draft Articles commentary art 8 [12]. See also Marjorie Zieck, 'Codification of the Law of Diplomatic Protection: The First Eight Articles' (2001) 14 *Leiden Journal of International Law* 209, 232; CSR1951 schedule [15] concerning CTDs (discussed in Section E).

[151] ILC Draft Articles commentary art 8 [11]. The ILC follows *Barcelona Traction* (see Section D).

internationally wrongful act of the state of nationality of the refugee';[152] in such cases, diplomatic protection to CSR1951 refugees would be denied.[153] The commentary justifies the qualification on policy grounds;[154] it posits that refugees may have serious complaints about their treatment in their state of origin, and allowing diplomatic protection in such cases means 'open[ing] the floodgates for international litigation'.[155] The commentary further suggests that fear of demands for such action by refugees may deter states from accepting refugees.[156]

Article 8(3) thus exposes difficulties in developing the (traditional) law of diplomatic protection in an era when human rights are strongly avowed but unsatisfactorily protected.[157] Indeed, the fact that claims on behalf of refugees may arise from circumstances which caused their plight and which underlie their well-founded fear of being persecuted is a potent reason to *encourage* protection rather than restrict it.[158] Moreover, the claim that entitling states of asylum, at their discretion, to exercise diplomatic protection would deter such states from admitting refugees is unpersuasive in view of the many positive (and costly) obligations that these states have already undertaken (arguably, in good faith) under CSR1951 regarding recognised refugees residing in their territory.

Nonetheless, read in concert with Article 8(2), the forward-looking nature of Article 8(3) should be acknowledged. Recognised CSR1951 refugees who reside habitually in states of asylum may now be given protection abroad in circumstances arising from their post-asylum travels and interactions. In any event, as was noted in Section E, travel to their state of origin may be either prohibited by their state of asylum or take place on rare or infrequent occasions. Thus, in light of the general resilience of the nationality requirement, the protection-enhancing agenda of the ILC Draft Articles is laudable, even though it has opted for a rather cautious approach. Indeed, it is contended that the

---

[152] ILC Draft Articles art 8(3).

[153] CSR1951 refugees may still initiate proceedings before supra-national tribunals or the Human Rights Committee. However, as was noted in Section C, the remedies offered by international human rights treaty bodies are rather limited and are often ineffective.

[154] Cf. Luke Lee, 'The Right to Compensation: Refugees and States of Asylum' (1986) 80(3) *American Journal of International Law* 532, 560–64 (arguing that, based on principles of *state responsibility*, there are plausible grounds for holding a state of origin liable for compensation to its refugees-nationals for the harm caused to them and to their state of asylum, as well as to UNHCR, in appropriate cases, for expenses incurred by care and maintenance of refugees).

[155] ILC Draft Articles commentary art 8 [10].   [156] Ibid.   [157] Crawford (n 10) 36.

[158] James L Kateka, 'John Dugard's Contribution to the Topic of Diplomatic Protection' (2007) 20 *Leiden Journal of International Law* 921, 926–7.

rationales guiding the ILC Draft Articles are applicable, *mutatis mutandis*, to entitlements of CSR1951 refugees *in* their states of asylum.

G Concluding Remarks

International law has long recognised the pertinence and significance of protection of nationals abroad. The value of such protection lies not only in the actual instances of its exercise, but in its availability, in the power that lies behind it, and in the resulting respect and security that a national enjoys as a normal accompaniment of his stay abroad.[159] The customary right of a national to receive real-time consular assistance abroad, codified in the widely ratified VCCR, remains unparalleled in its effective contribution to facilitating international travel and overcoming vulnerabilities, especially in emergency situations and when legal aid is sought.

It is contended that the advent of human rights treaties and their tribunals or review bodies has not rendered obsolete the protection of nationals abroad: such instruments offer limited remedies and enforcement is often ineffective. Indeed, resort to proceedings before the ICJ concerning ill treatment of foreign nationals in the US criminal justice system indicates that protection abroad retains its pedigree in the eyes of both states and individuals.

This chapter argues that a rights-centred approach to protection abroad curtails traditionally unfettered state discretion as to whether and when to exercise such protection. The ILC Draft Articles follow the *Barcelona Traction* ratio by stipulating that, at present, in *international* law, states cannot be required to protect their nationals abroad; nevertheless, recent years have witnessed a rights-centred jurisprudence in domestic courts leading to the potential emergence of a qualified duty to give due consideration to requests for protection abroad or to provide justifications for refusal to provide such protection. Moreover, some domestic constitutions entitle citizens to protection abroad. In recent developments that signify the importance of protection abroad, EU treaties now enunciate a judicially enforceable right of EU citizens to enjoy the protection of consular and diplomatic authorities of other MS on a par with the level of protection these MS provide their citizens when they travel to a non-EU state.

It is contended that these developments reflect a growing acknowledgement that protection obligations may extend extra-territorially. The bond

---

[159] Lauterpacht (n 21) 335.

between citizens and their (democratic) state manifests itself, *inter alia*, in citizens confiding trust in their state's commitment[160] to make representations on their behalf when they travel abroad and are in need of assistance or redress; citizenship is thus imbued with an extra-territorial dimension.[161] As Hansen contends, claiming protection abroad is not an entitlement of which most people will ever need to avail themselves of, but rights are not defined by the probability that they will be needed.[162]

The (revived) prominence of protection abroad highlights the vulnerability of CSR1951 refugees whose 'bond of nationality' with their state of nationality is (temporarily) severed: their status entails *ipso facto* that they do *not* enjoy the protection of their state. As recognised CSR1951 refugees residing in an asylum state, they enjoy a 'bundle' of rights that they may exercise in that state, and are also entitled to state of asylum–issued CTD to facilitate their travel. However, when travelling outside their state of asylum using their CTD, they are unable to enjoy the protection that their state of asylum offers to its own nationals.

Indeed, the 'nationality of claims' requirement which stood at the heart of the institution of diplomatic protection at the time CSR1951 was drafted still does so today. However, sixty years later, the ILC decided to 'carve out' an exception to the nationality requirement, for refugee protection by their state of asylum. The ILC Draft Articles' *lex ferenda* stipulation authorising states of asylum to exercise diplomatic protection on behalf of recognised and habitually resident refugees acknowledges their predicament and transposes human rights considerations to the traditional diplomatic protection arena.[163]

---

[160] Kim Barry, 'Home and Away: The Construction of Citizenship in an Emigration Context' (2006) 81 *NYU Law Review* 11, 33 (arguing in relation to kidnappings of foreign workers in Iraq in the mid 2000s that, the willingness of certain emigration state governments to protect and defend their citizens abroad became a test of those states' commitment to their entire citizenry, residents and emigrants alike).

[161] Cf. Nicholas Barber, *The Constitutional State* (Oxford University Press 2011) 41 (contending that it is a constitutive rule of states that their primary purpose is the advancement of the well-being of their members).

[162] Randall Hansen, 'The Poverty of Postnationalism: Citizenship, Immigration, and the New Europe' (2009) 38(1) *Theory and Society* 1, 12.

[163] Cf. David Kennedy, *The Dark Sides of Virtue: Reassessing International Humanitarianism* (Princeton University Press 2004) 203 (asserting that diplomatic protection cannot be fully analogised with refugee protection, since the former primarily concerns reciprocal rights of sovereign states, and the fact that a national gets 'protected' is secondary). See also Thomas M Franck, *The Empowered Self: Law and Society in the Age of Individualism* (Oxford University Press 2001) 197 (sceptically noting that states rarely have an interest in private causes of their subjects, especially if by taking their cases they risk antagonising

A rights-centred approach to protection abroad entails that, by taking up the claim of its national, a state also serves a broader interest of ensuring that its citizens are accorded proper treatment in accordance with human rights standards, an interest that ought to be shared by other states as well.[164] The state of asylum that has issued the CTDs used by CSR1951 refugees is (and, indeed, should be) legitimately interested in the way they are treated abroad. The state of asylum is also the state that is most likely to enjoy the confidence and trust of its refugees.

It is contended in this chapter and, indeed, in the book as a whole that CSR1951 refugees are a special category of non-citizen residents: their predicament are also of a *political* nature, and are evident when they travel outside their state of asylum without effective state protection. While the ILC Draft Articles may have had to adopt a cautious approach to reach consensus, it is submitted that a stronger commitment to state protection abroad would be welcome. States should be generally expected to protect rights of their citizens upon request where and when they can reasonably do so, and equally they should extend protection to 'their' CSR1951 refugees *as if they were their nationals.*

Analogies can be drawn between the rights-centred approach of the ILC Draft Articles to protection abroad of CSR1951 refugees, manifested by the partial exception to the nationality requirement, and the analysis in this book of the scope of protection that recognised CSR1951 refugees ought to enjoy *in* their states of asylum. The vulnerability of CSR1951 refugees is manifested when they travel outside their state of asylum, and the ILC Draft Articles seek to ameliorate it, albeit partially, by explicitly authorising states of asylum to provide protection abroad to their recognised CSR1951 refugees. Nevertheless, it is *in* their state of asylum where the predicament of recognised CSR1951 refugees is most significant. It manifests itself in their exclusion from the political community of that state, while they remain estranged from the political community of their state of origin for an indeterminate and potentially protracted period. Chapter 8 addresses their possible enfranchisement in elections of their states of asylum.

---

fellow-sovereigns with whom they have mutually beneficial relations. Equally, states may resort to excessive recourse, making an individual's private claim a *cause célèbre* that is disproportionate to the inflicted wrong).

[164] Leigh (n 9) 456.

8

Enfranchisement of Recognised CSR1951 Refugees in Elections of Their States of Asylum

A Introduction

Ours is a global legal order where rights to permanent security of residence in a state and the right to return to it are (usually) citizenship-dependent;[1] where states are held responsible for protecting rights of their nationals at home,[2] and, to a considerably lesser, yet normatively and practically significant extent abroad;[3] and where the right to vote is claimed and increasingly exercised by expatriates[4] in light of its protective and expressive purposes.[5]

Nearly all recognised CSR1951 refugees[6] are excluded from voting in elections of their states of asylum qua non-citizen residents. It was argued in Chapter 2 that their electoral exclusion is not incompatible with conventional interpretations of international refugee law and international human rights law obligations undertaken by states of asylum. This chapter argues that enfranchisement of recognised CSR1951 refugees in elections of their states of asylum is normatively desirable.

Citizenship-based eligibility coupled with cumbersome naturalisation requirements result in electoral exclusion of non-citizen residents for potentially protracted periods. This book does not appraise naturalisation requirements *as such*;[7] nevertheless, several observations are in order.

First, it is contended, *contra* ethnic nationalists, that naturalisation should be generally accessible and reasonably attainable on a non-discriminatory basis.[8] A time-dependent right to acquire full membership

---

[1] See Chapter 1.   [2] See Chapter 2.   [3] See Chapter 7.   [4] See Chapter 6.
[5] See Chapter 3.   [6] CSR1951 art 1A(2).   [7] See Chapter 4.
[8] See e.g. Diane F Orentlicher, 'Citizenship and National Identity' in David Wippman (ed), *International Law and Ethnic Conflict* (Cornell University Press 1998) 296, 323 (contending that the democratic nature of a state of residence is fundamentally subverted by denying full citizenship to long-time residents). See also Dora Kostakopoulou, *The Future Governance of Citizenship* (Oxford University Press 2008) 6 (contending that 'long term residents are "outsiders" since they are permitted to enter the private realm of the state but are excluded

in the community where one establishes one's life by forming personal, social, and economic connections seems appropriate.[9] Second, while this book does not appraise the propriety of general naturalisation requirements (for instance, so-called citizenship tests), relaxation of such requirements will *ipso facto* facilitate naturalisation of non-citizen residents, including CSR1951 refugees. Third, it stands to reason that, should (more) states choose to adopt residence-based franchise in (all) their elections, CSR1951 refugees *qua* residents would be enfranchised.[10]

Nevertheless, the central claim of this book is that recognised CSR1951 refugees are a *special* category of resident non-citizens; they should be entitled to vote in elections of their states of asylum prior to naturalisation, even when non-citizen residents generally remain electorally excluded.

A pre-CSR1951 UN report noted that '[t]he refugee's disabilities arise from the fact that he neither possesses the ultimate possibility of returning to his own country, nor enjoys the protection of that country while away from it'.[11] In order for CSR1951 refugees to enjoy adequate state protection as long as they retain their refugee status, they should be entitled to rights that are (traditionally) considered *citizenship*-dependent.[12] Their state of asylum, acting *in loco civitatis*, is best placed to afford such rights to its recognised refugees.[13]

from the public realm'). Cf. David Miller, 'Democracy's Domain' (2009) *Philosophy and Public Affairs* 37(3) 219, 219–20 (applying the *coercion principle* to explain why states that deny citizenship to long-term immigrants who make their life in a new state are justifiably accused of violating democratic principles); David Miller, 'Immigrants, Nations, and Citizenship' (2008) 16(4) *Journal of Political Philosophy* 371, 375 (defining permanent residents as 'citizens in the making').

[9] See e.g. Joseph H Carens, *On Belonging* (Boston Review 2005), http://bostonreview.net/BR30.3/carens.php.

[10] Chapter 5.

[11] UNGA, *Refugees and Stateless Persons: Report of the Secretary General*, A/C.3/527 (26 October 1949) [20], www.unhcr.org/refworld/docid/3ae68beb10.html.

[12] See Patrick Weil, 'From Conditional to Secured and Sovereign: The New Strategic Link Between the Citizen and the Nation-State in a Globalised World' (2011) 9(3–4) *International Journal of Constitutional Law* 614, 622. Cf. Kiran Banerjee, 'Political Community of Fate or Postnational State? Tensions and Transformation in Contemporary German Citizenship' 13, http://ssrn.com/abstract=2019672 (describing the status of EU citizens who 'enjoy important political entitlements traditionally reserved to national citizens, including the right to local political participation, diplomatic and consular protection, and freedom of movement with regard to entering and exiting their state of residence').

[13] *Refugees and Stateless Persons* (n 11) [18] (noting that '[i]t is understood that the duty of protecting the refugees rests in the first instance upon the governments of countries in the territory of which the refugees are located'). Cf. James C Hathaway and Michelle Foster, *Law of Refugee Status* (2nd edn Cambridge University Press 2014) 21 (asserting that the rights . . . to be granted to persons who meet the definition . . . are directly related to the

Put differently, recognised CSR1951 refugees should enjoy full membership of the (political) community of their state of asylum for the indeterminate period during which they hold refugee status, so that, insofar as enfranchisement is concerned, they are treated by their state of asylum as if they were its citizens. Hence, states of asylum which retain citizenship-based eligibility[14] in some or all of[15] their elections should regard recognised CSR1951 refugees as if they were their citizens for voting eligibility purposes.[16]

Section B introduces the enfranchisement rationale; it is contended that enfranchisement of CSR1951 refugees is a desirable and achievable (political) remedy for the (political) predicament which forms a substantive part of the conceptual basis of their recognition. The analysis draws on the particular vulnerabilities of CSR1951 refugees, distinguishing them from other non-citizen residents.

Section C considers the expressive and protective significance of voting for individuals (Chapter 3) in the light of the particular predicament of CSR9151 refugees. It revisits the general arguments concerning citizenship models (Chapter 4) and the plausibility of citizenship voting qualifications (Chapter 5), emphasising how the subjection of CSR1951 refugees to unaccountable (to them, absent enfranchisement) power is compounded by the absence of available 'exit' options.

Section D asserts that recognition of CSR1951 refugees is an explicit acknowledgement by a state of asylum of their (political) predicament, and a principled commitment to act *in loco civitatis* to protect CSR1951 refugees as long as protection is required.[17] It is submitted that rationales underlying commitments to 'assimilation' (read: *integration*) are applicable to enfranchisement. While integration of refugees is a considerable

---

predicament of being outside one's country of origin . . . the alienage requirement ensures a match between the beneficiary class and the remedy provided by the Convention'.)

[14] *Compare* voting eligibility in New Zealand, considered in Section D.

[15] Some states extend voting rights to (some or all of their) non-citizen residents in local elections; see Chapter 2.

[16] Eligibility remains subject to individual competence; the appraisal thereof falls *outside the scope of the book*. Notably, as non-citizen residents, the comparator is the 'core electorate' (resident citizens). The core electorate concept is discussed in Ruvi Ziegler, 'Independence referendums and citizenship ab initio- a rejoinder' in Ruvi Ziegler, Jo Shaw, and Rainer Bauböck (eds), *Independence Referendums: Who Should Vote and Who Should be Offered Citizenship?* (Robert Schuman Centre for Advanced Studies 2014/90, EUI 2014) 59.

[17] See e.g. UNGA Declaration on Territorial Asylum, Preamble, GA/Res/2312 (XXII) 22 UN GAOR Supp (No 16) at 81, UN Doc A/6716 (1967) (noting that '[t]he grant of asylum by a State is a peaceful and humanitarian act and . . . as such it cannot be regarded as unfriendly by any other state').

challenge for states of asylum, enfranchisement may be a stepping stone on an integration path. Finally, it is conceded that CSR1951 refugees are likely to be drawn to or remain in rights-protecting states of asylum.[18]

B   The Enfranchisement Rationale

The predicament that CSR1951 refugees suffer is directly linked to their recognised status as persons in need of international protection. In the case of recognised CSR1951 refugees, the general vulnerabilities that non-citizens *qua non-citizens* suffer due to their physical alienage from the political community of their state of origin are compounded due to the circumstances that have led to their departure from their state of origin, and due to the *indeterminate* length of their stay in the state of asylum: neither open-ended nor with a specified endpoint.[19]

Chapter 1 highlighted that, absent exceptional circumstances, a state of asylum may not deport CSR1951 refugees. However, their security of residence is contingent on continuing to hold their refugee status. Article 1C of CSR1951 contains an *exhaustive* list of six clauses entailing cessation of CSR1951 refugee status. Of these, only Article 1C(3) is triggered by the state of asylum's actions: the provision stipulates that, if a CSR1951 refugee naturalises (usually by acquiring the nationality of her state of asylum), their refugee status would generally cease as CSR1951-based protection would no longer be required.[20]

---

[18] Cf. Matthew E Price, *Rethinking Asylum: History, Purpose and Limits* (Cambridge University Press 2009) 10 (asserting that public support for asylum has diminished due to a shift from a 'political' to a 'humanitarian' view of asylum).

[19] David Owen, 'Citizenship and the Marginalities of Migrants' (2013) 16(3) *Critical Review of International Social and Political Philosophy* 326, 331.

[20] CSR1951 art 1C(3): 'The Convention shall cease to apply to any person falling under the terms of Section A if ... [h]e has acquired a new nationality and enjoys the protection of the country of his new nationality'. It is possible, though considerably less likely, that CSR1951 refugees will take up citizenship of a third state and enjoy its effective protection, for instance through marriage. See UNHCR, *Handbook and Guidelines on Procedures and Criteria for Determining Refugee Status under the 1951 Convention and the 1967 Protocol Relating to the Status of Refugees* (reissued December 2011) [17] (stipulating that, to satisfy the conditions of art 1C(3), the new nationality must be effective, namely correspond to a genuine link between the individual and the state; and the refugee must be willing and able to avail herself of the protection of the government of her new nationality). Regarding refugee volition, see James C Hathaway and Michelle Foster, *Law of Refugee Status* (2nd edn Cambridge University Press 2014) 496–97 (citing delegates to the Conference of Plenipotentiaries who believed that it was not right to force a refugee to accept a new citizenship, yet suggesting that the provision does not expressly condition cessation on a voluntary act).

Crucially, *all* the other cessation clauses materialise as a result of occurrences that are beyond the control of the state of asylum. Three cessation clauses are triggered by the actions of *CSR1951 refugees* and require voluntariness, intent, and effective protection. According to Articles 1C(1) and 1C(2), respectively, refugees may re-avail themselves of the protection of their state of origin;[21] or they may re-acquire its nationality.[22] In both cases, it is assumed that the (political) ties between CSR1951 refugees and their state of origin have been mended. CSR1951 Refugees may voluntarily re-establish themselves in their state of origin, in which case they no longer suffer physical alienage therefrom.[23] In contradistinction, the Article 1C(5) and (6) cessation clauses concern changes in the state of origin that are of a fundamental, stable, and durable nature, and which indicate that CSR1951 refugees no longer require international protection.[24] Yet, neither CSR1951 refugees nor their states of asylum know *when* or, indeed, *whether* such changes in circumstances will occur. Refugee status is retained unless one or more of the above conditions is satisfied.[25]

---

[21] Ibid art 1C(1). See Handbook (n 20) [119] (stressing the need to show voluntariness, intent, and actual re-availment).

[22] Ibid art 1C(2). See Handbook (n 20) [126–28] (suggesting that nationality must be 'expressly or impliedly accepted' before cessation would be appropriate; nevertheless, if recognised refugees have full knowledge that their nationality will be restored automatically by their state of origin unless they opt out, they should signal their rejection; should a refugee decline an offer of nationality, the element of voluntary re-acquisition will be absent).

[23] Ibid art 1C(4). See e.g. Atle Grahl-Madsen, *The Status of Refugees in International Law* (Sijthoff 1966) 370 (noting that '[i]f he [the refugee] abandons his flight and goes home, it is only natural that he ceases to be considered a refugee'). Refugees may choose to return, risking persecution; and if their decision is made voluntarily, and reestablishment is durable, refugee status ceases.

[24] Ibid arts 1C(5), (6). These provisions have been traditionally invoked on a group basis, though textually individual determination is not precluded. See e.g. UNHCR EXCOM Conclusion No 69 'Cessation of Status' (9 October 1992) [a] (noting that '[s]tates must carefully assess the fundamental character of the changes in the country of nationality or origin, including the general human rights situation, as well as the particular cause of fear of persecution, in order to make sure in an objective and verifiable way that the situation which justified the granting of refugee status has ceased to exist'); and [b] (noting that 'an essential element in . . . assessment by states is the fundamental, stable, and durable character of the changes' and emphasising 'that the "ceased circumstances" cessation clauses shall not apply to refugees who continue to have a well-founded fear of persecution').

[25] See James C Hathaway, 'Why Refugee Law Still Matters' (2007) 8 *Melbourne Journal of International Law* 89, 96 (arguing that an erroneous insistence on an 'absolutist' linkage between refugee status and a right of *permanent* immigration raises the stakes for governments and harms asylum; refugee law requires that states of asylum receive refugees in dignity, but does not compel them to permanently redefine the nature of their own political community).

'The need to "respect a basic degree of stability for individual refugees"'[26] dictates that a 'refugee's status should not in principle be subject to frequent review to the detriment of his sense of security, which international protection is intended to provide'.[27]

As noted in Chapter 1, *citizens*, unlike recognised CSR1951 refugees, enjoy permanent security of residence in their state(s) of nationality.[28] It is an indispensable marker of belonging to a state;[29] it may even be argued that the expulsion of non-citizens is a manifestation of the privileged status of citizens.[30] The 'indefeasible right to remain... is what makes the status [of citizen] irreplaceable'.[31] Freedom from deportation enables

---

[26] Handbook (n 20) [135].

[27] UNHCR, *Summary Conclusions: Cessation of Refugee Status* (Lisbon Expert Roundtable 3–4 May 2001) [12].

[28] An explicit prohibition on expulsion of *nationals* can be found in e.g. Protocol IV to the Convention for the Protection of Human Rights and Fundamental Freedoms securing certain rights and freedoms other than those already included in the Convention and in the First Protocol thereto (adopted 16 September 1963, entered into force 2 May 1968) ETS No 046 art 3(1): 'No one shall be expelled, by means either of an individual or of a collective measure, from the territory of the State of which he is a national'. See Clarissa Rile Hayward, 'The Dark Side of Citizenship: Membership, Territory and the (Anti-) Democratic Polity' (2011) 9(1) *Issues in Legal Scholarship* (Article 5) 3 (drawing an analogy between the state and a club, and arguing that '[a] polity does not admit a resident alien as a member when it grants her some rights any more than a club admits a guest as a member when it allows her to use its facilities and enjoy its services. Guests would be present, and protected, and given (equal) access to club facilities, but at the pleasure of the officers and the members of the club').

[29] Indicatively, in its *Note on the Interpretation of Article 1E of the 1951 Convention Relating to the Status of Refugees* (UNHCR 2009) [13–15] UNHCR posits that, for the purposes of determining the applicability of the provision (discussed in Chapter 2), rights and obligations 'need not be identical in every respect to those enjoyed by nationals of the country in question' and that '[t]he status envisaged in Article 1E should normally only be temporary, followed by formal acquisition of the nationality of the country concerned'. Notably, however, it is posited that '[n]o difference is allowed as regards protection from forced removal. Persons to whom the application of Article 1E is considered must like nationals be protected against deportation and expulsion'.

[30] Bridget Anderson, Matthew J Gibney, and Emanuela Paoletti, 'Citizenship, Deportation and the Boundaries of Belonging' (2011) 15 *Citizenship Studies* 547, 548 (contending that 'the act of expulsion simultaneously rids the state of an unwanted individual and affirms the political community's idealised view of what membership should (or should not) mean'); Peter Marden, 'Mapping Territoriality' in David Graham and Nana Poku (eds), *Migration, Globalisation, and Human Security* (Routledge 2000) 47, 57 (asserting that the right to unqualified indefinite residence is a key attribute of nationality; conversely, vulnerability to exclusion or expulsion signifies non-belonging).

[31] Cristina M Rodriguez, 'Review of Peter J Spiro, *Beyond Citizenship: American Citizenship after Globalization*' (2009) 103 *American Journal of International* Law 180, 187. See also Cristina M Rodriguez, 'The Citizenship Paradox in a Transnational Age' (2008) 106 *Michigan Law Review* 1111, 1120–21.

citizens to pursue long-term projects, knowing that they may remain in the state.[32] Importantly, the justificatory bases for the non-deportability of CSR1951 refugees distinguishes them from other non-citizens including non-CSR1951 refugees stateless persons.

The cogency of human rights obligations that a state undertakes towards *all* persons within its jurisdiction is pertinently tested regarding CSR1951 refugees:[33] Recognised CSR1951 refugees cannot or will not return to their state of origin, and so cannot (regain) the full scope of rights protection in that state; hence, they have no effective 'exit' option from their state of asylum, but have to rely exclusively on that state's protection.

The *political* predicament of CSR1951 refugees is thus distinguishable from that of voluntary migrants (who may or may not be 'migrant workers').[34] It is also distinguishable from the predicament of 'stateless persons' *as such* which is first and foremost due to their lack of *de jure* nationality:[35] resolution of the statelessness predicament *requires* the acquisition of a nationality.[36] Moreover, stateless persons do not necessarily suffer physical alienage from their state of habitual residence:

---

[32] Dominic Abrams and Michael A Hogg, *Social Identity and Social Cognition* (Blackwell Publishing 1999) 266 (asserting that '[p]eople have a fundamental need to feel certain about their world and their place within it . . . and that [u]ncertainty is aversive because it is ultimately associated with reduced control over one's life').

[33] See Yaesmin Soysal, *The Limits of Citizenship* (University of Chicago 1994) 143 (suggesting that the notion of 'universal personhood' as a basis of membership resonates most clearly in the case of 'political refugees' whose status in the host polities rests exclusively on an appeal to human rights).

[34] Migrant Workers Convention art 2(1) defines a 'migrant worker' as 'a person who is to be engaged, is engaged or has been engaged in a remunerated activity in a State of which he or she is not a national'.

[35] As noted in the Introduction, the Convention Relating to the Status of Statelessness Persons (adopted 28 September 1954, entered into force 6 June 1960) 360 UNTS 117 art 1 defines a 'stateless person' as 'a person who is not considered as a national by any State under the operation of its law'. See also Preamble [3]: '[c]onsidering that only those stateless persons who are also refugees are covered by the Convention Relating to the Status of Refugees of 28 July 1951, and that there are many stateless persons who are not covered by that Convention'.

[36] See e.g. the Convention on Reduction of Statelessness, (adopted 30 August 1961, entered into force 13 December 1975) 989 UNTS 175 Preamble ('considering it desirable to reduce statelessness by international agreement'); see also European Convention on Nationality (ECN) (adopted 6 November 1997, entered into force 1 March 2000) ETS No 066 art 4 (stipulating under 'Principles' that (a) 'everyone has the right to a nationality' and (b) 'statelessness shall be avoided') and art 2(a) (defining nationality as 'the legal bond between an individual and a State').

oftentimes, they are stateless where they were born and have continuously resided.[37]

It was argued in Chapter 6 that states increasingly provide their expatriates access to OCV procedures. In contrast, CSR1951 refugees *qua* expatriates are highly unlikely to have access to OCV procedures, should their state of origin generally offer them to its nationals abroad, in light of the fact that they have left their state of origin involuntarily and despite the fact that they are stakeholders in its elections. Unlike OCV of voluntary expatriates or of CFMs in post-conflict elections, access of CSR1951 refugees to OCV procedures requires the (largely unattainable) cooperation of the CSR1951 refugee, the state of asylum, and the state of origin; genuine impediments are unavoidable.[38]

Chapter 7 demonstrated that, when travelling outside their state of asylum, CSR1951 refugees cannot turn to representatives of their state of origin and request its diplomatic protection in the event of ill treatment, nor can they expect to receive consular assistance therefrom. Consequently, CSR1951 refugees have no recourse to protection abroad should mistreatment occur. It was submitted that, alongside the existing requirement that states of asylum *shall* issue CTDs to recognised refugees which afford these refugees an unconditional right to return to the issuing state as if they were its nationals,[39] states of asylum should extend to their recognised refugees the same protection abroad that these states grant their own nationals when they travel abroad; and, indeed, that states ought to grant such protection to their nationals in suitable cases.

Atle Grahl-Madsen has characterised the absence of protection *outside* the state's territory as 'a symptom of a deep-rooted conflict between CSR1951 refugees and their states of origin that is based on a well-founded fear of persecution' and which inhibits them from returning.[40] Importantly, while state protection abroad and proper access to OCV procedures require the consent, cooperation, or acquiescence of another state, a commitment to enfranchise CSR1951 refugees is an *internal matter* for the

---

[37] Ruma Mandal, *Protection Mechanisms outside of the 1951 Convention ('Complementary Protection')* (Legal and Protection Policy Research Series PPLA/2005/02 June 2005) [33].

[38] Cf. Migrant Workers Convention art 41(1) guarantees migrant workers and members of their families 'the right to participate in public affairs of their State of origin and to vote and to be elected at elections' of their *state of origin*.

[39] CSR1951 art 28 and sch sec 13(1) ('[e]ach Contracting State undertakes that the holder of a travel document issued by it in accordance with Article 28 of this Convention shall be readmitted to its territory at any time during the period of its validity'). See also EUQD art 25.

[40] Status of Refugees (n 23) 98–100.

state of asylum.[41] Moreover, the case for extending protection is dependent on establishing the entitlement of nationals to such protection. In contrast, states of asylum may autonomously decide to entitle CSR1951 refugees to vote in their elections; while, as demonstrated in Chapter 2, human rights treaties do not require states to enfranchise non-citizens, states may choose to do so, exercising sovereignty.

It is therefore argued that, in the case of CSR1951 refugees, disaggregation of citizenship-dependent rights should be three-fold. First, when travelling abroad, they should enjoy unqualified readmission to their state of asylum. Contracting states to CSR1951 are already required to issue refugees CTDs that guarantee their readmission. Second, when CSR1951 refugees travel outside their state of asylum using their state of asylum–issued CTD *in lieu* of their passport, the state of asylum should afford them its protection abroad as if they were its nationals; in turn, nationals increasingly, though still not universally, have recourse to state protection abroad. The ILC Draft Articles on Diplomatic Protection endorse the above proposition. Third, the central claim of this book, namely that it is normatively desirable to enfranchise CSR1951 refugees in elections of their state of asylum, notwithstanding generally applicable citizenship-based eligibility criteria.

By enfranchising CSR1951 refugees, their state of asylum will be recognising that, for an indeterminate period, CSR1951 refugees have no other political community to return to or turn to for protection;[42] the state of asylum is best placed to 'step in' and let recognised CSR1951 refugees into its political space for such time as they are in need of its protection.

Advocates of *residence*-based voting eligibility (see Chapter 5) argue that it should be applied to all non-citizen residents, including voluntary migrants who have access to OCV procedures of their state of origin, enjoy its protection abroad, and are able to return to it at will.[43]

---

[41] See Chapter 5 (noting that, in general, participation in elections of institutions of two states does not violate equality principles, notwithstanding particular issues arising in the context of supra-national institutions like the EU).

[42] See Rainer Bauböck, 'The Rights and Duties of External Citizenship' (2009) 13(5) *Citizenship Studies* 475, 482 (submitting that '[t]he core of external citizenship is the right to return ... the return option is an important element in migrants' overall bundle of citizenship rights, no matter whether they are individually likely to choose it').

[43] Cf. Kostakopoulou (n 8) (advocating a *domicile*-based 'a-national citizenship'). She further notes that refugees 'do not acquire domicile unless they decide to settle in the host country for an indefinite period' whereas '[a] refugee ... who decides to remain in the host country even though he can return home could establish domicile'. Ibid 114. On her model, it is unclear *when* refugees would acquire electoral participation rights in their state of asylum.

Nevertheless, this book asserts that recognised CSR1951 refugees have *stronger* inclusion claims than other non-citizen residents[44] due to their 'civic limbo'.[45]

It ought to be emphasised, that extending citizenship-based rights to recognised CSR1951 refugees does not absolve states of asylum from their CSR1951 obligation to 'as far as possible facilitate the assimilation and naturalisation of refugees'.[46] A longer term view would acknowledge that CSR1951 refugee protection cannot isolate itself from its primary objective, namely the re-establishment of the refugee within a community:[47] the situation of CSR1951 refugees is 'abnormal and should not be regarded as permanent'.[48]

See, in contrast, Ulrich K Preuss, 'Migration – A Challenge to Modern Citizenship' (1998) 4(3) *Constellations* 307, 314 (arguing that membership in a political community requires deeper, more existential and emotional kind of commonness than common residence within the boundaries of a given territory).

[44] Bauböck (n 42) 477 (contending that, in the main, 'denizenship' and long-term external citizenship are two sides of the coin, and the normative framework through which migrants' claim to equal respect and concern should be assessed ought to involve both states of residence and states of origin. He suggests that we 'abandon not the norm of equal respect and concern for all citizens, but the notion that this demand is exclusively addressed to the government of a single country').

[45] Owen (n 19) 332.

[46] CSR1951 art 34. See also ECN art 6(4) (Acquisition of Nationality): '[E]ach state shall facilitate in its internal law the acquisition of its nationality for ... (g) ... recognised refugees lawfully and habitually resident on its territory'. The Explanatory Notes [52] postulate that 'state parties still retain their discretion to decide whether to grant their nationality to such applicants [recognised refugees]'. See also Council of Europe, Committee of Ministers, Recommendation R84 (21) on the Acquisition by Refugees of Nationality of the Host Country (14 November 1984) (reiterating that 'the acquisition of the nationality of the host country by refugees who wish to do so and by their children constitutes the most effective means of ensuring their integration in that country' and recommending that 'member states consider the fact of being a refugee as a favourable element for the purposes of the procedure for granting nationality ... for example by reducing the required period of residence'). The resolution recalled Resolution 70(2) on the Acquisition by Refugees of the Nationality of Their Country of Residence (26 January 1970) and Recommendation 564 of the Consultative Assembly of the Council of Europe (1969) [1(b)] (which invited member states to facilitate naturalisation 'by making every effort to remove or at least reduce, legal obstacles to naturalisation such as the minimum period of residence when it exceeds five years, the costs of naturalisation when it exceeds the financial possibilities of the majority of refugees, the length of time elapsing between the receipt of applications for naturalisation and their consideration, and the requirement that refugees should prove the loss of their former nationality').

[47] Guy S Goodwin-Gill, 'The Language of Protection' (1989) 1(1) *International Journal of Refugee Law* 1, 17.

[48] Atle Grahl-Madsen, *Commentary on the Refugee Convention 1951, Articles 2–11, 13–37* (Division of International Protection 1997) (1963) 247.

While UNHCR reiterates that 'voluntary repatriation, in safety and dignity, where and when feasible, remains the most preferred solution in the majority of refugee situations'[49] it could be argued that, in protracted situations, like other long-term residents, CSR1951 refugees may develop a strong attachment to their host community and wish to remain there.[50]

However, even when naturalisation eventually takes place, CSR1951 refugees will have remained excluded from electoral processes during the (protracted) period between recognition and naturalisation. Moreover, CSR1951 manifests a tension between, on the one hand, obligations undertaken by a state of asylum following recognition and, on the other, finding a durable long-term solution for refugees in one of three states: their state of origin, the state of asylum or through resettlement a third state.[51] The circumstances which give rise to CSR1951 refugee status may change *after* naturalisation has taken place[52] whereas citizenship is, in principle, a life-long status.[53]

---

[49] UNHCR EXCOM Conclusion No 104 (LVI) 'Local Integration' (7 October 2005) preamble.

[50] Jeff Crisp, 'No Solutions in Sight: The Problem of Protracted Refugee Situations in Africa' (2003) 22(4) *Refugee Survey Quarterly* 114, 143. See also Will Kymlicka and Wayne Norman, 'Citizenship in Diverse Societies: Issues, Contexts, Concepts' in Will Kymlicka and Wayne Norman (eds), *Citizenship in Diverse Societies* (Oxford University Press 2000) 1, 21. Cf. Joan Fitzpatrick, 'Cessation of Refugee Status and Withdrawal of Temporary Protection' (1999) 13 *Georgetown Immigration Law Journal 343*, 350 (suggesting that 'victims of severe past persecution may be traumatised by forced return to the scene of their suffering even if their persecutors have since been routed; conversely, many forced migrants feel such a strong attachment to their homes that they self-repatriate even before conditions are safe sparing the state of refuge the delicate task of deciding when to withdraw protection . . .').

[51] Cf. Nicholas Van Hear, 'Refugees in Diaspora: From Durable Solutions to Transnational Relations' (2006) 23(1) *Refuge* 9.

[52] See e.g. *Lazerevic v SSHD* [1997] EWCA Civ 1007 (Brown LJ) (holding that '[i]t is a matter for the secretary of state whether, in the long term, refugees are to be allowed to settle in the UK. He is it seems to me, perfectly entitled to give them sanctuary here only for the limited period of their actual need, returning them to their countries of origin once their conflicts end and their borders re-open. Article 1C(5) [of CSR1951] expressly so allows').

[53] Cf. United States, *Citizenship Laws of the World* (Office of Personnel Management 2001), www.opm.gov/extra/investigate/is-01.pdf (outlining reasons invoked by states for denationalization, including acquisition of another citizenship, political activity in another State such as voting, holding office, and serving in the military, failure to renew one's passport, residence abroad, obtaining citizenship via fraudulent means, divorce, or being deemed a 'security threat'). See also Matthew J Gibney, 'Should Citizenship be Conditional' (RSC Working Paper Series No 75 July 2011) 10–11, www.rsc.ox.ac.uk/publications/working-papers-folder_contents/RSCworkingpaper75.pdf (noting that, historically, the acceptance of the state's right to execute helps explain why the right to strip citizenship was rarely questioned, as for most liberal thinkers the stripping of citizenship in

Indeed, while liberalising naturalisation procedures is commendable, and may go hand in hand with a general rights-based approach,[54] states seem keen to retain sovereign discretion regarding naturalisation, not least because of the life-long implications of granting state citizenship;[55] this observation holds even if one objects in principle to Weis' position that '[a] state cannot be compelled to grant its nationality, even after a long waiting period, to a refugee settled in its territory'.[56] It is submitted that, disaggregation of citizenship-dependent rights ameliorates *current* protection needs of CSR1951 refugees, and is thus well within the integration-led spirit of CSR1951, in the light of contemporary rights-centred understanding of the obligations that are owed to recognised refugees.

An ancillary concern that is raised in the CSR1951 refugee context by making electoral rights *contingent* on naturalisation regards the (still quite prevalent) prohibition on multiple nationalities. The number of states that allow their citizens to hold dual citizenship has grown;[57] indeed, the state of asylum should be expected to forgo a requirement that CSR1951 refugee applicants renounce their former citizenship, not least in light of their 'soft' Article 34 obligations to facilitate naturalisation. Yet, states of

---

conjunction with banishment was viewed as a humane alternative to the death penalty). *See also generally* Audrey Macklin, 'Citizenship Revocation, the Privilege to Have Rights and the Production of the Alien' (2014) 40(1) *Queens Law Journal* 1.

[54] Roxana Barbulescu, 'Mobile Union Citizens Should have Portable Voting Rights within the EU' in Rainer Bauböck, Philippe Cayla and Catriona Seth, *Should EU Citizens Living in Other Member States Vote There in National Elections* (EUI RSCAS Working Paper No 2012/32 July 2012) 37 (claiming that a state that extends voting rights to non-citizens is also more likely to have liberal naturalisation policies).

[55] See e.g. *R (AHK and others) v Secretary of State of the Home Department* [2009] EWCA Civ 287 [10] (holding that 'the grant of British citizenship under Section 6(1) of the 1981 Act is not a fundamental human right'). Cf. Committee on International Assistance to Refugees, *Report by the Committee* (submitted to the Council of the League of Nations, Geneva on 3 January 1939) pt ii conclusions [9] (noting that '[t]he refugee problem has, as its corollaries, the problems of assimilation and naturalization in the states of asylum or immigration. This is a very complex question, because it involves both the sovereignty of the state that is either prepared or not prepared to grant its citizenship to these exiles and the sincerity of the immigrants' determination to become loyal citizens of another country... [e]very state must itself decide each individual case'.).

[56] Paul Weis, *The Refugee Convention, 1951: The Travaux Préparatoires Analysed with a Commentary* (Grotius Publications 1995) 23.

[57] See David Reichel, *Do Legal Regulations Hinder Naturalisation? Citizenship Policies and Naturalisation Rates in Europe* (European University Institute Working paper RSCAS 2011/51 2011) 5 (noting that only two EU MS, Estonia and Lithuania, allow no exceptions to their general prohibition on dual nationality).

asylum only control *their* naturalisation policy.[58] The state of origin may, under its domestic laws, disallow the acquisition of new citizenship:[59] the refugee would then potentially lose their citizenship, compromising their right to return.[60] Indeed, CSR1951 refugees may wish to retain their attachment to their state of origin in view of the (hopefully temporary) nature of their persecution;[61] thus, in the case of CSR1951 refugees, making enjoyment of citizenship-dependent rights contingent on their naturalisation is disconcerting.[62]

C   The Fundamentality of Voting: Citizenship Voting Qualifications Revisited

It was demonstrated in Chapter 3 that, there are both expressive (intrinsic) and protective (instrumental) reasons for valuing participation, and that they should be considered mutually reinforcing.[63] Electoral participation is considered to be an autonomy-enhancing act, which can potentially legitimate other political involvement in society, and which manifests human dignity, as well as professes the enjoyment of equal worth, concern, and respect of society.

Admittedly, the ability of CSR1951 refugees to live a fully autonomous life in their state of asylum in the sense of making *life-long* plans is significantly inhibited by the fact that their residence in that state may indeed be temporary. The state of asylum has an interest in retaining the possibility of excluding them if and when the need for international

---

[58]   EUDO, Modes of Acquisition (Recognised Refugees), http://eudo-citizenship.eu/modes-of-acquisition/190/?search=1&idmode=A22#.UIETFG9gZho.

[59]   See e.g. Ruth Rubio-Marin (ed), *Human Rights and Immigration* (Oxford University Press 2014) 128 (conditioning her model of near-automatic naturalisation of resident non-citizens on their state of origin tolerating multiple nationality).

[60]   Rainer Bauböck, 'Boundaries and Birthright' (2011) 9 *Issues in Legal Scholarship* (Article 3) 5.

[61]   See e.g. Tomas Hammar, 'Dual Citizenship and Political Integration' (1985) 19(3) *International Migration Review* 438, 440 (arguing that '[w]hile political refugees often want to give up their old citizenship, there are, on the other hand, also many who for political reasons want to keep it').

[62]   See e.g. Egon F Kunz, 'Exile and Resettlement: Refugee Theory' (1981) 15 *International Migration Review* 42, 42–43 (arguing that individuals who are forced to leave their homes will often have a much stronger desire to return than those who leave voluntarily, and differentiating between refugees who 'cling to their [pre-displacement] identity and anticipate return and those who eagerly embrace their new life, leaving the old behind').

[63]   David Owen, 'Transnational Citizenship and Rights of Political Participation' (Normative Orders Working Paper No 6 2011) 3, http://publikationen.ub.uni-frankfurt.de/frontdoor/index/index/docId/22387.

protection is no longer required; this interest comes into tension with the interest of CSR1951 refugees in living a fully autonomous life. CSR1951 refugees may nonetheless choose to make provisional plans in view of prospects of possible naturalisation, and a social recognition that they may have a stake in society (even if its temporal scope is yet to be decided) manifested through electoral inclusion can in and of itself be autonomy enhancing.[64]

Now, non-inclusion of refugees *qua* non-citizen residents can be distinguished from the indignity entailed for instance by the exclusion in some jurisdictions of convicted adult citizens. Nevertheless, a sense of equal worth and belonging to a community, not least the community in which one habitually resides, is valuable to all persons. Sassen contends that the sense of belonging of CSR1951 refugees is thrown into question both in their state of origin and in their state of asylum, as without citizenship in the latter they are 'denied not only political rights but also the capacity to speak politically and the right to be heard'.[65]

From a 'republican' perspective, the predicament of CSR1951 refugees is pertinently *political*, having had their ties with the political community of their state of origin severed for an indeterminate period; it is thus both symbolically and conceptually significant for them to be embraced into the political community of their state of asylum.[66] As Arendt postulated, '[t]he fundamental deprivation of human rights [and citizenship] is manifested first and above all in the deprivation of a place in the world [a political space] which makes opinions significant and actions effective'.[67] Arendt maintained that the political sphere is the sphere of equality in which

---

[64] It was noted in Chapter 2 that some states set up consultative bodies for non-citizens *in lieu* of entitling them to participate in electoral processes. While such bodies may be considered autonomy enhancing, their consultative nature signals (political) inferiority both to the non-citizens and to society more generally.

[65] Saskia Sassen, 'The Repositioning of Citizenship' in Alison Brysk and Gershon Shafir (eds), *People Out of Place: Globalisation, Human Rights and the Citizenship Gap* (Routledge 2004) 191, 191–92.

[66] It was noted in previous chapters that CSR1951 refugees may be stateless, that is they have fled their state of habitual residence (where they are likely to have been electorally excluded). In such cases, absent persecution, they should have been given the opportunity to acquire their state of origin's citizenship. See also James Bohman, *Democracy across Borders: From Demos to Demoi* (MIT Press 2007) 112 (noting that '[t]he right to nationality is thus not a mere right to protection. It is a positive normative power that includes all the enabling participatory conditions for social and political rights, and it creates obligations for the international community to all persons lacking membership status or place in an ongoing or functioning political community').

[67] Hannah Arendt, *The Origins of Totalitarianism* (Harcourt 1967) 296, 298.

individuals are judged by their actions and opinions and not by irrelevant personal characteristics, and 'the loss of a polity itself expels [a person] from humanity'.[68] For Arendt, those who are situated outside the polis or the state are deprived not of their speech, but of a place in which their speech makes sense – their words become mere noise.[69] Indeed, recognition and inclusion in their state of asylum could mirror-image the conditions that prompted their departure from their state of origin.

Now, absent electoral rights in the state of asylum, CSR1951 refugees have other ways of expressing themselves politically: they can contribute to public discourse, for instance, by writing newspaper columns, by using social media and other channels of communication, by protest and lobbying, and by joining civil society organisations. Nevertheless, it is contended that their electoral non-inclusion casts a wide shadow on other forms of political participation on three main counts. First, questions may be posed by (full) members as to legitimacy of their interventions *qua* non-members;[70] moreover, states may be reluctant to allow non-citizens generally, and CSR1951 refugees in particular, to engage in political activities (see Chapter 2). Second, due to their non-inclusion, CSR1951 refugees may feel less engaged with the political process; if their state of asylum does not consider them as equal participants and is sending them a message of non-inclusion, they may be less inclined to get involved in its politics. Third, in view of the non-permanent (albeit indeterminate) nature of their status in the host state, the public nature of non-electoral means of political participation may deter CSR1951 refugees from causing public stir lest they will be subject to retaliatory measures. Thus, it is contended that, for *enfranchised* persons, having access to non-electoral means of political engagement reinforces their status, whereas for CSR1951 refugees its effective contribution is rather limited.

---

[68] Ibid 297. See also Alison Kesby, *The Right to Have Rights* (Oxford University Press 2012) 70.

[69] Hannah Arendt, *The Human Condition* (University of Chicago Press 1998) 27. In 'Introduction into Politics' in *The Promise of Politics* (Schocken Books 2005) 93, she conceptualises political freedom in spatial terms, underscoring that, for her, the loss of a political community entails the loss of the very space in which one can actualize the capacity for freedom.

[70] See e.g. Heather L Johnson, 'These Fine Lines: Locating Noncitizenship in Political Protest in Europe' (2015) 19(8) *Citizenship Studies* 951, 955 (exploring refugee protest camps in Europe in light of the prevailing notion that political action or agency from outside of citizenship, by noncitizens, is seen as illegitimate, and troubling, recognising that 'moving beyond citizenship as the guiding framework for understanding political agency, in theory or in practice, is difficult').

It was suggested in Chapter 2 that, in international human rights law and international refugee law, CSR1951 refugees are entitled to rights in their states of asylum. Nevertheless, political clout (which CSR1951 refugees crucially lack for an indeterminate period) is required for these rights to be properly respected, protected and fulfilled by states of asylum. Indeed, as Chapter 3 demonstrated, voting is also *instrumentally* significant as a means for expressing individual preferences, especially for members of marginalised groups whose voice is otherwise either sidelined or ignored by policy-makers.

Decision-makers arguably lack an incentive to give proper consideration to rights and interests of non-enfranchised populations. They may deny them access to *intangible* resources, such as involvement in policy consultations and meetings during constituency visits; whereas decisions affecting tangible resources (such as welfare benefits) are likely to be made in the (political) absence of the non-enfranchised.[71] Indeed, even if (some) rights are 'trumps',[72] it would not be reasonable to argue that electoral rights have no instrumental function in protecting (other) rights; for instance, if CSR1951 refugees are not heard by the decision-makers, and not represented in political parties, councils, and parliaments, then politicians are less likely to take their interests into account.[73] Hence, while enfranchised disempowered groups or persons such as CSR1951 refugees may require special institutional protection or 'virtual representation' by civil society organisations, such measures ought to supplement rather than replace their electoral participation.[74] While other citizens may use their own electoral rights to articulate interests of refugees, they would not be able to encapsulate these interests in full.

Now, the potential significance of enfranchisement of CSR1951 refugees affects but does not resolve the question whether, as non-citizens, they should be entitled to vote in elections of their state of asylum. It is

---

[71] See e.g. Pieter Bevelander, 'Naturalisation and Social Inclusion' in OECD, *Naturalisation: A Passport for the Better Integration of Immigrants?* (2011) 238 (the article considers socio-economic ramifications of excluding migrants from electoral processes and of their naturalisation).

[72] Ronald Dworkin, *Taking Rights Seriously* (Duckworth 1978) xi.

[73] Hammar (n 61) 439; see also Gaim Kibreab, 'Citizenship Rights and Repatriation of Refugees' (2003) 37(1) *International Migration Review* 24, 58.

[74] The US Supreme Court famously stipulated in *US v Carolene Products*, 304 US 144 (1938) n4 that 'more searching judicial inquiry' may be called for where 'prejudice against discrete and insular minorities . . . curtail[s] the operation of those political processes ordinarily to be relied upon to protect minorities'. Hence, the question is whether access to the political process is *sufficient* rather than whether it should be *substituted* by other means.

submitted that the arguments for an inseparability position, presented in Chapter 5, are considerably weaker in relation to recognised CSR1951 refugees whereas the *residence*-based eligibility argument are weightier.

It was asserted that, social cohesion is largely dependent on having an (exclusive) common (civic) identity, symbolised by enfranchisement, and that naturalisation is thus a necessary step towards inclusion. However, if asylum is an expressive act of a state, sending a welcoming message to those in need, it seems reasonable to suggest that it may strengthen the state's collective identity as a (political) community that is committed to rights protection.

It was also argued that voters should be loyal to their state, and that state citizenship (indeed, on certain accounts, *exclusive* citizenship), which has previously manifested allegiance to a ruler, now manifests loyalty to the community. However, 'Tebbit tests' contrasting the loyalty of migrants to their state of asylum and to their state of origin seem particularly ill-suited in the case of recognised CSR1951 refugees, especially when the latter's fear of persecution stems from the actions of a persecutory state.[75] As the Coalition for Immigrant and Refugee Rights and the National Immigrant Justice Center argued before a US federal court in *Bluman*, 'the notion that those who come to the U.S. for the express purpose of escaping persecution by their own government are likely to then support some "foreign" interest – presumably that of their persecutor – in U.S. elections is nothing short of absurd'.[76]

According to the 'stakeholder principle', voters should have a long-term interest in the polity's well-being; citizenship guarantees a permanent connection between an individual and her state, which in turn generates such interest.[77] It is unclear whether CSR1951 refugees are necessarily going to have a long-term stake in the polity's well-being, as their length of stay is indeterminate. It was noted above that CSR1951 refugees are unable to make life-long plans (until and unless they naturalise); it could

---

[75] See http://barrettsonthisday.anorak.co.uk/uncategorized/1814/tebbit-proposes-cricket-test.html.

[76] *Bluman et al v Federal Election Commission*, 800 F Supp 2d 281 (D.D.C. 2011) *Amici Curiae* (3 October 2011) 13.

[77] Rainer Bauböck, 'Stakeholder Citizenship and Transnational Political Participation: A Normative Evaluation of External Voting' (2007) 75 *Fordham Law Review* 2393 (see also Chapter 5). Elsewhere, Bauböck argues that 'Past and future subjections are not justifying grounds for inclusion, but empirical indicators for a genuine link that is itself the justifying reason for inclusion from a stakeholder perspective' Rainer Bauböck, 'Morphing the Demos into the Right Shape: Normative Principles for Enfranchising Resident Aliens and Expatriate Citizens' (2015) 22(5) *Democratization* 820, 825.

be similarly argued that they are also unable to consider the life-long plans of the polity.

Three responses may be given.

First, CSR1951 refugees are still distinguishable from migrant workers, students, or other temporary residents in that their length of stay is not *fixed* but rather *indeterminate*; it may turn out to be protracted and reach a point at which, according to a state's general naturalisation laws, citizenship may be sought. It cannot be easy for a state of asylum to make assumptions about the long-term stakes of a CSR1951 refugee when analyses depend on circumstances that lie outside that state's control.[78]

Second, the fate of CSR1951 refugees is tied to their state of asylum to a far greater extent than the fate of voluntary migrants who can return to their state of origin. Indeed, their fate may often be more effectively and meaningfully tied to the fate of the community than the link between citizens holding multiple citizenships and a state whose citizenship they hold nominally without residing therein. It is thus not unreasonable to assume that refugees' interest in the well-being of their state of asylum is real.

Third, the state of asylum may decide to naturalise refugees, and relax its requirements for doing so. Notwithstanding possible revocation of the refugee's previous nationality by her state of origin, there is a reasonable chance that he or she will eventually naturalise. It is thus possible that, should the state of asylum decide to make the refugee a permanent member, he or she will become one, thereby guaranteeing a life-long stake in the well-being of the polity. On this view, it is plausible to consider (at least some) CSR1951 refugees as 'citizens in the making'. It should not fall

---

[78] Ruth Rubio-Marin, *Immigration as a Democratic Challenge: Citizenship and Inclusion in Germany and the United States* (Cambridge University Press 2000) 55. In the UK, certain non-citizen residents that do not have indefinite leave to remain are enfranchised in *all* elections, including the general election. According to the Representation of the People Act 1983 c2 s4(6), persons entitled to be registered as parliamentary or local government elector include, alongside a British citizen and a citizen of the Republic of Ireland (who does not require leave to enter or remain in the UK as per the Ireland Act 1949 c 41), a 'qualifying Commonwealth citizen'. The latter is either (a) not a person who requires leave under the Immigration Act 1971 c77 s2(1)(b) to enter or remain in the UK or (b) is such a person but *for the time being* has . . . *any description of such leave* (emphases added). Commonwealth countries: www.electoralcommission.org.uk/_data/assets/electoral_commission_pdf_file/0009/79515/List-of-eligible-countries.pdf. For a critique of the UK general election franchise, see Peter Goldsmith, *Citizenship: Our Common Bond* (2008) 75–6 (submitting that 'the right to vote is one of the hallmarks of the political status of citizens; it is not a means of expressing closeness between countries').

on the individual refugee to be excluded because the state of asylum may *eventually* choose to exercise its prerogative not to naturalise her.

It was also contended that citizenship *qua* citizenship has become devalued because of the decoupling of rights therefrom; enfranchisement remains a tangible benefit that incentivises naturalisation. Nevertheless, it seems sensible to claim that, for recognised CSR1951 refugees, the 'currency' of naturalisation is particularly strong and requires no additional incentives in view of their 'civic and social limbo'.

Chapter 5 has also explored arguments for *domicile*-based suffrage. These arguments include the normative significance of subjection to unaccountable power; the notion of dependency compounded by the unavailability of a viable 'exit' option; and the unfairness entailed by exclusion of persons sharing social burdens, primarily, though not exclusively, through taxation. Regarding the latter argument, it may be suggested that, absent an 'exit' option, CSR1951 refugees are quite likely to contribute their time and energy to their host society. However, even if the above argument does not carry greater weight for recognised CSR1951 refugees than for other non-citizens, the former two do, for the following reasons.

Persons are vulnerable to domination to the extent that they are dependent on a relationship where a power-holder can exercise arbitrary (that is, unaccountable) power over them. Elections are an important (though not an exclusive) means of making the exercise of power accountable, not just on polling day, but throughout public life: incumbents are constantly aware of the possibility that they may be replaced if they fail to engage their constituents and respond to their interests, and so are their opponents.

By comparison, decision-makers may consider it unnecessary to devote time and attention to the interests and views of the electorally excluded, and are less likely to take their views into account when formulating policies. Absent enfranchisement, immigrants are less likely to be consulted regarding new policies affecting their employment, housing, or welfare rights; visits to their neighbourhoods are more likely to address grievances of *citizens* (often voiced against migrants). For CSR1951 refugees, enfranchisement will not close the accountability gap, especially as pending deportation would still cast a wide shadow, but it may narrow it: they would be more likely to enjoy civil rights and other protections if they enjoy rights of political participation.[79] Democratic iterations do not

---

[79] Sarah Song, 'Democracy and Noncitizen Voting Rights' (2009) 13(6) *Citizenship Studies* 607, 614.

only change existing membership norms, but they also afford refugees the opportunity to make their voices heard.[80]

Indeed, it stands to reason that the absence of accountability of the state to its non-enfranchised population may be a cause for concern, as governments may not feel obliged to justify policy changes to the same extent (if at all) and to be responsive to their interests through the democratic process. This concern is compounded when the 'exit costs' of leaving the state are high, and when the non-citizen does not have a powerful home state ready to hold the host state accountable for rights violations.[81] Hence, the more non-citizen residents are subject to discrimination and prejudice, the greater the value of the protection of their state of origin and of an 'exit option',[82] both absent in the case of CSR1951 refugees.

In terms of vulnerability caused by lack of access to accountability mechanisms and high 'exit' costs, the predicament of recognised CSR9151 refugees may be contrasted with the situation faced by EU SCNs, that is EU nationals living in another EU MS. It was noted in previous chapters that SCNs may enjoy protection abroad when they travel outside the EU: if their state of nationality is not present in that non-EU state, other EU MS are required to provide protection as if the SCNs were their nationals. SCNs are legally entitled to vote in local and in elections to the European Parliament, and nationals of most EU MS have access to OCV. Significantly, SCNs, in principle, can return to their state of nationality *at any time* should they wish to.

The length of stay in their state of residence increases the dependence of SCNs on that state, and may make the (legal) 'exit' option less relevant. However, on the spectrum of non-citizen populations, CSR1951 refugees have a substantially stronger case residence-based eligibility than SCNs (notwithstanding the potency of EU law rights-based arguments).[83]

---

[80] Bonnie Honig, 'Another Cosmopolitanism? Law and Politics in the New Europe' in Seyla Benhabib (ed), *Another Cosmopolitanism: Hospitality, Sovereignty, and Democratic Iterations* (Oxford University Press 2006) 102, 107.

[81] Meghan Benton, 'The Tyranny of the Enfranchised Majority? The Accountability of States to their Non-Citizen Population' (2010) 16(4) *Res Publica* 397, 408 (asserting that the most effective pressure on the US to free detainees held at Guantanamo was mounted by liberal democracies whose nationals had been detained).

[82] Ruth Rubio-Marin, 'Transnational Politics and the Democratic Nation-State: Normative Challenges of Expatriate Voting and Nationality Retention of Emigrants' (2006) 81 *NYU Law Review* 117, 123.

[83] Cf. art 42(3) of the Migrant Workers Convention, enunciating that '[m]igrant workers may enjoy political rights in the State of employment if that State . . . grants them such rights'. This provision follows art 41, which pronounces the *right* to migrant workers to

D   Recognition, Integration, and Public Resistance

1   The Meaning of Recognition

A decision to admit a person as a CSR1951 refugee signifies a commitment on the part of a state of asylum to extend its protection to individuals whose own state has *failed to protect* by action or omission. It was noted above that, at the time CSR1951 refugees are recognised, neither they nor their state of asylum know when or indeed whether the circumstances that have led to the departure will change. Upon recognition, short of affording permanent membership, the state of asylum, having admitted refugees, undertakes to host and protect them for as long as such protection is required.[84]

Matthew Price suggests that asylum is a political instrument: viewing it as a humanitarian instrument is a 'conceptual error'.[85] For Price, a decision to grant asylum is *condemnatory* as it 'constitutes a means to condemn persecutory regimes, eventually leading to their reform and to solving the root cause of refugee flows by promoting the rule of law and human rights'.[86] He considers individual refugees as means to achieve a broader policy goal, namely condemnation as a foreign policy tool. Adopting an 'accountability approach' to recognition, Price notes that in circumstances where non-state actors are responsible for persecution, the state of origin cannot be condemned and so asylum should not be granted.[87]

It is notable that, while considering asylum to be an exclusively *political* practice, Price suggests that 'the right to vote cannot be a measure for persecution';[88] he describes the human rights approach to persecution as 'over-inclusive'.[89] Price asserts that the state of asylum should extend

vote in elections of their states of origin, and art 23, which pronounces their right to have access to their state of origin's diplomatic and consular services. Hence, despite the fact that migrant workers do not suffer political alienage from their state of origin, states of employment should consider favourably their electoral inclusion. For further discussion of Out-of-Country voting, see Chapter 6.

[84] See e.g. Jean-François Durieux, 'Three Asylum Paradigms' (2013) 20(2) *International Journal on Minority and Group Rights* 147, 156 (distinguishing the CSR1951 'admission' paradigm from 'rescue' and 'inhuman treatment' paradigms, and noting that 'faithful implementation of [1951] Convention standards favours the assimilation of refugees within their new communities'). See also Alexander Betts, 'The Normative Terrain of the Global Refugee Regime' (2015) 29(4) *Ethics & International Affairs* 363, 368 (noting that, for Durieux, persecution is distinctive for two reasons: it leaves no alternative route for protection and it often enables states to admit people based on affinity with their plight, given the individualized nature of persecution).

[85] *Rethinking Asylum* (n 18) 13.   [86] Ibid 75.   [87] Ibid 155.   [88] Ibid 116.   [89] Ibid.

'membership in a new political community'.[90] However, he devotes very little attention to the scope of membership, and fails to consider the temporal dimension thereof or, indeed, the possibility that repatriation may be feasible in future.

In contrast, it is submitted that the political predicament of CSR1951 refugees makes them a special category of non-citizen residents. Assuming failure of state protection, the analysis considers the effects of physical and political alienage on individual refugees whether their well-founded fear of persecution emanates from state or from non-state actors.[91] The claim is that, by recognising persons as CSR1951 refugees, a state of asylum acknowledges their political predicament, and aims to ameliorate it, not (necessarily) by condemning another regime, but by acting in loco civitatis. While according to Price's account, asylum *necessarily* carries a condemnatory expressive message,[92] this book views asylum as cementing an expressive commitment to extend protection, acting *in loco civitatis* for an indefinite period.

2   Commitment to Refugee Integration

Recognised refugees often face considerable challenges in adapting to new cultures and languages, while separated from family and social support networks. It was previously noted that, Article 34 of CSR1951 requires Contracting States 'so far as possible' to facilitate 'the assimilation and naturalisation' of CSR1951 refugees. While the provision does not establish formal obligations, states should, *inter alia*, give 'favourable consideration to requests for naturalization received from refugees' and reduce 'the financial obstacles which procedural charges and costs may pose to destitute refugees'.[93] Indeed, while Article 34 does not *require* Contracting States to naturalise refugees,[94] a state that fails to provide a path to naturalisation would at the very least be expected to provide a cogent explanation: recognised refugees must have access to state institutions to facilitate their integration.[95]

---

[90] Ibid 248.   [91] See Chapter 1.

[92] Matthew E Price, 'Politics or Humanitarianism? Recovering the Political Roots of Asylum' (2004) 19 *Georgetown Immigration Law Journal* 277, 295.

[93] Grahl-Madsen (n 48) 245, quoting Ad Hoc Committee on Statelessness and Related Problems, *Memorandum by the Secretary-General* (1950) UN Doc E/AC.32/2 p 50.

[94] See e.g. *Abuissa v MJELR* [2010] IEHC 366 (Ireland).

[95] James C Hathaway, *Rights of Refugees under International Law* (Cambridge University Press 2005) 989. See also the December 2012 judgment of the Irish Supreme Court in

UNHCR acknowledges that 'local integration is a sovereign decision' exercised by states 'considering the specific circumstances of each refugee situation'.[96] Nonetheless, it 'notes that the 1951 Convention and its 1967 Protocol set out rights and minimum standards for the treatment of refugees that are geared towards the process of integration' and describes local integration as a process entailing the 'host state granting refugees a secure legal status and a progressively wider range of rights and entitlements that are broadly commensurate with those enjoyed by its citizens and, over time, the possibility of naturalisation'.[97]

The obligation in Article 34 to facilitate 'assimilation' precedes 'naturalisation'. Indeed, logically, '[b]y facilitating "assimilation" the Contracting State is to a certain extent also facilitating the naturalization of refugees'.[98] Grahl-Madsen argued that, states should lay 'foundations, or stepping stones, so that the refugee may familiarise himself with the language, customs, and way of life of the nation among whom he lives, so that he – without any feeling of coercion – may be more readily integrated in the economic, social and cultural life of his country of refuge'.[99]

It was noted in Chapter 2 that, according to the *Travaux*, the term 'assimilation' refers to *integration*. Rosa Da Costa postulates that 'the international community has always rejected the notion that CSR1951 refugees should be expected to abandon their own culture and way of life so as to become indistinguishable from nationals of the host

---

Mallak v Minister for Justice Equality and Law Reform [2012] IRSC 59. The applicant, a Syrian national recognised as a CSR1951 refugee in Ireland, applied for naturalisation; his application was denied, and no reasons were given save for reliance on the minister's absolute discretion. The Supreme Court quashed the decision, holding that 'the Minister was under a duty to provide [Mr Mallak] with reasons for his decision to refuse his application for naturalisation' and that 'his failure to do so deprived the [Mr Mallak] of any meaningful opportunity either to make a new application for naturalisation or to challenge the decision on substantive grounds'.

[96] UNHCR EXCOM Conclusion No 109 (LXI) 'Protracted Refugee Situations' (8 December 2009) [h]. As a matter of best practice, UNHCR suggests that the required period of residence for refugees in order to be eligible for naturalisation would not exceed five years. See Rosa Da Costa, *Rights of Refugees in the Context of Integration: Legal Standards and Recommendations* (UNHCR Legal and Protection Policy Research Series Department of International Protection 2006) 186.

[97] UNHCR EXCOM Conclusion No 104 (LVI) 'Local Integration' (7 October 2005) [d] and [l].

[98] Grahl-Madsen (n 48) 247.

[99] Ibid. See Alice Edwards, 'Human Rights, Refugees and the Right to 'Enjoy' Asylum' (2005) 17(2) *International Journal of Refugee Law* 295, 307 (defining naturalisation as the formalisation of the local integration solution).

community'.[100] CSR1951 refugee integration is arguably a 'dynamic and multifaceted two-way process which requires efforts by all parties concerned, including a preparedness on the part of refugees to adapt to the host society without having to forego their own cultural identity, and a corresponding readiness on the part of host communities and public institutions to welcome refugees and meet the needs of a diverse population'.[101]

The EU Qualification Directive (EUQD) provides a helpful comparison. Article 34 thereof, entitled 'Access to Integration Facilities', stipulates that '[i]n order to facilitate the integration of beneficiaries of international protection into society, Member States shall ensure access to integration programmes which they consider to be appropriate so as to take into account the specific needs of beneficiaries of refugee status . . . or create pre-conditions which guarantee access to such programmes'.[102]

The EUQD should be read in tandem with the Long-Term Residents Directive whose application was extended in 2011 to beneficiaries of international protection, including CSR1951 refugees.[103] The accompanying notes suggest that, on the adoption of the amended directive, beneficiaries shall 'enjoy equality of treatment with citizens of the Member State of residence on a wide range of economic and social matters' so that 'long-term residence status [will constitute] a genuine instrument for the integration of long-term residents into the society in which they live'.[104]

---

[100] Rosa Da Costa (n 96) 9 (citing Nehemiah Robinson, *Convention relating to the Status of Refugees: Its History and Interpretation, a Commentary* (Institute of Jewish Affairs 1953) 142, 166).

[101] UNHCR, *Note on the Integration of Refugees in the European Union* (May 2007) [1].

[102] Recital [47] notes that such facilities include 'where appropriate, language training and the provision of information concerning individual rights and obligations relating to their protection status in the Member State concerned'. Art 20(1) (General rules) stipulates that '[t]his Chapter shall be without prejudice to the rights laid down in the Geneva Convention'.

[103] Directive 2011/51/EU of the European Parliament and of the Council of 11 May 2011 amending Council Directive 2003/109/EC of 25 November 2003 [Concerning the Status of Third-Country Nationals who are Long-Term Residents] to Extend its Scope to Beneficiaries of International Protection OJ L 132/1, 19 May 2011.

[104] Ibid [6]. In art 9(3), the Directive considers the implications of changes regarding a beneficiary's eligibility for international protection. The provision stipulates that 'member states may withdraw the long-term residence status in the event of the revocation of, ending of or refusal to renew international protection . . . if the long-term resident status was obtained on the basis of international protection'.

3   Integration and Enfranchisement: New Zealand's Best Practices

For many states, the benefits of offering asylum to refugees used to out-weigh the costs, as refugees were culturally similar, helped to meet labour shortages, arrived in manageable numbers, and reinforced ideological or strategic objectives.[105] Today, refugee integration poses challenges for states of asylum, due in part to ethnic, linguistic, and other differences between CSR1951 refugees and the receiving population.

Nevertheless, although cultural similarities undoubtedly smooth inte-gration, the ethnicity of a refugee population should not predicate the durable solutions available to them.[106] It was noted earlier that, the assumption underlying refugee recognition is that the length of stay is *indeterminate:* refugees may remain in the state of asylum for protracted periods. Seen in this light, it is in the state's interest to mitigate the challenges posed by integration.[107] While enfranchisement can be seen a reward for integration, the better view is that it should be considered a means for facilitating integration.

It may be argued that, coerced exile may impinge on the integration process, as refugees may orient themselves towards eventual return; never-theless, refugees may be inclined to develop ties to the community within which they reside and a human need to build a new life following severe trauma.[108] A state of asylum that decides to enfranchise its refugees will be sending them (as well as the public at large) a message of integration and inclusion.[109]

It was noted in Section C that voting rights may be instrumentally important to protect rights of refugees. Enfranchised refugees are likely

---

[105] Erika Feller, *The 1951 Convention at 50: New Challenges for the International Refugee Protection Regime* (Presentation to the Lauterpacht Research Centre for International Law 17 October 2000) 4.

[106] Alexandra Fielden, *Local Integration: An Under-Reported Solution to Protracted Refugee Situations* (New Issues in Refugee Research Working Paper No 158 2008) 6.

[107] Cf. Diane Barnes, 'Resettled Refugees' Attachment to their Original and Subsequent Homelands: Long-Term Vietnamese Refugees in Australia' (2001) 14 *Journal of Refugee Studies* 394, 409–10 (suggesting that 'the danger of [host] countries not taking positive steps to promote the full social inclusion of people whom they accept as refugees is that this can lead to a withdrawal of their emotional commitment to, and social engagement with, the [host] country. Refugees who perceive themselves to be excluded . . . may continue to reside there, but turn inwards and identify themselves in term of their ethnic minority status').

[108] Fitzpatrick (n 50) 348.

[109] See e.g. Alastair Ager and Alison Strang, 'Understanding Integration: A Conceptual Framework' (2008) 21(2) *Journal of Refugee Studies* 166, 181.

to be empowered, better able, and hopefully more willing to enrich their host society. European Council on Refugees and Exiles (ECRE) posits that allowing recognised refugees to have access to decision-making processes and the political life of the state of durable asylum is 'key to ensuring a two-way process of integration involving refugees and host societies on an equitable basis'.[110]

In a survey conducted among recognised refugees in Scotland during the run-up to the 2010 UK General Elections, the right to vote was emphasised as one of the main reasons for wishing to attain British citizenship. Interviewees suggested that enfranchisement would be particularly meaningful in view of their pre-flight experiences in their state of origin.[111]

New Zealand's electoral legislation offers an intriguing model for refugee integration, *inter alia*, through enfranchisement. Since 1975, New Zealand entitles *all* permanent residents to vote in *all* of its elections, provided that they have continuously resided in New Zealand for no less than one year.[112] New Zealand has thus adopted a domicile-based franchise.

Pertinently to this book, those recognised as CSR1951 refugees pursuant to New Zealand legislation[113] can straight away apply for residence on the basis of that recognition,[114] even though 'the grant of residence does not automatically follow the recognition of a refugee'.[115] If the residence application is successful, she will become an eligible voter within a year. In the parliamentary debate, the government representative noted that '[t]he bill... strengthens New Zealand's already highly regarded refugee determination system... reflects best-practice standards internationally'.[116]

It is also noteworthy that, under the New Zealand Immigration Act (NZIA), 'every New Zealand citizen has by virtue of his or her citizenship

---

[110] European Council of Refugees and Exiles, *Position on the Integration of Refugees in Europe* (December 2002) [26]. See also European Council of Refugees and Exiles, *Good Practice Guide on the Integration of Refugees in the European Union* (2001) 36.

[111] Emma Stewart and Gareth Mulvey, *Becoming British Citizens? Experiences and Opinions of Refugees Living in Scotland* (Scottish Refugee Council and Strathclyde University February 2011) 39.

[112] Electoral Act 1993 No 87, §74(1)(a)(ii), (b).

[113] New Zealand Immigration Act 2009 No 51, §129(1) (NZIA). New Zealand acceded to CSR1951 on 30 June 1960 and to the New York Protocol on 6 August 1973; CSR1951 is appended to the NZIA as Schedule 1.

[114] Immigration New Zealand, Operational Manual (19 August 2013) §C.5.15.1, www .immigration.govt.nz/opsmanual/.

[115] Ibid §C5.15.5.a.

[116] NZIA, first reading (2 November 2007) David Cunlife (Minister of Immigration), www.parliament.nz/en-NZ/PB/Legislation/Bills/4/7/d/00DBHOH_BILL8048_1-Immigration-Bill.htm.

the right to enter and be in New Zealand at any time'[117] whereas 'a person who is not a New Zealand citizen may . . . enter and be in New Zealand only if the person is the holder of a visa granted under this Act and . . . has been granted entry permission'.[118] The NZIA clarifies that recognised refugees may only be deported based on CSR1951 Article 32(1) or Article 33 grounds,[119] unless one of the Article 1C cessation grounds applies.[120]

The New Zealand model of post-recognition permanent residence status that is easily obtainable by refugees and which entails full enfranchisement after one year is an example of best practices by a CSR1951 Contracting State. Nevertheless, it is acknowledged that the geographical location of New Zealand may have an effect on its (liberal) legislative policies.

4   The Public Resistance Challenge

Refugees living in states of asylum where their rights are protected, where they have definite prospects for naturalisation or permanent residence, and where favourable structural factors enable them to enjoy a decent standard of living tend to remain even if the conditions that prompted their displacement are eliminated.[121] Indeed, the link between rights protection, empowerment, integration, and the possibility of naturalisation cannot be denied. One of the reasons why some African governments keep refugees in spatially segregated sites is, arguably, to prevent their incorporation into host societies, so that once the circumstances that prompted their displacement and flight have changed, repatriation is easily enforceable.[122]

Hence, states of asylum may 'worry' that the electoral inclusion of CSR1951 refugees will become a pull factor for new refugees and a push factor against voluntary repatriation of already recognised CSR1951 refugees. Moreover, governments that are increasingly accountable to

---

[117] NZIA, §13(1).   [118] NZIA, §14(1)(b).
[119] NZIA, §164(1).   [120] NZIA, §143(b)(i).
[121] Kibreab (n 73) 63. Kibreab argues that 'the fact that nationals of the same countries displaced by identical factors responded differently to the elimination of the factors that prompted displacement depending on where they resided clearly suggests that return movements are motivated, on the one hand, by lack of civil, political and economic rights and, on the other, by unfavorable structural conditions manifested in lack of economic and social capacity of absorption in states of asylum rather than by the desire to belong to particular places or communities of origin'. Ibid 58.
[122] Gaim Kibreab, 'Revisiting the Debate on People, Place, Identity and Displacement' (1999) 12(4) *Journal of Refugee Studies* 387, 400.

public opinion on questions of immigration may be tempted to tighten their refugee policies in response to these negative public perceptions.[123]

Gibney argues that the conflict between respect for the rights of refugees and the provision of asylum is real: just as rights impose constraints on what can be legitimately done to refugees, so they place limits on what can be legitimately done for them.[124] Nevertheless, it may be contended that resistance to electoral inclusion crystallises the symbolic inclusive significance thereof, namely the importance that full members of the political community of the state of asylum attach to their membership. On this account, non-inclusion signals unwillingness to (fully) integrate CSR1951 refugees.

Now, there can be no doubt that a functioning state cannot operate a scheme of refugee protection without solid public support. The argument advanced here is that, for a Contracting State that acknowledges its existing obligations, enfranchising recognised CSR1951 refugees would be in the spirit of the Convention and its commitment thereto, and is arguably likely to make refugee integration more attainable.

Public resistance to absorption of refugees can usually be expected to appear earlier on, at the eligibility stage,[125] and may explain restrictive interpretations of CSR1951 which lead to low recognition rates. Indeed, as Fitzpatrick and Bonan argue, 'the best assimilated and long-resident refugees do not present a likely target for public discontent'.[126] It is submitted that, by opting to recognise persons as CSR1951 refugees, a Contracting State has already chosen a path; enfranchisement of CSR1951 refugees in its elections would be a natural step forward.

E   Concluding Remarks

Political theorists have long been considering the desirability of a link between eligibility to vote and state citizenship as a manifestation of full membership in a political community; the mutually reinforcing

---

[123] Ibid 403.

[124] Matthew J Gibney, *The Ethics and Politics of Asylum* (Cambridge University Press 2004) 249–50.

[125] See e.g. Catherine Dauvergne, 'Refugee Law and the Measure of Globalisation' in Savitri Taylor (ed), *Nationality, Refugee Status and State Protection Law in Context* (Federation Press 2005) 62, 76 (arguing that refugee law is becoming a key point of response to a perceived challenge to national sovereignty within a discourse of democratic politics).

[126] See Joan Fitzpatrick and Rafael Bonoan, 'Cessation of Refugee Status' in Erika Feller, Volker Türk, and Frances Nicholson (eds), *Refugee Protection in International Law* (Cambridge University Press 2003) 491, 543.

POLITICAL PREDICAMENT AND REMEDIES

significance of territoriality and nationality in a global order where sovereign states, ultimately, retain control over their borders and membership lies at the heart of these analyses. In turn, refugee law scholars have been pondering the suitability of the CSR1951 refugee regime and the availability of durable solutions for recognised refugees.

This book considers the predicament of persons who satisfy the CSR1951 refugee definition during the indeterminate period between their recognition and the realisation of a durable solution. By conceptualising the political predicament of recognised CSR1951 refugees *qua non-citizens* in their state of asylum, the book brings together elements of the political theory and refugee law discourses.

It is argued that recognised CSR1951 refugees suffer from a special 'protection gap' which may be mitigated by expanding the scope of legal obligations under CSR1951, in line with the overarching aim to provide rights that would constitute surrogate or substitute national protection.[127] Hence, CSR1951 refugees are relevantly different from other non-citizen residents, and the case for their enfranchisement is stronger. The closing chapter presented the enfranchisement rationale; it then applied the fundamentality of voting framework to the case of CSR1951 refugees, and scrutinised relevant themes in the voting-citizenship debate. Finally, it explored possible links between integration and enfranchisement.

It is nevertheless acknowledged that *some* of the arguments that are advanced in this book can be applied, *mutatis mutandis*, to other groups of non-citizens, particularly other forced migrants. Moreover, a different conceptualisation of the voting-citizenship 'nexus' may broadly affect legal entitlements of non-citizen residents, including CSR1951 refugees. This book has aimed to contribute to the conceptualisation of the relations between individuals and their state by opening up avenues for further legal and political inquiry.

[127] Law of Refugee Status (n 20) 51.

BIBLIOGRAPHY

Monographs, Edited Books, and Articles

Abrams, Dominic and Hogg, Michael *Social Identity and Social Cognition* (Blackwell Publishing 1999)

Adelman, Howard 'Modernity, Globalization, Refugees and Displacement' in Alastair Ager (ed), *Refugees: Perspectives on the Experience of Forced Migrants* (Continuum 1999) 85

Agamben, Giorgio *Homo Sacer: Sovereign Power and Bare Life* (Stanford University Press 1998)

Ager, Alastair and Strang, Alison 'Understanding Integration: A Conceptual Framework' (2008) 21(2) *Journal of Refugee Studies* 166

Albert, Matthew 'Prima Facie Determination of Refugee Status' (Refugee Studies Centre, Working Paper Series No 55 January 2010)

Aleinikoff, T Alexander *Citizenship Policies for an Age of Migration* (Carnegie 2002)
'Citizens, Aliens, Membership and the Constitution' (1990) 7 *Constitutional Commentary* 9
'Theories of Loss of Citizenship' (1986) 84 *Michigan Law Review* 1471

Aleinikoff, T Alexander, and Klusmeyer, Douglas (eds) *Citizenship Policies for an Age of Migration* (Carnegie 2002)

Alexy, Robert *A Theory of Constitutional Rights* (Oxford University Press 2002)

Amerasinghe, Chittharanjan F *Diplomatic Protection* (Oxford University Press 2008)

An-Na'im, Abdullahi Ahmed 'State Responsibility under International Human Rights Law to Change Religious and Customary Laws' in Rebecca Cook (ed), *Human Rights of Women: National and International Perspectives* (University of Pennsylvania Press 1994) 167

Anderson, Bridget 'What Does 'The Migrant' Tell Us about the (Good) Citizen?' (University of Oxford Centre for Migration, Policy and Society, Working Paper No 94 2012)

Anderson, Bridget, Gibney Matthew J, and Paoletti, Emanuela 'Citizenship, Deportation and the Boundaries of Belonging' (2011) 15 *Citizenship Studies* 547

Anker, Deborah 'Refugee Law, Gender, and the Human Rights Paradigm' (2002) 15 *Harvard Human Rights Journal* 133

Anker, Deborah and Marouf, Famta E 'Socioeconomic Rights and Refugee Status: Deepening the Dialogue between Human Rights and Refugee Law' (2009) 103 *American Journal of International Law* 784

Arendt, Hannah 'Introduction into Politics' in *The Promise of Politics* (Schocken-Books 2005) 93

'We Refugees' in Marc Robinson (ed), *Altogether Elsewhere: Writers on Exile* (5th edn Faber and Faber 1994) 110

The Human Condition (University of Chicago Press 1989)

The Origins of Totalitarianism (Harcourt 1967)

Badhwar, Neera K 'Moral Agency, Commitment and Impartiality' (1996) 13(1) *Social Philosophy and Policy* 1

Baehr, Peter R 'Democracy and the Right to Political Participation' in David P Forsythe (ed), *Encyclopaedia of Human Rights* (Oxford University Press 2009)

Banerjee, Kiran 'Political Community of Fate or Postnational State? The Persistence of the Other in Contemporary German Citizenship' (conference paper)

Barber, Nicholas *The Constitutional State* (Oxford University Press 2011)

Barbulescu, Roxana 'Mobile Union Citizens Should Have Portable Voting Rights within the EU' in Rainer Baubök, Philippe Cayla, and Catriona Seth, *Should EU Citizens Living in Other Member States Vote There in National Elections* (European University Institute RSCAS 2012/32 July 2012)

Batchelor, Carol 'Statelessness and the Problem of Resolving Nationality Status' (1998) 10 *International Journal of Refugee Law* 156

Baubök, Rainer 'Morphing the Demos into the Right Shape: Normative Principles for Enfranchising Resident Aliens and Expatriate Citizens' (2015) 22(5) *Democratization* 820

'Boundaries and Birthright' (2011) 9 *Issues in Legal Scholarship* (Article 3)

'The Rights and Duties of External Citizenship' (2009) 13(5) *Citizenship Studies* 475

'Stakeholder Citizenship and Transnational Political Participation: A Normative Evaluation of External Voting' (2007) 75 *Fordham Law Review* 2393

'Expansive Citizenship: Voting beyond Territory and Membership' (2005) 38 *Political Science and Politics* 683

'Towards a Political Theory of Migrant Transnationalism' (2003) 37 *International Migration Review* 700

Transnational Citizenship: Membership and Rights in International Migration (Edward Elgar 1994)

Immigration and the Boundaries of Citizenship (Centre for Research in Ethnic Relations, University of Warwick 1992)

Baubök, Rainer, and Goodman, Sarah Wallace *Naturalisation* (EUDO, Citizenship Policy Brief No 2 2011)

Banerjee, Kiran 'Political Community of Fate or Postnational State? Tensions and Transformation in Contemporary German Citizenship' (SSRN)

Barnes, Diane 'Resettled Refugees' Attachment to Their Original and Subsequent Homelands: Long-Term Vietnamese Refugees in Australia' (2001) 14 *Journal of Refugee Studies* 394

Barry, Kim 'Home and Away: The Construction of Citizenship in an Emigration Context' (2006) 81 *NYU Law Review* 11

    The Frontiers of Democracy: The Right to Vote and Its Limits (Palgrave Macmillan 2009)

Beckman, Ludvig 'Who Should Vote? Conceptualizing Universal Suffrage in Studies of Democracy' (2007) 15(1) *Democratization* 29

    'Citizenship and Voting Rights: Should Resident Aliens Vote?' (2006) 10(2) *Citizenship Studies* 153

Beiner, Ronald *Liberalism, Nationalism, Citizenship: Essays on the Problem of Political Community* (University of British Columbia Press 2003)

    'Introduction: Why Citizenship Constitutes a Theoretical Problem in the Last Decade of the Twentieth Century' in Ronald Beiner (ed), *Theorizing Citizenship* (SUNY Press 1995)

    What's the Matter with Liberalism (University of California Press 1992)

Benhabib, Seyla *The Rights of Others* (Harvard University Press 2004)

    'Citizens, Residents and Aliens in a Changing World' (1999) 66 *Social Research* 708

Benhabib, Seyla, and Resnik, Judith 'Introduction' in Seyla Benhabib and Judith Resnik (eds), *Migrations and Mobility: Citizenship, Borders and Gender* (NYU Press 2009)

Bennouna, Mohamed Special Rapporteur, *Preliminary Report on Diplomatic Protection*, ILC Report, 50th session (2000)

Benton, Meghan 'The Tyranny of the Enfranchised Majority? The Accountability of States to their Non-Citizen Population' (2010) 16(4) *Res Publica* 397

Benton, Meghan, and Caroline Bettinger-Lopez and Bassina Farbernblum, 'Book Review of David Weissbrodt, *The Human Rights of Non-Citizens* (Oxford University Press 2008)' (UNSW, Research Series paper No 46 2010)

Berlin, Isaiah 'Two Concepts of Liberty' in Isaiah Berlin (ed), *Four Essays on Liberty* (Oxford University Press 1969)

Betts, Alexander 'The Normative Terrain of the Global Refugee Regime' (2015) 29(4) *Ethics & International Affairs* 363

Bevelander, Pieter 'Naturalisation and Social Inclusion' in *Naturalisation: A Passport for the Better Integration of Immigrants?* (OECD 2011)

Beyani, Chaloka 'Introduction' in Paul Weis, *The Refugee Convention 1951: the Travaux Préparatoires Analysed with a Commentary* (Cambridge University Press 1995) 8

Bhabha, Jacqueline 'Internationalist Gatekeepers? The Tension between Asylum Advocacy and Human Rights' (2002) 15 *Harvard Human Rights Journal* 155

Blais, Andre, Massicotte, Louis and Yoshinaka, Antoine 'Deciding Who Has the Right to Vote: A Comparative Analysis of Election Laws' (2001) 20 *Electoral Studies* 41

Blank, Yishai 'Spheres of Citizenship' (2007) 8(2) *Theoretical Inquiries in Law* 411

Bohman, James *Democracy across Borders: From Demos to Demoi* (MIT Press 2007)

Borchard, Edwin *The Diplomatic Protection of Citizens Abroad* (Banks, 1922)

    'Basic Elements of Diplomatic Protection of Citizens Abroad' (1913) 7 *American Journal of International Law* 497

Bosniak, Linda 'The Meaning of Citizenship' (2011) 9 *Issues in Legal Scholarship* (Article 12)

    'Persons and Citizens in Constitutional Thought' (2010) 8(1) *International Journal of Constitutional Law* 9

    'Citizenship, Non-citizenship and the Trans-nationalization of Domestic Work' in Seyla Benhabib and Judith Resnik (eds), *Migrations and Motilities: Citizenship, Borders and Gender* (NYU Press 2009) 127

    'Being Here: Ethical Territoriality and the Rights of Immigrants' (2007) 8(2) *Theoretical Inquiries in Law* 389

    'Denationalising Citizenship' in T Alexander Aleinikoff and Douglas Klusmeyer (eds), *Citizenship Today: Global Perspectives and Practices* (Carnegie 2001) 237

Bossuyt, Marc J *Guide to the Travaux Préparatoires of the International Covenant on Civil and Political Rights* (Nijhof 1987)

Brettschneider, Corey *Democratic Rights: The Substance of Self-Government* (Princeton University Press 2007)

Brilmayer, Lea 'From "Contract" to "Pledge": The Structure of International Human Rights Agreements' (2006) *British Yearbook of Human Rights* 163

    'Shaping and Sharing in Democratic Theory: Toward a Political Philosophy of Interstate Equality' (1987) 15 *Florida State University Law Review* 389

Brownlie, Ian *Principles of Public International Law* (7th edn Oxford University Press 2008)

Brubaker, Rogers *Citizenship and Nationhood in France and Germany* (Harvard University Press 1992)

Buchanan, Allen 'Justice as Reciprocity versus Subject-Centered Justice' (1990) 19(3) *Philosophy and Public Affairs* 227

Burton, Velmer S 'The Consequences of Official Labels: A Research Note on Rights Lost by the Mentally Ill, Mentally Incompetent and Convicted Felons' (1990) 26(3) *Community Mental Health Journal* 267

Caney, Simon *Justice beyond Borders: A Global Political Theory* (Oxford University Press 2005)

Capps, Patrick *Human Dignity and the Foundations of International Law* (Hart 2009)

Carens, Joseph H *Who Belongs: The Ethics of Immigration* (on file with author)

On Belonging (Boston Review 2005)

'Who Should Get In? The Ethics of Immigration Admissions' (2003) 17(1) *Ethics and International Affairs* 95

Culture, Citizenship, and Community (Oxford University Press 2000)

'The Philosopher and the Policymaker: Two Perspectives on the Ethics of Immigration with Special Attention to the Problem of Restricting Asylum' in Kay Hailbronner et al (eds), *Immigration Admissions: The Search for Workable Policies in Germany and the United States* (Berghahn Books 1997) 3

'Refugees and the Limits of Obligation' (1992) 6 *Public Affairs Quarterly* 31

'Who Belongs? Theoretical and Legal Questions about Birthright Citizenship in the United States' (1987) 37 *University of Toronto Law Journal* 413

'Aliens and Citizens: The Case for Open Borders' (1987) 49 *Review of Politics* 251

Carter, Caroline 'The Right to Vote for Non-Resident Citizens: Considered through the Example of East Timor' (2011) 46 *Texas International Law Journal* 655

Cassese, Antonio (ed) *UN Law/Fundamental Rights: Two Topics in International Law* (Sijthoff & Noordhoff 1979)

Castles, David 'Globalisation and the Ambiguities of National Citizenship' in Rainer Bauböck and John Rundell (eds), *Blurred Boundaries: Migration, Ethnicity, Citizenship* (Ashgate 1998)

Castiglione, Dario, Santoro, Emilio and Bellamy, Richard *Lineages of European Citizenship: Rights, Belonging, and Participation in Eleven Nation-states* (Palgrave Macmillan 2004)

Castles, Stephen and Davidson, Alastair *Citizenship and Migration: Globalization and the Politics of Belonging* (Routledge 2000)

Cerna, Christina M 'Impact on the Right to Consular Notification' in Menno T Kamminga and Martin Scheinin (eds), *The Impact of Human Rights Law on General International Law* (Oxford University Press 2009)

'The Right to Consular Notification as a Human Right' (2008) 31 *Suffolk Transnational Law Review* 419

'Universal Democracy: An International Legal Right or the Pipe Dream of the West?' (1995) 27 *NYU Journal of International Law and Politics* 289

Chetail, Vincent 'Are Refugee Rights Human Rights? An Unorthodox Questioning of the Relations between Refugee Law and Human Rights Law' in Ruth Rubio Marin (ed), *Human Rights and Immigration* (Oxford University Press 2014)

'Voluntary Repatriation in Public International Law: Concepts and Contents' (2004) 23(3) *Refugee Survey Quarterly* 1

Cholbi, Michael 'A Felon's Right to Vote' (2002) 21 *Law and Philosophy* 543

Cholewinski, Ryszard *Migrant Workers in International Human Rights Law: Their Protection in Countries of Employment* (Clarendon Press 1997)

Christiano, Thomas 'Voting and Democracy' (1995) 25(3) *Canadian Journal of Philosophy* 394

Christoffersen, Jonas 'Impact on General Principles of Treaty Interpretation' in Menno T Kamminga and Martin Scheinin (eds), *The Impact of Human Rights Law on General International Law* (Oxford University Press 2009) 37

Clark, Tom 'Rights Based Refuge: The Potential of the 1951 Convention and the Need for Authoritative Interpretation' (2004) 16(4) *International Journal of Refugee Law*

Clark, Tom, and Crépeau, François 'Mainstreaming Refugee Rights: The 1951 Refugee Convention and International Human Rights Law' (1999) 17(4) *Netherlands Quarterly of Human Rights* 389

Cohen, Elizabeth *The Myth of Full Citizenship: A Comparative Study of Semi-Citizenship in Democratic Polities* (PhD dissertation, Yale University 2003)

Cohen, Joshua 'For a Democratic Society' in Samuel Freeman (ed), *The Cambridge Companion to Rawls* (Cambridge University Press 2003)

Cohn, Jean L 'Changing Paradigms of Citizenship and the Exclusiveness of the Demos' (1999) 14 *International Sociology* 245

Coles, Gervase JL 'The Human Rights Approach to the Solution of the Refugee Problem: A Theoretical and Practical Enquiry' in Alan E Nash and John P Humphrey (eds), *Human Rights and the Protection of Refugees under International Law* (The Institute for Research on Public Policy 1988)

Collyer, Michael 'A Geography of Extra-Territorial Citizenship: Explanations of External Voting' (2014) 2(1) *Migration studies* 55

Cox, Adam 'Temporal Dimension of Voting Rights' (2007) 93 *Virginia Law Review* 361

Crawford, James 'The ILC Articles on Diplomatic Protection' (2006) 31 *South Africa Yearbook International Law* 19

'Democracy and the Body of International Law' in Gregory H Fox and Brad Roth (eds), *Democratic Governance and International Law* (Cambridge University Press 2000)

Craven, Matthew 'Human Rights in the Realm of Power: Sanctions and Extraterritoriality' in Fons Coomans and Menno T Kamminga (eds), *Extraterritorial Application of Human Rights Treaties* (Hart 2004) 233

Crisp, Jeff 'No Solutions in Sight: The Problem of Protracted Refugee Situations in Africa' (2003) 22(4) *Refugee Survey Quarterly* 114

D'Souza, Frances and Crisp, Jeff *The Refugee Dilemma* (Minority Rights Group Report No 43, 1985)

Dagger, Richard *Civic Virtues: Rights, Citizenship and Republican Liberalism* (Oxford University Press 1997)

Dahl, Robert *On Democracy* (Yale University Press 1998)
  Democracy and Its Critics (Yale University Press 1989)
Dauvergne, Catherine 'Refugee Law and the Measure of Globalisation' in Savitri
  Taylor (ed), *Nationality, Refugee Status and State Protection Law in Context*
  (Federation Press 2005) 62
Davy, Ulrike 'Article 32: Expulsion' in Andreas Zimmermann (ed), *The 1951 Con-
  vention Relating to the Status of Refugees and its 1967 Protocol: A Commentary*
  (Oxford University Press 2011)
Da Costa, Rosa *Rights of Refugees in the Context of Integration* (UNHCR 2006)
De Vattel, Emer *The Law of Nations or the Principles of Natural Law
  Applied to the Conduct and to the Affairs of Nations and Sovereigns*
  (1758)
Deng, Francis Mading 'The UN and the Protection of Human Rights: The Global
  Challenge of Internal Displacement' (2001) 5 *Washington University Journal
  of Law and Policy* 141
Denza, Eileen *Diplomatic Law: A Commentary on the Vienna Convention on Diplo-
  matic Relations* (3rd edn Oxford University Press 2008)
Derrida, Jacques *On Hospitality* (Stanford University Press 2000)
Diner, Dan Dan Diner, 'Nation, Migration and Memory: On Historical Concepts
  of Citizenship' (1998) 4(3) *Constellations* 293
Donnelly, Jack *Universal Human Rights in Theory and Practice* (2nd edn Cornell
  University Press 2003)
  'Cultural Relativism and Universal Human Rights' (1984) 6 *Human Rights
  Quarterly* 400
Douglas, Joshua 'Is the Right to Vote Really Fundamental?' (2008) 18 *Cornell Journal
  of Law and Public Policy* 143
Dowty, Alan *Closed Borders: The Contemporary Assault on Free Movement* (Yale
  University Press 1997)
Dugard, John 'Diplomatic Protection' in Max Planck Encyclopaedia of Public
  International Law (2006)
  'Diplomatic Protection and Human Rights: The Draft Articles of the Interna-
  tional Law Commission' (2005) 24 *Australian Yearbook International Law*
  75
  Special Rapporteur, *First Report on Diplomatic Protection* (2001)
  Special Rapporteur, *Seventh Report on Diplomatic Protection* (2005)
Durieux, Jean-François 'Three Asylum Paradigms' (2013) 20(2) *International Jour-
  nal on Minority and Group Rights* 147
Dworkin, Ronald *Sovereign Virtue* (Harvard University Press 2000)
  'What is Equality?' (1987) 22 *University of Simon Fraser Law Review* 1
  Taking Rights Seriously (Duckworth 1978)
Earnest, David C 'The Enfranchisement of Resident Aliens: Variations and expla-
  nations' (2015) 22(5) *Democratization* 861

'Neither Citizen nor Stranger: Why States Enfranchise Resident Aliens' (2006) 58(2) *World Politics* 242

Voting Rights for Resident Aliens: Nationalism, Postnationalism and Sovereignty in an Era of Mass Migration (PhD dissertation, George Washington University 2004)

Edwards, Alice 'Human Rights, Refugees and the Right to 'Enjoy' Asylum' (2005) 17(2) *International Journal of Refugee Law* 295

Eleftheriadis, Pavlos *Legal Rights* (Oxford University Press 2008)

Elster, Jon 'Deliberation and Constitution Making' in Jon Elster (ed), *Deliberative Democracy* (Cambridge University Press 1998)

Ely, John H *Democracy and Distrust: A Theory of Judicial Review* (Harvard University Press 1980)

Endicott, Timothy 'The Logic of Freedom and Power' in Samantha Besson and John Tasioulas (eds), *The Philosophy of International Law* (Oxford University Press 2010) 245

Escarameia, Paula 'Professor Dugard as an Innovator in the World of the International Law Commission' (2007) 20 *Leiden Journal of International Law* 931

Evans, Tony *The Politics of Human Rights* (2nd edn Pluto Press 2005)

Ewald, Alec '"Civil Death": The Ideological Paradox of Criminal Disenfranchisement Law in the United States' (2002) 2002 *Wisconsin Law Review* 1045

Fahrmeir, Andreas *Citizenship: The Rise and Fall of a Modern Concept* (Yale University Press 2007)

Falk, Richard 'Accountability, Asylum and Sanctuary: Challenging Our Political and Legal Imagination' in Ved P Nanda (ed), *Refugee Law and Policy: International and US Responses* (Greenwood Press Inc 1989)

Farer, Tom 'How the International System Copes with Involuntary Migration' (1995) 17 *Human Rights Quarterly* 72

Farrior, Stephanie 'International Human Rights Treaties and the Rights of Female Refugees' in Anne Bayefsky (ed), *Human Rights and Refugees, Internally Displaced Persons and Migrant Workers* (Nijhoff 2006)

Feldblum, Miriam 'Reconfiguring Citizenship in Europe' in Christian Joppke (ed), *Challenges to the Nation-State* (Oxford University Press 1998)

Feller, Erika 'Asylum, Migration and Refugee Protection: Realities, Myths and the Promise of Things to Come' (2006) 18 (3–4) *International Journal of Refugee Law* 509

'Refugees Are Not Migrants' (2005) 25(4) *Refugee Survey Quarterly* 27

'International Refugee Protection 50 Years On: The Protection Challenges of the Past, Present and Future' (2001) 83 (843) *International Review of the Red Cross* 581

'The UN and the Protection of Human Rights: The Evolution of the International Refugee Protection Regime' (2001) 5 *Washington University Journal of Law and Policy* 129

'The 1951 Convention at 50: New Challenges for the International Refugee Protection Regime' (Presentation to the Lauterpacht Research Centre for International Law 17 October 2000)

Feria-Tinta, Mónica 'Due Process and the Right to Life in the Context of the Vienna Convention on Consular Relations: Arguing the LaGrand Case' (2001) 12(2) *European Journal of International Law* 363

Fielden, Alexandra *Local Integration: An Under-Reported Solution to Protracted Refugee Situations* (UNHCR New Issues in Refugee Research Working Paper No 158 2008)

Finnis, John M 'Nationality, Alienage and Constitutional Principle' (2007) 123 *Law Quarterly Review* 41

Fishkin, Joseph 'Equal Citizenship and the Individual Right to Vote' (2011) 86 *Indiana Law Journal* 1289

Fitzpatrick, Joan 'The Unreality of International Law in the US and the LaGrand Case' (2002) 27 *Yale Journal of International Law* 427

'The End of Protection: Legal Standards for Cessation of Refugee Status and Withdrawal of Temporary Protection' (1998–1999) 13 *Georgetown Immigration Law Journal* 343

'Revitalizing the 1951 Refugee Convention' (1996) 9 *Harvard Human Rights Journal* 229

Fitzpatrick, Joan, and Bonoan, Rafael 'Cessation of Refugee Status' in Volker Türk and Erika Feller (eds), *Refugee Protection in International Law* (Cambridge University Press 2003)

Fitzpatrick, Joan, and Nicholson, Frances 'Cessation (Article 1C)' in Erika Feller, Volker Türk, and Frances Nicholson (eds), *Refugee Protection in International Law* (Cambridge University Press 2003)

Fletcher, George 'Disenfranchisement as Punishment: Reflections on the Radical Uses of Infamia' (1999) 46 *UCLA Law Review* 1895

Foner, Eric *Reconstruction, America's Unfinished Revolution 1863–1877* (Harper & Row 1988)

Ford, Richard 'City-States and Citizenship' in T Alexander Aleinikoff and Charles Klusmeyer (eds), *Citizenship Today: Global Perspectives and Practices* (Carnegie 2001)

Fortin, Antonio 'The Meaning of Protection in the Refugee Definition' (2001) 12(4) *International Journal of Refugee Law* 548

Fox, Gregory 'The Right to Political Participation in International Law' in Gregory H Fox and Brad Roth (eds), *Democratic Governance and International Law* (Cambridge University Press 2000)

'The Right to Political Participation in International Law' (1992) 17 *Yale Journal of International Law* 539

Franck, Thomas *The Empowered Self: Law and Society in the Age of Individualism* (Oxford University Press 2001)

'The Emerging Right to Democratic Governance' (1992) 86 *American Journal of International Law* 46

Franke, Mark FN 'Political Exclusion of Refugees in the Ethics of International Relations' in Patrick Hayden (ed), *The Ashgate Research Companion to Ethics and International Relations* (Ashgate 2009) 309

Frazer, Elizabeth *The Problems of Communitarian Politics: Unity and Conflict* (Oxford University Press 1999)

Furman, Jesse 'Political Illiberalism: The Paradox of Disenfranchisement and the Ambivalence of Rawlsian Justice' (1997) 106 *Yale Law Journal* 1197

Gallagher, Dennis and Schowengerdt, Anna 'Participation of Refugees in Postconflict Elections' in Krishna Kumar (ed), *Postconflict Elections, Democratization, and International Assistance* (Lynne Rienner Publishers 1998)

Gardner, James A 'The Dignity of Voters' (2010) 64 *University of Miami Law Review* 435

'Liberty, Community and the Constitutional Structure of Political Influence: A Reconsideration of the Right to Vote' (1997) 145(4) *University of Pennsylvania Law Review* 893

Gavison, Ruth 'Immigration and the Human Rights Discourse' (2010) 43(2) *Israel Law Review* 1

Gewirth, Alan 'Are there any Absolute Rights?' In Jeremy Waldron (ed), *Theories of Rights* (Oxford University Press 1984) 91

Ghoshal, Animesh, Crowley, Thomas M 'Refugees and Immigrants: A Human Rights Dilemma' (1983) 5(3) *Human Rights Quarterly* 327

Gibney, Matthew J *Should Citizenship be Conditional?* (RSC Working Paper Series No 75 July 2011)

'The Rights of Non-Citizens to Membership' in Caroline Sawyer and Brad K Blitz (eds), *Statelessness in the European Union* (Cambridge University Press 2011)

The Ethics and Politics of Asylum (Cambridge University Press 2004)

Gibney, Matthew J, and Hansen, Randall *Deportation and the Liberal State: the Forcible Return of Asylum Seekers and Unlawful Migrants in Canada, Germany and the United Kingdom* (UNHCR 2003)

Gigauri, George *Resolving the Liberal Paradox: Citizen Rights and Alien Rights in the UK* (RSC Working Paper No 31 July 2008)

Goldsmith, Jack, and Posner, Eric A *The Limits of International Law* (Oxford University Press 2005)

Goldsmith, Peter *Citizenship: Our Common Bond* (UK Ministry of Justice 2008)

Goodhart, Michael *Democracy as Human Rights: Freedom and Equality in the Age of Globalization* (Routledge 2005)

Goodin, Robert 'Enfranchising All Affected Interests, and Its Alternatives' (2007) 35(1) *Philosophy and Public Affairs* 40

'What Is So Special about Our Fellow Countrymen?' (1988) 98 *Ethics* 663

Goodwin-Gill, Guy S 'The Politics of Refugee Protection' (2008) 27(1) *Refugee Survey Quarterly* 8

Free and Fair Elections (Inter-Parliamentary Union 2006)

Refugees and Their Human Rights (RSC Working Paper No 17 2004)

'Asylum 2001: A Convention and a Purpose' (2001) 13 *International Journal of Refugee Law* 1

'Migration: International Law and Human Rights' in Bimal Ghosh (ed), *Managing Migration* (Oxford University Press 2000) 160

'Who to Protect, How ... and the Future?' (1997) 9(1) *International Journal of Refugee Law* 1

'International Law and Human Rights: Trends Concerning International Migrants and Refugees' (1989) 23(3) *International Migration Review* 526

'The Language of Protection' (1989) 1(1) *International Journal of Refugee Law* 1

'Voluntary Repatriation: Legal and Policy Issues' in Gil Loescher and Laila Monahan (eds), *Refugees and International Relations* (Clarendon Press 1989) 255

'Non-refoulement and the New Asylum Seekers' (1986) 26(4) *Virginia Journal of International Law* 897

International Law and the Movement of Persons between States (Clarendon Press 1978)

Goodwin-Gill, Guy S, and McAdam, Jane *The Refugee in International Law* (3rd edn Oxford University Press 2007)

Grace, James *External and Absentee Voting in Challenging the Norms and Standards of Election Administration* (IFES 2007)

Enfranchising Conflict Forced Migrants (IOM 2003)

The Electoral Rights of Conflict Forced Migrants: A Review of Relevant Legal Norms and Instruments (IOM 2003)

Grace, James, and Mooney, Erin 'Peacebuilding through the Electoral Participation of Displaced Populations' 28(1) (2009) *Refugee Survey Quarterly* 95

Graham, David T and Poku, Nana *Migration, Globalisation and Human Security* (Psychology Press 2009)

Grahl-Madsen, Atle 'Protection of Refugees by Their Country of Origin' (1985–1986) 11 *Yale Journal of International Law* 362

The Status of Refugees in International Law (Sijthoff 1966)

Commentary on the Refugee Convention 1951, Articles 2–11, 13–37 (1963)

Griffin, James *On Human Rights* (Oxford University Press 2008)

Habermas, Jürgen *The Postnational Constellation* (Polity Press 2001)

Between Facts and Norms (Polity Press 1996)

'Three Normative Models of Democracy' in Seyla Benhabib (ed), *Democracy and Difference: Contesting the Boundaries of the Political* (Princeton University Press 1996)

Haddad, Emma *The Refugee in International Society: Between Sovereigns* (Cambridge University Press 2008)

'The Refugee: The Individual between Sovereigns' (2003) 17(3) *Global Society* 297

'Refugee Protection: A Clash of Values' (2003) 7(3) *International Journal of Human Rights* 1

Hamilton, Vivian E 'Democratic Inclusion, Cognitive Development, and the Age of Electoral Majority' (2012) 77(4) *Brooklyn Law Review* 1

Hammar, Tomas *Democracy and the Nation State: Aliens, Denizens and Citizens in a World of International Migration* (Aldershot 1990)

'Dual Citizenship and Political Integration' (1985) 19(3) *International Migration Review* 438

Hampshire, James 'Becoming Citizens: Naturalisation in the Liberal State', in Gideon Calder, Peter Cole and Jonathan Seglow (eds), *Citizenship Acquisition and National Belonging* (Palgrave 2010) 74

Hansen, Randall 'The Poverty of Postnationalism: Citizenship, Immigration, and the New Europe' (2009) 38(1) *Theory and Society* 1

Hanson, Michael *Survey of the Principal Legal Aspects of the Refugee Question at the Present Time* (1938)

Harper-Ho, Virginia 'Noncitizen Voting Rights: The History, the Law and Current Prospects for Change' (2000) 21 *Immigration and Nationality Law Review* 477

Harvey, Colin 'Time for Reform? Refugees, Asylum-Seekers, and Protection under International Human Rights Law' (2015) 34 *Refugee Survey Quarterly* 43

Hathaway, James C 'Why Refugee Law Still Matters' (2007) 8 *Melbourne Journal of International Law* 89

The Rights of Refugees under International Law (Cambridge University Press 2005)

'The Rights of States to Repatriate Former Refugees' (2005) 20 *Ohio State Journal on Dispute Resolution* 175

'What's in a Label?' (2005) 5(1) *European Journal of Migration and Law* 1

'The Meaning of Repatriation' (1997) 9(4) *International Journal of Refugee Law* 551

'A Reconsideration of the Underlying Premise of Refugee Law' (1990) 31 *Harvard International Law Journal* 129

'The Evolution of Refugee Law' (1984) 33 *International and Comparative Law Quarterly* 348

Hathaway, James C, and Foster, Michele *The Law of Refugee Status* (2nd edn Cambridge University Press 2014)

Hathaway, James C, and Neve, Alexander 'Making International Refugee Law Relevant Again' (1998) 10 *Harvard Human Rights Law Journal* 115

Hayduk, Ron 'Democracy for All: Restoring Immigrant Voting Rights in the United States' (2004) 26(4) *New Political Science* 499

Hayward, Clarissa Rile 'The Dark Side of Citizenship: Membership, Territory and the (Anti-) Democratic Polity' (2011) 9 *Issues in Legal Scholarship* (Article 5)

Heater, Derek *What Is Citizenship?* (Polity Press 1999)

> *Citizenship: The Civic Ideal in World History, Politics and Education* (Longman 1990)

Held, David *Models of Democracy* (Polity Press 1996)

> *Democracy and the Global Order: From the Modern State to Cosmopolitan Governance* (Polity Press 1995)

Helton, Arthur C 'What Is Refugee Protection? A Question Revisited' in Niklaus Steiner, Matthew J Gibney, Gil Loescher (eds), *Problems of Protection: The UNHCR, Refugees and Human Rights* (Routledge 2003)

Henkin, Louis 'Protecting the World's Exiles: The Human Rights of Noncitizens' (2000) 22(1) *Human Rights Quarterly* 280

> 'Human Rights and State Sovereignty' (1995/6) 25 (1/2) *Georgia Journal of Comparative and International Law* 31

> 'Refugees and Their Human Rights' (1994–1995) 18 *Fordham International Law Journal* 1079

Higgins, Rosalyn *Problems and Process: International Law and How We Use It* (Clarendon Press 1995)

> 'Derogations under Human Rights Treaties' (1976–7) 48 *British Yearbook International Law* 281

Honig, Bonnie 'Another Cosmopolitanism? Law and Politics in the New Europe' in Seyla Benhabib (ed), *Another Cosmopolitanism: Hospitality, Sovereignty, and Democratic Iterations* (Oxford University Press 2006) 102

Humphrey, John 'Political and Related Rights' in Theodor Meeron (ed), *Human Rights in International Law: Legal and Policy Issues* (Oxford University Press 1986) 171

Hurschka, Constantin 'Article 15' in Andreas Zimmermann (ed), *The 1951 Convention Relating to the Status of Refugees and 1967 Protocol* (Oxford University Press 2011) 571

Ignatieff, Michael 'The Myth of Citizenship' in Ronald Beiner (ed), *Theorizing Citizenship* (SUNY Press 1995) 53

Itchikawa, Minako *Citizenship, Human Rights and State Sovereignty in International Relations* (PhD thesis, University of Keele 2004)

Jackson, Vicky 'Citizenships, Federalisms and Gender' in Seyla Benhabib and Judith Resnik (eds), *Migrations and Motilities: Citizenship, Borders and Gender* (NYU Press 2009) 439

Jacobson, David *Rights across Borders: Immigration and the Decline of Citizenship* (Johns Hopkins University Press 1996)

Jennings, Ivor *The Approach to Self-Government* (Cambridge University Press 1958)

Jennings, Robert 'Speech on the Report of the International Court of Justice' (1992) 86 *American Journal of International Law* 249

'Sovereignty and International Law' in Gerard Kreijen (ed), *State, Sovereignty and International Governance* (2002) 29

Jennings, Robert, and Watts Arthur (eds) *Oppenheim's International Law* (9th edn Oxford University Press 2008) (1905)

Johns, Alecia 'The Case for Political Candidacy as a Fundamental Human Right' (2016) 16 *Human Rights Law Review* 29

Johnson, Heather L 'These Fine Lines: Locating Noncitizenship in Political Protest in Europe' (2015) 19(8) *Citizenship Studies* 951

Jones, Peter *Rights* (Macmillan 1994)

Joppke, Christian 'The Inevitable Lightening of Citizenship' in Ricard Zapata-Barrero (ed), *Citizenship Policies in the Age of Diversity* (CIDON Foundation 2009) 37

Immigration and the Nation-State: The United States, Germany, and Great Britain (Oxford University Press 2000)

'Asylum and State Sovereignty: A Comparison of the US, Germany and Britain' in Christian Joppke (ed), *Challenge to the Nation State: Immigration in Western Europe and the US* (Oxford University Press 1998) 110

Jordan, Bill, and Duvel, Franck (eds) *Migration* (Polity Press 2003)

Kadish, Mark J 'Article 36 of the Vienna Convention on Consular Relations: A Search for the Right to Consul' (1997) 18 *Michigan Journal of International Law* 565

Kagan, Michael 'We Live in a Country of UNHCR: The UNHCR Surrogate State and Refugee Policy in the Middle East' (UNHCR New Issues in Refugee Research No 201 February 2011)

Kälin, Walter 'Non-State Agents of Persecution and the Inability of the State to Protect' in International Association of Refugee Law, *The Changing Nature of Persecution* (Institute of Public Law University of Berne October 2000)

Kamminga, Menno T 'Final Report on the Impact of International Human Rights Law on General International Law' in Menno T Kamminga and Martin Scheinin (eds), *The Impact of International Human Rights Law on General International Law* (Oxford University Press 2009)

Kant, Immanuel *Perpetual Peace: A Philosophical Sketch* (W Hastie trans 1891) (1795)

Kateb, George 'The Moral Distinctiveness of Representative Democracy' (1981) 91 *Ethics* 357

Kateka, James L 'John Dugard's Contribution to the Topic of Diplomatic Protection' (2007) 20 *Leiden Journal of International Law* 921

Katz, Richard *Democracy and Elections* (Oxford University Press 1997)

Kelsen, Hans *General Theory of Law and State* (Anders Wedberg Trans, Russell & Russell 1961)

Kennedy, David *The Dark Sides of Virtue: Reassessing International Humanitarianism* (Princeton University Press 2004)

'Residential Associations as State Actors: Regulating the Impact of Gated Communities on Non-members' (1995) 105 (3) *Yale Law Journal* 761

Keyssar, Alexander *The Right to Vote: the Contested History of Democracy in the United States* (Basic Books 2000)

Kibreab, Gaim 'Citizenship Rights and Repatriation of Refugees' (2003) 37(1) *International Migration Review* 24

'Revisiting the Debate on People, Place, Identity and Displacement' (1999) 12(4) *Journal of Refugee Studies* 387

Kingsbury, Damien 'Universalism and Exceptionalism in Asia' in Damien Kingsbury and Leena Avonius (eds), *Human Rights in Asia: A Reassessment of the Asian Values Debate* (Palgrave Macmillan 2008)

Knop, Karen 'Citizenship, Public and Private' (2008) 71 *Law and Contemporary Problems* 309

Kommers, Donald P *The Constitutional Jurisprudence of the Federal Republic of Germany* (Duke University Press 1997) 197

Korn, David A *Exodus within Borders: An Introduction to the Crisis of Internal Displacement* (Brookings Institution Press 1999)

Kostakopoulou, Theodora *The Future Governance of Citizenship* (Cambridge University Press 2008)

Krasner, Stephen *Sovereignty, Organized Hypocrisy* (Princeton University Press, 1997)

Krenz, Frank 'The Refugee as a Subject of International Law' (1966) *International and Comparative Law Quarterly* 90

Kritzman-Amir, Tally *Socioeconomic Refugees* (PhD dissertation, Faculty of Law Tel-Aviv University 2009)

Kukathas, Chandran 'Liberalism, Communitarianism, and Political Community' (1996) 13(1) *Society Philosophy and Policy* 80

Kunz, Egon F 'Exile and Resettlement: Refugee Theory' (1981) 15 *International Migration Review* 42

Künzli, Annemarieke 'Exercising Diplomatic Protection: The Fine Line between Litigation, Demarches and Consular Assistance' (2006) 66 *ZaöRV* 321

Kymlicka, Will 'Social Unity in a liberal State' (1996) 13(1) *Social Philosophy and Policy* 105

'Return of the Citizen: A Survey of Recent Work on Citizenship Theory' in
  Ronald Beiner (ed), *Theorizing Citizenship* (SUNY Press 1995)
Kymlicka, Will, and Norman, Wayne 'Citizenship in Diverse Societies: Issues, Con-
  texts, Concepts' in Will Kymlicka and Wayne Norman (eds), *Citizenship in
  Diverse Societies* (Oxford University Press 2000) 21
Lacy, Brett *Building Accountability, Legitimacy and Peace: Refugees, Internally Dis-
  places Persons, and the Right to Political Participation* (International Founda-
  tion for Electoral Systems 2004)
Lafleur, Jean-Michel 'The Enfranchisement of Citizens Abroad: Variations and
  Explanations' (2015) 22(5) *Democratization* 840
Lambert, Hélène 'Article 2: General Obligations' in Andreas Zimmermann (ed),
  The 1951 Convention Relating to the Status of Refugees and 1967 Protocol
  (Oxford University Press 2011)
  Seeking Asylum: Comparative Law and Practice in Selected European Countries
  (Nijhoff 1995)
Lardy, Heather 'Citizenship and the Right to Vote' (1997) 17(1) *Oxford Journal of
  Legal Studies* 76
Lauterpacht, Hersch 'Allegiance, Diplomatic Protection, and Criminal Jurisdiction
  over Aliens' (1945–1947) 9 *Cambridge Law Journal* 330
  'Foreword' in Paul Weis, *Nationality and Statelessness in International Law*
  (2nd edn Sijthoff & Noordhoff 1979)
Lavi, Shai 'Citizenship Revocation as Punishment: On the Modern Duties of Cit-
  izens and Their Criminal Breach' (2011) 61(4) *University of Toronto Law
  Journal* 783
Lee, Luke *Consular Law and Practice* (Oxford University Press 1991)
  'The Right to Compensation: Refugees and States of Asylum' (1986) 80(3)
  American Journal of International Law 532
Leigh, Guy 'Nationality and Diplomatic Protection' (1971) 20 *International and
  Comparative Law Quarterly* 453
Legomsky, Stephen H 'Citizens' Rights and Human Rights' (2010) 43(1) *Israel Law
  Review* 67
  'Why Citizenship' (1994) 35 *Virginia Journal of International Law* 279
Lenard, Patti Tamara 'Residence and the Right to Vote' (2015) 16 *International
  Migration and Integration* 119
Levin, Michael *The Spectre of Democracy: The Rise of Modern Democracy as Seen by
  Its Critics* (Macmillan 1992)
Levinson, Sanford 'Suffrage and Community: Who Should Vote?' (1989) 41 *Florida
  Law Review* 545
Lister, Matthew 'Who Are Refugees' (2013) 32(5) *Law and Philosophy* 645
Lister, Ruth 'Citizenship in the Immigration Context' (2010–2011) 70 *Maryland
  Law Review* 175
  'Children and Citizenship' (2007) 8(2) *Theoretical Inquiries in Law* 695

Locke, John *The Second Treatise of Civil Government* (first published 1690 Blackwell 1946)
  Two Treatises of Government (first published 1690 Peter Laslett ed, Cambridge University Press 1960)
Lopez-Guerra, Claudio 'Should Expatriates Vote?' (2005) 12 *Journal of Political Philosophy* 216
Long, Katy *Voting with Their Feet: A Review of Refugee Participation and the Role of UNHCR in Country of Origin Elections and Other Political Processes* (UNHCR 2010)
MacDonald, David R Difference and Belonging: Liberal Citizenship and Modern Multiplicity (PhD thesis, LSE 2002)
Macedo, Stephen *Liberal Virtues* (Clarendon Press 1991)
Macklin, Audrey 'Citizenship Revocation, the Privilege to Have Rights and the Production of the Alien' (2014) 40(1) *Queens Law Journal* 1
Mandal, Ruma *Political Rights of Refugees* (UNHCR 2003)
  Protection Mechanisms Outside of the 1951 Convention ('Complementary Protection') (UNHCR 2005)
Mann, Itamar 'Refugees' (2011) 2e *Mafteah* 81
Manza, Jeff and Uggen, Christopher *Locked Out: Felon Disenfranchisement and American Democracy* (Oxford University Press 2006)
Marden, Peter 'Mapping Territoriality' in David Graham and Nana Poku (eds), *Migration, Globalisation, and Human Security* (Routledge 2000)
Marshall, Trevor H and Bottomore, Tom *Citizenship and Social Class* (Pluto Press 1992) (1950)
Martin, David A 'New Rules on Dual Nationality for a Democratizing Globe: Between Rejection and Embrace' (1999) 14 *Georgetown Immigration Law Journal* 1
  'Due Process and Membership in the National Community: Political Asylum and Beyond' (1983) 44 *University of Pittsburgh Law Review* 165
Marx, Reinhard 'Article 1E' in Andreas Zimmermann (ed), *The 1951 Convention Relating to the Status of Refugees and 1967 Protocol* (Oxford University Press 2011) 571
Mason, Andrew *Community, Solidarity and Belonging: Levels of Community and their Normative Significance* (Cambridge University Press 2000)
Massey, Hugh *UNHCR and De Facto Statelessness* (UNHCR April 2010)
Massicotte, Louis, Blais, Andre, and Yoshinaka, Antoine *Establishing the Rules of the Game: Election Laws in Democracies* (University of Toronto Press 2004)
Mathew, Penelope 'Review: James Hathaway, The Rights of Refugees under International Law (Cambridge University Press 2005)' (2008) 102(1) *American Journal of International Law* 206
  'Lest We Forget: Australia's Policy on East Timorese Asylum Seekers' (1999) 11(1) *International Journal of Refugee Law* 7

Mazzeschi, Riccardo Pisillo 'The Relationship between Human Rights and the Rights of Aliens and Immigrants' in Ulrich Fastenrath, Rudolf Geiger et al (eds), *From Bilateralism to Community Interest* (Oxford University Press 2011)

'Impact on the Law of Diplomatic Protection' in Menno T Kamminga and Martin Scheinin (eds), *The Impact of Human Rights Law on General International Law* (Oxford University Press 2009)

McAdam, Jane *Complementary Protection in International Refugee Law* (Oxford University Press 2007)

McCorquodale, Robert 'The Individual and the International Legal System' in Malcolm Evans (ed), *International Law* (3rd edn Oxford University Press 2010)

McCrudden, Christopher 'A Common Law of Human Rights? Transnational Judicial Conversations on Human Rights' (2000) 20 *Oxford Journal of Legal Studies* 499

'Human Dignity and Judicial Interpretation of Human Rights' (2008) 19(4) *European Journal of International Law* 655

McDougal, Myres S, Lasswell, Harold D, and Chen, Lung-Chu 'The Protection of Aliens from Discrimination and World Public Order: Responsibility of States Conjoined with Human Rights' (1976) 70 *American Journal of International Law* 459

McGinnis, John and Somin, Ilya 'Democracy and International Human Rights Law' (2009) 84(4) *Notre Dame Law Review* 1739

Michelman, Frank 'Parsing "a Right to have Rights"' (1996) 3(2) *Constellations* 200

'Conceptions of Democracy in American Constitutional Argument: Voting Rights' (1989) 41 *Florida Law Review* 439

Milano, Enrico 'Diplomatic Protection and Human Rights before the International Court of Justice: Refashioning Tradition?' (2005) 35 *Netherlands Yearbook International Law* 85

Milanović, Marko *Extraterritorial Application of Human Rights Treaties: Law, Principles and Policy* (Oxford University Press 2011)

Mill, John Stuart *Representative Government* (1861)

'Thoughts on Parliamentary Reform' in John Robson (ed), *The Collected Works of John Stuart Mill* (Liberty Fund 2006)

Miller, David 'Immigrants, Nations, and Citizenship' (2008) 16(4) *Journal of Political Philosophy* 371

'Democracy's Domain' (2009) 37(3) *Philosophy and Public Affairs* 219

Citizenship and National Identity (Polity Press 2000)

'Bounded Citizenship' in Kimberly Hutchings and Roland Dannreuther (eds), *Cosmopolitan Citizenship* (Macmillan 1999) 60

On Nationality (Clarendon Press 1995)

Milner, James *Refugees and the Peace-Building Process* (UNHCR 2011)

Mitchell, David 'Undermining Individual and Collective Citizenship: The Impact of Exclusion Laws on the African-American Community' (2007) 34 *Fordham Urban Law Journal* 833

Möller, Kai 'Balancing and the Structure of Constitutional Rights' (2007) 5(3) *International Journal of Constitutional Law* 453

Montesquieu, Charles de Secondat, Baron de *The Spirit of Laws* (first published 1748, Thomas Nugent tr, Printed for J Collingwood 1823)

Montgomery, J Randal 'Components of Refugee Adaptation' (1996) 30 *International Migration Review* 679

Morris, Lydia 'Managing Contradiction: Civic Stratification and Migrants' rights' (2003) 37(1) *International Migration Review* 74

Morsink, Johannes *Inherent Human Rights: Philosophical Roots of the Universal Declaration* (University of Philadelphia Press 2009)

Munro, Daniel 'Integration through Participation: Noncitizen Resident Voting Rights in an Era of Globalisation' (2008) 9(1) *Journal of International Migration and Integration* 43

Murphy, Sean 'The Expulsion of Aliens and Other Topics: The Sixty-Fourth Session of the International Law Commission' (2013) 107(1) *American Journal of International Law* 164

Mutua, Makau 'Standards Setting in Human Rights: Critique and Prognosis' (2007) 29(3) *Human Rights Quarterly* 547

Human Rights: A Political and Cultural Critique (University of Pennsylvania Press 2002)

Nagy, Boldizsar 'The Frontiers of the Sovereign' in Anne Bayefsky (ed), *Human Rights and Refugees, Internally Displaced Persons and Migrant Workers* (Nijhoff 2006) 91

Nathwani, Niraj *Rethinking Refugee Law* (Nijhoff 2003)

Navarro, Carlos 'The Political Rights of Migrant Workers and External Voting' in *Voting from Abroad: The International IDEA Handbook on External Voting* (IDEA 2007)

Neuman, Gerald L 'We the People: Alien Suffrage in German and American Perspective' (1991–1992) 13 *Michigan Journal of International Law* 259

'Aliens and Equal Protection: Why Not the Right to Vote?' (1977) 75 *Michigan Law Review* 1092

Nolan, Aoilfe 'The Child as "Democratic Citizen" – Challenging the Participation Gap' [2010] *Public Law* 126

Noll, Gregor *Rejected Asylum Seekers: The Problem of Return* (UNHCR 1999)

Nowak, Manfred *UN Covenant on Civil and Political Rights: CCPR Commentary* (2nd revised edn Engel 2005)

Nussbaum, Martha *Capabilities as Fundamental Entitlements: Sen and Social Justice* (Hitotsubashi University 2002)

O'Connell, Rory 'Realising Political Equality: The European Court of Human Rights and Positive Obligations in a Democracy' (2010) 61(3) *Northern Ireland Law Quarterly* 263

Okowa, Pohebe 'Issues of Admissibility and the Law on International Responsibility' in Malcolm Evans (ed), *International Law* (3rd edn Oxford University Press 2010)

Oppenheim, Lassa and Lauterpacht, Hersch *International Law: A Treatise* (Longmans 1955)

Owen, David 'Citizenship and the Marginalities of Migrants' (2013) 16(3) *Critical Review of International Social and Political Philosophy* 326

    In Loco Civitatis (on file with author)

    'Transnational Citizenship and Rights of Political Participation' (Normative Orders Working Paper No 06 2011)

    'Resident Aliens, Non-resident Citizens and Voting Rights' in Gideon Calder, Peter Cole and Jonathan Seglow (eds), *Citizenship Acquisition and National Belonging* (Palgrave 2010) 63

Parekh, Bhikhu 'Finding a Proper Place for Human Rights' in Kate Tunstall (ed), *Displacement, Asylum, Migration* (Oxford Amnesty Lectures 2004, Oxford University Press 2006)

    'Three Theories of Immigration' in Sarah Spencer (ed), *Strangers and Citizens: A Positive Approach to Migrants and Refugees* (Rivers Oram Press 1994)

Paternan, Carol *Participation and Democratic Theory* (Cambridge University Press 1970)

Persau, Santhosh *Protecting Refugees and Asylum-Seekers under the ICCPR* (UNHCR, New Issues in Refugee Research No 132 November 2006)

Perry, Michael 'Secular Viewpoints, Religious Viewpoints and the Morality of Human Rights' (Emory University School of Law Public Law and Legal Theory Research Paper Series 102–10)

Perry, Stephen 'Immigration, Justice and Culture' in Warren Schwartz (ed), *Justice in Immigration* (Cambridge University Press 1995)

Peter, Fabienne 'The Human Right to Political Participation' (2013) 7(2) *Journal of Ethics & Social Philosophy* 1

Pettit, Philip *Republicanism: A Theory of Freedom and Government* (Oxford University Press 1997)

Pettus, Katherine *Felony Disenfranchisement in the Contemporary United States: An Ancient Practice in a Modern Polity* (PhD dissertation, Columbia University 2002)

Pildes, Richard 'What Kind of Right Is "the Right to Vote"' (2007) 93 *Virginia Law Review in Brief* 43

Plender, Richard *Basic Documents on International Migration Law* (Nijhoff 1997)

    International Migration Law (revised 2nd edn Nijhoff 1988)

Pobjoy, Jason 'Treating Like Cases Alike' (2010) 34)(1) *Melbourne University Law Review* 181

Pogge, Thomas *World Poverty and Human Rights: Cosmopolitan Responsibilities and Reforms* (Polity Press 2008)

Prather, Lauren, and Herron, Erik S 'Enfranchising Displaced Voters: Lessons from Bosnia-Herzegovina' (2007) 6(4) *Election Law Journal* 354

Preuss, Ulrich K 'Migration – A Challenge to Modern Citizenship' (1998) 4(3) *Constellations* 307

Price, Matthew E *Rethinking Asylum: History, Purpose and Limits* (Cambridge University Press 2009)

　'Politics or Humanitarianism? Recovering the Political Roots of Asylum' (2004) 19 *Georgetown Immigration Law Journal* 277

Przeworski, Adam 'Minimalist Conception of Democracy: A Defense' in Ian Shapiro and Casiano Hacker-Cordón (eds), *Democracy's Value* (Cambridge University Press 1999)

Pupavac, Vanessa 'Refugees in the Sick Role: Stereotyping Refugees and Eroding Refugee Rights' (New Issues in Refugee Research No 127 August 2006)

Quigley, John B, Aceves, William J, and Shank, S Adele *The Law of Consular Access: A Documentary Guide* (Routledge 2010)

Raskin, James 'Legal Aliens, Local Citizens: The Historical, Constitutional and Theoretical Meanings of Alien Suffrage' (1993) 41(4) *University of Pennsylvania Law Review* 1391

Raz, Joseph 'Legal Rights' in Joseph Raz (ed), *Ethics in the Public Domain* (Clarendon Press 1995)

　The Morality of Freedom (Clarendon Press 1986)

　'Right-Based Moralities' in Jeremy Waldron (ed), *Theories of Rights* (Oxford University Press 1984) 191

Rawls, John *The Law of Peoples* (Harvard University Press 1999)

　Political Liberalism (Columbia University Press 1996)

　A Theory of Justice (Harvard University Press 1971)

Rehman, Javaid *International Human Rights Law* (2nd edn Pearson 2010)

Reichel, David *Do Legal Regulations Hinder Naturalisation? Citizenship Policies and Naturalisation Rates in Europe* (European University Institute RSCAS 2011/51 2011)

Reiman, Jeffrey 'Liberal and Republican Arguments against Felon Disenfranchisement' (2005) 24(1) *Criminal Justice Ethics* 3

Reisman, Michael 'Sovereignty and Human Rights in Contemporary International Law' (1990) 84 *American Journal of International Law* 866

Richmond, Anthony H *Global Apartheid: Refugees, Racism and the New World Order* (Oxford University Press 1994)

Ritzer, George 'Rethinking Globalization: Glocalization/Grobalization and Something/Nothing' (2003) 21(3) *Sociological Theory* 193

Rivers, Julian 'Proportionality and Variable Intensity of Review' (2006) 65 *Cambridge Law Journal* 174

Roberts, Adam 'More Refugees, Less Asylum: A Regime in Transformation' (1998) 11(4) *Journal of Refugee Studies* 375

Roberts, Bayard *Guide to Forced Migration and Electoral Participation* (Forced Migration Online 2003)

Robinson, Nehemiah *Convention Relating to the Status of Refugees: Its History and Interpretation, a Commentary* (Institute of Jewish Affairs 1953)

    The Universal Declaration of Human Rights: Its Origin, Significance, Application and Interpretation (Institute of Jewish Affairs 1950)

Rodriguez, Cristina M 'Review of Peter J Spiro, Beyond Citizenship: American Citizenship after Globalization' (2009) 103 *American Journal of International Law* 180

    'The Citizenship Paradox in a Transnational Age' (2008) 106 *Michigan Law Review* 1111

Rosas, Allan 'Article 21' in Gudmundur Alfredson and Asbjorn Eide (eds), *The Universal Declaration of Human Rights: A Common Standard of Achievement* (Nijhoff 1999) 431

Rosberg, Gerald M 'Aliens and Equal Protection: Why Not the Right to Vote?' (1977) 75(5–6) *Michigan Law Review* 1092

Rousseau, Jean-Jacques *On the Social Contract* (first published 1762, Judith Masters tr, St Martin's Press 1978)

Rubio-Marin, Ruth *Human Rights and Immigration* (Cambridge University Press 2014)

    'Transnational Politics and the Democratic Nation-State: Normative Challenges of Expatriate Voting and Nationality Retention of Emigrants' (2006) 81 *NYU Law Review* 117

    Immigration as a Democratic Challenge: Citizenship and Inclusion in Germany and the United States (Cambridge University Press 2000)

Sadurski, Wojciech 'Legitimacy, Political Equality, and Majority Rule' (2008) 21 *Ratio Juris* 39

Saliceti, Alessandro I 'The Protection of EU Citizens Abroad' (2011) 17(1) *European Public Law* 91

Sandel, Michael J *Liberalism and the Limits of Justice* (2nd edn, Cambridge University Press 1998)

Sassen, Saskia 'The Repositioning of Citizenship' in Alison Brysk and Gershon Shafir (eds), *People Out of Place: Globalisation, Human Rights and the Citizenship Gap* (Routledge 2004)

Saunders, Ben 'Majority Rule and Procedural Equality' (2010) 23(1) *Ratio Juris* 113

    Republicanism and Abstention (on file with author)

Schall, Jason 'The Consistency of Felon Disenfranchisement with Citizenship Theory' (2006) 22 *Harvard Blackletter Law Review* 53

Schauer, Fredrick 'Community, Citizenship and the Search for National Identity' (1986) 84 *Michigan Law Review* 1504

Schwarzenberger, Georg *International Law* (3rd edn Stevens 1957)

Seglow, Jonathan 'Arguments for Naturalisation' (2008) 57(5) *Political Studies* 788

Sen, Amartya *The Idea of Justice* (Penguin 2009)

    Development as Freedom (Oxford University Press 1999)

    'Human Rights and Economic Achievements' in Joanna Bauer and Daniel Bell (eds), *The East Asian Challenge for Human Rights* (Cambridge University Press 1999)

Shachar, Ayelet *The Birthright Lottery: Citizenship and Global Inequality* (Harvard University Press 2009)

    'The Future of National Citizenship: Going, Going, Gone?' (2009) 59 *University of Toronto Law Journal* 579

Shacknove, Andrew 'Who Is a Refugee?' (1985) 95 *Ethics* 274

Shearer, Ivan and Opeskin, Brian 'Nationality and Statelessness' in Brian Opeskin, Richard Perruchoud and Jillyanne Redpath-Cross (eds), *Foundations of International Migration Law* (Cambridge University Press 2012) 93

Shklar, Judith N *American Citizenship: The Quest for Inclusion* (Harvard University Press 1991)

Shuck, Peter 'The Devaluation of American Citizenship' in Peter Shuck (ed), *Citizens, Strangers and In-Betweens: Essays on Immigration and Citizenship* (Westview Press 1998)

Skordas, Achilles 'Article 7' in Andreas Zimmermann (ed), *The 1951 Convention Relating to the Status of Refugees and 1967 Protocol* (Oxford University Press 2011) 571

Sloane, Robert D 'Breaking the Genuine Link: The Contemporary International Legal Regulation of Nationality' (2009) 50 *Harvard International Law Journal* 1

Spinner, Jeff *The Boundaries of Citizenship* (Johns Hopkins University Press 1994)

Spiro, Peter J '*Citizenship and Diaspora: A State Home for Transnational Politics?*' in Terrance Lyons and Peter Mandaville (eds), *Politics from Afar: Transnational Diasporas and Networks* (Hurst/Columbia University Press 2011)

    'A New International Law of Citizenship' (2011) 105(4) *American Journal of International Law* 694

Springrose, Linda J 'Strangers in a Strange Land' (1999–2000) 14 *Georgetown Immigration Law Journal* 185

Soguk, Nevzat *States and Strangers: Refugees and the Displacement of Statecraft* (University of Minnesota Press 1999)

Song, Sarah 'Democracy and Noncitizen Voting Rights' (2009) 13(6) *Citizenship Studies* 607

Soysal, Yaesmin *The Limits of Citizenship* (University of Chicago 1994)

'Changing Citizenship in Europe: Remarks on Post-national Membership and the National State' in David Cesarani and Mary Fulbrook (eds), *Citizenship, Nationality, and Migration in Europe* (Routledge 1996) 24

Stasinopolous, Panos 'EU Citizenship as a Battle of the Concepts: Travailleur v Citoyen' (2011) 4(2) *European Journal of Legal Studies* 74

Steinbock, Daniel J 'Interpreting the Refugee Definition' (1998) 45 *UCLA Law Review* 733

Steiner, Henry 'Do Human Rights Require a Particular Form of Democracy?' in Eugene Cotran and Adel O Sherif (eds), *Democracy, Human Rights and Islam* (Kluwer 1999) 193

'Political Participation as a Human Right' (1988) 1 *Harvard Human Rights Yearbook* 77

Stewart, Emma and Mulvey, Gareth *Becoming British Citizens? Experiences and Opinions of Refugees Living in Scotland* (Scottish Refugee Council and Strathclyde University February 2011)

Suhrke, Astri 'Burden-Sharing during Refugee Emergencies: The Logic of Collective versus National Action' (1998) 11(4) *Journal of Refugee Studies* 396

Sweeney, James 'Margin of Appreciation, Cultural Relativity, and the European Court of Human Rights in the post Cold-War Era' (2004) 54 *International and Comparative Law Quarterly* 459

Tahbaz, Christopher C, and Takkenberg, Alex *The Collected Travaux Préparatoires of the 1951 Geneva Convention Relating to the Status of Refugees* (Dutch Refugee Council 1990)

Talbott, William *Which Rights Should Be Universal?* (Oxford University Press 2005)

Tambakaki, P *Human Rights, or Citizenship?* (Birkbeck Law Press 2010)

Tamir, Yael *Liberal Nationalism* (Princeton University Press 1993)

Taylor, Charles 'The Dynamics of Democratic Exclusion' (1998) 9(4) *Journal of Democracy* 143

'The Politics of Recognition' in Amy Gutmann (ed), *Multiculturalism: Examining the Politics of Recognition* (Princeton University Press 1994) 25

'Cross-Purposes: The Liberal-Communitarian Debate' in Nancy Rosenblum (ed), *Liberalism and the Moral Life* (Harvard University Press 1989)

Tesón, Fernando *A Philosophy of International Law* (Westview Press 1998)

Tiburcio, Carmen *The Human Rights of Aliens under International and Comparative Law* (Nijhoff 2001)

Torpey, John *The Invention of the Passport* (Cambridge University Press 2000)

Tribe, Lawrence *American Constitutional Law* (2nd edn Foundation Press 1988)

Türk, Volker 'Non-State Agents of Persecution' in Vincent Chetail and V Gowlland-Debbas (eds), *Switzerland and the International Protection of Refugees* (Kluwer 2002) 95

Van Gunsteren, Herman R 'Admission to Citizenship' (1988) 98 *Ethics* 731

Van Hear, Nicholas 'Refugees in Diaspora: From Durable Solutions to Transnational Relations' (2006) 23(1) *Refuge* 9

Van Waas, Laura *Nationality Matters* (Intersentia 2008)

Vedsted-Hansen, Jens 'Article 28/Schedule' in Andreas Zimmerman (ed), *The 1951 Convention relating to the Status of Refugees and Its 1951 Protocol: A Commentary* (Oxford University Press 2011)

Vermeer-Künzli, Annemarieke 'As If: The Legal Fiction in Diplomatic Protection' (2007) 18 *European Journal of International Law* 37

'Case Concerning Mexican Nationals' (2005) 18 *Leiden Journal of International Law* 49

Vink, Maarten P and de Groot, Gerard-Rene *Loss of Citizenship* (EUDO Citizenship Policy Brief No 3 2012)

'Citizenship Attribution in Western Europe: International Framework and Domestic Trends' (2010) 36(5) *Journal of Ethnic and Migration Studies* 713

Vucetic, Srdjan 'Democracies and International Human Rights: Why Is There No Place for Migrant Workers?' (2007) 11(4) *International Journal of Human Rights* 403

Waldron, Jeremy 'Teaching Cosmopolitan Right' in Kevin McDonough and Walter Feinberg (eds), *Citizenship and Education in Liberal-Democratic Societies* (Oxford University Press 2003) 23

Law and Disagreement (Clarendon Press 1999)

'Participation: The Right of Rights' (1998) 98(3) *Proceedings of the Aristotelian Society* 307

'A Right-Based Critique of Constitutional Rights' (1993) 13(1) *Oxford Journal of Legal Studies* 18

Liberal Rights (Cambridge University Press 1993)

'Special Ties and Natural Duties' (1993) 22(1) *Philosophy and Public Affairs* 3

Walker, Kristen 'Defending the 1951 Convention Definition of Refugee' (2002–2003) 17 *Georgetown Immigration Law Journal* 583

Walzer, Michael 'Spheres of Affection' in Joshua Cohen (ed), *For Love of Country?* (Beacon Press 1996)

Spheres of Justice: A Defense of Pluralism and Equality (Robertson 1983)

'Citizenship' in Terence Ball, James Farr, and Russell Hanson (eds), *Political Innovation and Conceptual Change* (Cambridge University Press 1982) 216

Obligations: Essays on Disobedience, War, and Citizenship (Clarion Books 1970)

Weil, Patrick 'From Conditional to Secured and Sovereign: The New Strategic Link Between the Citizen and the Nation-State in a Globalised World' (2011) 9(3–4) *International Journal of Constitutional Law* 614

Weiler, Joseph HH 'To be a European Citizen – Eros and Civilization' (1997) 4(4) *Journal of European Public Policy* 495

Weiner, Myron 'Ethics, National Sovereignty and the Control of Immigration' (1996) 30 *International Migration Review* 171

Weis, Paul *The Refugee Convention 1951: The Travaux Préparatoires Analysed with a Commentary* (Grotius Publications 1995)

    Nationality and Statelessness in International Law (2nd edn Sijthoffand Noordhoof 1979)

    'Human Rights and Refugees' (1971) 1 *Israel Yearbook on Human Rights* 35

    'The 1967 Protocol Relating to the Status of Refugees and Some Questions Relating to the Law of Treaties' (1967) *British Yearbook of International Law* 39

    'The United Nations Convention on the Reduction of Statelessness 1961' (1962) 11 *International and Comparative Law Quarterly* 1073

    Nationality and Statelessness in International Law (Stevens 1956)

    'The International Protection of Refugees' (1954) 48 *American Journal of International Law* 193

Weissbrodt, David *The Human Rights of Non-Citizens* (Oxford University Press 2008)

Weissbrodt, David, and Divine, Michael 'Unequal Access to Human Rights: The Categories of Noncitizenship' (2015) 19(8) *Citizenship Studies* 870

Weissbrodt, David, and Meili, Stephen 'Human Rights and Protection of Non-Citizens: Whither Universality and Indivisibility of Rights?' (2009) 28(4) *Refugee Survey Quarterly* 34

Wheatley, Stephen *The Democratic Legitimacy of International Law* (Hart 2010)

Williams, Melissa 'Non-Territorial Boundaries of Citizenship' in Seyla Benhabib, Ian Shapiro and Danilo Petranovic (eds), *Identities, Affiliations, and Allegiances* (Cambridge University Press 2007)

Wilsner, David 'Non-State Actors and the Definition of a Refugee in the United Kingdom: Protection, Accountability or Culpability?' (2003) 15(1) *International Journal of Refugee Law* 68

Winkler, Adam 'Expressive Voting' (1993) 68 *NYU Law Review* 330

Woodward, John 'Commentary: Liberalism and Migration' in Brian Barry and Robert Goodin (eds), *Free Movement: Ethical Issues in the Transnational Migration of People and of Money* (Harvester Wheatsheaf 1992) 59

Worster, William T 'The Contemporary International Law of the Right to Receive Asylum' (2014) 26(4) *International Journal of Refugee Law* 477

Wyman, Katryna M 'Sinking States' in Daniel H Cole and Elinor Ostrom (eds), *Property in Land and Other Resources* (Lincoln Institute of Land Policy 2012)

Zieck, Marjorie 'Codification of the Law of Diplomatic Protection: The First Eight Articles' (2001) 14 *Leiden Journal of International Law* 209

    UNHCR and Voluntary Repatriation of Refugees (Nijhoff 1997)

Ziegler, Reuven (Ruvi) 'Voting Eligibility: Strasbourg's Timidity' in Katja S Ziegler, Elizabeth Wicks and Loveday Hodson (eds), *The UK and European Human Rights: A Strained Relationship?* (Hart 2015) 165

'Legal Outlier, Again? U.S. Felon Suffrage: Comparative and International Human Rights Perspectives' (2011) 29(2) *Boston University International Law Journal* 197

'The French Headscarves Ban: Intolerance or Necessity?' (2006) 40(1) *John Marshall Law Review* 235

Shaw, Jo and Bauböck, Rainer (eds) *Independence Referendums: Who Should Vote and Who Should be Offered Citizenship?* (Robert Schuman Centre for Advanced Studies 2014/90 EUI 2014)

Zilbershats, Yaffa *The Human Right to Citizenship* (Transnational Publishing 2002)

'Reconsidering the Concept of Citizenship' (2001) 36 *Texas International Law Journal* 689

Other Sources

Canada, Law Commission *Citizenship and Identity* (Sage 1999)

CARE *Report on Consular and Diplomatic Protection: Legal Framework in the EU Member States* (2010)

Committee on International Assistance to Refugees *Report by the Committee* (submitted to the Council of the League of Nations, Geneva, 3 January 1939)

Committee on Social, Economic and Cultural Rights General Comment No 20: *Non-Discrimination in Economic, Social and Cultural Rights* (2 July 2009)

Committee on the Elimination of Discrimination against Women General Recommendation No 21: *Equality in Marriage and Family* (1994)

Committee on the Elimination of Racial Discrimination General Recommendation No 30: *Discrimination against Non-citizens* (10 January 2004)

Concluding Observations (Netherlands) (2004)

General Recommendation No 22: Article 5 and Refugees and Displaced Persons (1996)

Committee on Migrant Workers Report, CMW/C/ALB/CO/1 of 22 February 2010 (Albania)

Report, CMW/C/DZA/1 of 22 June 2008 (Algeria)

Report, CMW/C/AZE/CO/1 of 19 May 2009 (Azerbaijan)

Report, CMW/C/BIH/CO/1 of 3 June 2009 (BiH)

Report, CMW/C/BOL/CO/1 of 29 April 2008 (Bolivia)

Report, CMW/C/CHL/CO/1 of 19 October 2011 (Chile)

Report, CMW/C/COL/CO/1 of 22 May 2009 (Colombia)

Report, CMW/C/ECU/2 of 26 January 2010 (Ecuador)

Report, CMW/C/EGY/CO/1 of 25 May 2007 (Egypt)

Report, CMW/C/SLV/CO/1 of 4 February 2009 (El Salvador)

Report, CMW/C/GTM/CO/1 of 18 October 2011 (Guatemala)

Report, CMW/C/MLI/CO/1 of 31 May 2006 (Mali)

Report, CMW/C/MEX/1 of 18 November 2005 (Mexico)

Report, CMW/C/PRY/1 of 23 February 2011 (Paraguay)
Report, CMW/C/PHL/CO/1 of 22 May 2009 (Philippines)
Report, CMW/C/SEN/1 of 4 January 2010 (Senegal)
Report, CMW/C/LKA/CO/1 of 19 October 2009 (Sri Lanka)
Council of Europe, Committee of Ministers *Thematic Monitoring Report presented by the Secretary General and Decisions on Follow-up Action taken by the Committee of Ministers* (19 October 2005)
    Recommendation R84 (21) *The Acquisition by Refugees of Nationality of the Host Country* (14 November 1984)
Council of Europe, Committee on Migration, Refugees and Demography *Report on Participation of Immigrants and Foreign Residents in Political Life in the Council of Europe Member States* (22 December 2000)
Council of Europe, European Commission for Democracy through Law *Report on Out-of-Country Voting* (17–18 June 2011)
    European Code of Good Practice in Electoral Matters (30 October 2002)
Council of Europe, Parliamentary Assembly Andreas Gross, Rapporteur, *The State of Democracy in Europe: Specific Challenges Facing European Democracies: The Case of Diversity and Migration* (6 June 2008)
    Recommendation No 1714 (2005)
    Resolution No 1459, *Abolition of Restrictions on the Right to Vote* (2005)
    Recommendation No 1650, *Links between Europeans Living Abroad and Their Countries of Origin* (2004)
    Recommendation No R(86), *The Exercise in the State of Residence by Nationals of Other Member States of the Right to Vote in the Elections of the State of Origin* (21 March 1986)
    Recommendation No 799 (1977), *The Political Rights and Position of Aliens* (25 January 1977)
    Resolution 70(2), *The Acquisition by Refugees of the Nationality of Their Country of Residence* (26 January 1970)
    European Code of Good Practice in Electoral Matters, Opinion 190/2002 (5–6 July and 18–19 October 2002)
European Council of Refugees and Exiles *Position on the Integration of Refugees in Europe* (December 2002)
    Good Practice Guide on the Integration of Refugees in the European Union (2001)
European Union Commission, *Proposed Council Directive on Consular Protection for Citizens of the Union Abroad* (2011)
    Commission, *Consular Protection for EU Citizens in Third Countries* (March 2011)
    Commission, *EU Citizenship Report 2010: Dismantling the Obstacles to EU Citizens' rights* (October 2010)
    Recommendation CM/Rec (2009): *The Nationality of Children*

Human Rights Committee Concluding Observations (Portugal) (2003); Belgium (2004); Latvia (2004)

General Comment No 31: *The Nature of the General Legal Obligation imposed on States Parties to the Covenant* (29 March 2004)

General Comment No 27: *Freedom of Movement* (Article 12) (2 November 1999)

General Comment No 25 (57): *The Right to Take Part in the Conduct of Public Affairs, Voting Rights and the Right of Equal Access to Public Service* (Article 25) (27 August 1996)

General Comment No 18: *Non Discrimination* (10 November 1989)

General Comment No 15: *The Position of Aliens under the Covenant* (11 April 1986)

General Comment No 12: *Article 1* (13 March 1984)

Institute for Democracy and Electoral Assistance *Voting from Abroad: The International IDEA Handbook on External Voting* (2007)

Intergovernmental Committee on Refugees *Memorandum: Statelessness and some of its Causes: An Outline* (UNRRA 1946)

International Law Commission *Draft Articles on Expulsion of Aliens*, ILC Report, 64th session (2012)

Draft Articles on Diplomatic Protection, ILC Report, 58th session (2006)

Articles on Responsibility of States for Internationally Wrongful Acts, ILC Report, 53rd session (2001)

Nationality, including Statelessness, *Report on Present Statelessness*, Yearbook of the International Law Commission (1954)

Michigan Guidelines on Nexus to a Convention Ground *Guidelines Reflecting the Consensus of Participants at the Second Colloquium on Challenges in International Refugee Law* (23–25 March 2001)

New Zealand, Immigration New Zealand, *Operational Manual* (March 2012)

United Kingdom, Foreign and Commonwealth Office *Human Rights and Democracy: the 2011 Report* (April 2012)

United Nations, Ad Hoc Committee on Refugees and Stateless Persons *Draft Report of the Ad Hoc Committee on Statelessness and Related Problems* (15 February 1950)

United Nations, High Commissioner for Refugees *Guide for Issuance of Machine-Readable Convention Travel Documents for Refugees and Stateless Persons* (October 2012)

EXCOM, *Note on International Protection* (1–5 October 2012)

Handbook and Guidelines on Procedures and Criteria for Determining Refugee Status under the 1951 Convention and the 1967 Protocol Relating to the Status of Refugees (reissued December 2011)

The Participation of Refugees in Elections of Their Country of Nationality and the Role of UNHCR (2010)

Note on the Interpretation of Article 1E of the 1951 Convention Relating to the Status of Refugees (March 2009)

EXCOM Conclusion No 109 'Protracted Refugee Situations' (8 December 2009)

Guidance Note on Refugee Claims Relating to Sexual Orientation and Gender Identity (21 November 2008)

Note on the Integration of Refugees in the European Union (May 2007)

Written Submissions on Behalf of the Intervener in *R (Al Rawi and others) v Secretary of State for Foreign and Commonwealth Affairs* (12 July 2006)

Guidelines on International Protection, *The Application of Article 1A(2) of the 1951 Convention and/or 1967 Protocol Relating to the Status of Refugees to Victims of Trafficking and Persons at Risk of Being Trafficked* (7 April 2006)

EXCOM Conclusion No 104 'Local Integration' (7 October 2005)

EXCOM Conclusion No 103 'The Provision of Diplomatic Protection including through Complementary Forms of Protection' (7 October 2005)

Handbook for Repatriation and Reintegration Activities (May 2004)

Guidelines on International Protection: Cessation of Refugee Status under Articles 1C(5) and (6) of the Convention (2003)

Refugee Protection: A Guide to International Refugee Law (1 December 2001)

Note on International Protection (13 September 2001)

Summary Conclusions: Cessation of Refugee Status, Lisbon Expert Roundtable (3–4 May 2001)

Note on International Protection (7 July 2000)

The Cessation Clauses: Guidelines on Their Application (26 April 1999)

Introduction to International Protection: UNHCR Emergency Management Training Program (1 July 1999)

The State of the World's Refugees: A Humanitarian Agenda (1997)

EXCOM Conclusion No 69 'Cessation of Status' (9 October 1992)

EXCOM 'The Application of the Ceased Circumstances Clause in the 1951 Convention' (20 December 1991)

EXCOM Conclusion No 62 (xli), *Note on International Protection* (5 October 1990)

Note on Expulsion of Refugees (24 August 1977)

United States of America Department of State, *Citizenship Laws of the World* (2001)

INDEX

Abbassi UK Court of Appeal, 174
African Charter of Human and
  Peoples' Rights, 55
agents of persecution
  interpretations of, 28–9
Al Rawi UK Court of Appeal,
  187–8
Alexy, Robert, 86
American Convention on Human
  Rights, 55
An-Na'im, Abdullahi Ahmed, 82–3
Arendt, Hannah, 103, 207–8
Aristotle
  republican citizenship, 100–1
  view of an ideal political life, 78
assimilation of CSR1951 refugees,
  45–6
asylum
  as a political instrument, 214–15
  definition, 23
  grant of territorial asylum, 23–4
  inchoate right to, 23–5
  right to, 23
asylum seekers, 9–10
Australian High Court, 182

Barcelona Traction International Court
  of Justice, 172, 187
Bauböck, Rainer, 91, 96, 98–9, 122–3
Bellinger, John, 171
Benhabib, Seyla, 113
Benthamite democracy, 87
Berlin, Isaiah, 76
Bluman US Federal Court, 210
Bonoan, Rafael, 221
Breard, Angel Francisco, 168
Brubaker, Rogers, 90, 110

Cabell US Supreme Court, 114
Carens, Joseph, 18–19, 20–1, 22–3, 94,
  97, 103
Chetail, Vincent, 25, 26
Chile
  non-citizen voting, 56
citizenship
  as a bundle of rights, 91–2
  communitarian perspectives,
    105–6
  comparison with non-statist
    association membership, 91
  criterion for participation in
    elections, 4–5
  defining, 89–91
  EU citizenship, 99, 124
  human dimension of states, 89–90
  inclusive and exclusive aspects,
    89–91
  international functions of, 15
  interrelationship with
    enfranchisement, 113–20
  liberal perspectives, 95–100
    equal citizenship and the role of
      participation, 95–7
    identity and attachment, 97–9
    prioritisation of citizens, 99–100
  multi-dimensional character,
    92–5
  multiple citizenships, 103–5
  republican perspectives, 100–5
    equal citizenship and the role of
      participation, 100–2
    identity and attachment, 102–5
    multiple citizenships, 103–5
    prioritisation of citizens, 105
  right to, 35–6

253

Lightning Source UK Ltd.
Milton Keynes UK
UKOW06n0746060117
291496UK00001B/2/P